The Best Of
Alex
2011

C000004539

Charles Peattie & Russell Taylor

Masterley Publishing

The Best Of Alex 2011

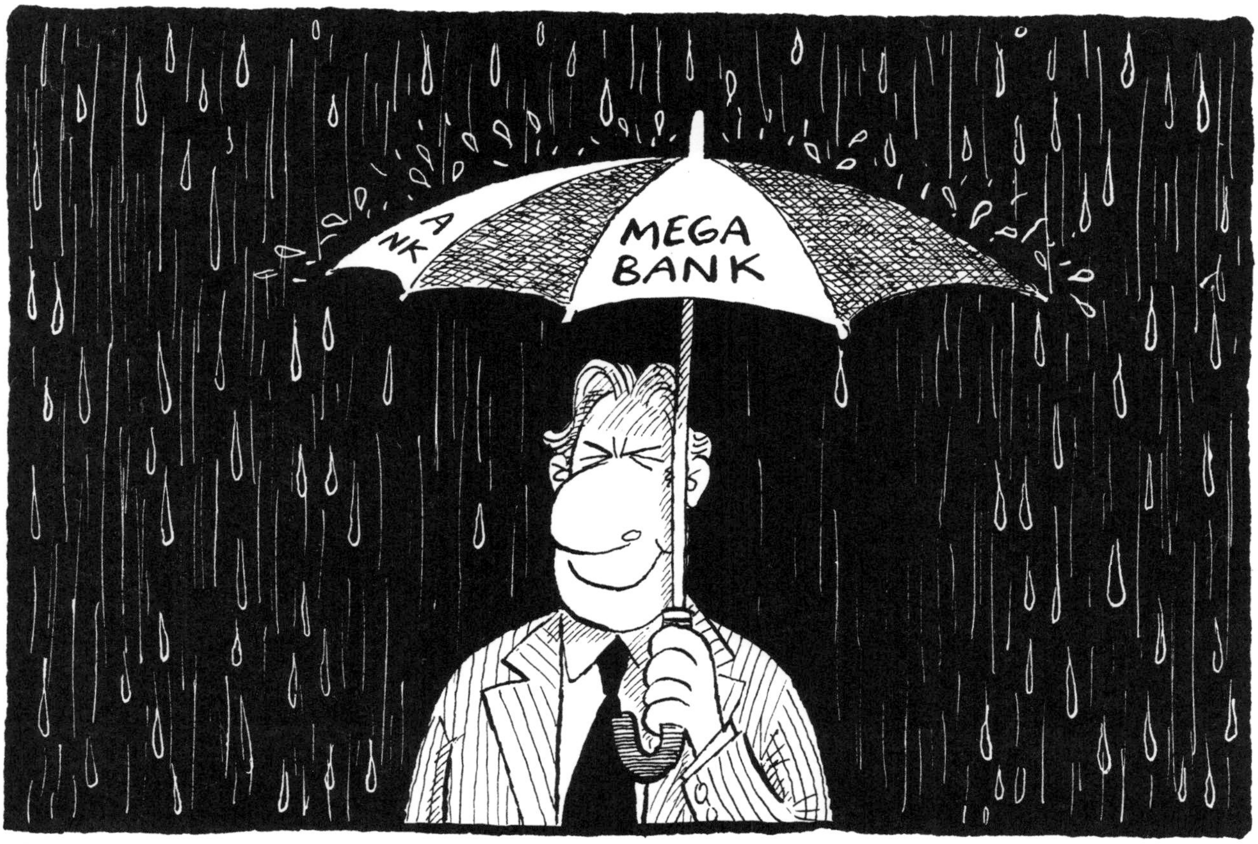
MEGA BANK

First Published in 2011 by MASTERLEY PUBLISHING

Layout and Artwork: Suzette Field

ISBN: 978 1 85375 827 0

Printed and bound by CPI Group (UK) Ltd, Croydon, CR0 4YY

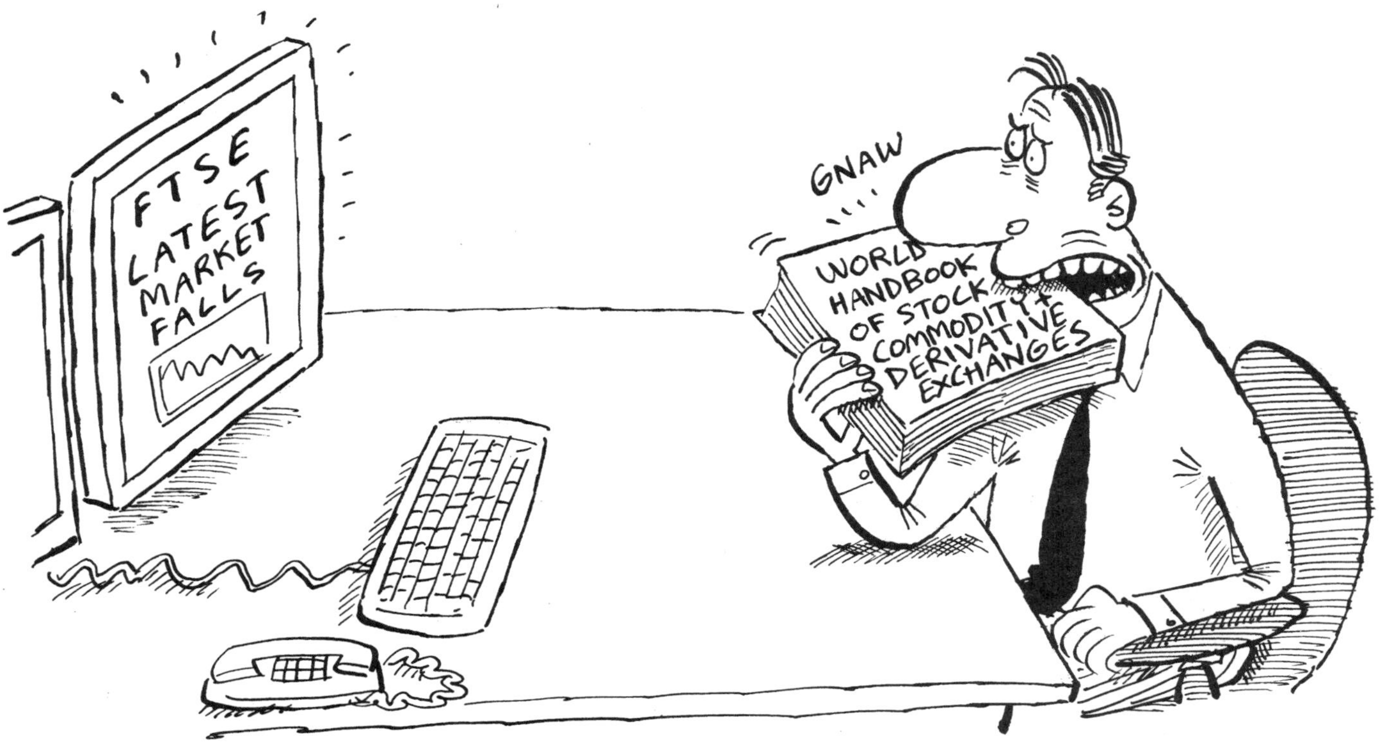
FTSE
LATEST MARKET FALLS
GNAW
WORLD HANDBOOK OF STOCK COMMODITY + DERIVATIVE EXCHANGES

Our usual gratitude goes to our generous sponsors.

FTSE Group (FTSE) is the world-leader in the creation and management of index solutions.

Mondo Visione provides vital knowledge about the world's exchanges and trading venues.

FOREWORD

A question that we are often asked by readers is: what comes first in creating an Alex cartoon: the words or the pictures? The answer is neither. What comes first is the lunch. Lunch is an integral part of our job. In the same way that Alex will ply a CFO with wine to get him to blurt out some price sensitive information about his company, we dine with the real life Alexes who tell us all about the arcane world they work in.

You see we don't need to make up much stuff. A lot of what you'll read in this book comes straight from the horse's mouth. In fact our job is frequently to tone down the stories we're told, so that our non-City readership (and there are quite a few of them) won't conclude that we are taking too many liberties with our satirical licence.

Sometimes we wonder what's in it for the guys who find themselves (or rather their banks) picking up the tab for these lunches with us. Perhaps it's a sort of confessional for them. In a world of corporate conformity it gives them the chance to divulge their real opinion about the people that blight their lives: bosses, clients, compliance officers etc.

Or maybe it's that it allows them to unburden themselves of a mindset that is as taboo as sexism or ageism in the financial workplace, namely: pessimism. Whatever their private opinions may be, in the City everyone has to be unremittingly bullish in public: about their bonuses, about their business, about the state of the economy..

But for the last three years we have been hearing pretty much the same message from nearly all the bankers, brokers, traders and financial PR people who we lunch with. It's usually expressed along the lines of "Well, I don't know.. This market looks like pants to me and there's a load more bad stuff in the pipeline. But everyone else seems to think it's going to be okay"

This is what they tell us in private. In public they remain as unremittingly upbeat as ever. That's because a general mood of confidence sustains markets and stops the economy going down the tubes.

It's all very worrying.

Do they think that as satirists and social commentators we have so little influence on public opinion that it's safe for them to tell us this stuff? Or are we expected to respect the sanctity of the upmarket French restaurant and not reveal anything said in it?

Sometimes we wonder what would happen if all those people found out that everyone else was (like them) seemingly merely putting on a macho display of bullishness in public while inwardly quaking..

No, it's probably best not to go there.. In fact it's probably best to go to a restaurant, while you still have a job and expense account, and have a nice lunch. And if you need someone to come with you we're always available.

Charles Peattie Russell Taylor

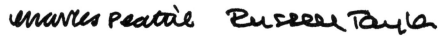

Charles Peattie and Russell Taylor

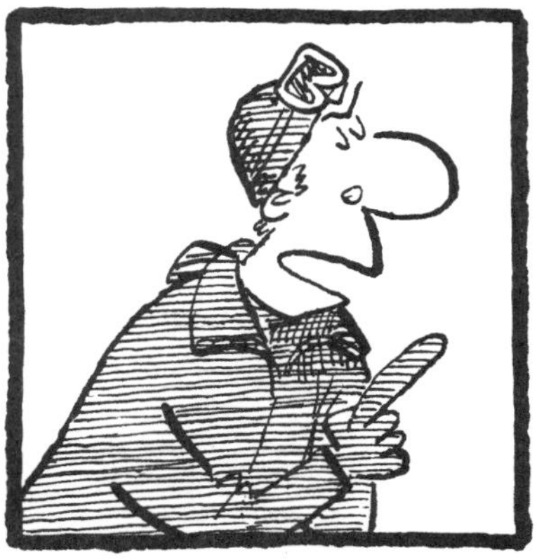

Alex - investment banker

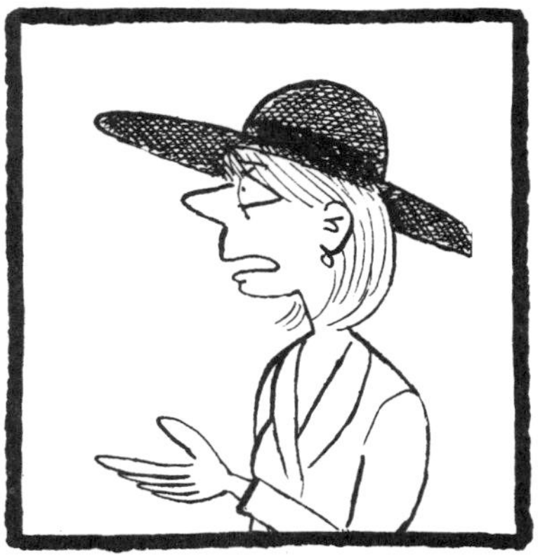

Penny - Alex's wife

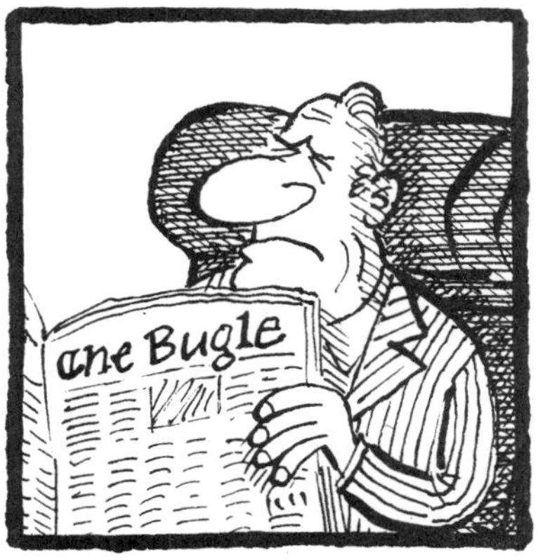
the Bugle

Rupert - senior banker

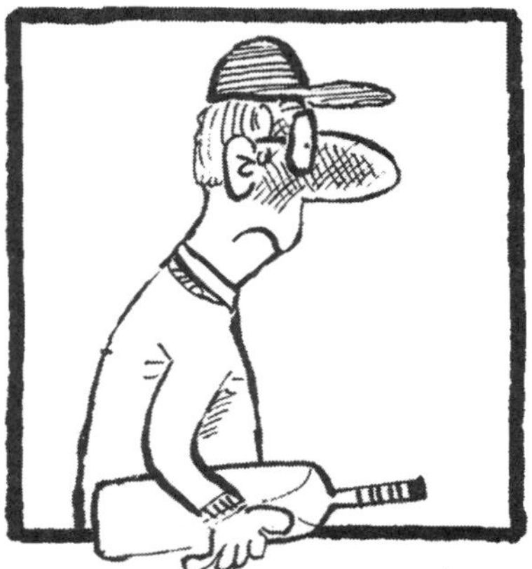

Clive - Alex's colleague

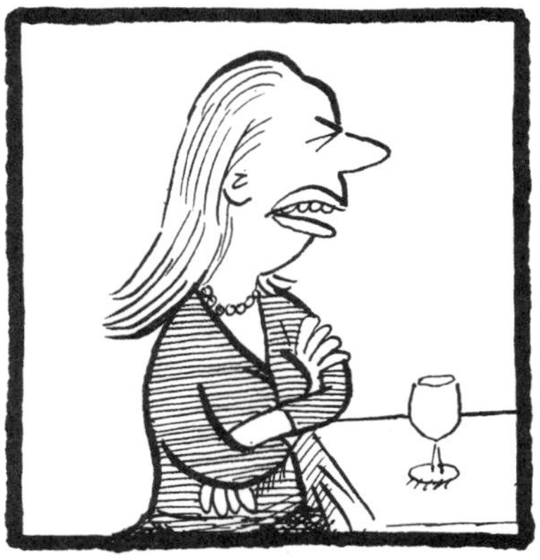

Bridget - Clive's wife

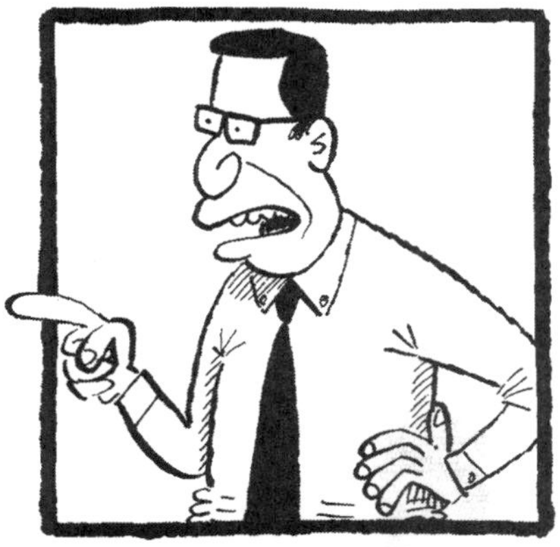

Cyrus - Alex's boss

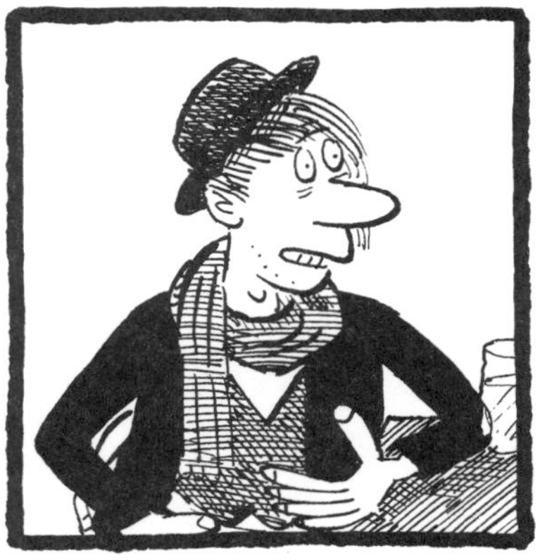

Christopher - Alex's son

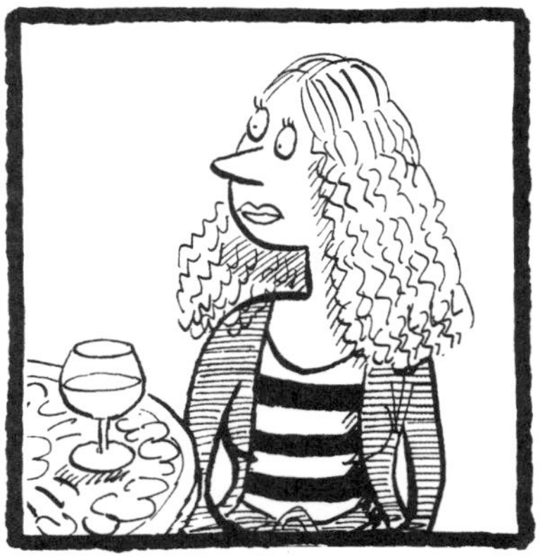

Sophie - Christopher's girlfriend

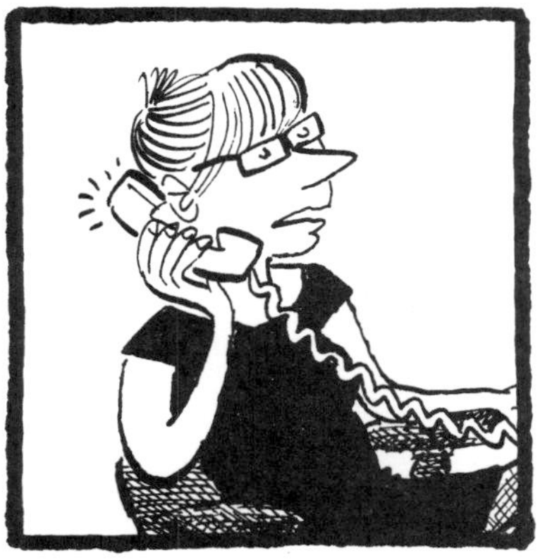

Sara - headhunter

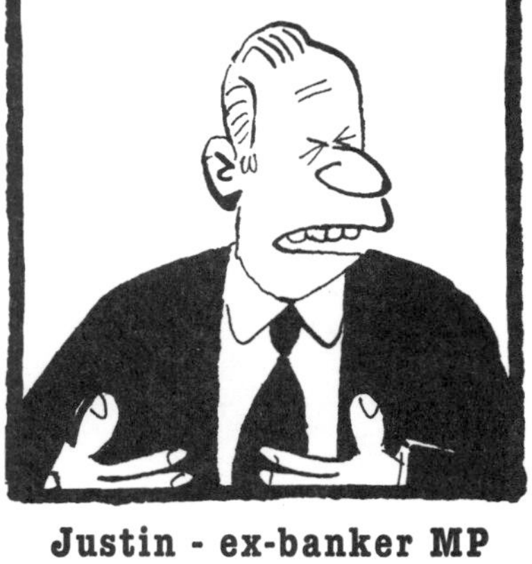

Justin - ex-banker MP

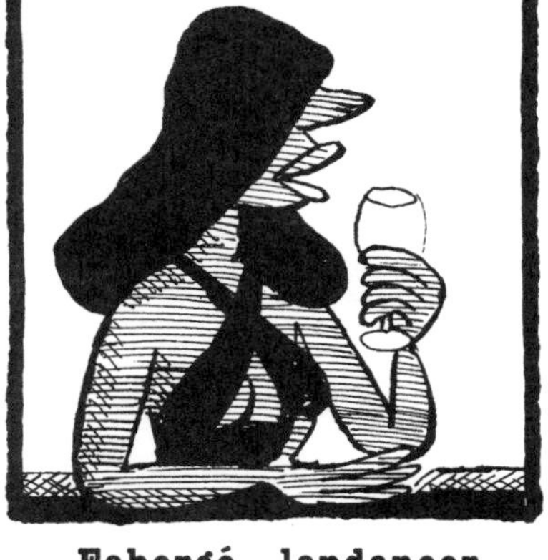

Fabergé - lapdancer

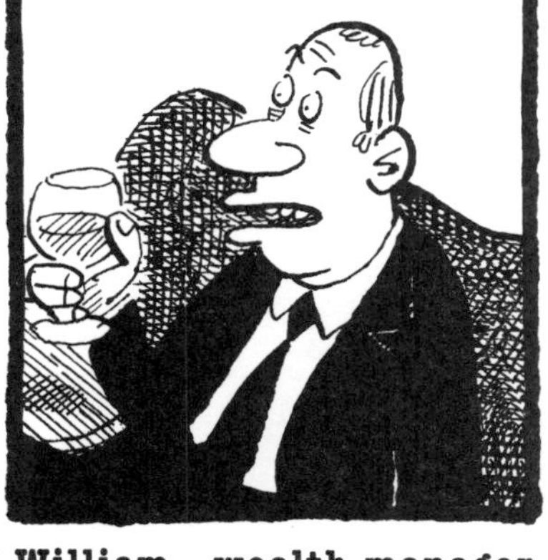

William - wealth manager

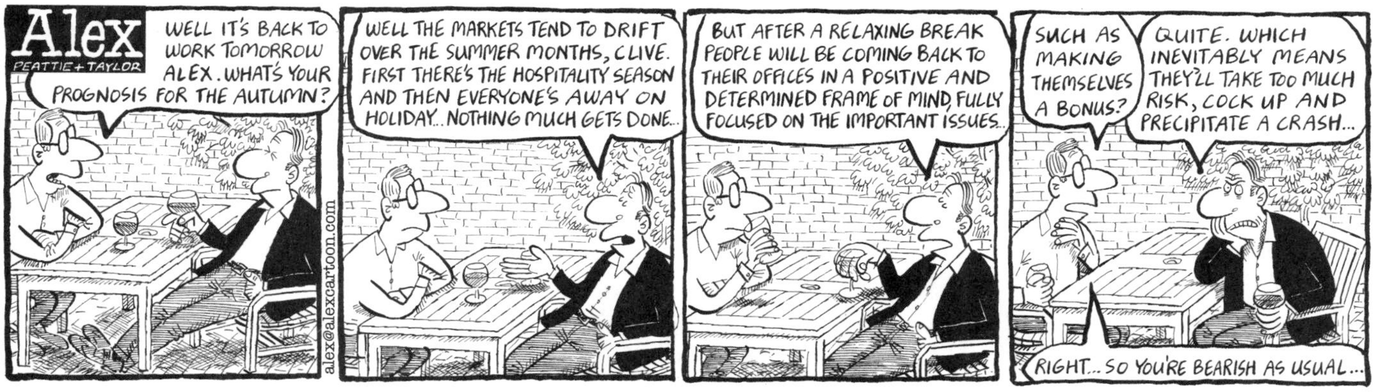
Alex
PEATTIE + TAYLOR
WELL IT'S BACK TO WORK TOMORROW ALEX. WHAT'S YOUR PROGNOSIS FOR THE AUTUMN?
WELL THE MARKETS TEND TO DRIFT OVER THE SUMMER MONTHS, CLIVE. FIRST THERE'S THE HOSPITALITY SEASON AND THEN EVERYONE'S AWAY ON HOLIDAY... NOTHING MUCH GETS DONE...
alex@alexcartoon.com
BUT AFTER A RELAXING BREAK PEOPLE WILL BE COMING BACK TO THEIR OFFICES IN A POSITIVE AND DETERMINED FRAME OF MIND, FULLY FOCUSED ON THE IMPORTANT ISSUES...
SUCH AS MAKING THEMSELVES A BONUS?
QUITE. WHICH INEVITABLY MEANS THEY'LL TAKE TOO MUCH RISK, COCK UP AND PRECIPITATE A CRASH...
RIGHT... SO YOU'RE BEARISH AS USUAL...

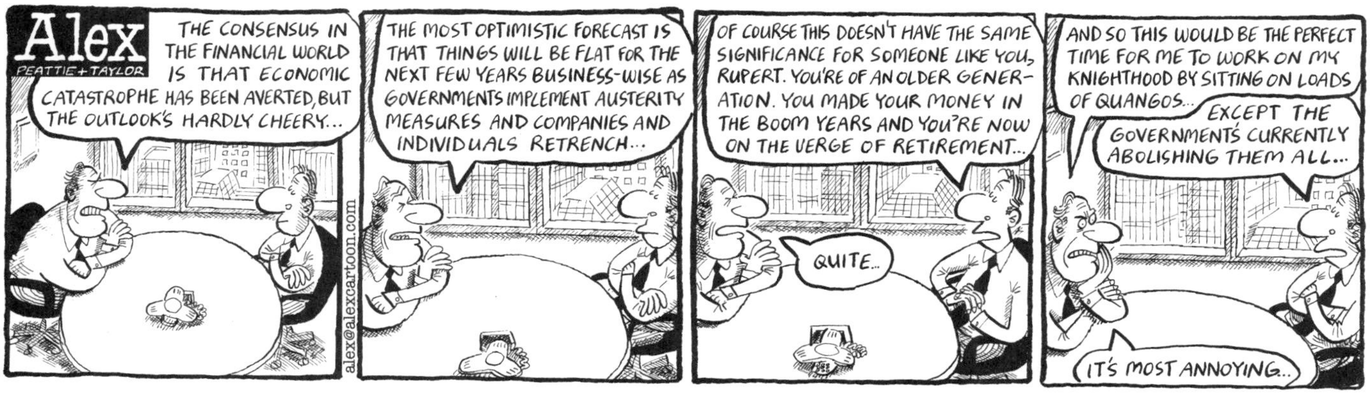
Alex
PEATTIE + TAYLOR
THE CONSENSUS IN THE FINANCIAL WORLD IS THAT ECONOMIC CATASTROPHE HAS BEEN AVERTED, BUT THE OUTLOOK'S HARDLY CHEERY...
THE MOST OPTIMISTIC FORECAST IS THAT THINGS WILL BE FLAT FOR THE NEXT FEW YEARS BUSINESS-WISE AS GOVERNMENTS IMPLEMENT AUSTERITY MEASURES AND COMPANIES AND INDIVIDUALS RETRENCH...
alex@alexcartoon.com
OF COURSE THIS DOESN'T HAVE THE SAME SIGNIFICANCE FOR SOMEONE LIKE YOU, RUPERT. YOU'RE OF AN OLDER GENERATION. YOU MADE YOUR MONEY IN THE BOOM YEARS AND YOU'RE NOW ON THE VERGE OF RETIREMENT...
QUITE...
AND SO THIS WOULD BE THE PERFECT TIME FOR ME TO WORK ON MY KNIGHTHOOD BY SITTING ON LOADS OF QUANGOS...
EXCEPT THE GOVERNMENT'S CURRENTLY ABOLISHING THEM ALL...
IT'S MOST ANNOYING...

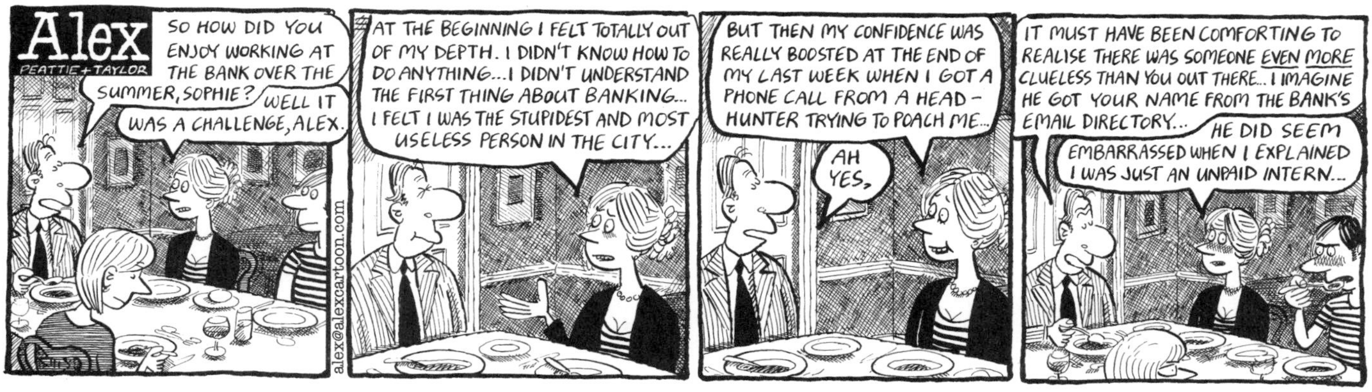
Alex
PEATTIE + TAYLOR
SO HOW DID YOU ENJOY WORKING AT THE BANK OVER THE SUMMER, SOPHIE?
WELL IT WAS A CHALLENGE, ALEX.
AT THE BEGINNING I FELT TOTALLY OUT OF MY DEPTH. I DIDN'T KNOW HOW TO DO ANYTHING... I DIDN'T UNDERSTAND THE FIRST THING ABOUT BANKING... I FELT I WAS THE STUPIDEST AND MOST USELESS PERSON IN THE CITY...
alex@alexcartoon.com
BUT THEN MY CONFIDENCE WAS REALLY BOOSTED AT THE END OF MY LAST WEEK WHEN I GOT A PHONE CALL FROM A HEAD-HUNTER TRYING TO POACH ME...
AH YES,
IT MUST HAVE BEEN COMFORTING TO REALISE THERE WAS SOMEONE EVEN MORE CLUELESS THAN YOU OUT THERE... I IMAGINE HE GOT YOUR NAME FROM THE BANK'S EMAIL DIRECTORY...
HE DID SEEM EMBARRASSED WHEN I EXPLAINED I WAS JUST AN UNPAID INTERN...

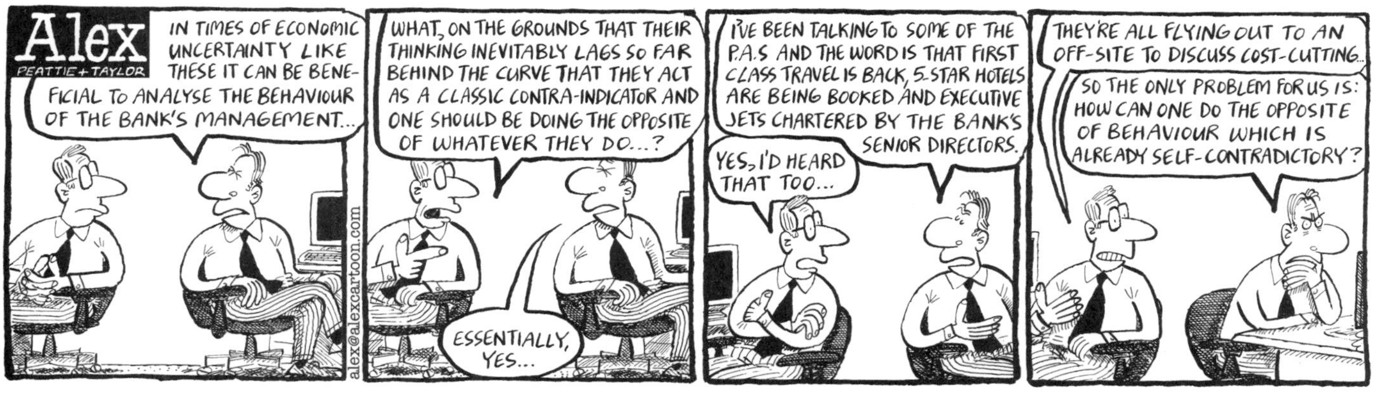
Alex
PEATTIE + TAYLOR
IN TIMES OF ECONOMIC UNCERTAINTY LIKE THESE IT CAN BE BENEFICIAL TO ANALYSE THE BEHAVIOUR OF THE BANK'S MANAGEMENT...
WHAT, ON THE GROUNDS THAT THEIR THINKING INEVITABLY LAGS SO FAR BEHIND THE CURVE THAT THEY ACT AS A CLASSIC CONTRA-INDICATOR AND ONE SHOULD BE DOING THE OPPOSITE OF WHATEVER THEY DO...?
ESSENTIALLY, YES...
alex@alexcartoon.com
I'VE BEEN TALKING TO SOME OF THE P.A.S AND THE WORD IS THAT FIRST CLASS TRAVEL IS BACK, 5-STAR HOTELS ARE BEING BOOKED AND EXECUTIVE JETS CHARTERED BY THE BANK'S SENIOR DIRECTORS.
YES, I'D HEARD THAT TOO...
THEY'RE ALL FLYING OUT TO AN OFF-SITE TO DISCUSS COST-CUTTING...
SO THE ONLY PROBLEM FOR US IS: HOW CAN ONE DO THE OPPOSITE OF BEHAVIOUR WHICH IS ALREADY SELF-CONTRADICTORY?

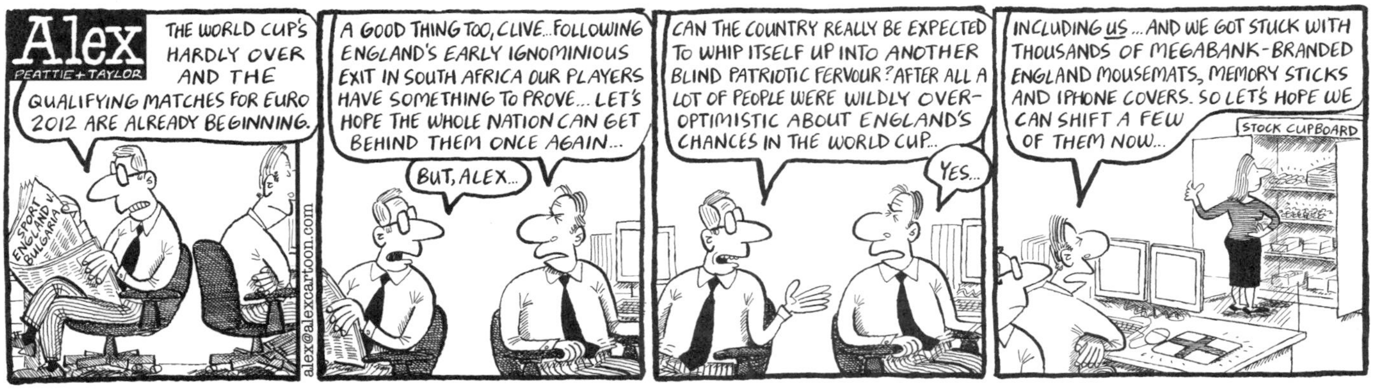
Alex
PEATTIE + TAYLOR
THE WORLD CUP'S HARDLY OVER AND THE QUALIFYING MATCHES FOR EURO 2012 ARE ALREADY BEGINNING.
SPORT ENGLAND V BULGARIA
alex@alexcartoon.com
A GOOD THING TOO, CLIVE... FOLLOWING ENGLAND'S EARLY IGNOMINIOUS EXIT IN SOUTH AFRICA OUR PLAYERS HAVE SOMETHING TO PROVE... LET'S HOPE THE WHOLE NATION CAN GET BEHIND THEM ONCE AGAIN...
BUT, ALEX...
CAN THE COUNTRY REALLY BE EXPECTED TO WHIP ITSELF UP INTO ANOTHER BLIND PATRIOTIC FERVOUR? AFTER ALL A LOT OF PEOPLE WERE WILDLY OVER-OPTIMISTIC ABOUT ENGLAND'S CHANCES IN THE WORLD CUP...
YES...
INCLUDING US... AND WE GOT STUCK WITH THOUSANDS OF MEGABANK-BRANDED ENGLAND MOUSEMATS, MEMORY STICKS AND IPHONE COVERS. SO LET'S HOPE WE CAN SHIFT A FEW OF THEM NOW...
STOCK CUPBOARD

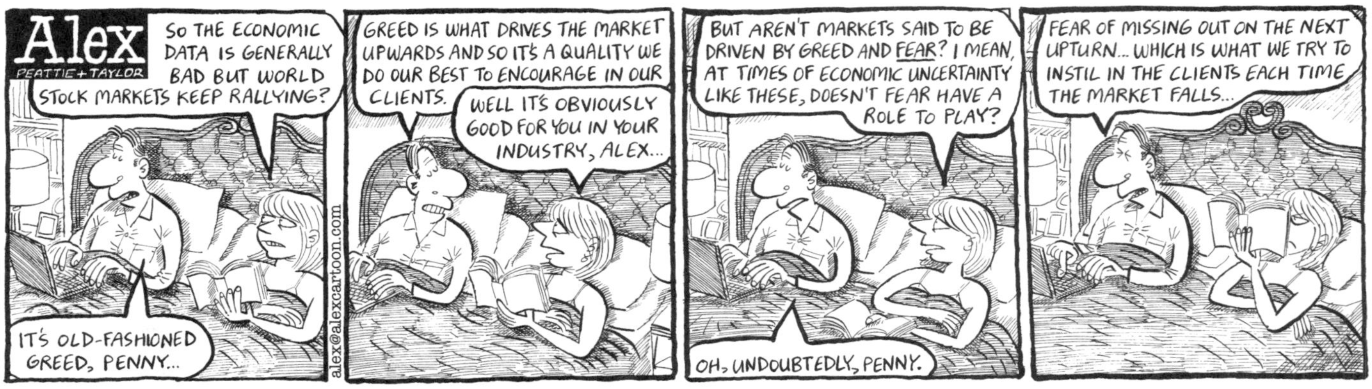
Alex
PEATTIE + TAYLOR
SO THE ECONOMIC DATA IS GENERALLY BAD BUT WORLD STOCK MARKETS KEEP RALLYING?
IT'S OLD-FASHIONED GREED, PENNY...
alex@alexcartoon.com
GREED IS WHAT DRIVES THE MARKET UPWARDS AND SO IT'S A QUALITY WE DO OUR BEST TO ENCOURAGE IN OUR CLIENTS.
WELL IT'S OBVIOUSLY GOOD FOR YOU IN YOUR INDUSTRY, ALEX...
BUT AREN'T MARKETS SAID TO BE DRIVEN BY GREED AND FEAR? I MEAN, AT TIMES OF ECONOMIC UNCERTAINTY LIKE THESE, DOESN'T FEAR HAVE A ROLE TO PLAY?
OH, UNDOUBTEDLY, PENNY.
FEAR OF MISSING OUT ON THE NEXT UPTURN... WHICH IS WHAT WE TRY TO INSTIL IN THE CLIENTS EACH TIME THE MARKET FALLS...

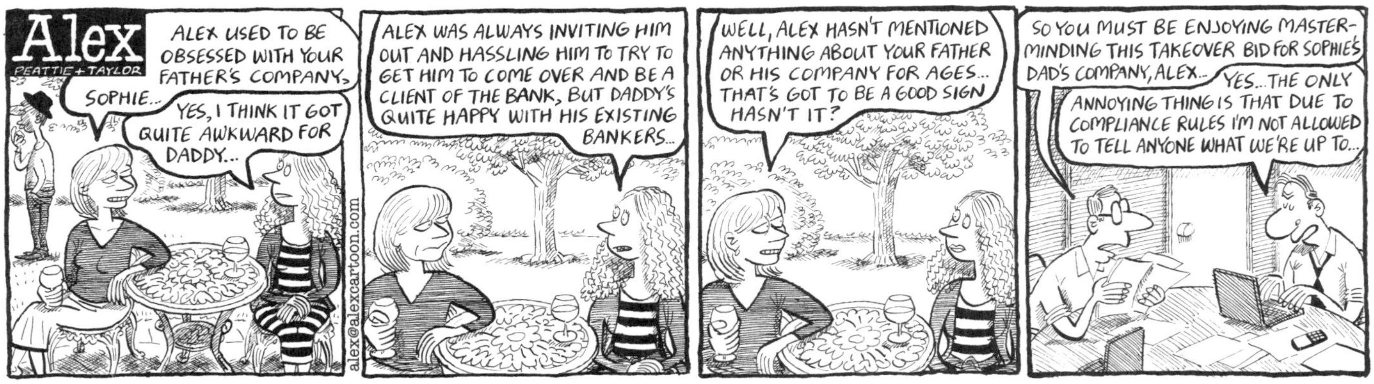
Alex
PEATTIE + TAYLOR
ALEX USED TO BE OBSESSED WITH YOUR FATHER'S COMPANY, SOPHIE...
YES, I THINK IT GOT QUITE AWKWARD FOR DADDY...
alex@alexcartoon.com
ALEX WAS ALWAYS INVITING HIM OUT AND HASSLING HIM TO TRY TO GET HIM TO COME OVER AND BE A CLIENT OF THE BANK, BUT DADDY'S QUITE HAPPY WITH HIS EXISTING BANKERS...
WELL, ALEX HASN'T MENTIONED ANYTHING ABOUT YOUR FATHER OR HIS COMPANY FOR AGES... THAT'S GOT TO BE A GOOD SIGN HASN'T IT?
SO YOU MUST BE ENJOYING MASTER-MINDING THIS TAKEOVER BID FOR SOPHIE'S DAD'S COMPANY, ALEX...
YES... THE ONLY ANNOYING THING IS THAT DUE TO COMPLIANCE RULES I'M NOT ALLOWED TO TELL ANYONE WHAT WE'RE UP TO...

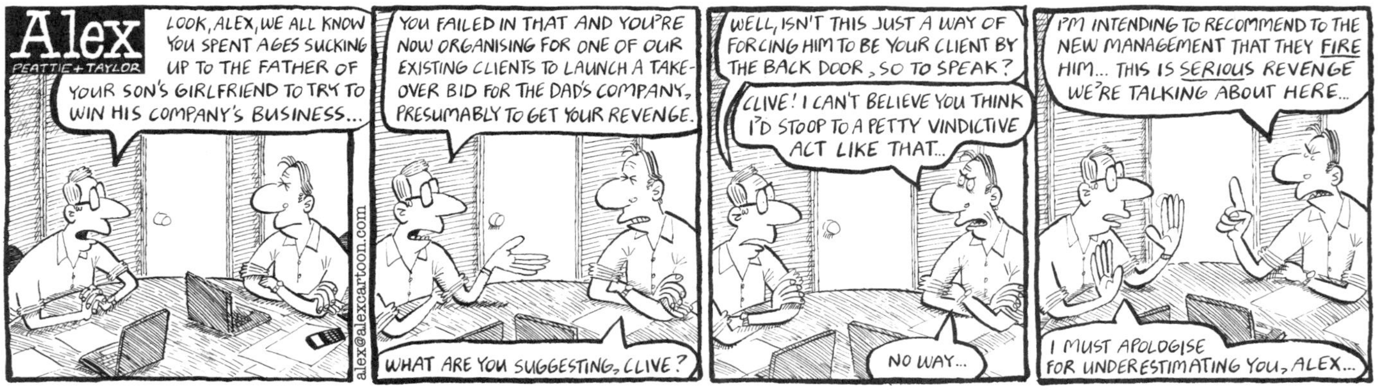
Alex
PEATTIE + TAYLOR
LOOK, ALEX, WE ALL KNOW YOU SPENT AGES SUCKING UP TO THE FATHER OF YOUR SON'S GIRLFRIEND TO TRY TO WIN HIS COMPANY'S BUSINESS...
alex@alexcartoon.com
YOU FAILED IN THAT AND YOU'RE NOW ORGANISING FOR ONE OF OUR EXISTING CLIENTS TO LAUNCH A TAKE-OVER BID FOR THE DAD'S COMPANY, PRESUMABLY TO GET YOUR REVENGE.
WHAT ARE YOU SUGGESTING, CLIVE?
WELL, ISN'T THIS JUST A WAY OF FORCING HIM TO BE YOUR CLIENT BY THE BACK DOOR, SO TO SPEAK?
CLIVE! I CAN'T BELIEVE YOU THINK I'D STOOP TO A PETTY VINDICTIVE ACT LIKE THAT...
NO WAY...
I'M INTENDING TO RECOMMEND TO THE NEW MANAGEMENT THAT THEY FIRE HIM... THIS IS SERIOUS REVENGE WE'RE TALKING ABOUT HERE...
I MUST APOLOGISE FOR UNDERESTIMATING YOU, ALEX...

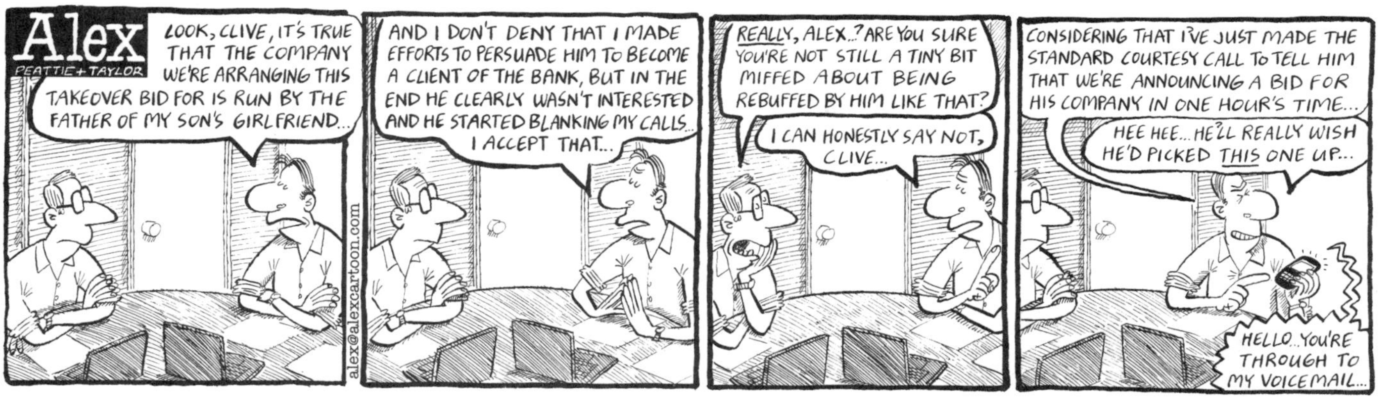
Alex
PEATTIE + TAYLOR
LOOK, CLIVE, IT'S TRUE THAT THE COMPANY WE'RE ARRANGING THIS TAKEOVER BID FOR IS RUN BY THE FATHER OF MY SON'S GIRLFRIEND...
AND I DON'T DENY THAT I MADE EFFORTS TO PERSUADE HIM TO BECOME A CLIENT OF THE BANK, BUT IN THE END HE CLEARLY WASN'T INTERESTED AND HE STARTED BLANKING MY CALLS... I ACCEPT THAT...
REALLY, ALEX..? ARE YOU SURE YOU'RE NOT STILL A TINY BIT MIFFED ABOUT BEING REBUFFED BY HIM LIKE THAT?
I CAN HONESTLY SAY NOT, CLIVE...
CONSIDERING THAT I'VE JUST MADE THE STANDARD COURTESY CALL TO TELL HIM THAT WE'RE ANNOUNCING A BID FOR HIS COMPANY IN ONE HOUR'S TIME...
HEE HEE... HE'LL REALLY WISH HE'D PICKED THIS ONE UP...
HELLO... YOU'RE THROUGH TO MY VOICEMAIL...
alex@alexcartoon.com

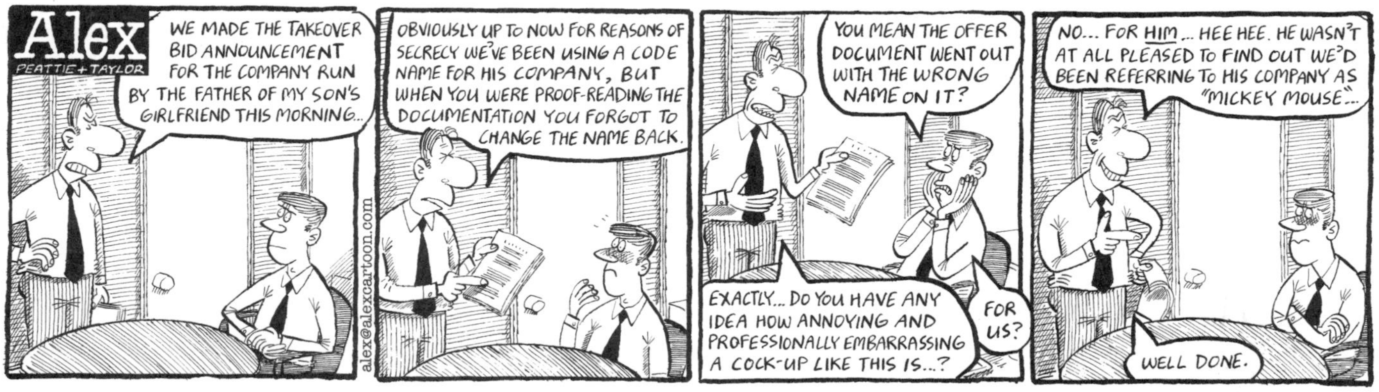
Alex
PEATTIE + TAYLOR
WE MADE THE TAKEOVER BID ANNOUNCEMENT FOR THE COMPANY RUN BY THE FATHER OF MY SON'S GIRLFRIEND THIS MORNING...
OBVIOUSLY UP TO NOW FOR REASONS OF SECRECY WE'VE BEEN USING A CODE NAME FOR HIS COMPANY, BUT WHEN YOU WERE PROOF-READING THE DOCUMENTATION YOU FORGOT TO CHANGE THE NAME BACK.
YOU MEAN THE OFFER DOCUMENT WENT OUT WITH THE WRONG NAME ON IT?
EXACTLY... DO YOU HAVE ANY IDEA HOW ANNOYING AND PROFESSIONALLY EMBARRASSING A COCK-UP LIKE THIS IS...?
FOR US?
NO... FOR HIM... HEE HEE. HE WASN'T AT ALL PLEASED TO FIND OUT WE'D BEEN REFERRING TO HIS COMPANY AS "MICKEY MOUSE"...
WELL DONE.
alex@alexcartoon.com

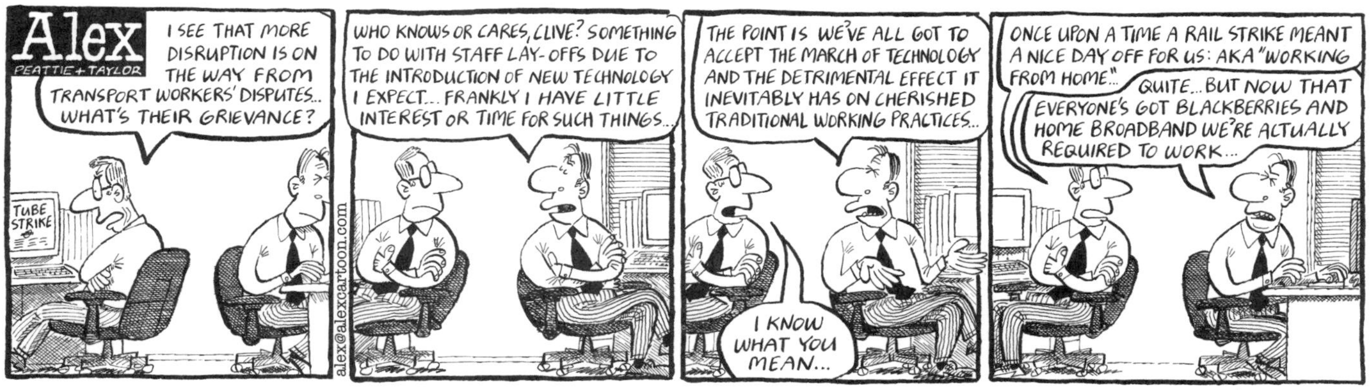
Alex
PEATTIE + TAYLOR
I SEE THAT MORE DISRUPTION IS ON THE WAY FROM TRANSPORT WORKERS' DISPUTES... WHAT'S THEIR GRIEVANCE?
TUBE STRIKE
WHO KNOWS OR CARES, CLIVE? SOMETHING TO DO WITH STAFF LAY-OFFS DUE TO THE INTRODUCTION OF NEW TECHNOLOGY I EXPECT... FRANKLY I HAVE LITTLE INTEREST OR TIME FOR SUCH THINGS...
THE POINT IS WE'VE ALL GOT TO ACCEPT THE MARCH OF TECHNOLOGY AND THE DETRIMENTAL EFFECT IT INEVITABLY HAS ON CHERISHED TRADITIONAL WORKING PRACTICES...
I KNOW WHAT YOU MEAN...
ONCE UPON A TIME A RAIL STRIKE MEANT A NICE DAY OFF FOR US: AKA "WORKING FROM HOME".
QUITE... BUT NOW THAT EVERYONE'S GOT BLACKBERRIES AND HOME BROADBAND WE'RE ACTUALLY REQUIRED TO WORK...
alex@alexcartoon.com

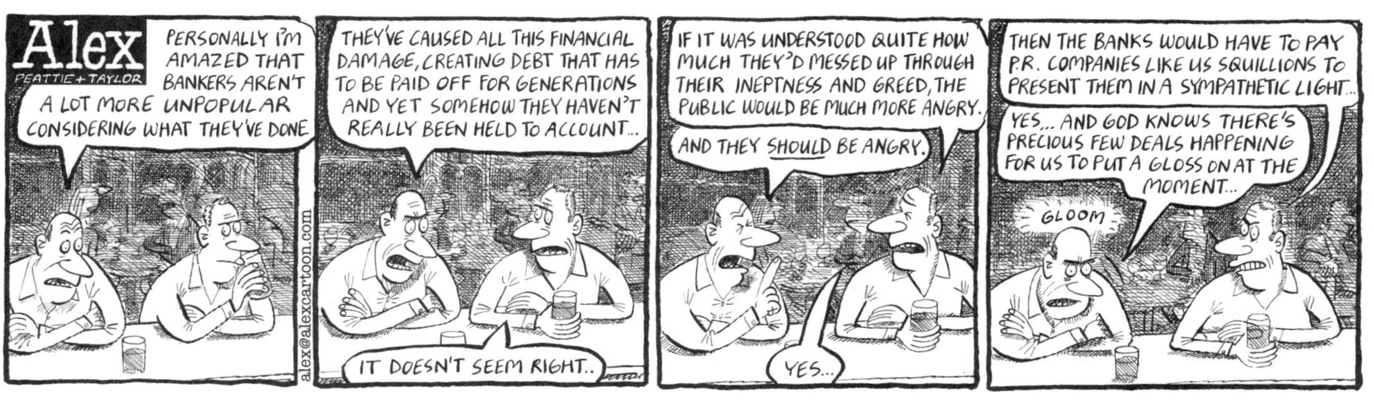
Alex
PEATTIE + TAYLOR
PERSONALLY I'M AMAZED THAT BANKERS AREN'T A LOT MORE UNPOPULAR CONSIDERING WHAT THEY'VE DONE
THEY'VE CAUSED ALL THIS FINANCIAL DAMAGE, CREATING DEBT THAT HAS TO BE PAID OFF FOR GENERATIONS AND YET SOMEHOW THEY HAVEN'T REALLY BEEN HELD TO ACCOUNT...
IT DOESN'T SEEM RIGHT..
IF IT WAS UNDERSTOOD QUITE HOW MUCH THEY'D MESSED UP THROUGH THEIR INEPTNESS AND GREED, THE PUBLIC WOULD BE MUCH MORE ANGRY.
AND THEY SHOULD BE ANGRY.
YES...
THEN THE BANKS WOULD HAVE TO PAY P.R. COMPANIES LIKE US SQUILLIONS TO PRESENT THEM IN A SYMPATHETIC LIGHT...
YES... AND GOD KNOWS THERE'S PRECIOUS FEW DEALS HAPPENING FOR US TO PUT A GLOSS ON AT THE MOMENT...
GLOOM
alex@alexcartoon.com

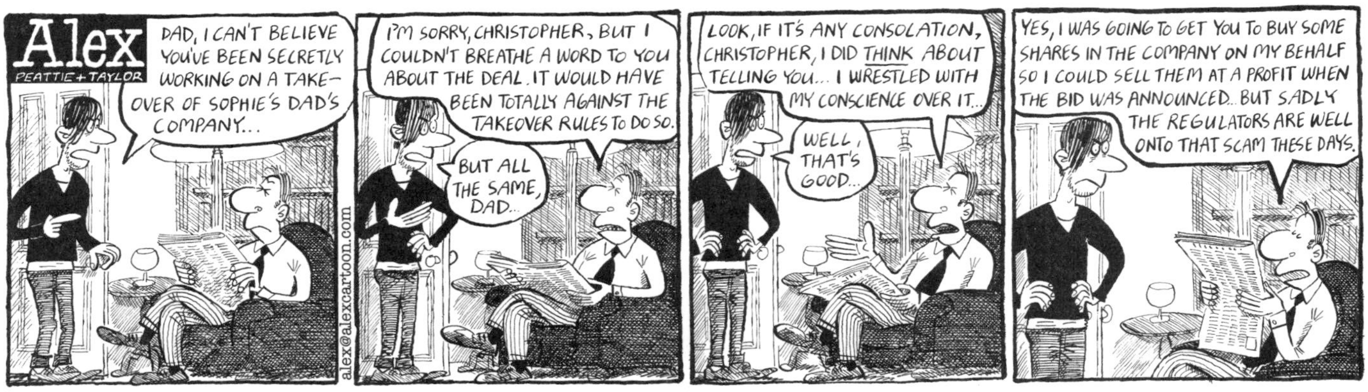
Alex
PEATTIE + TAYLOR
DAD, I CAN'T BELIEVE YOU'VE BEEN SECRETLY WORKING ON A TAKE-OVER OF SOPHIE'S DAD'S COMPANY...
alex@alexcartoon.com
I'M SORRY, CHRISTOPHER, BUT I COULDN'T BREATHE A WORD TO YOU ABOUT THE DEAL. IT WOULD HAVE BEEN TOTALLY AGAINST THE TAKEOVER RULES TO DO SO.
BUT ALL THE SAME, DAD...
LOOK, IF IT'S ANY CONSOLATION, CHRISTOPHER, I DID THINK ABOUT TELLING YOU... I WRESTLED WITH MY CONSCIENCE OVER IT...
WELL, THAT'S GOOD...
YES, I WAS GOING TO GET YOU TO BUY SOME SHARES IN THE COMPANY ON MY BEHALF SO I COULD SELL THEM AT A PROFIT WHEN THE BID WAS ANNOUNCED.. BUT SADLY THE REGULATORS ARE WELL ONTO THAT SCAM THESE DAYS.

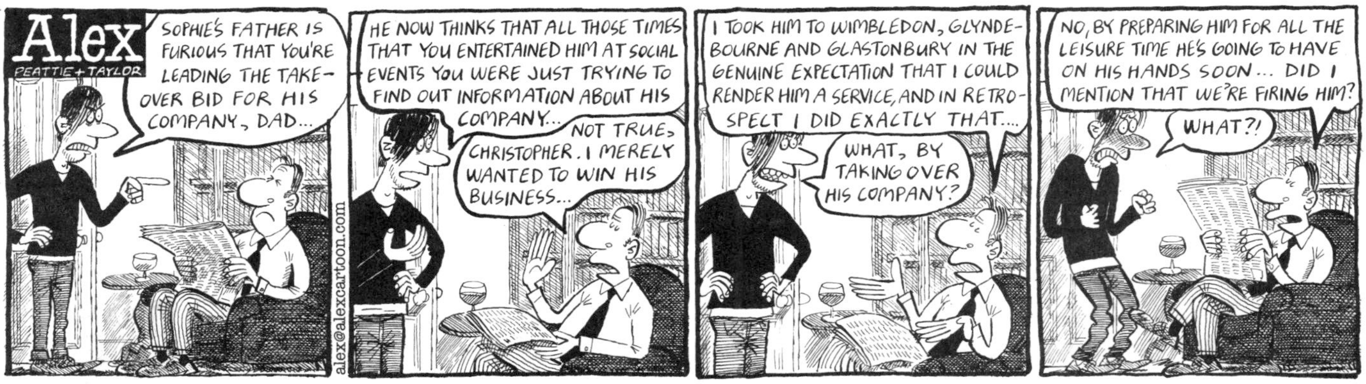
Alex
PEATTIE + TAYLOR
SOPHIE'S FATHER IS FURIOUS THAT YOU'RE LEADING THE TAKE-OVER BID FOR HIS COMPANY, DAD...
alex@alexcartoon.com
HE NOW THINKS THAT ALL THOSE TIMES THAT YOU ENTERTAINED HIM AT SOCIAL EVENTS YOU WERE JUST TRYING TO FIND OUT INFORMATION ABOUT HIS COMPANY...
NOT TRUE, CHRISTOPHER. I MERELY WANTED TO WIN HIS BUSINESS...
I TOOK HIM TO WIMBLEDON, GLYNDE-BOURNE AND GLASTONBURY IN THE GENUINE EXPECTATION THAT I COULD RENDER HIM A SERVICE, AND IN RETRO-SPECT I DID EXACTLY THAT....
WHAT, BY TAKING OVER HIS COMPANY?
NO, BY PREPARING HIM FOR ALL THE LEISURE TIME HE'S GOING TO HAVE ON HIS HANDS SOON... DID I MENTION THAT WE'RE FIRING HIM?
WHAT?!

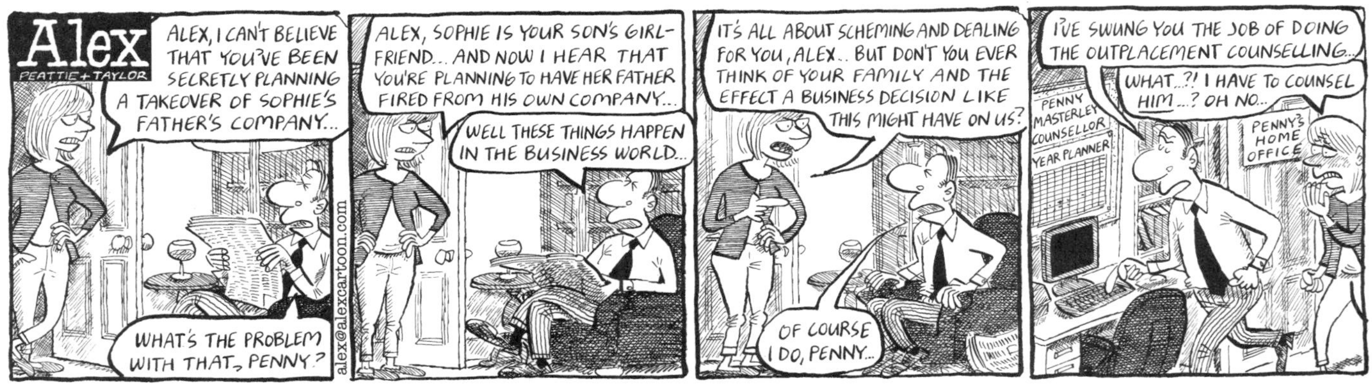
Alex
PEATTIE + TAYLOR
ALEX, I CAN'T BELIEVE THAT YOU'VE BEEN SECRETLY PLANNING A TAKEOVER OF SOPHIE'S FATHER'S COMPANY...
WHAT'S THE PROBLEM WITH THAT, PENNY?
alex@alexcartoon.com
ALEX, SOPHIE IS YOUR SON'S GIRL-FRIEND... AND NOW I HEAR THAT YOU'RE PLANNING TO HAVE HER FATHER FIRED FROM HIS OWN COMPANY...
WELL THESE THINGS HAPPEN IN THE BUSINESS WORLD...
IT'S ALL ABOUT SCHEMING AND DEALING FOR YOU, ALEX.. BUT DON'T YOU EVER THINK OF YOUR FAMILY AND THE EFFECT A BUSINESS DECISION LIKE THIS MIGHT HAVE ON US?
OF COURSE I DO, PENNY...
I'VE SWUNG YOU THE JOB OF DOING THE OUTPLACEMENT COUNSELLING...
WHAT..?! I HAVE TO COUNSEL HIM...? OH NO...
PENNY MASTERLEY COUNSELLOR YEAR PLANNER
PENNY'S HOME OFFICE

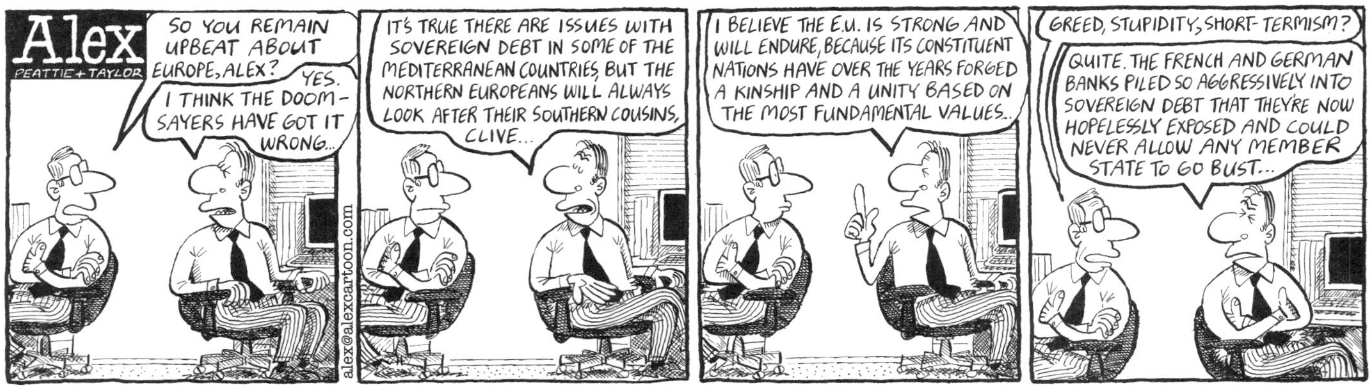
Alex
PEATTIE + TAYLOR
SO YOU REMAIN UPBEAT ABOUT EUROPE, ALEX?
YES. I THINK THE DOOM-SAYERS HAVE GOT IT WRONG...
alex@alexcartoon.com
IT'S TRUE THERE ARE ISSUES WITH SOVEREIGN DEBT IN SOME OF THE MEDITERRANEAN COUNTRIES, BUT THE NORTHERN EUROPEANS WILL ALWAYS LOOK AFTER THEIR SOUTHERN COUSINS, CLIVE...
I BELIEVE THE E.U. IS STRONG AND WILL ENDURE, BECAUSE ITS CONSTITUENT NATIONS HAVE OVER THE YEARS FORGED A KINSHIP AND A UNITY BASED ON THE MOST FUNDAMENTAL VALUES...
GREED, STUPIDITY, SHORT-TERMISM?
QUITE. THE FRENCH AND GERMAN BANKS PILED SO AGGRESSIVELY INTO SOVEREIGN DEBT THAT THEY'RE NOW HOPELESSLY EXPOSED AND COULD NEVER ALLOW ANY MEMBER STATE TO GO BUST...

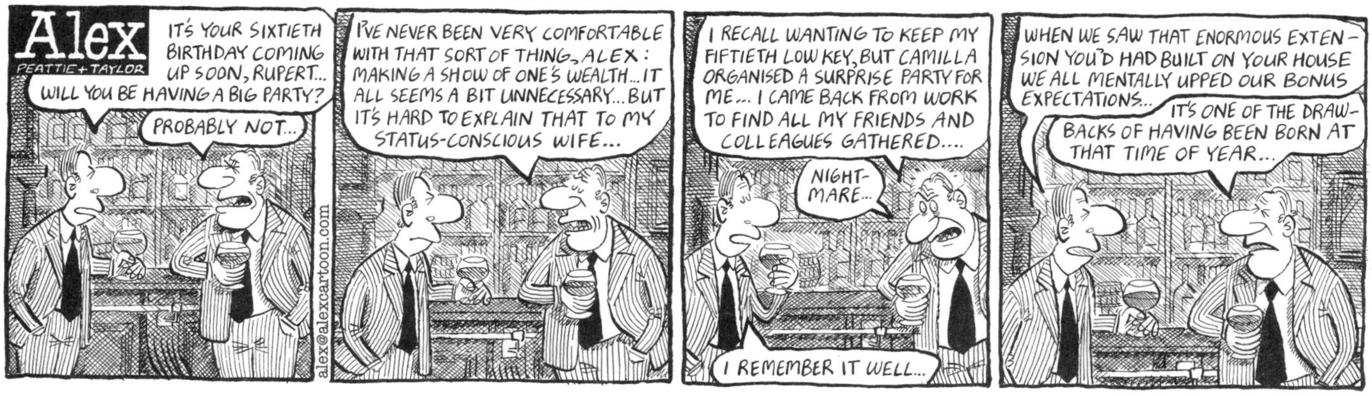
Alex
PEATTIE + TAYLOR
IT'S YOUR SIXTIETH BIRTHDAY COMING UP SOON, RUPERT... WILL YOU BE HAVING A BIG PARTY?
PROBABLY NOT...
I'VE NEVER BEEN VERY COMFORTABLE WITH THAT SORT OF THING, ALEX: MAKING A SHOW OF ONE'S WEALTH... IT ALL SEEMS A BIT UNNECESSARY... BUT IT'S HARD TO EXPLAIN THAT TO MY STATUS-CONSCIOUS WIFE...
alex@alexcartoon.com
I RECALL WANTING TO KEEP MY FIFTIETH LOW KEY, BUT CAMILLA ORGANISED A SURPRISE PARTY FOR ME... I CAME BACK FROM WORK TO FIND ALL MY FRIENDS AND COLLEAGUES GATHERED....
NIGHT-MARE...
I REMEMBER IT WELL...
WHEN WE SAW THAT ENORMOUS EXTEN-SION YOU'D HAD BUILT ON YOUR HOUSE WE ALL MENTALLY UPPED OUR BONUS EXPECTATIONS...
IT'S ONE OF THE DRAW-BACKS OF HAVING BEEN BORN AT THAT TIME OF YEAR...

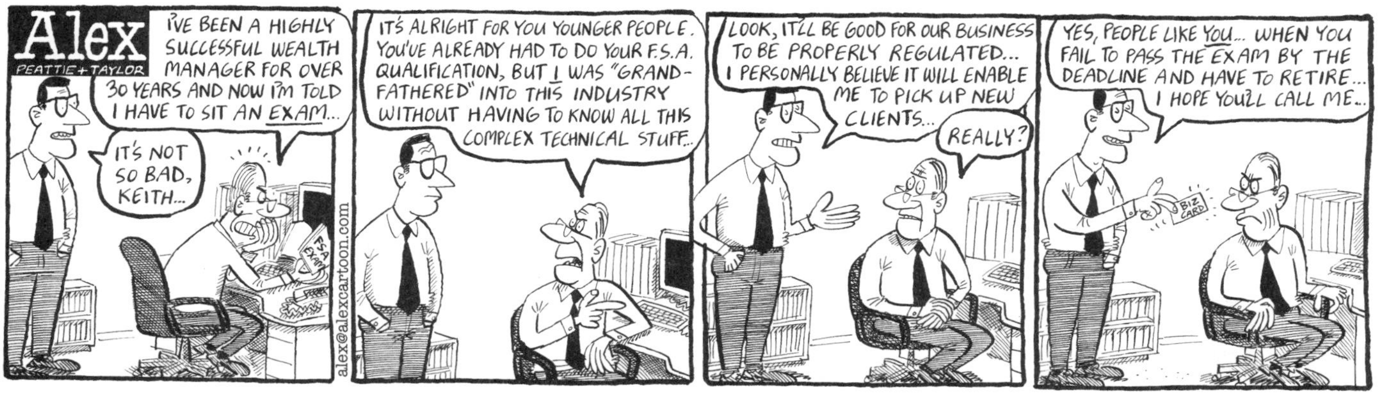
Alex
PEATTIE + TAYLOR
I'VE BEEN A HIGHLY SUCCESSFUL WEALTH MANAGER FOR OVER 30 YEARS AND NOW I'M TOLD I HAVE TO SIT AN EXAM...
IT'S NOT SO BAD, KEITH...
IT'S ALRIGHT FOR YOU YOUNGER PEOPLE. YOU'VE ALREADY HAD TO DO YOUR F.S.A. QUALIFICATION, BUT I WAS "GRAND-FATHERED" INTO THIS INDUSTRY WITHOUT HAVING TO KNOW ALL THIS COMPLEX TECHNICAL STUFF...
alex@alexcartoon.com
LOOK, IT'LL BE GOOD FOR OUR BUSINESS TO BE PROPERLY REGULATED... I PERSONALLY BELIEVE IT WILL ENABLE ME TO PICK UP NEW CLIENTS...
REALLY?
YES, PEOPLE LIKE YOU... WHEN YOU FAIL TO PASS THE EXAM BY THE DEADLINE AND HAVE TO RETIRE... I HOPE YOU'LL CALL ME...
BIZ CARD

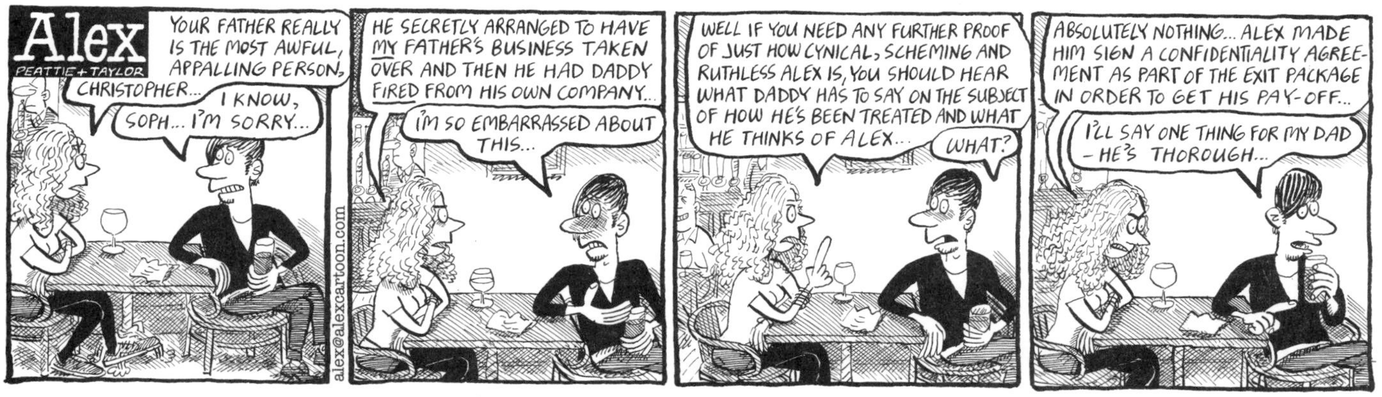
Alex
PEATTIE + TAYLOR
YOUR FATHER REALLY IS THE MOST AWFUL, APPALLING PERSON, CHRISTOPHER...
I KNOW, SOPH... I'M SORRY...
HE SECRETLY ARRANGED TO HAVE MY FATHER'S BUSINESS TAKEN OVER AND THEN HE HAD DADDY FIRED FROM HIS OWN COMPANY...
I'M SO EMBARRASSED ABOUT THIS...
alex@alexcartoon.com
WELL IF YOU NEED ANY FURTHER PROOF OF JUST HOW CYNICAL, SCHEMING AND RUTHLESS ALEX IS, YOU SHOULD HEAR WHAT DADDY HAS TO SAY ON THE SUBJECT OF HOW HE'S BEEN TREATED AND WHAT HE THINKS OF ALEX...
WHAT?
ABSOLUTELY NOTHING... ALEX MADE HIM SIGN A CONFIDENTIALITY AGREE-MENT AS PART OF THE EXIT PACKAGE IN ORDER TO GET HIS PAY-OFF...
I'LL SAY ONE THING FOR MY DAD - HE'S THOROUGH...

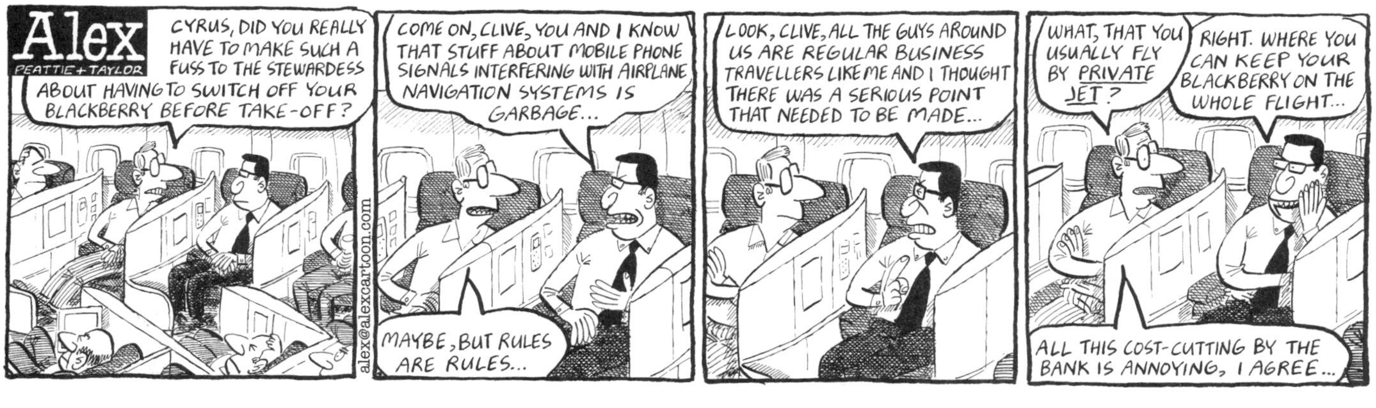
Alex
PEATTIE + TAYLOR
CYRUS, DID YOU REALLY HAVE TO MAKE SUCH A FUSS TO THE STEWARDESS ABOUT HAVING TO SWITCH OFF YOUR BLACKBERRY BEFORE TAKE-OFF?
COME ON, CLIVE, YOU AND I KNOW THAT STUFF ABOUT MOBILE PHONE SIGNALS INTERFERING WITH AIRPLANE NAVIGATION SYSTEMS IS GARBAGE...
MAYBE, BUT RULES ARE RULES...
alex@alexcartoon.com
LOOK, CLIVE, ALL THE GUYS AROUND US ARE REGULAR BUSINESS TRAVELLERS LIKE ME AND I THOUGHT THERE WAS A SERIOUS POINT THAT NEEDED TO BE MADE...
WHAT, THAT YOU USUALLY FLY BY PRIVATE JET?
RIGHT. WHERE YOU CAN KEEP YOUR BLACKBERRY ON THE WHOLE FLIGHT...
ALL THIS COST-CUTTING BY THE BANK IS ANNOYING, I AGREE...

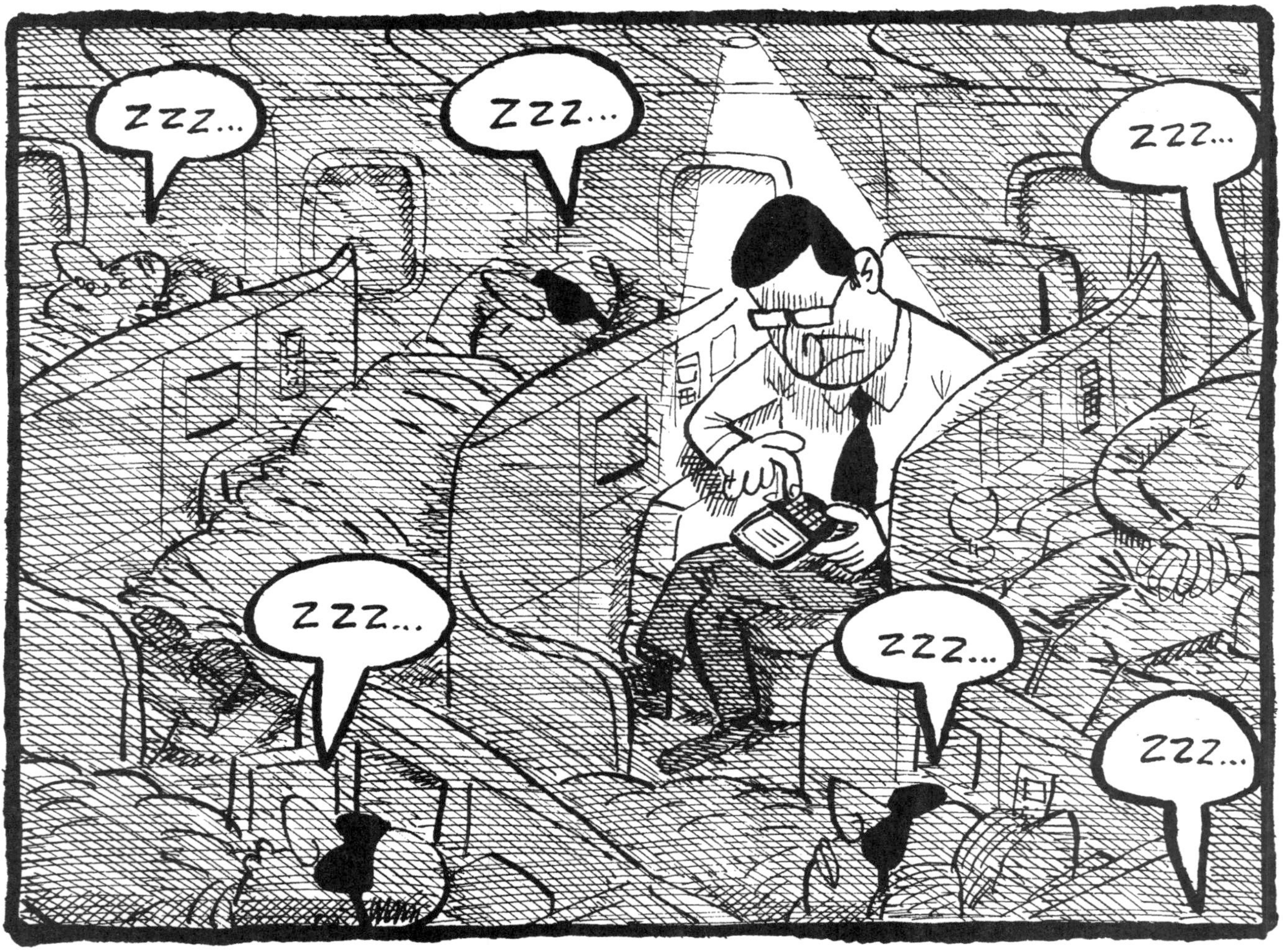
ZZZ...
ZZZ...
ZZZ...
ZZZ...
ZZZ...
ZZZ...

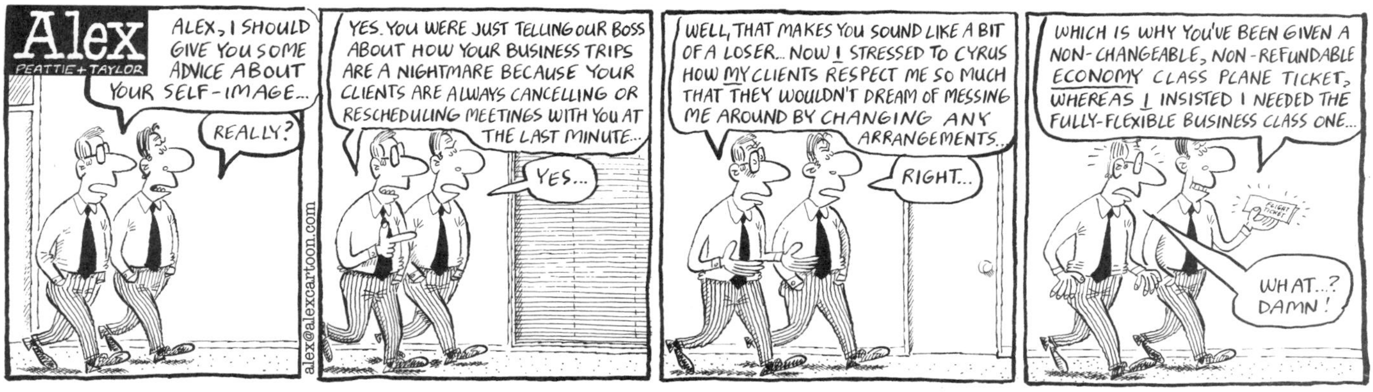
Alex
PEATTIE + TAYLOR
ALEX, I SHOULD GIVE YOU SOME ADVICE ABOUT YOUR SELF-IMAGE...
REALLY?
alex@alexcartoon.com
YES. YOU WERE JUST TELLING OUR BOSS ABOUT HOW YOUR BUSINESS TRIPS ARE A NIGHTMARE BECAUSE YOUR CLIENTS ARE ALWAYS CANCELLING OR RESCHEDULING MEETINGS WITH YOU AT THE LAST MINUTE...
YES...
WELL, THAT MAKES YOU SOUND LIKE A BIT OF A LOSER... NOW I STRESSED TO CYRUS HOW MY CLIENTS RESPECT ME SO MUCH THAT THEY WOULDN'T DREAM OF MESSING ME AROUND BY CHANGING ANY ARRANGEMENTS...
RIGHT...
WHICH IS WHY YOU'VE BEEN GIVEN A NON-CHANGEABLE, NON-REFUNDABLE ECONOMY CLASS PLANE TICKET, WHEREAS I INSISTED I NEEDED THE FULLY-FLEXIBLE BUSINESS CLASS ONE...
WHAT...? DAMN!

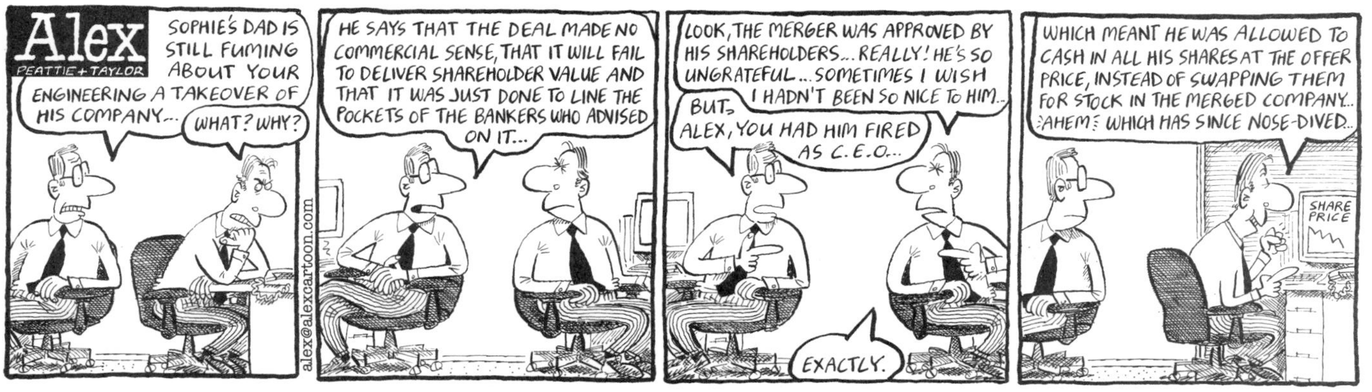
Alex
PEATTIE + TAYLOR
SOPHIE'S DAD IS STILL FUMING ABOUT YOUR ENGINEERING A TAKEOVER OF HIS COMPANY...
WHAT? WHY?
alex@alexcartoon.com
HE SAYS THAT THE DEAL MADE NO COMMERCIAL SENSE, THAT IT WILL FAIL TO DELIVER SHAREHOLDER VALUE AND THAT IT WAS JUST DONE TO LINE THE POCKETS OF THE BANKERS WHO ADVISED ON IT...
LOOK, THE MERGER WAS APPROVED BY HIS SHAREHOLDERS... REALLY! HE'S SO UNGRATEFUL... SOMETIMES I WISH I HADN'T BEEN SO NICE TO HIM...
BUT, ALEX, YOU HAD HIM FIRED AS C.E.O...
EXACTLY.
WHICH MEANT HE WAS ALLOWED TO CASH IN ALL HIS SHARES AT THE OFFER PRICE, INSTEAD OF SWAPPING THEM FOR STOCK IN THE MERGED COMPANY... AHEM WHICH HAS SINCE NOSE-DIVED...
SHARE PRICE

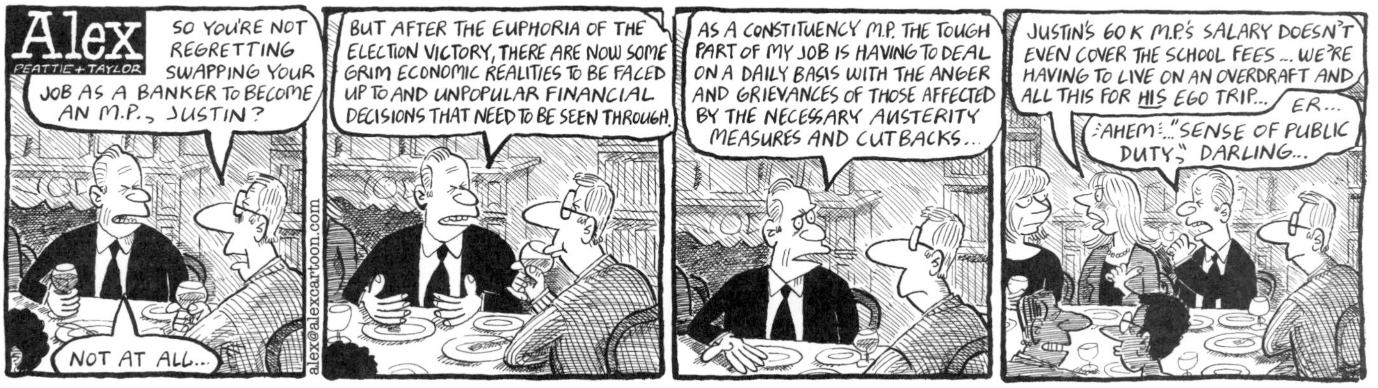
Alex
PEATTIE + TAYLOR
SO YOU'RE NOT REGRETTING SWAPPING YOUR JOB AS A BANKER TO BECOME AN M.P., JUSTIN?
NOT AT ALL...
alex@alexcartoon.com
BUT AFTER THE EUPHORIA OF THE ELECTION VICTORY, THERE ARE NOW SOME GRIM ECONOMIC REALITIES TO BE FACED UP TO AND UNPOPULAR FINANCIAL DECISIONS THAT NEED TO BE SEEN THROUGH.
AS A CONSTITUENCY M.P. THE TOUGH PART OF MY JOB IS HAVING TO DEAL ON A DAILY BASIS WITH THE ANGER AND GRIEVANCES OF THOSE AFFECTED BY THE NECESSARY AUSTERITY MEASURES AND CUTBACKS...
JUSTIN'S 60 K M.P.'S SALARY DOESN'T EVEN COVER THE SCHOOL FEES... WE'RE HAVING TO LIVE ON AN OVERDRAFT AND ALL THIS FOR HIS EGO TRIP...
ER...
AHEM... "SENSE OF PUBLIC DUTY," DARLING...

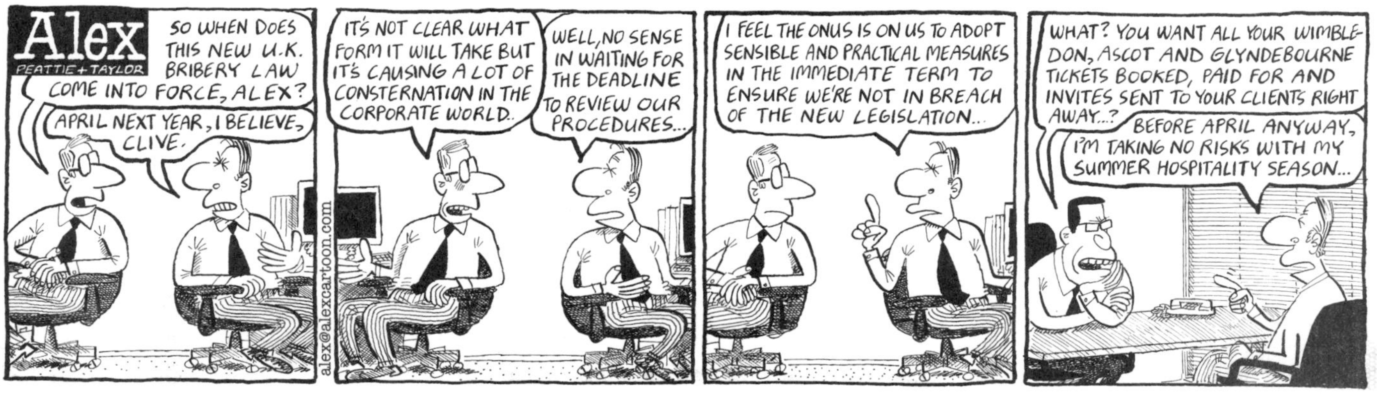
Alex
PEATTIE + TAYLOR
SO WHEN DOES THIS NEW U.K. BRIBERY LAW COME INTO FORCE, ALEX?
APRIL NEXT YEAR, I BELIEVE, CLIVE.
alex@alexcartoon.com
IT'S NOT CLEAR WHAT FORM IT WILL TAKE BUT IT'S CAUSING A LOT OF CONSTERNATION IN THE CORPORATE WORLD.
WELL, NO SENSE IN WAITING FOR THE DEADLINE TO REVIEW OUR PROCEDURES...
I FEEL THE ONUS IS ON US TO ADOPT SENSIBLE AND PRACTICAL MEASURES IN THE IMMEDIATE TERM TO ENSURE WE'RE NOT IN BREACH OF THE NEW LEGISLATION...
WHAT? YOU WANT ALL YOUR WIMBLEDON, ASCOT AND GLYNDEBOURNE TICKETS BOOKED, PAID FOR AND INVITES SENT TO YOUR CLIENTS RIGHT AWAY...?
BEFORE APRIL ANYWAY, I'M TAKING NO RISKS WITH MY SUMMER HOSPITALITY SEASON...

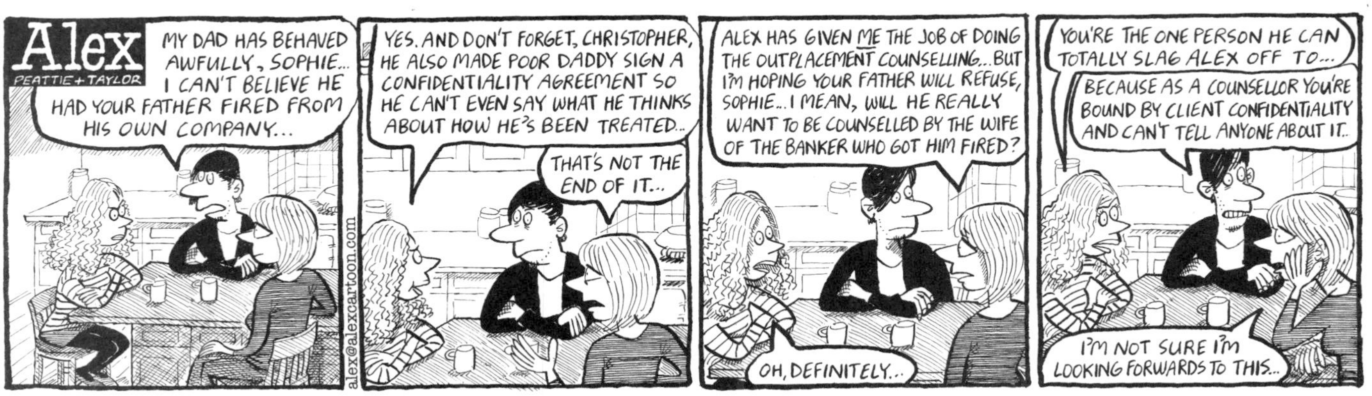
Alex
PEATTIE + TAYLOR
MY DAD HAS BEHAVED AWFULLY, SOPHIE... I CAN'T BELIEVE HE HAD YOUR FATHER FIRED FROM HIS OWN COMPANY...
YES. AND DON'T FORGET, CHRISTOPHER, HE ALSO MADE POOR DADDY SIGN A CONFIDENTIALITY AGREEMENT SO HE CAN'T EVEN SAY WHAT HE THINKS ABOUT HOW HE'S BEEN TREATED..
THAT'S NOT THE END OF IT...
alex@alexcartoon.com
ALEX HAS GIVEN ME THE JOB OF DOING THE OUTPLACEMENT COUNSELLING...BUT I'M HOPING YOUR FATHER WILL REFUSE, SOPHIE... I MEAN, WILL HE REALLY WANT TO BE COUNSELLED BY THE WIFE OF THE BANKER WHO GOT HIM FIRED?
OH, DEFINITELY...
YOU'RE THE ONE PERSON HE CAN TOTALLY SLAG ALEX OFF TO...
BECAUSE AS A COUNSELLOR YOU'RE BOUND BY CLIENT CONFIDENTIALITY AND CAN'T TELL ANYONE ABOUT IT..
I'M NOT SURE I'M LOOKING FORWARDS TO THIS...

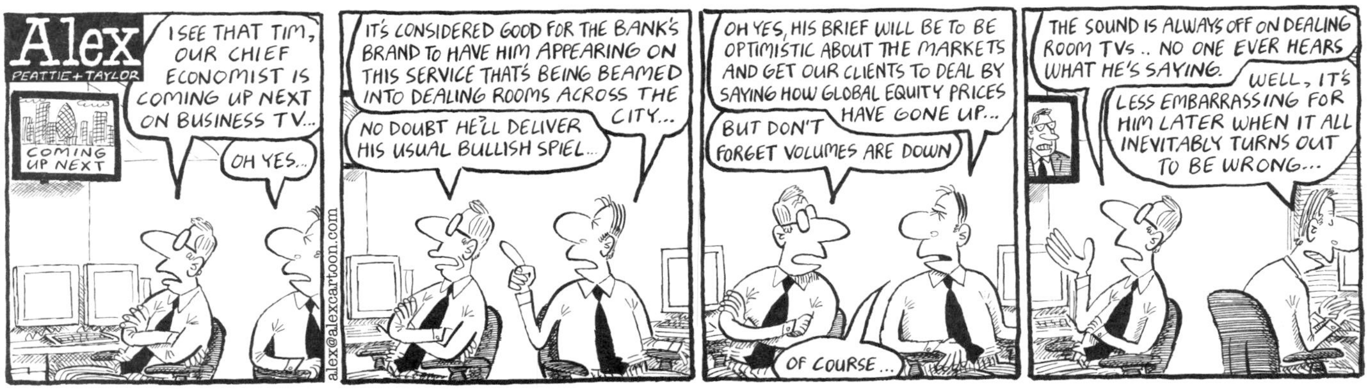
Alex
PEATTIE + TAYLOR
COMING UP NEXT
I SEE THAT TIM, OUR CHIEF ECONOMIST IS COMING UP NEXT ON BUSINESS TV...
OH YES...
alex@alexcartoon.com
IT'S CONSIDERED GOOD FOR THE BANK'S BRAND TO HAVE HIM APPEARING ON THIS SERVICE THAT'S BEING BEAMED INTO DEALING ROOMS ACROSS THE CITY...
NO DOUBT HE'LL DELIVER HIS USUAL BULLISH SPIEL...
OH YES, HIS BRIEF WILL BE TO BE OPTIMISTIC ABOUT THE MARKETS AND GET OUR CLIENTS TO DEAL BY SAYING HOW GLOBAL EQUITY PRICES HAVE GONE UP...
BUT DON'T FORGET VOLUMES ARE DOWN
OF COURSE...
THE SOUND IS ALWAYS OFF ON DEALING ROOM TVs .. NO ONE EVER HEARS WHAT HE'S SAYING.
WELL, IT'S LESS EMBARRASSING FOR HIM LATER WHEN IT ALL INEVITABLY TURNS OUT TO BE WRONG...

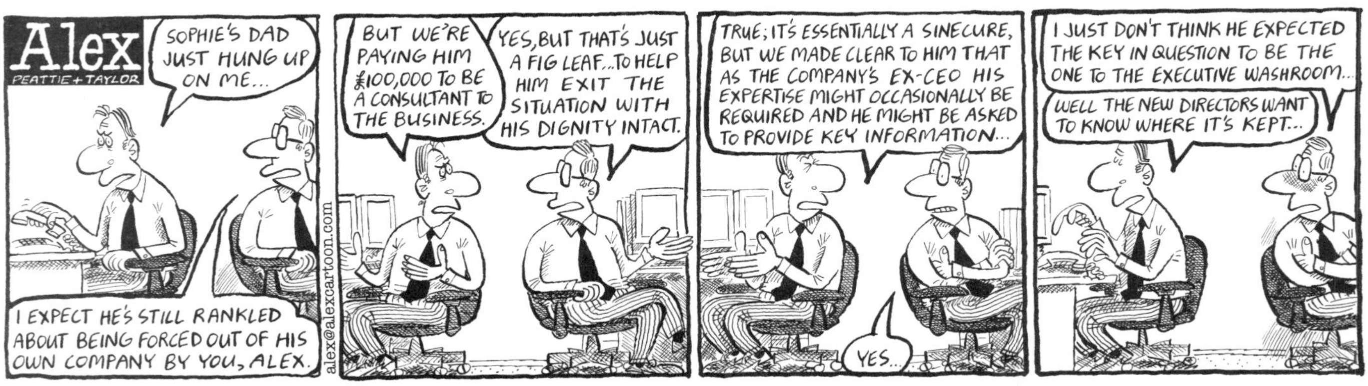
Alex
PEATTIE + TAYLOR
SOPHIE'S DAD JUST HUNG UP ON ME...
I EXPECT HE'S STILL RANKLED ABOUT BEING FORCED OUT OF HIS OWN COMPANY BY YOU, ALEX.
alex@alexcartoon.com
BUT WE'RE PAYING HIM £100,000 TO BE A CONSULTANT TO THE BUSINESS.
YES, BUT THAT'S JUST A FIG LEAF...TO HELP HIM EXIT THE SITUATION WITH HIS DIGNITY INTACT.
TRUE; IT'S ESSENTIALLY A SINECURE, BUT WE MADE CLEAR TO HIM THAT AS THE COMPANY'S EX-CEO HIS EXPERTISE MIGHT OCCASIONALLY BE REQUIRED AND HE MIGHT BE ASKED TO PROVIDE KEY INFORMATION...
YES...
I JUST DON'T THINK HE EXPECTED THE KEY IN QUESTION TO BE THE ONE TO THE EXECUTIVE WASHROOM...
WELL THE NEW DIRECTORS WANT TO KNOW WHERE IT'S KEPT...

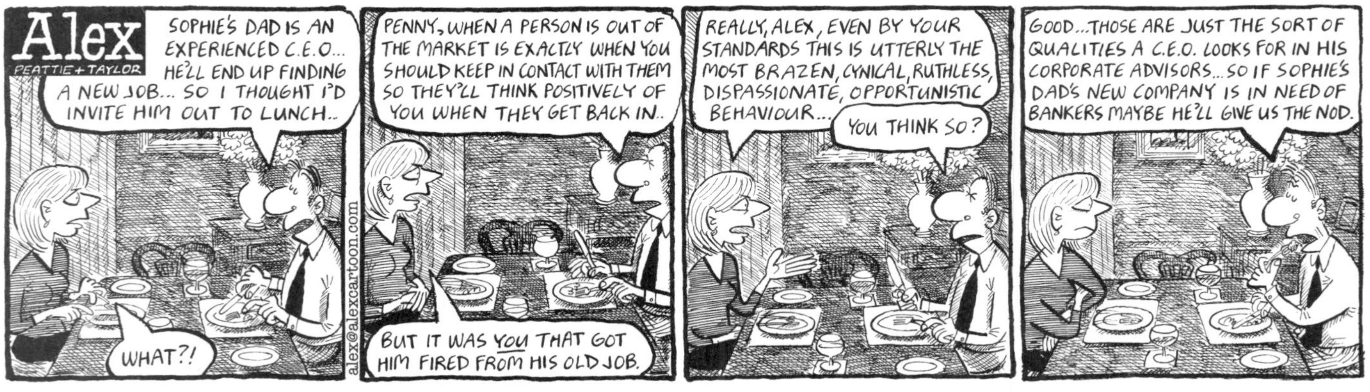
Alex
PEATTIE + TAYLOR
SOPHIE'S DAD IS AN EXPERIENCED C.E.O... HE'LL END UP FINDING A NEW JOB... SO I THOUGHT I'D INVITE HIM OUT TO LUNCH..
WHAT?!
alex@alexcartoon.com
PENNY, WHEN A PERSON IS OUT OF THE MARKET IS EXACTLY WHEN YOU SHOULD KEEP IN CONTACT WITH THEM SO THEY'LL THINK POSITIVELY OF YOU WHEN THEY GET BACK IN..
BUT IT WAS YOU THAT GOT HIM FIRED FROM HIS OLD JOB.
REALLY, ALEX, EVEN BY YOUR STANDARDS THIS IS UTTERLY THE MOST BRAZEN, CYNICAL, RUTHLESS, DISPASSIONATE, OPPORTUNISTIC BEHAVIOUR...
YOU THINK SO?
GOOD...THOSE ARE JUST THE SORT OF QUALITIES A C.E.O. LOOKS FOR IN HIS CORPORATE ADVISORS...SO IF SOPHIE'S DAD'S NEW COMPANY IS IN NEED OF BANKERS MAYBE HE'LL GIVE US THE NOD.

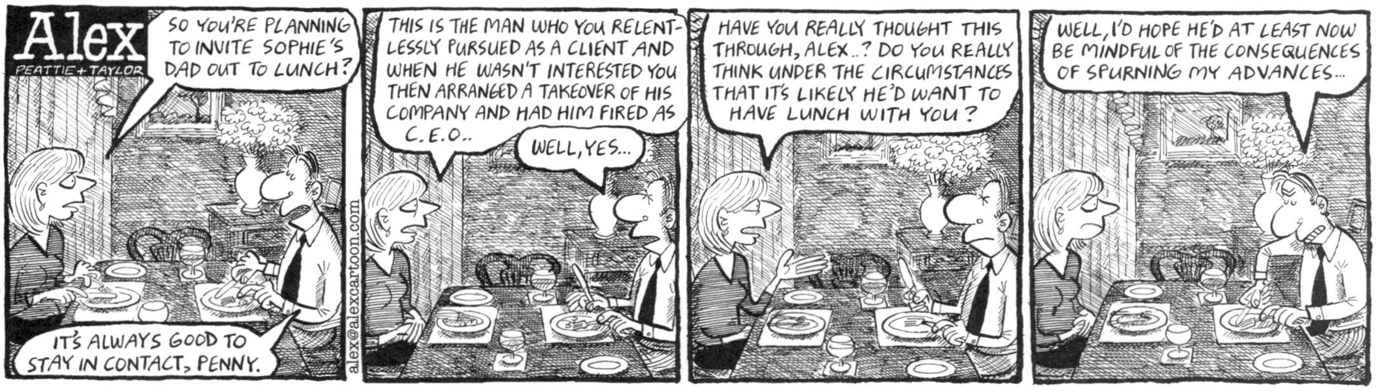
Alex
PEATTIE + TAYLOR
SO YOU'RE PLANNING TO INVITE SOPHIE'S DAD OUT TO LUNCH?
IT'S ALWAYS GOOD TO STAY IN CONTACT, PENNY.
alex@alexcartoon.com
THIS IS THE MAN WHO YOU RELENTLESSLY PURSUED AS A CLIENT AND WHEN HE WASN'T INTERESTED YOU THEN ARRANGED A TAKEOVER OF HIS COMPANY AND HAD HIM FIRED AS C.E.O..
WELL, YES...
HAVE YOU REALLY THOUGHT THIS THROUGH, ALEX..? DO YOU REALLY THINK UNDER THE CIRCUMSTANCES THAT IT'S LIKELY HE'D WANT TO HAVE LUNCH WITH YOU?
WELL, I'D HOPE HE'D AT LEAST NOW BE MINDFUL OF THE CONSEQUENCES OF SPURNING MY ADVANCES...

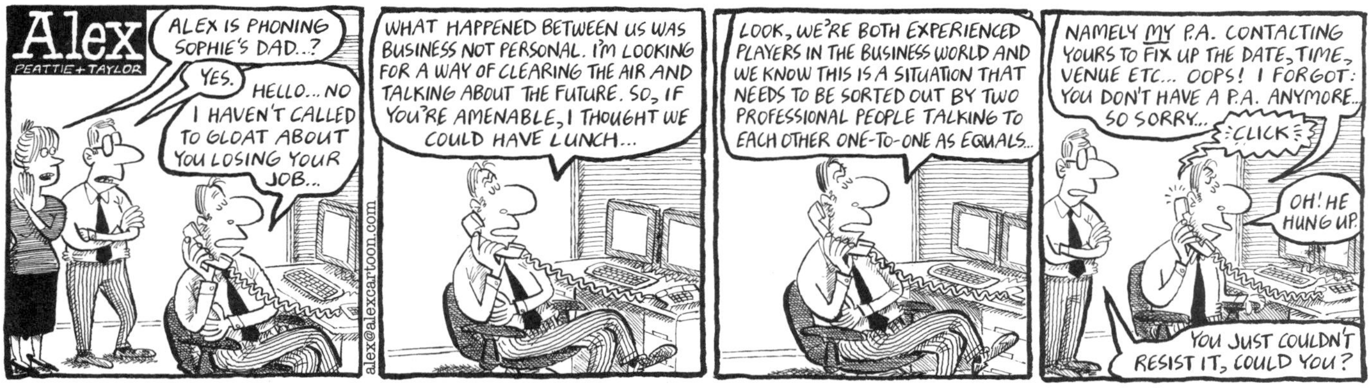
Alex
PEATTIE + TAYLOR
ALEX IS PHONING SOPHIE'S DAD...?
YES.
HELLO... NO I HAVEN'T CALLED TO GLOAT ABOUT YOU LOSING YOUR JOB...
alex@alexcartoon.com
WHAT HAPPENED BETWEEN US WAS BUSINESS NOT PERSONAL. I'M LOOKING FOR A WAY OF CLEARING THE AIR AND TALKING ABOUT THE FUTURE. SO, IF YOU'RE AMENABLE, I THOUGHT WE COULD HAVE LUNCH...
LOOK, WE'RE BOTH EXPERIENCED PLAYERS IN THE BUSINESS WORLD AND WE KNOW THIS IS A SITUATION THAT NEEDS TO BE SORTED OUT BY TWO PROFESSIONAL PEOPLE TALKING TO EACH OTHER ONE-TO-ONE AS EQUALS...
NAMELY MY P.A. CONTACTING YOURS TO FIX UP THE DATE, TIME, VENUE ETC... OOPS! I FORGOT: YOU DON'T HAVE A P.A. ANYMORE... SO SORRY...
CLICK
OH! HE HUNG UP.
YOU JUST COULDN'T RESIST IT, COULD YOU?

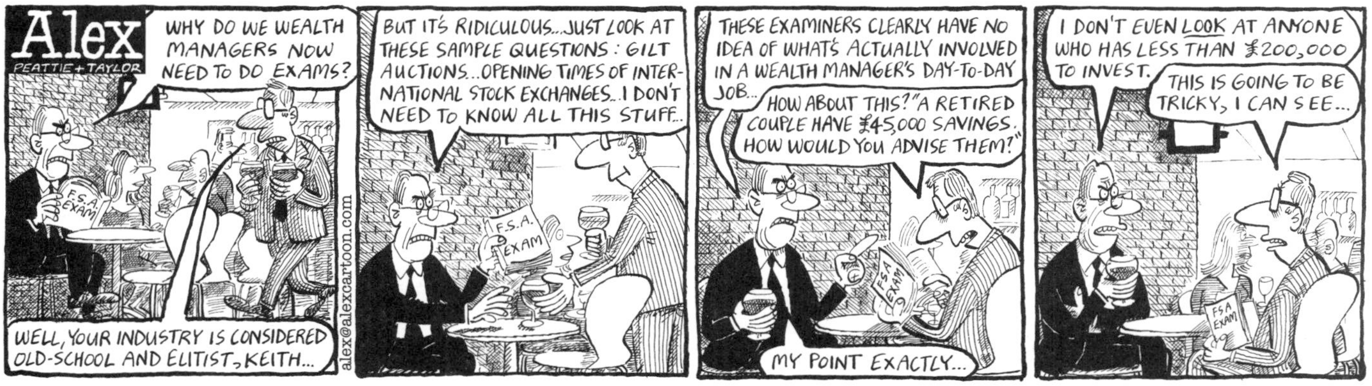
Alex
PEATTIE + TAYLOR
WHY DO WE WEALTH MANAGERS NOW NEED TO DO EXAMS?
F.S.A. EXAM
WELL, YOUR INDUSTRY IS CONSIDERED OLD-SCHOOL AND ELITIST, KEITH...
alex@alexcartoon.com
BUT IT'S RIDICULOUS... JUST LOOK AT THESE SAMPLE QUESTIONS: GILT AUCTIONS... OPENING TIMES OF INTERNATIONAL STOCK EXCHANGES... I DON'T NEED TO KNOW ALL THIS STUFF...
F.S.A. EXAM
THESE EXAMINERS CLEARLY HAVE NO IDEA OF WHAT'S ACTUALLY INVOLVED IN A WEALTH MANAGER'S DAY-TO-DAY JOB...
HOW ABOUT THIS?" A RETIRED COUPLE HAVE £45,000 SAVINGS. HOW WOULD YOU ADVISE THEM?"
F.S.A. EXAM
MY POINT EXACTLY...
I DON'T EVEN LOOK AT ANYONE WHO HAS LESS THAN £200,000 TO INVEST.
THIS IS GOING TO BE TRICKY, I CAN SEE...
F.S.A. EXAM

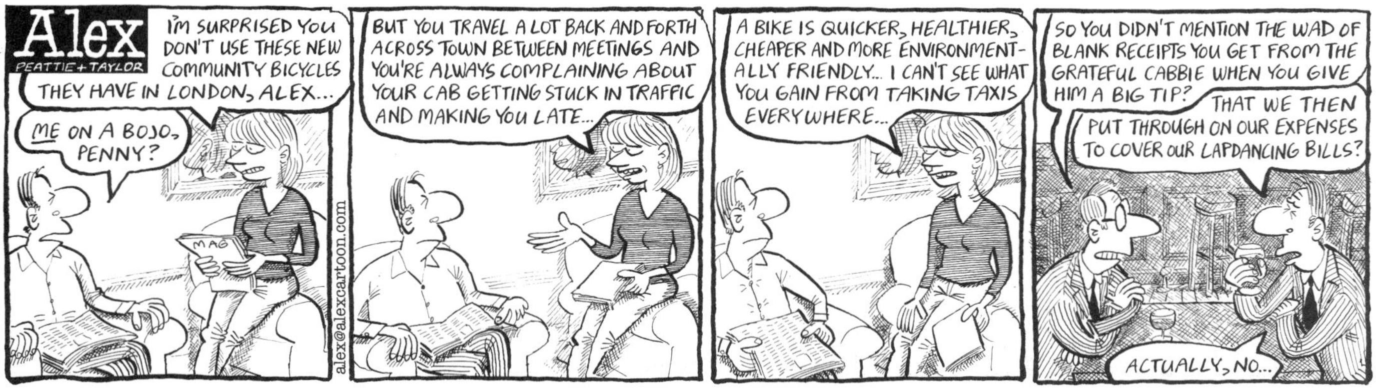
Alex
PEATTIE + TAYLOR
I'M SURPRISED YOU DON'T USE THESE NEW COMMUNITY BICYCLES THEY HAVE IN LONDON, ALEX...
ME ON A BOJO, PENNY?
MAG
alex@alexcartoon.com
BUT YOU TRAVEL A LOT BACK AND FORTH ACROSS TOWN BETWEEN MEETINGS AND YOU'RE ALWAYS COMPLAINING ABOUT YOUR CAB GETTING STUCK IN TRAFFIC AND MAKING YOU LATE...
A BIKE IS QUICKER, HEALTHIER, CHEAPER AND MORE ENVIRONMENTALLY FRIENDLY... I CAN'T SEE WHAT YOU GAIN FROM TAKING TAXIS EVERYWHERE...
SO YOU DIDN'T MENTION THE WAD OF BLANK RECEIPTS YOU GET FROM THE GRATEFUL CABBIE WHEN YOU GIVE HIM A BIG TIP?
THAT WE THEN PUT THROUGH ON OUR EXPENSES TO COVER OUR LAPDANCING BILLS?
ACTUALLY, NO...

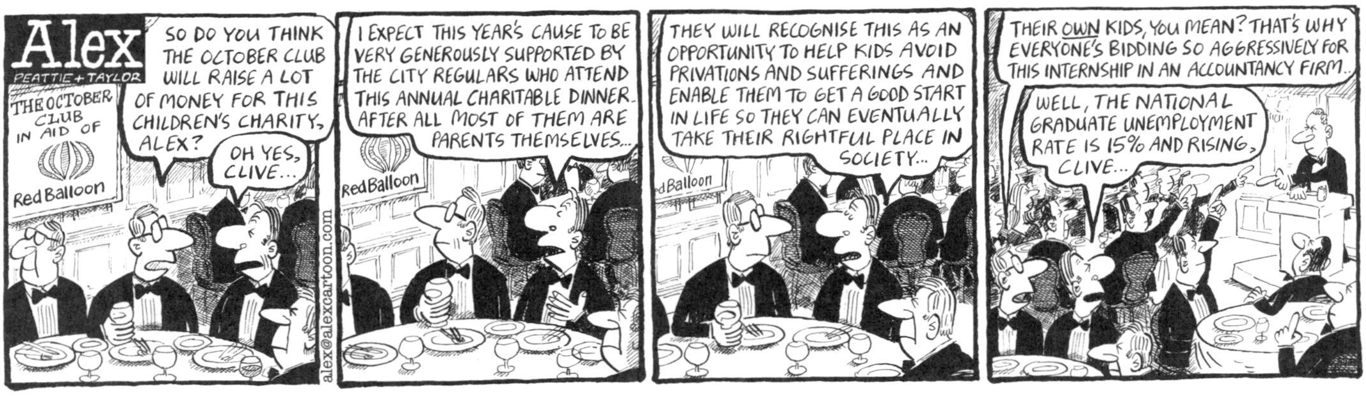
Alex
PEATTIE + TAYLOR
THE OCTOBER CLUB IN AID OF
Red Balloon
SO DO YOU THINK THE OCTOBER CLUB WILL RAISE A LOT OF MONEY FOR THIS CHILDREN'S CHARITY, ALEX?
OH YES, CLIVE...
alex@alexcartoon.com
I EXPECT THIS YEAR'S CAUSE TO BE VERY GENEROUSLY SUPPORTED BY THE CITY REGULARS WHO ATTEND THIS ANNUAL CHARITABLE DINNER. AFTER ALL MOST OF THEM ARE PARENTS THEMSELVES...
Red Balloon
THEY WILL RECOGNISE THIS AS AN OPPORTUNITY TO HELP KIDS AVOID PRIVATIONS AND SUFFERINGS AND ENABLE THEM TO GET A GOOD START IN LIFE SO THEY CAN EVENTUALLY TAKE THEIR RIGHTFUL PLACE IN SOCIETY...
THEIR OWN KIDS, YOU MEAN? THAT'S WHY EVERYONE'S BIDDING SO AGGRESSIVELY FOR THIS INTERNSHIP IN AN ACCOUNTANCY FIRM...
WELL, THE NATIONAL GRADUATE UNEMPLOYMENT RATE IS 15% AND RISING, CLIVE...

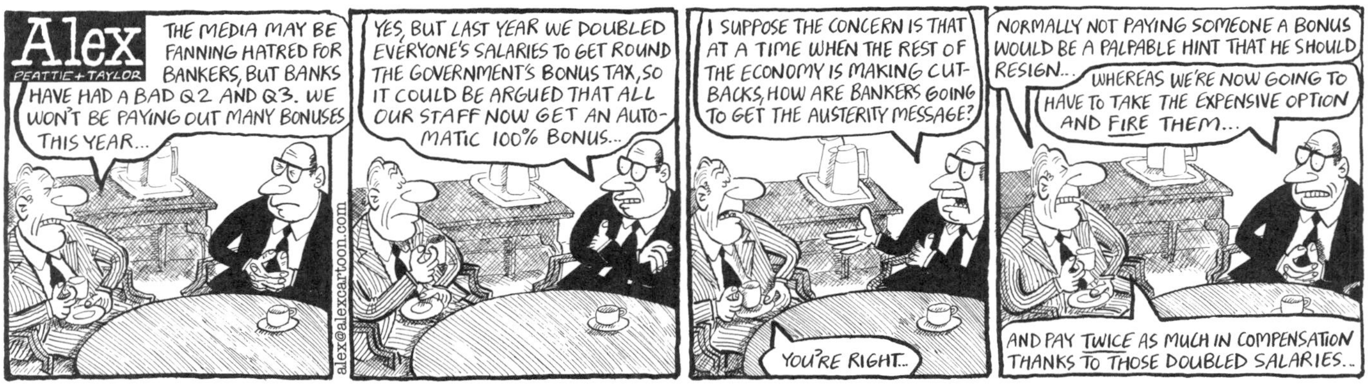
Alex
PEATTIE + TAYLOR
THE MEDIA MAY BE FANNING HATRED FOR BANKERS, BUT BANKS HAVE HAD A BAD Q2 AND Q3. WE WON'T BE PAYING OUT MANY BONUSES THIS YEAR...
alex@alexcartoon.com
YES, BUT LAST YEAR WE DOUBLED EVERYONE'S SALARIES TO GET ROUND THE GOVERNMENT'S BONUS TAX, SO IT COULD BE ARGUED THAT ALL OUR STAFF NOW GET AN AUTOMATIC 100% BONUS...
I SUPPOSE THE CONCERN IS THAT AT A TIME WHEN THE REST OF THE ECONOMY IS MAKING CUTBACKS, HOW ARE BANKERS GOING TO GET THE AUSTERITY MESSAGE?
YOU'RE RIGHT...
NORMALLY NOT PAYING SOMEONE A BONUS WOULD BE A PALPABLE HINT THAT HE SHOULD RESIGN...
WHEREAS WE'RE NOW GOING TO HAVE TO TAKE THE EXPENSIVE OPTION AND FIRE THEM...
AND PAY TWICE AS MUCH IN COMPENSATION THANKS TO THOSE DOUBLED SALARIES...

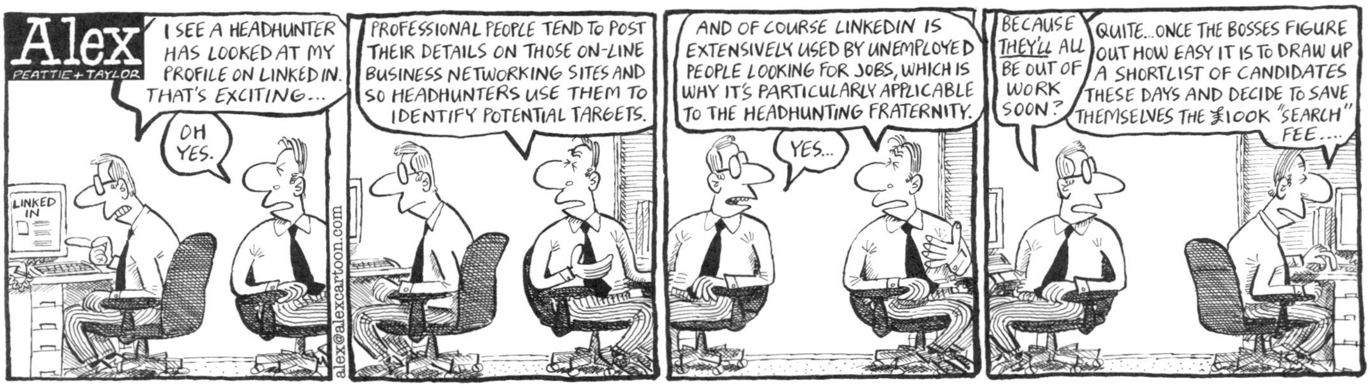
Alex
PEATTIE + TAYLOR
I SEE A HEADHUNTER HAS LOOKED AT MY PROFILE ON LINKED IN. THAT'S EXCITING...
OH YES.
LINKED IN
alex@alexcartoon.com
PROFESSIONAL PEOPLE TEND TO POST THEIR DETAILS ON THOSE ON-LINE BUSINESS NETWORKING SITES AND SO HEADHUNTERS USE THEM TO IDENTIFY POTENTIAL TARGETS.
AND OF COURSE LINKEDIN IS EXTENSIVELY USED BY UNEMPLOYED PEOPLE LOOKING FOR JOBS, WHICH IS WHY IT'S PARTICULARLY APPLICABLE TO THE HEADHUNTING FRATERNITY.
YES...
BECAUSE THEY'LL ALL BE OUT OF WORK SOON?
QUITE... ONCE THE BOSSES FIGURE OUT HOW EASY IT IS TO DRAW UP A SHORTLIST OF CANDIDATES THESE DAYS AND DECIDE TO SAVE THEMSELVES THE £100K "SEARCH" FEE....

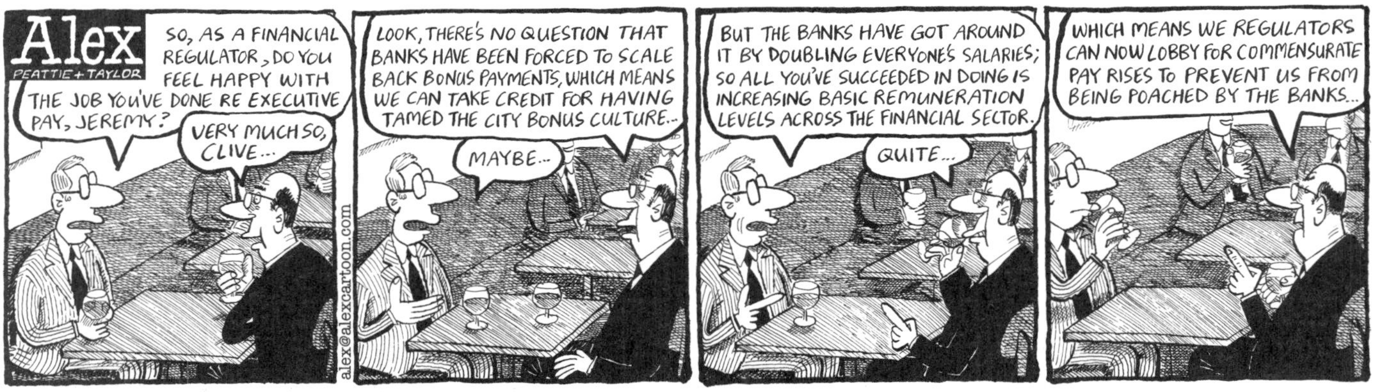
Alex
PEATTIE + TAYLOR
SO, AS A FINANCIAL REGULATOR, DO YOU FEEL HAPPY WITH THE JOB YOU'VE DONE RE EXECUTIVE PAY, JEREMY?
VERY MUCH SO, CLIVE...
alex@alexcartoon.com
LOOK, THERE'S NO QUESTION THAT BANKS HAVE BEEN FORCED TO SCALE BACK BONUS PAYMENTS, WHICH MEANS WE CAN TAKE CREDIT FOR HAVING TAMED THE CITY BONUS CULTURE...
MAYBE...
BUT THE BANKS HAVE GOT AROUND IT BY DOUBLING EVERYONE'S SALARIES; SO ALL YOU'VE SUCCEEDED IN DOING IS INCREASING BASIC REMUNERATION LEVELS ACROSS THE FINANCIAL SECTOR.
QUITE...
WHICH MEANS WE REGULATORS CAN NOW LOBBY FOR COMMENSURATE PAY RISES TO PREVENT US FROM BEING POACHED BY THE BANKS...

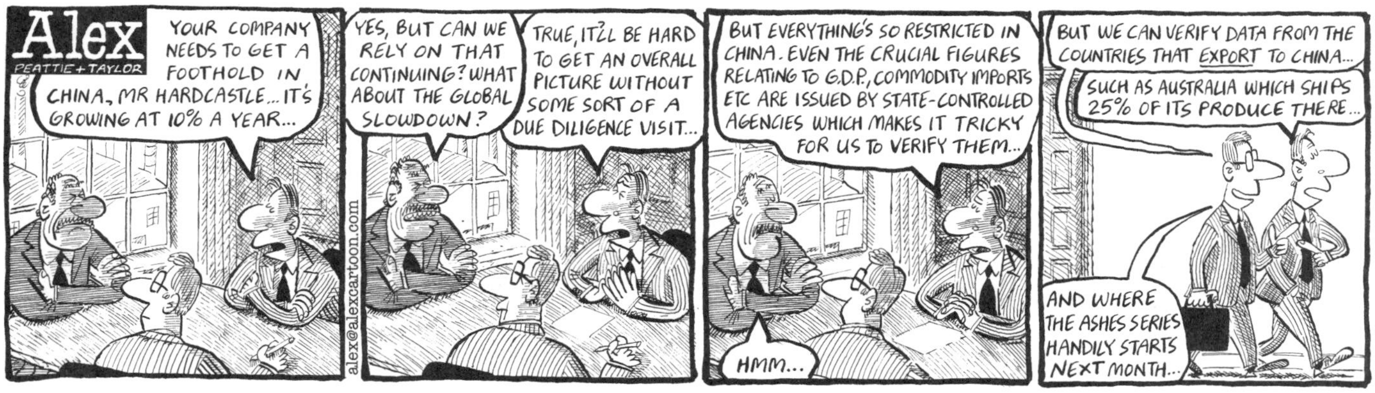
Alex
PEATTIE+TAYLOR
YOUR COMPANY NEEDS TO GET A FOOTHOLD IN CHINA, MR HARDCASTLE... IT'S GROWING AT 10% A YEAR...
YES, BUT CAN WE RELY ON THAT CONTINUING? WHAT ABOUT THE GLOBAL SLOWDOWN?
TRUE, IT'LL BE HARD TO GET AN OVERALL PICTURE WITHOUT SOME SORT OF A DUE DILIGENCE VISIT...
alex@alexcartoon.com
BUT EVERYTHING'S SO RESTRICTED IN CHINA. EVEN THE CRUCIAL FIGURES RELATING TO G.D.P., COMMODITY IMPORTS ETC ARE ISSUED BY STATE-CONTROLLED AGENCIES WHICH MAKES IT TRICKY FOR US TO VERIFY THEM...
HMM...
BUT WE CAN VERIFY DATA FROM THE COUNTRIES THAT EXPORT TO CHINA...
SUCH AS AUSTRALIA WHICH SHIPS 25% OF ITS PRODUCE THERE...
AND WHERE THE ASHES SERIES HANDILY STARTS NEXT MONTH...

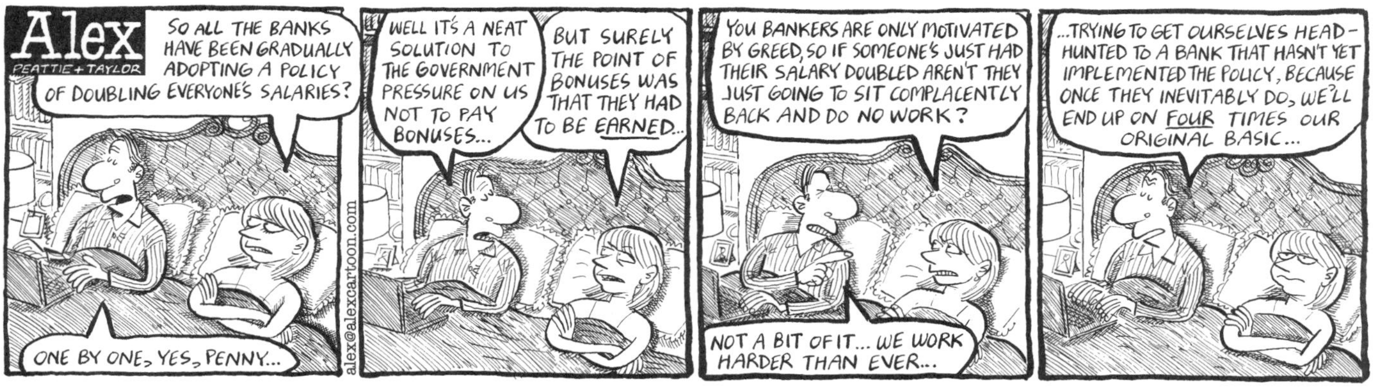
Alex
PEATTIE+TAYLOR
SO ALL THE BANKS HAVE BEEN GRADUALLY ADOPTING A POLICY OF DOUBLING EVERYONE'S SALARIES?
ONE BY ONE, YES, PENNY...
WELL IT'S A NEAT SOLUTION TO THE GOVERNMENT PRESSURE ON US NOT TO PAY BONUSES...
BUT SURELY THE POINT OF BONUSES WAS THAT THEY HAD TO BE EARNED...
alex@alexcartoon.com
YOU BANKERS ARE ONLY MOTIVATED BY GREED, SO IF SOMEONE'S JUST HAD THEIR SALARY DOUBLED AREN'T THEY JUST GOING TO SIT COMPLACENTLY BACK AND DO NO WORK?
NOT A BIT OF IT... WE WORK HARDER THAN EVER...
...TRYING TO GET OURSELVES HEAD-HUNTED TO A BANK THAT HASN'T YET IMPLEMENTED THE POLICY, BECAUSE ONCE THEY INEVITABLY DO, WE'LL END UP ON FOUR TIMES OUR ORIGINAL BASIC...

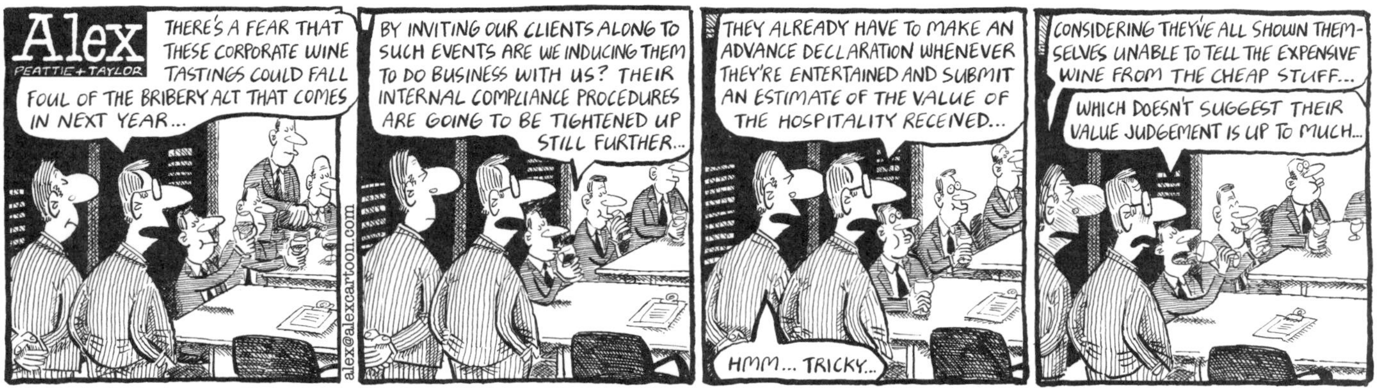
Alex
PEATTIE+TAYLOR
THERE'S A FEAR THAT THESE CORPORATE WINE TASTINGS COULD FALL FOUL OF THE BRIBERY ACT THAT COMES IN NEXT YEAR...
BY INVITING OUR CLIENTS ALONG TO SUCH EVENTS ARE WE INDUCING THEM TO DO BUSINESS WITH US? THEIR INTERNAL COMPLIANCE PROCEDURES ARE GOING TO BE TIGHTENED UP STILL FURTHER...
alex@alexcartoon.com
THEY ALREADY HAVE TO MAKE AN ADVANCE DECLARATION WHENEVER THEY'RE ENTERTAINED AND SUBMIT AN ESTIMATE OF THE VALUE OF THE HOSPITALITY RECEIVED...
HMM... TRICKY...
CONSIDERING THEY'VE ALL SHOWN THEMSELVES UNABLE TO TELL THE EXPENSIVE WINE FROM THE CHEAP STUFF...
WHICH DOESN'T SUGGEST THEIR VALUE JUDGEMENT IS UP TO MUCH...

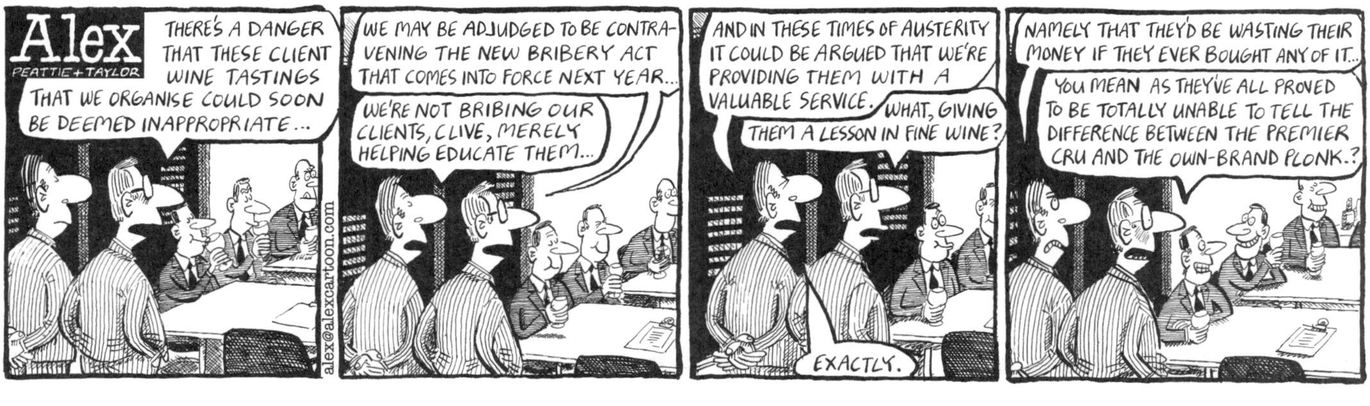
Alex
PEATTIE+TAYLOR
THERE'S A DANGER THAT THESE CLIENT WINE TASTINGS THAT WE ORGANISE COULD SOON BE DEEMED INAPPROPRIATE...
alex@alexcartoon.com
WE MAY BE ADJUDGED TO BE CONTRAVENING THE NEW BRIBERY ACT THAT COMES INTO FORCE NEXT YEAR...
WE'RE NOT BRIBING OUR CLIENTS, CLIVE, MERELY HELPING EDUCATE THEM...
AND IN THESE TIMES OF AUSTERITY IT COULD BE ARGUED THAT WE'RE PROVIDING THEM WITH A VALUABLE SERVICE.
WHAT, GIVING THEM A LESSON IN FINE WINE?
EXACTLY.
NAMELY THAT THEY'D BE WASTING THEIR MONEY IF THEY EVER BOUGHT ANY OF IT...
YOU MEAN AS THEY'VE ALL PROVED TO BE TOTALLY UNABLE TO TELL THE DIFFERENCE BETWEEN THE PREMIER CRU AND THE OWN-BRAND PLONK?

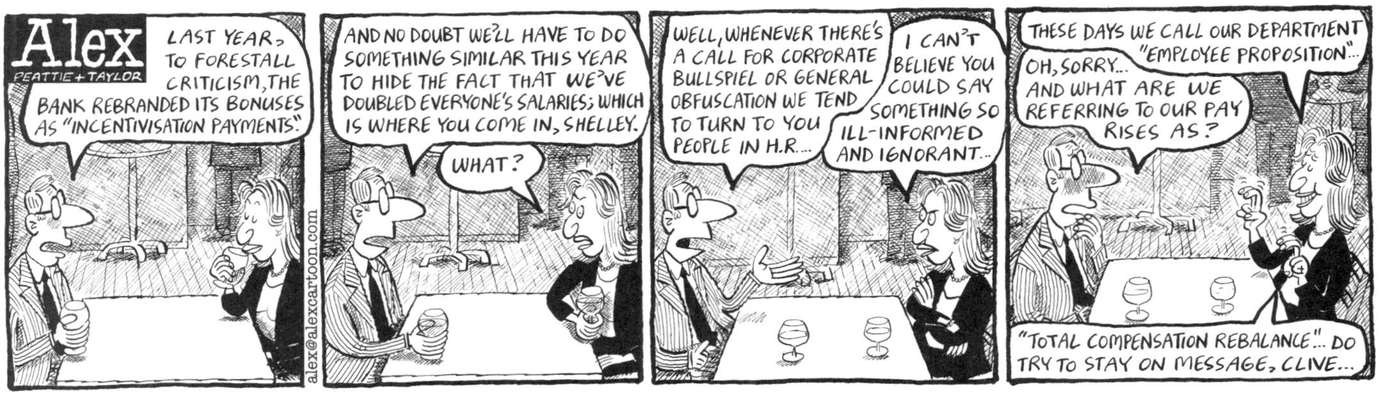
Alex
PEATTIE + TAYLOR
LAST YEAR, TO FORESTALL CRITICISM, THE BANK REBRANDED ITS BONUSES AS "INCENTIVISATION PAYMENTS."
alex@alexcartoon.com
AND NO DOUBT WE'LL HAVE TO DO SOMETHING SIMILAR THIS YEAR TO HIDE THE FACT THAT WE'VE DOUBLED EVERYONE'S SALARIES; WHICH IS WHERE YOU COME IN, SHELLEY.
WHAT?
WELL, WHENEVER THERE'S A CALL FOR CORPORATE BULLSPIEL OR GENERAL OBFUSCATION WE TEND TO TURN TO YOU PEOPLE IN H.R....
I CAN'T BELIEVE YOU COULD SAY SOMETHING SO ILL-INFORMED AND IGNORANT...
THESE DAYS WE CALL OUR DEPARTMENT "EMPLOYEE PROPOSITION"...
OH, SORRY... AND WHAT ARE WE REFERRING TO OUR PAY RISES AS?
"TOTAL COMPENSATION REBALANCE"... DO TRY TO STAY ON MESSAGE, CLIVE...

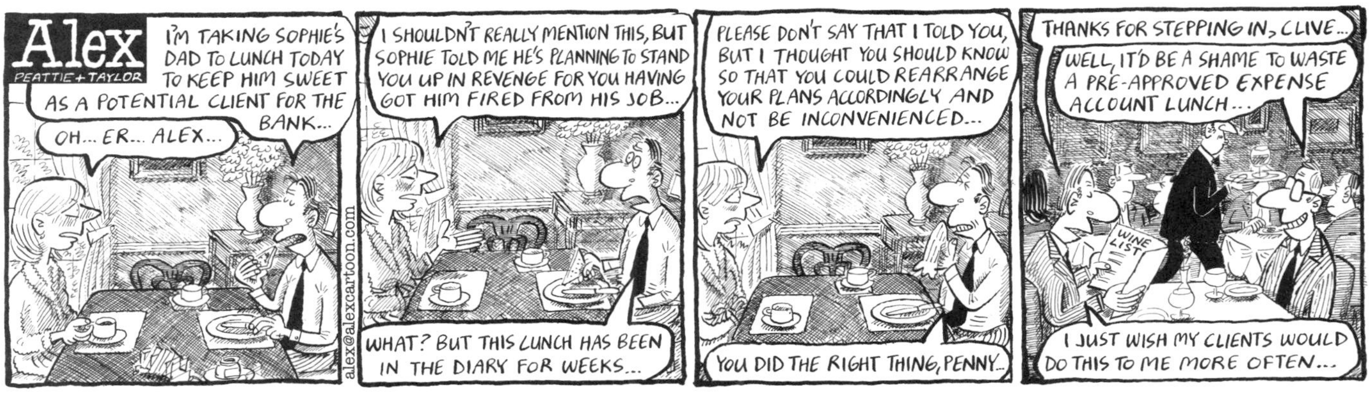
Alex
PEATTIE + TAYLOR
I'M TAKING SOPHIE'S DAD TO LUNCH TODAY TO KEEP HIM SWEET AS A POTENTIAL CLIENT FOR THE BANK...
OH... ER... ALEX...
alex@alexcartoon.com
I SHOULDN'T REALLY MENTION THIS, BUT SOPHIE TOLD ME HE'S PLANNING TO STAND YOU UP IN REVENGE FOR YOU HAVING GOT HIM FIRED FROM HIS JOB...
WHAT? BUT THIS LUNCH HAS BEEN IN THE DIARY FOR WEEKS...
PLEASE DON'T SAY THAT I TOLD YOU, BUT I THOUGHT YOU SHOULD KNOW SO THAT YOU COULD REARRANGE YOUR PLANS ACCORDINGLY AND NOT BE INCONVENIENCED...
YOU DID THE RIGHT THING, PENNY...
THANKS FOR STEPPING IN, CLIVE...
WELL, IT'D BE A SHAME TO WASTE A PRE-APPROVED EXPENSE ACCOUNT LUNCH...
WINE LIST
I JUST WISH MY CLIENTS WOULD DO THIS TO ME MORE OFTEN...

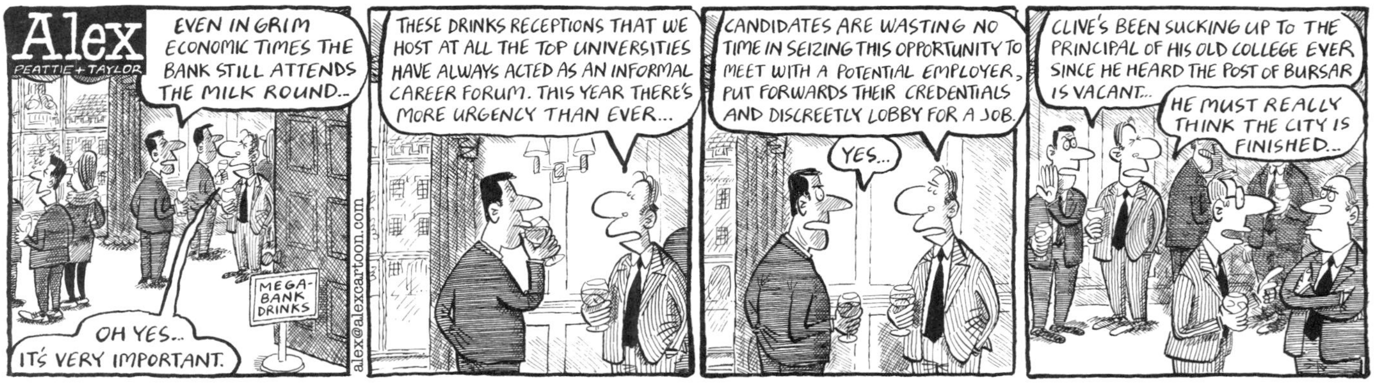
Alex
PEATTIE + TAYLOR
EVEN IN GRIM ECONOMIC TIMES THE BANK STILL ATTENDS THE MILK ROUND...
MEGA-BANK DRINKS
OH YES... IT'S VERY IMPORTANT.
alex@alexcartoon.com
THESE DRINKS RECEPTIONS THAT WE HOST AT ALL THE TOP UNIVERSITIES HAVE ALWAYS ACTED AS AN INFORMAL CAREER FORUM. THIS YEAR THERE'S MORE URGENCY THAN EVER...
CANDIDATES ARE WASTING NO TIME IN SEIZING THIS OPPORTUNITY TO MEET WITH A POTENTIAL EMPLOYER, PUT FORWARDS THEIR CREDENTIALS AND DISCREETLY LOBBY FOR A JOB.
YES...
CLIVE'S BEEN SUCKING UP TO THE PRINCIPAL OF HIS OLD COLLEGE EVER SINCE HE HEARD THE POST OF BURSAR IS VACANT...
HE MUST REALLY THINK THE CITY IS FINISHED...

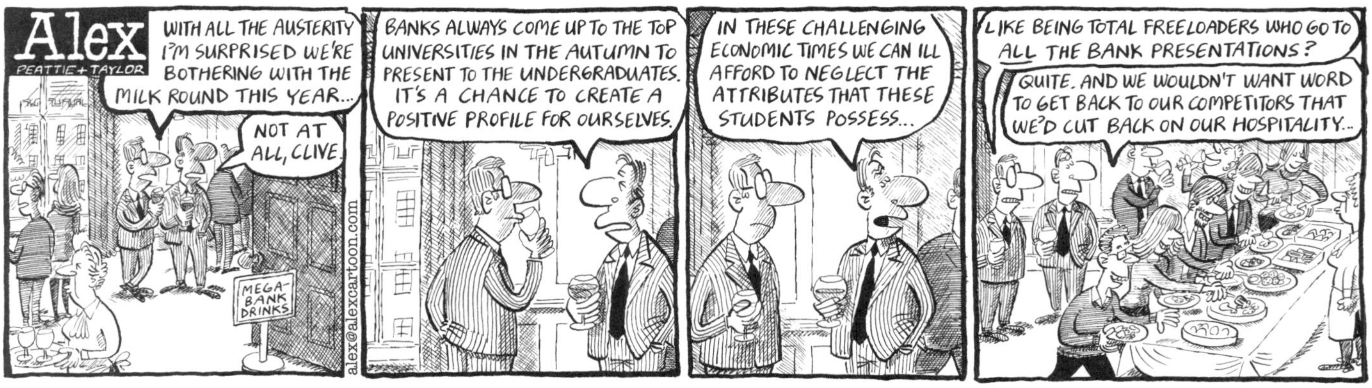
Alex
PEATTIE + TAYLOR
WITH ALL THE AUSTERITY I'M SURPRISED WE'RE BOTHERING WITH THE MILK ROUND THIS YEAR...
NOT AT ALL, CLIVE.
MEGA-BANK DRINKS
alex@alexcartoon.com
BANKS ALWAYS COME UP TO THE TOP UNIVERSITIES IN THE AUTUMN TO PRESENT TO THE UNDERGRADUATES. IT'S A CHANCE TO CREATE A POSITIVE PROFILE FOR OURSELVES.
IN THESE CHALLENGING ECONOMIC TIMES WE CAN ILL AFFORD TO NEGLECT THE ATTRIBUTES THAT THESE STUDENTS POSSESS...
LIKE BEING TOTAL FREELOADERS WHO GO TO ALL THE BANK PRESENTATIONS?
QUITE. AND WE WOULDN'T WANT WORD TO GET BACK TO OUR COMPETITORS THAT WE'D CUT BACK ON OUR HOSPITALITY...

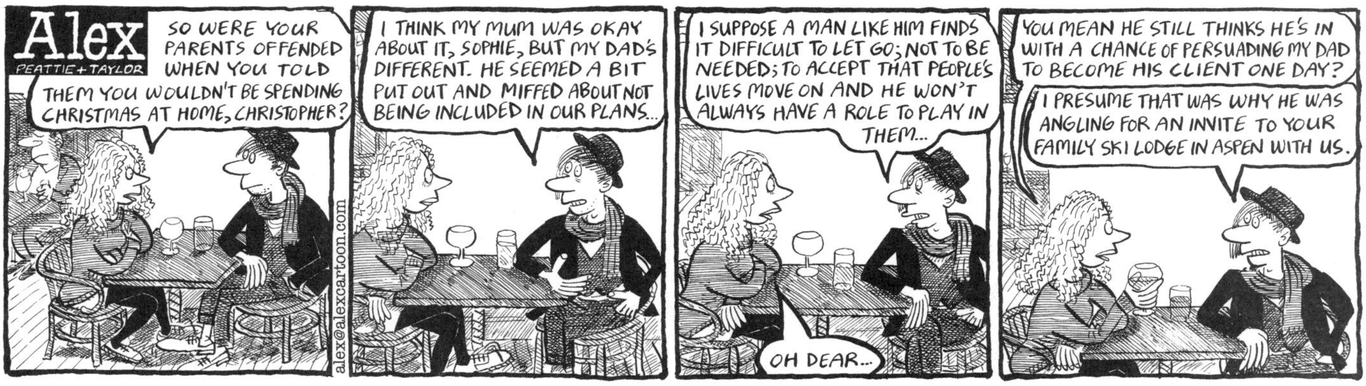
Alex
PEATTIE + TAYLOR
SO WERE YOUR PARENTS OFFENDED WHEN YOU TOLD THEM YOU WOULDN'T BE SPENDING CHRISTMAS AT HOME, CHRISTOPHER?
I THINK MY MUM WAS OKAY ABOUT IT, SOPHIE, BUT MY DAD'S DIFFERENT. HE SEEMED A BIT PUT OUT AND MIFFED ABOUT NOT BEING INCLUDED IN OUR PLANS...
alex@alexcartoon.com
I SUPPOSE A MAN LIKE HIM FINDS IT DIFFICULT TO LET GO; NOT TO BE NEEDED; TO ACCEPT THAT PEOPLE'S LIVES MOVE ON AND HE WON'T ALWAYS HAVE A ROLE TO PLAY IN THEM...
OH DEAR...
YOU MEAN HE STILL THINKS HE'S IN WITH A CHANCE OF PERSUADING MY DAD TO BECOME HIS CLIENT ONE DAY?
I PRESUME THAT WAS WHY HE WAS ANGLING FOR AN INVITE TO YOUR FAMILY SKI LODGE IN ASPEN WITH US.

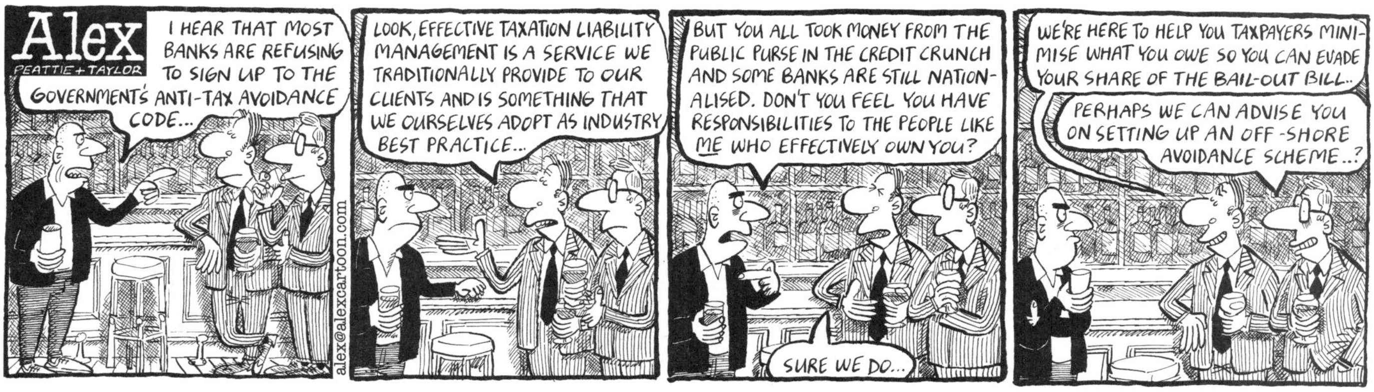
Alex
PEATTIE + TAYLOR
I HEAR THAT MOST BANKS ARE REFUSING TO SIGN UP TO THE GOVERNMENT'S ANTI-TAX AVOIDANCE CODE...
LOOK, EFFECTIVE TAXATION LIABILITY MANAGEMENT IS A SERVICE WE TRADITIONALLY PROVIDE TO OUR CLIENTS AND IS SOMETHING THAT WE OURSELVES ADOPT AS INDUSTRY BEST PRACTICE...
alex@alexcartoon.com
BUT YOU ALL TOOK MONEY FROM THE PUBLIC PURSE IN THE CREDIT CRUNCH AND SOME BANKS ARE STILL NATIONALISED. DON'T YOU FEEL YOU HAVE RESPONSIBILITIES TO THE PEOPLE LIKE ME WHO EFFECTIVELY OWN YOU?
SURE WE DO...
WE'RE HERE TO HELP YOU TAXPAYERS MINIMISE WHAT YOU OWE SO YOU CAN EVADE YOUR SHARE OF THE BAIL-OUT BILL...
PERHAPS WE CAN ADVISE YOU ON SETTING UP AN OFF-SHORE AVOIDANCE SCHEME...?

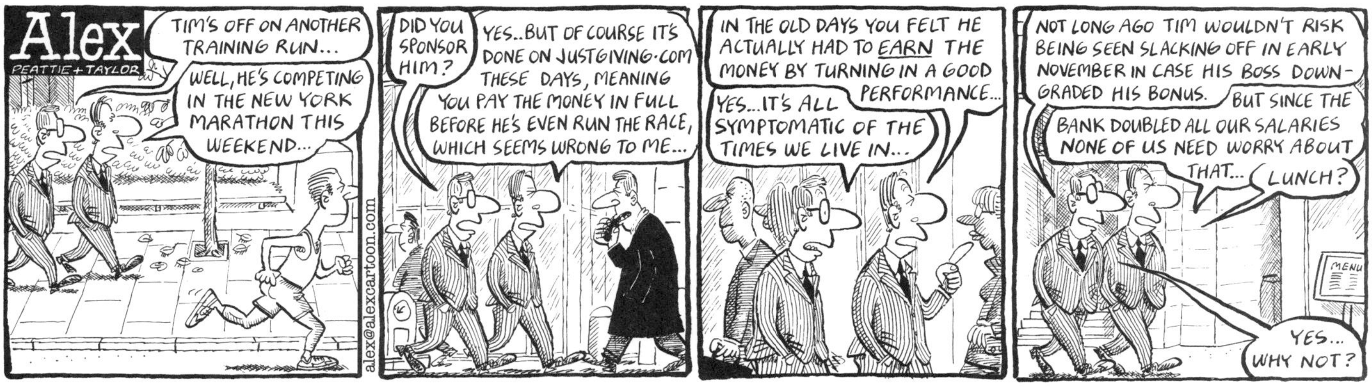
Alex
PEATTIE + TAYLOR
TIM'S OFF ON ANOTHER TRAINING RUN...
WELL, HE'S COMPETING IN THE NEW YORK MARATHON THIS WEEKEND...
alex@alexcartoon.com
DID YOU SPONSOR HIM?
YES...BUT OF COURSE IT'S DONE ON JUSTGIVING.COM THESE DAYS, MEANING YOU PAY THE MONEY IN FULL BEFORE HE'S EVEN RUN THE RACE, WHICH SEEMS WRONG TO ME...
IN THE OLD DAYS YOU FELT HE ACTUALLY HAD TO EARN THE MONEY BY TURNING IN A GOOD PERFORMANCE...
YES...IT'S ALL SYMPTOMATIC OF THE TIMES WE LIVE IN...
NOT LONG AGO TIM WOULDN'T RISK BEING SEEN SLACKING OFF IN EARLY NOVEMBER IN CASE HIS BOSS DOWNGRADED HIS BONUS.
BUT SINCE THE BANK DOUBLED ALL OUR SALARIES NONE OF US NEED WORRY ABOUT THAT...
LUNCH?
MENU
YES... WHY NOT?

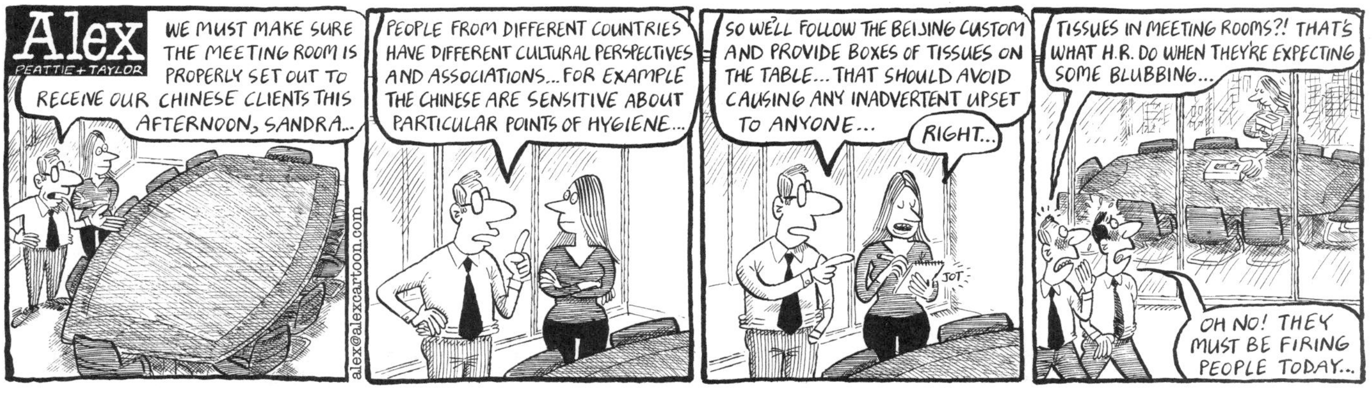
Alex
PEATTIE + TAYLOR
WE MUST MAKE SURE THE MEETING ROOM IS PROPERLY SET OUT TO RECEIVE OUR CHINESE CLIENTS THIS AFTERNOON, SANDRA...
alex@alexcartoon.com
PEOPLE FROM DIFFERENT COUNTRIES HAVE DIFFERENT CULTURAL PERSPECTIVES AND ASSOCIATIONS...FOR EXAMPLE THE CHINESE ARE SENSITIVE ABOUT PARTICULAR POINTS OF HYGIENE...
SO WE'LL FOLLOW THE BEIJING CUSTOM AND PROVIDE BOXES OF TISSUES ON THE TABLE... THAT SHOULD AVOID CAUSING ANY INADVERTENT UPSET TO ANYONE...
RIGHT...
JOT
TISSUES IN MEETING ROOMS?! THAT'S WHAT H.R. DO WHEN THEY'RE EXPECTING SOME BLUBBING...
OH NO! THEY MUST BE FIRING PEOPLE TODAY...

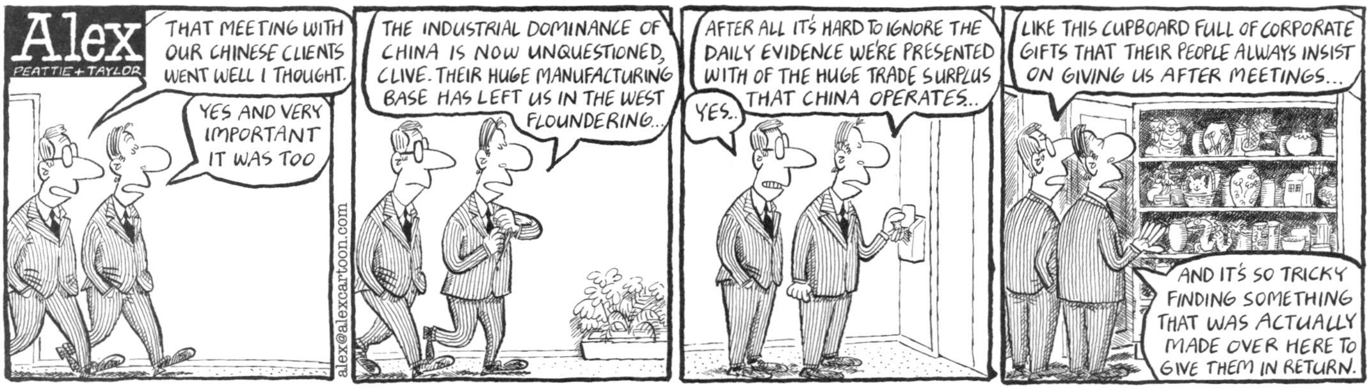
Alex
PEATTIE+TAYLOR
THAT MEETING WITH OUR CHINESE CLIENTS WENT WELL I THOUGHT.
YES AND VERY IMPORTANT IT WAS TOO
alex@alexcartoon.com
THE INDUSTRIAL DOMINANCE OF CHINA IS NOW UNQUESTIONED, CLIVE. THEIR HUGE MANUFACTURING BASE HAS LEFT US IN THE WEST FLOUNDERING...
AFTER ALL IT'S HARD TO IGNORE THE DAILY EVIDENCE WE'RE PRESENTED WITH OF THE HUGE TRADE SURPLUS THAT CHINA OPERATES..
YES..
LIKE THIS CUPBOARD FULL OF CORPORATE GIFTS THAT THEIR PEOPLE ALWAYS INSIST ON GIVING US AFTER MEETINGS...
AND IT'S SO TRICKY FINDING SOMETHING THAT WAS ACTUALLY MADE OVER HERE TO GIVE THEM IN RETURN.

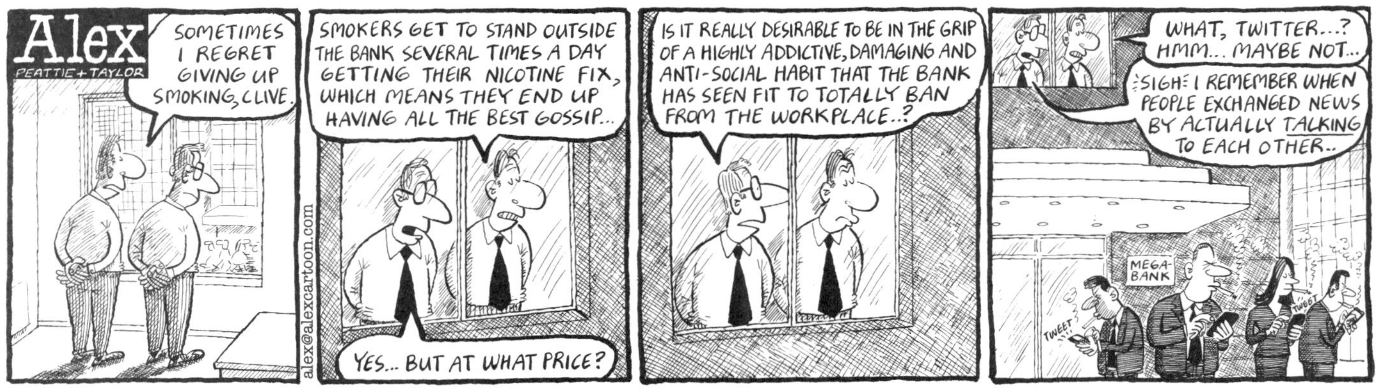
Alex
PEATTIE+TAYLOR
SOMETIMES I REGRET GIVING UP SMOKING, CLIVE.
alex@alexcartoon.com
SMOKERS GET TO STAND OUTSIDE THE BANK SEVERAL TIMES A DAY GETTING THEIR NICOTINE FIX, WHICH MEANS THEY END UP HAVING ALL THE BEST GOSSIP...
YES... BUT AT WHAT PRICE?
IS IT REALLY DESIRABLE TO BE IN THE GRIP OF A HIGHLY ADDICTIVE, DAMAGING AND ANTI-SOCIAL HABIT THAT THE BANK HAS SEEN FIT TO TOTALLY BAN FROM THE WORKPLACE..?
WHAT, TWITTER...? HMM... MAYBE NOT...
=SIGH= I REMEMBER WHEN PEOPLE EXCHANGED NEWS BY ACTUALLY TALKING TO EACH OTHER..
MEGA-BANK
TWEET
TWEET

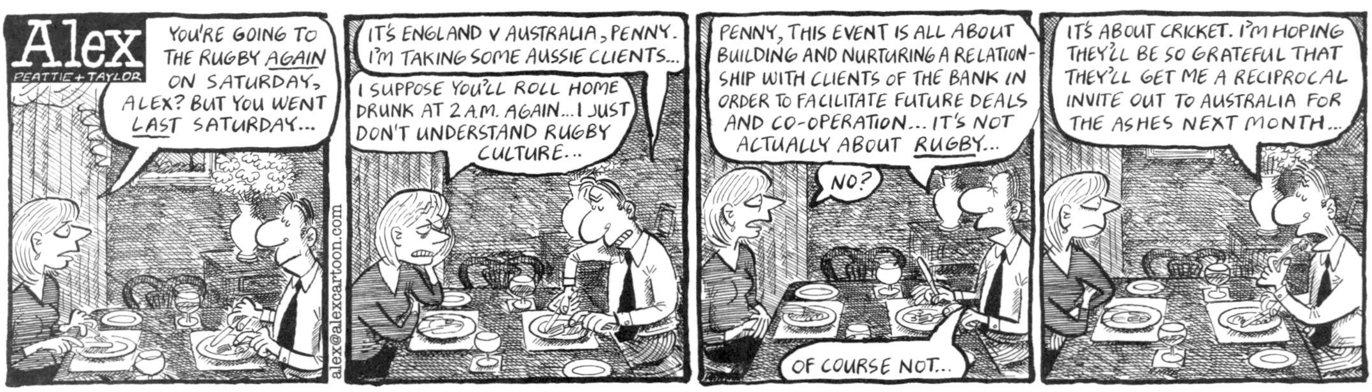
Alex
PEATTIE+TAYLOR
YOU'RE GOING TO THE RUGBY AGAIN ON SATURDAY, ALEX? BUT YOU WENT LAST SATURDAY...
alex@alexcartoon.com
IT'S ENGLAND V AUSTRALIA, PENNY. I'M TAKING SOME AUSSIE CLIENTS...
I SUPPOSE YOU'LL ROLL HOME DRUNK AT 2 A.M. AGAIN... I JUST DON'T UNDERSTAND RUGBY CULTURE...
PENNY, THIS EVENT IS ALL ABOUT BUILDING AND NURTURING A RELATIONSHIP WITH CLIENTS OF THE BANK IN ORDER TO FACILITATE FUTURE DEALS AND CO-OPERATION... IT'S NOT ACTUALLY ABOUT RUGBY...
NO?
OF COURSE NOT...
IT'S ABOUT CRICKET. I'M HOPING THEY'LL BE SO GRATEFUL THAT THEY'LL GET ME A RECIPROCAL INVITE OUT TO AUSTRALIA FOR THE ASHES NEXT MONTH...

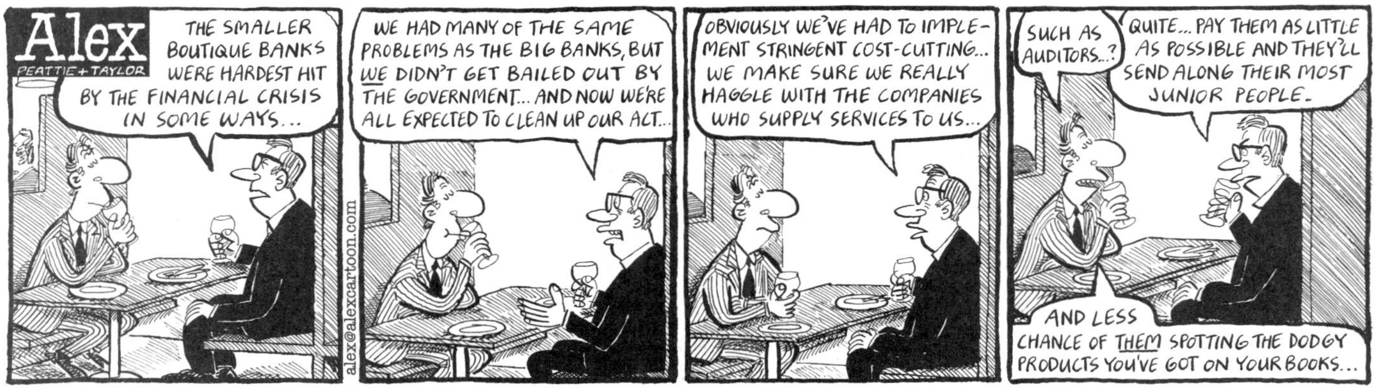
Alex
PEATTIE+TAYLOR
THE SMALLER BOUTIQUE BANKS WERE HARDEST HIT BY THE FINANCIAL CRISIS IN SOME WAYS...
alex@alexcartoon.com
WE HAD MANY OF THE SAME PROBLEMS AS THE BIG BANKS, BUT WE DIDN'T GET BAILED OUT BY THE GOVERNMENT... AND NOW WE'RE ALL EXPECTED TO CLEAN UP OUR ACT...
OBVIOUSLY WE'VE HAD TO IMPLEMENT STRINGENT COST-CUTTING... WE MAKE SURE WE REALLY HAGGLE WITH THE COMPANIES WHO SUPPLY SERVICES TO US...
SUCH AS AUDITORS...?
QUITE... PAY THEM AS LITTLE AS POSSIBLE AND THEY'LL SEND ALONG THEIR MOST JUNIOR PEOPLE.
AND LESS CHANCE OF THEM SPOTTING THE DODGY PRODUCTS YOU'VE GOT ON YOUR BOOKS...

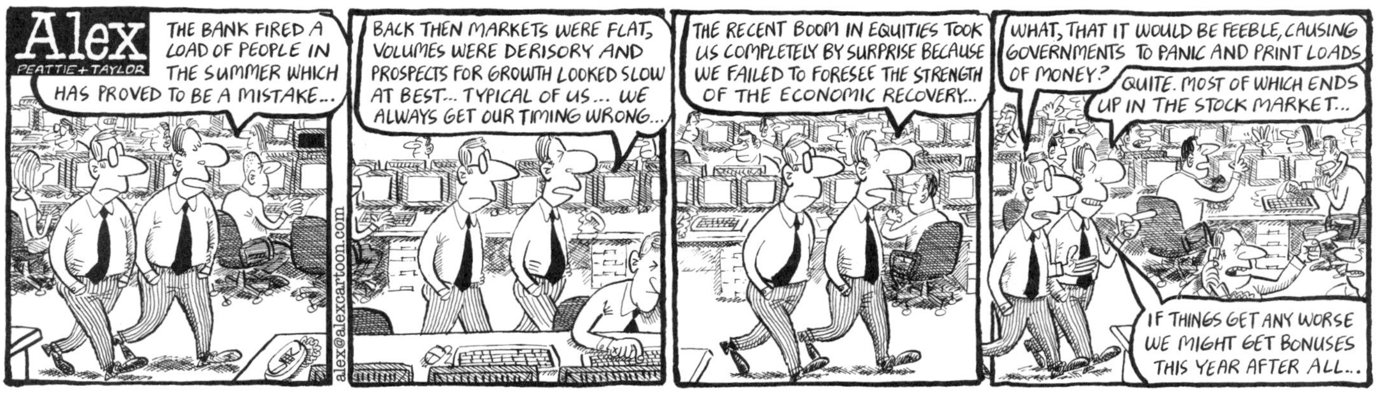
Alex
PEATTIE + TAYLOR
THE BANK FIRED A LOAD OF PEOPLE IN THE SUMMER WHICH HAS PROVED TO BE A MISTAKE...
BACK THEN MARKETS WERE FLAT, VOLUMES WERE DERISORY AND PROSPECTS FOR GROWTH LOOKED SLOW AT BEST... TYPICAL OF US... WE ALWAYS GET OUR TIMING WRONG...
alex@alexcartoon.com
THE RECENT BOOM IN EQUITIES TOOK US COMPLETELY BY SURPRISE BECAUSE WE FAILED TO FORESEE THE STRENGTH OF THE ECONOMIC RECOVERY...
WHAT, THAT IT WOULD BE FEEBLE, CAUSING GOVERNMENTS TO PANIC AND PRINT LOADS OF MONEY?
QUITE. MOST OF WHICH ENDS UP IN THE STOCK MARKET...
IF THINGS GET ANY WORSE WE MIGHT GET BONUSES THIS YEAR AFTER ALL...

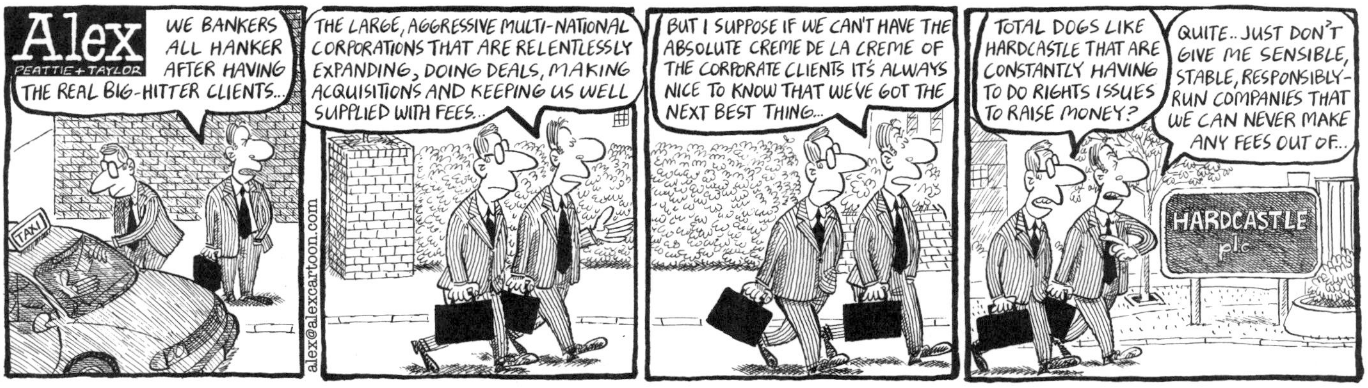
Alex
PEATTIE + TAYLOR
WE BANKERS ALL HANKER AFTER HAVING THE REAL BIG-HITTER CLIENTS...
TAXI
THE LARGE, AGGRESSIVE MULTI-NATIONAL CORPORATIONS THAT ARE RELENTLESSLY EXPANDING, DOING DEALS, MAKING ACQUISITIONS AND KEEPING US WELL SUPPLIED WITH FEES...
alex@alexcartoon.com
BUT I SUPPOSE IF WE CAN'T HAVE THE ABSOLUTE CREME DE LA CREME OF THE CORPORATE CLIENTS IT'S ALWAYS NICE TO KNOW THAT WE'VE GOT THE NEXT BEST THING...
TOTAL DOGS LIKE HARDCASTLE THAT ARE CONSTANTLY HAVING TO DO RIGHTS ISSUES TO RAISE MONEY?
QUITE.. JUST DON'T GIVE ME SENSIBLE, STABLE, RESPONSIBLY-RUN COMPANIES THAT WE CAN NEVER MAKE ANY FEES OUT OF...
HARDCASTLE plc

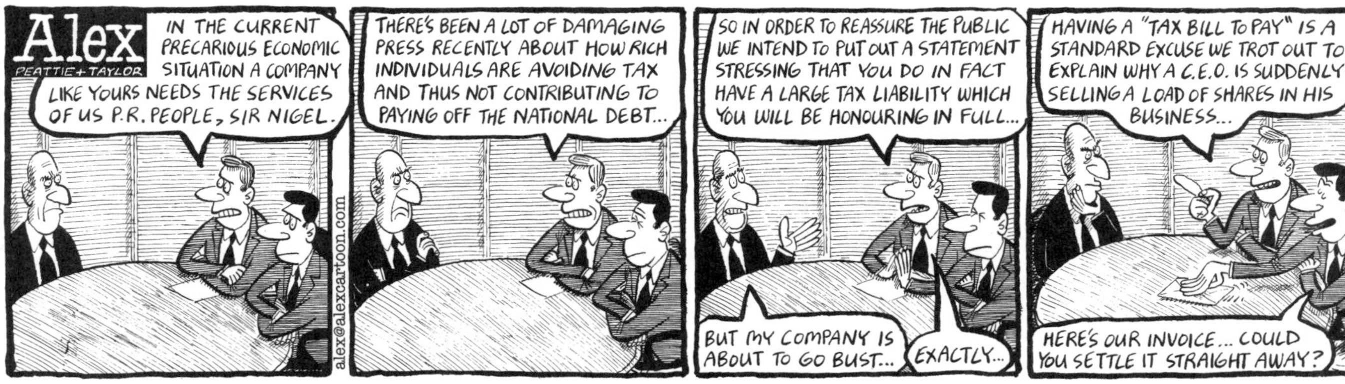
Alex
PEATTIE + TAYLOR
IN THE CURRENT PRECARIOUS ECONOMIC SITUATION A COMPANY LIKE YOURS NEEDS THE SERVICES OF US P.R. PEOPLE, SIR NIGEL.
THERE'S BEEN A LOT OF DAMAGING PRESS RECENTLY ABOUT HOW RICH INDIVIDUALS ARE AVOIDING TAX AND THUS NOT CONTRIBUTING TO PAYING OFF THE NATIONAL DEBT...
alex@alexcartoon.com
SO IN ORDER TO REASSURE THE PUBLIC WE INTEND TO PUT OUT A STATEMENT STRESSING THAT YOU DO IN FACT HAVE A LARGE TAX LIABILITY WHICH YOU WILL BE HONOURING IN FULL...
BUT MY COMPANY IS ABOUT TO GO BUST...
EXACTLY...
HAVING A "TAX BILL TO PAY" IS A STANDARD EXCUSE WE TROT OUT TO EXPLAIN WHY A C.E.O. IS SUDDENLY SELLING A LOAD OF SHARES IN HIS BUSINESS...
HERE'S OUR INVOICE... COULD YOU SETTLE IT STRAIGHT AWAY?

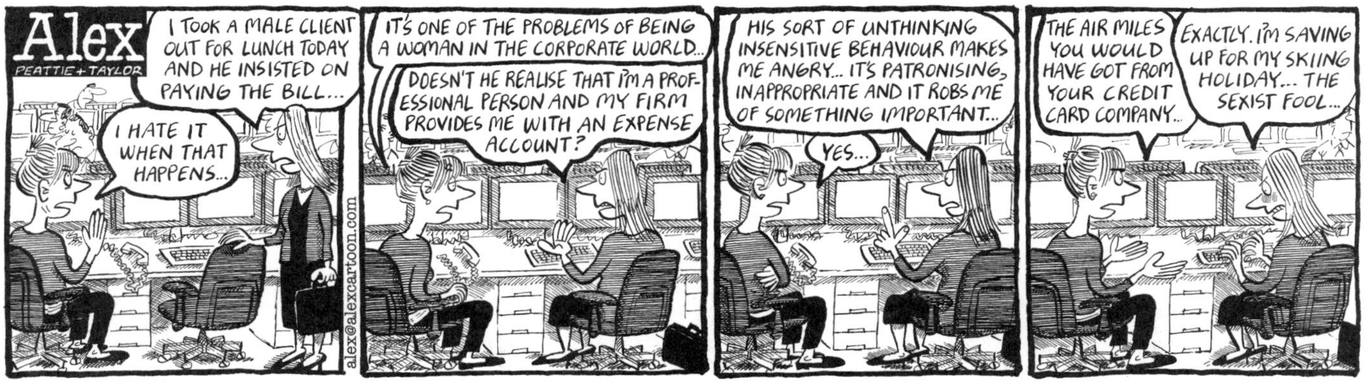
Alex
PEATTIE + TAYLOR
I TOOK A MALE CLIENT OUT FOR LUNCH TODAY AND HE INSISTED ON PAYING THE BILL...
I HATE IT WHEN THAT HAPPENS...
alex@alexcartoon.com
IT'S ONE OF THE PROBLEMS OF BEING A WOMAN IN THE CORPORATE WORLD...
DOESN'T HE REALISE THAT I'M A PROFESSIONAL PERSON AND MY FIRM PROVIDES ME WITH AN EXPENSE ACCOUNT?
HIS SORT OF UNTHINKING INSENSITIVE BEHAVIOUR MAKES ME ANGRY... IT'S PATRONISING, INAPPROPRIATE AND IT ROBS ME OF SOMETHING IMPORTANT...
YES...
THE AIR MILES YOU WOULD HAVE GOT FROM YOUR CREDIT CARD COMPANY...
EXACTLY. I'M SAVING UP FOR MY SKIING HOLIDAY... THE SEXIST FOOL...

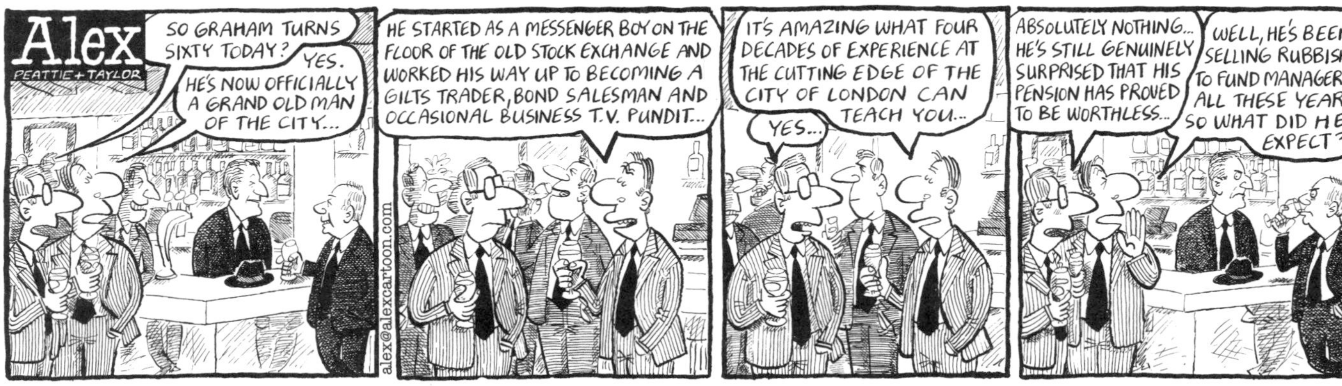
Alex
PEATTIE + TAYLOR
SO GRAHAM TURNS SIXTY TODAY?
YES.
HE'S NOW OFFICIALLY A GRAND OLD MAN OF THE CITY...
HE STARTED AS A MESSENGER BOY ON THE FLOOR OF THE OLD STOCK EXCHANGE AND WORKED HIS WAY UP TO BECOMING A GILTS TRADER, BOND SALESMAN AND OCCASIONAL BUSINESS T.V. PUNDIT...
alex@alexcartoon.com
IT'S AMAZING WHAT FOUR DECADES OF EXPERIENCE AT THE CUTTING EDGE OF THE CITY OF LONDON CAN TEACH YOU...
YES...
ABSOLUTELY NOTHING... HE'S STILL GENUINELY SURPRISED THAT HIS PENSION HAS PROVED TO BE WORTHLESS...
WELL, HE'S BEEN SELLING RUBBISH TO FUND MANAGERS ALL THESE YEARS SO WHAT DID HE EXPECT?

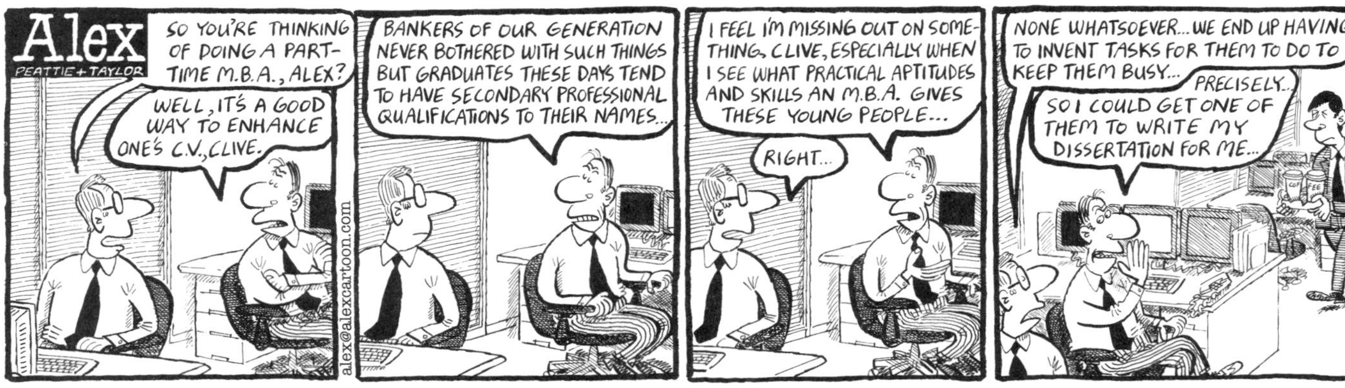
Alex
PEATTIE + TAYLOR
SO YOU'RE THINKING OF DOING A PART-TIME M.B.A., ALEX?
WELL, IT'S A GOOD WAY TO ENHANCE ONE'S C.V., CLIVE.
alex@alexcartoon.com
BANKERS OF OUR GENERATION NEVER BOTHERED WITH SUCH THINGS BUT GRADUATES THESE DAYS TEND TO HAVE SECONDARY PROFESSIONAL QUALIFICATIONS TO THEIR NAMES...
I FEEL I'M MISSING OUT ON SOMETHING, CLIVE, ESPECIALLY WHEN I SEE WHAT PRACTICAL APTITUDES AND SKILLS AN M.B.A. GIVES THESE YOUNG PEOPLE...
RIGHT...
NONE WHATSOEVER... WE END UP HAVING TO INVENT TASKS FOR THEM TO DO TO KEEP THEM BUSY...
PRECISELY...
SO I COULD GET ONE OF THEM TO WRITE MY DISSERTATION FOR ME...

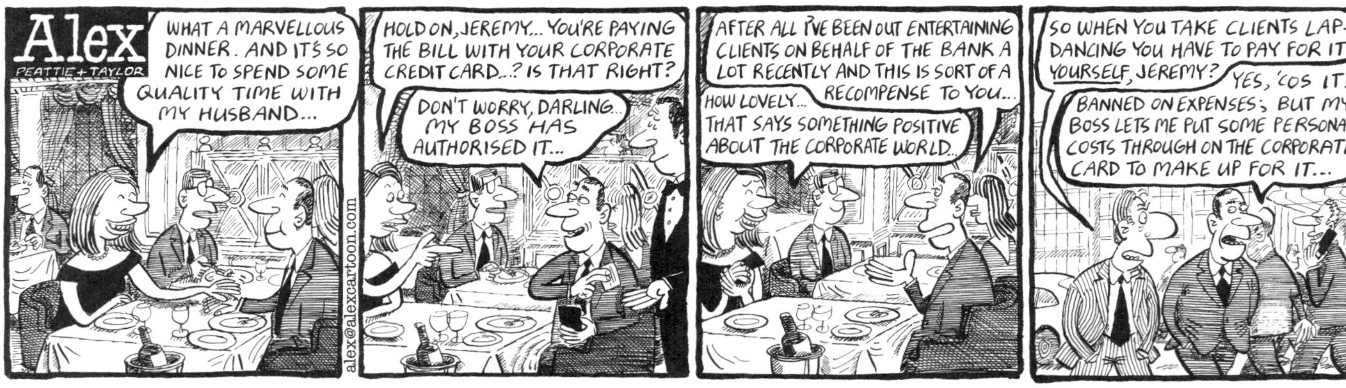
Alex
PEATTIE + TAYLOR
WHAT A MARVELLOUS DINNER. AND IT'S SO NICE TO SPEND SOME QUALITY TIME WITH MY HUSBAND...
alex@alexcartoon.com
HOLD ON, JEREMY... YOU'RE PAYING THE BILL WITH YOUR CORPORATE CREDIT CARD...? IS THAT RIGHT?
DON'T WORRY, DARLING... MY BOSS HAS AUTHORISED IT...
AFTER ALL I'VE BEEN OUT ENTERTAINING CLIENTS ON BEHALF OF THE BANK A LOT RECENTLY AND THIS IS SORT OF A RECOMPENSE TO YOU...
HOW LOVELY... THAT SAYS SOMETHING POSITIVE ABOUT THE CORPORATE WORLD...
SO WHEN YOU TAKE CLIENTS LAP-DANCING YOU HAVE TO PAY FOR IT YOURSELF, JEREMY?
YES, 'COS IT'S BANNED ON EXPENSES; BUT MY BOSS LETS ME PUT SOME PERSONAL COSTS THROUGH ON THE CORPORATE CARD TO MAKE UP FOR IT...

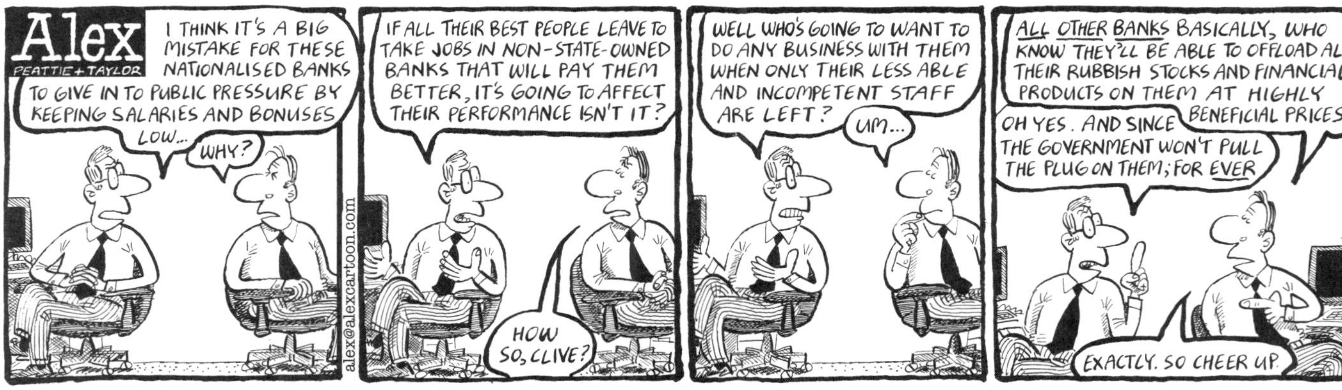
Alex
PEATTIE + TAYLOR
I THINK IT'S A BIG MISTAKE FOR THESE NATIONALISED BANKS TO GIVE IN TO PUBLIC PRESSURE BY KEEPING SALARIES AND BONUSES LOW...
WHY?
alex@alexcartoon.com
IF ALL THEIR BEST PEOPLE LEAVE TO TAKE JOBS IN NON-STATE-OWNED BANKS THAT WILL PAY THEM BETTER, IT'S GOING TO AFFECT THEIR PERFORMANCE ISN'T IT?
HOW SO, CLIVE?
WELL WHO'S GOING TO WANT TO DO ANY BUSINESS WITH THEM WHEN ONLY THEIR LESS ABLE AND INCOMPETENT STAFF ARE LEFT?
UM...
ALL OTHER BANKS BASICALLY, WHO KNOW THEY'LL BE ABLE TO OFFLOAD ALL THEIR RUBBISH STOCKS AND FINANCIAL PRODUCTS ON THEM AT HIGHLY BENEFICIAL PRICES...
OH YES. AND SINCE THE GOVERNMENT WON'T PULL THE PLUG ON THEM; FOR EVER
EXACTLY. SO CHEER UP.

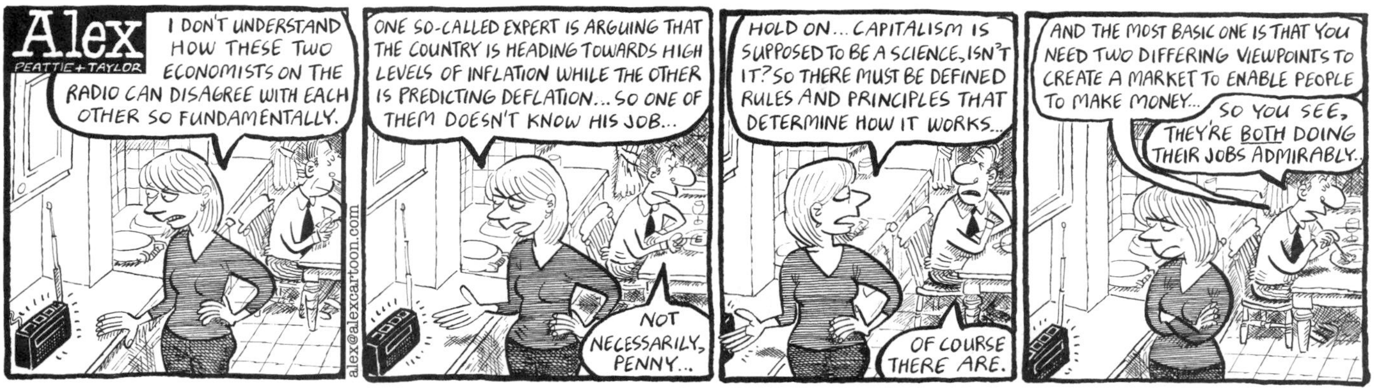
Alex
PEATTIE+TAYLOR
I DON'T UNDERSTAND HOW THESE TWO ECONOMISTS ON THE RADIO CAN DISAGREE WITH EACH OTHER SO FUNDAMENTALLY.
ONE SO-CALLED EXPERT IS ARGUING THAT THE COUNTRY IS HEADING TOWARDS HIGH LEVELS OF INFLATION WHILE THE OTHER IS PREDICTING DEFLATION... SO ONE OF THEM DOESN'T KNOW HIS JOB...
NOT NECESSARILY, PENNY...
alex@alexcartoon.com
HOLD ON... CAPITALISM IS SUPPOSED TO BE A SCIENCE, ISN'T IT? SO THERE MUST BE DEFINED RULES AND PRINCIPLES THAT DETERMINE HOW IT WORKS...
OF COURSE THERE ARE.
AND THE MOST BASIC ONE IS THAT YOU NEED TWO DIFFERING VIEWPOINTS TO CREATE A MARKET TO ENABLE PEOPLE TO MAKE MONEY...
SO YOU SEE, THEY'RE BOTH DOING THEIR JOBS ADMIRABLY...

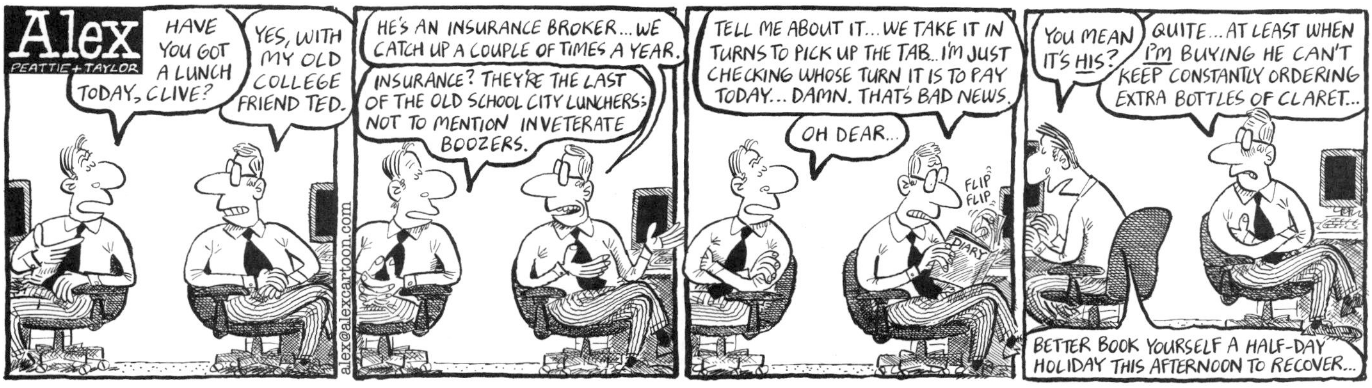
Alex
PEATTIE+TAYLOR
HAVE YOU GOT A LUNCH TODAY, CLIVE?
YES, WITH MY OLD COLLEGE FRIEND TED.
alex@alexcartoon.com
HE'S AN INSURANCE BROKER... WE CATCH UP A COUPLE OF TIMES A YEAR.
INSURANCE? THEY'RE THE LAST OF THE OLD SCHOOL CITY LUNCHERS; NOT TO MENTION INVETERATE BOOZERS.
TELL ME ABOUT IT... WE TAKE IT IN TURNS TO PICK UP THE TAB... I'M JUST CHECKING WHOSE TURN IT IS TO PAY TODAY... DAMN. THAT'S BAD NEWS.
OH DEAR...
FLIP FLIP
DIARY
YOU MEAN IT'S HIS?
QUITE... AT LEAST WHEN I'M BUYING HE CAN'T KEEP CONSTANTLY ORDERING EXTRA BOTTLES OF CLARET...
BETTER BOOK YOURSELF A HALF-DAY HOLIDAY THIS AFTERNOON TO RECOVER...

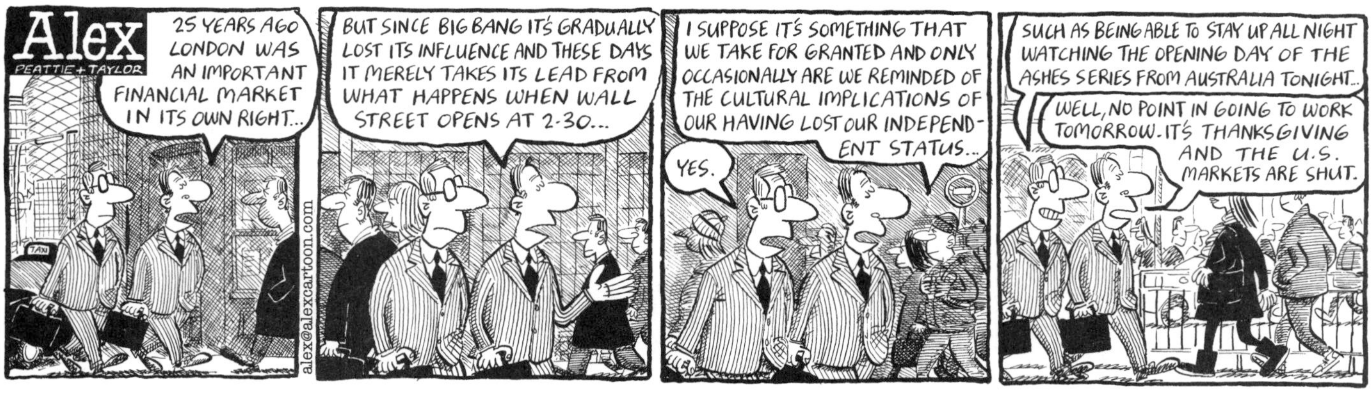
Alex
PEATTIE+TAYLOR
25 YEARS AGO LONDON WAS AN IMPORTANT FINANCIAL MARKET IN ITS OWN RIGHT...
TAXI
alex@alexcartoon.com
BUT SINCE BIG BANG IT'S GRADUALLY LOST ITS INFLUENCE AND THESE DAYS IT MERELY TAKES ITS LEAD FROM WHAT HAPPENS WHEN WALL STREET OPENS AT 2.30...
I SUPPOSE IT'S SOMETHING THAT WE TAKE FOR GRANTED AND ONLY OCCASIONALLY ARE WE REMINDED OF THE CULTURAL IMPLICATIONS OF OUR HAVING LOST OUR INDEPENDENT STATUS...
YES.
SUCH AS BEING ABLE TO STAY UP ALL NIGHT WATCHING THE OPENING DAY OF THE ASHES SERIES FROM AUSTRALIA TONIGHT...
WELL, NO POINT IN GOING TO WORK TOMORROW. IT'S THANKSGIVING AND THE U.S. MARKETS ARE SHUT.

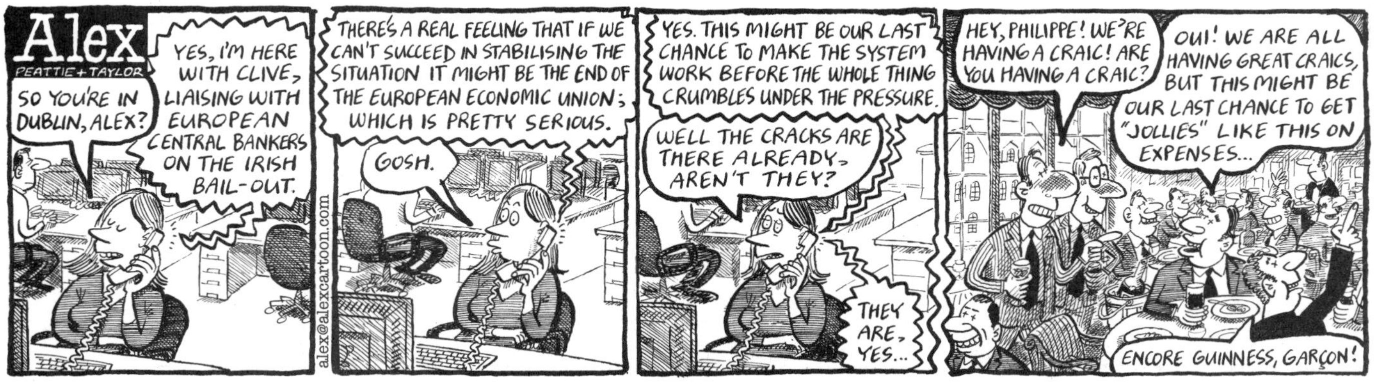
Alex
PEATTIE+TAYLOR
SO YOU'RE IN DUBLIN, ALEX?
YES, I'M HERE WITH CLIVE, LIAISING WITH EUROPEAN CENTRAL BANKERS ON THE IRISH BAIL-OUT.
alex@alexcartoon.com
THERE'S A REAL FEELING THAT IF WE CAN'T SUCCEED IN STABILISING THE SITUATION IT MIGHT BE THE END OF THE EUROPEAN ECONOMIC UNION; WHICH IS PRETTY SERIOUS.
GOSH.
YES. THIS MIGHT BE OUR LAST CHANCE TO MAKE THE SYSTEM WORK BEFORE THE WHOLE THING CRUMBLES UNDER THE PRESSURE.
WELL THE CRACKS ARE THERE ALREADY, AREN'T THEY?
THEY ARE, YES...
HEY, PHILIPPE! WE'RE HAVING A CRAIC! ARE YOU HAVING A CRAIC?
OUI! WE ARE ALL HAVING GREAT CRAICS, BUT THIS MIGHT BE OUR LAST CHANCE TO GET "JOLLIES" LIKE THIS ON EXPENSES...
ENCORE GUINNESS, GARÇON!

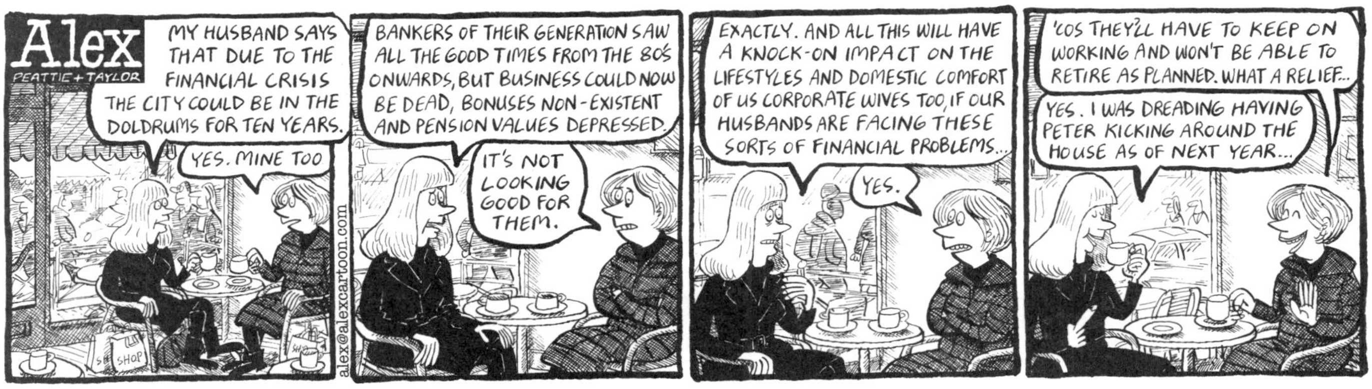
Alex
PEATTIE + TAYLOR
MY HUSBAND SAYS THAT DUE TO THE FINANCIAL CRISIS THE CITY COULD BE IN THE DOLDRUMS FOR TEN YEARS.
YES. MINE TOO
alex@alexcartoon.com
BANKERS OF THEIR GENERATION SAW ALL THE GOOD TIMES FROM THE 80's ONWARDS, BUT BUSINESS COULD NOW BE DEAD, BONUSES NON-EXISTENT AND PENSION VALUES DEPRESSED.
IT'S NOT LOOKING GOOD FOR THEM.
EXACTLY. AND ALL THIS WILL HAVE A KNOCK-ON IMPACT ON THE LIFESTYLES AND DOMESTIC COMFORT OF US CORPORATE WIVES TOO, IF OUR HUSBANDS ARE FACING THESE SORTS OF FINANCIAL PROBLEMS...
YES.
'COS THEY'LL HAVE TO KEEP ON WORKING AND WON'T BE ABLE TO RETIRE AS PLANNED. WHAT A RELIEF...
YES. I WAS DREADING HAVING PETER KICKING AROUND THE HOUSE AS OF NEXT YEAR...

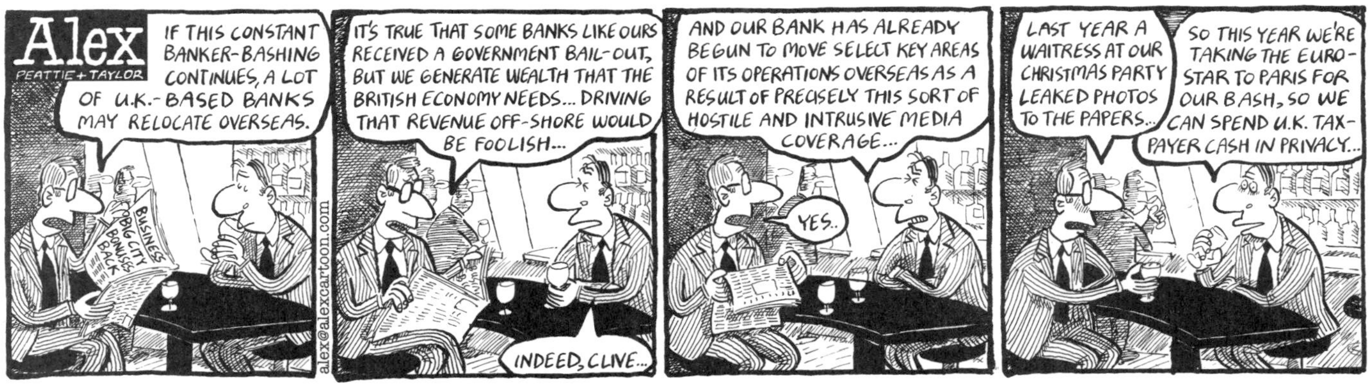
Alex
PEATTIE + TAYLOR
IF THIS CONSTANT BANKER-BASHING CONTINUES, A LOT OF U.K.-BASED BANKS MAY RELOCATE OVERSEAS.
alex@alexcartoon.com
IT'S TRUE THAT SOME BANKS LIKE OURS RECEIVED A GOVERNMENT BAIL-OUT, BUT WE GENERATE WEALTH THAT THE BRITISH ECONOMY NEEDS... DRIVING THAT REVENUE OFF-SHORE WOULD BE FOOLISH...
INDEED, CLIVE...
AND OUR BANK HAS ALREADY BEGUN TO MOVE SELECT KEY AREAS OF ITS OPERATIONS OVERSEAS AS A RESULT OF PRECISELY THIS SORT OF HOSTILE AND INTRUSIVE MEDIA COVERAGE...
YES..
LAST YEAR A WAITRESS AT OUR CHRISTMAS PARTY LEAKED PHOTOS TO THE PAPERS...
SO THIS YEAR WE'RE TAKING THE EURO-STAR TO PARIS FOR OUR BASH, SO WE CAN SPEND U.K. TAX-PAYER CASH IN PRIVACY...

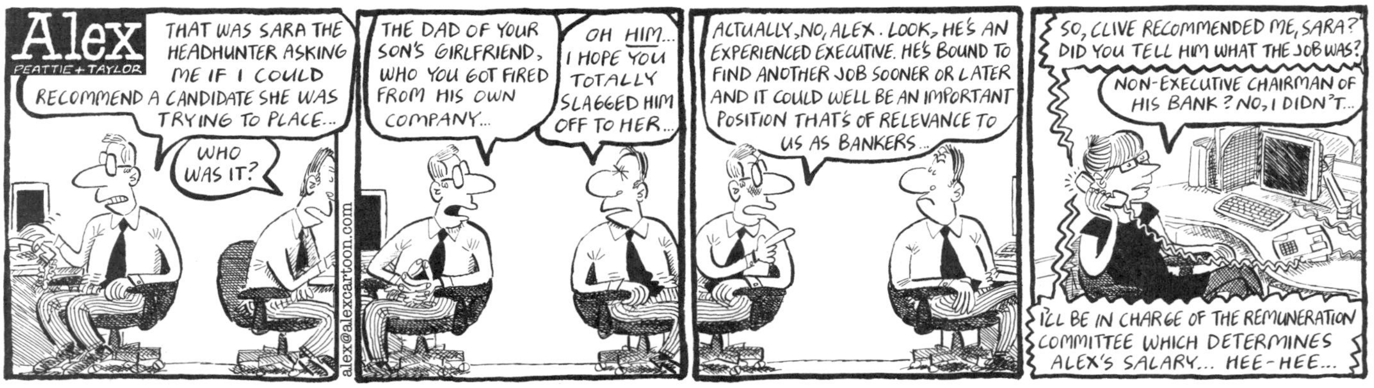
Alex
PEATTIE + TAYLOR
THAT WAS SARA THE HEADHUNTER ASKING ME IF I COULD RECOMMEND A CANDIDATE SHE WAS TRYING TO PLACE...
WHO WAS IT?
alex@alexcartoon.com
THE DAD OF YOUR SON'S GIRLFRIEND, WHO YOU GOT FIRED FROM HIS OWN COMPANY...
OH HIM... I HOPE YOU TOTALLY SLAGGED HIM OFF TO HER...
ACTUALLY, NO, ALEX. LOOK, HE'S AN EXPERIENCED EXECUTIVE. HE'S BOUND TO FIND ANOTHER JOB SOONER OR LATER AND IT COULD WELL BE AN IMPORTANT POSITION THAT'S OF RELEVANCE TO US AS BANKERS...
SO, CLIVE RECOMMENDED ME, SARA? DID YOU TELL HIM WHAT THE JOB WAS?
NON-EXECUTIVE CHAIRMAN OF HIS BANK? NO, I DIDN'T...
I'LL BE IN CHARGE OF THE REMUNERATION COMMITTEE WHICH DETERMINES ALEX'S SALARY... HEE-HEE...

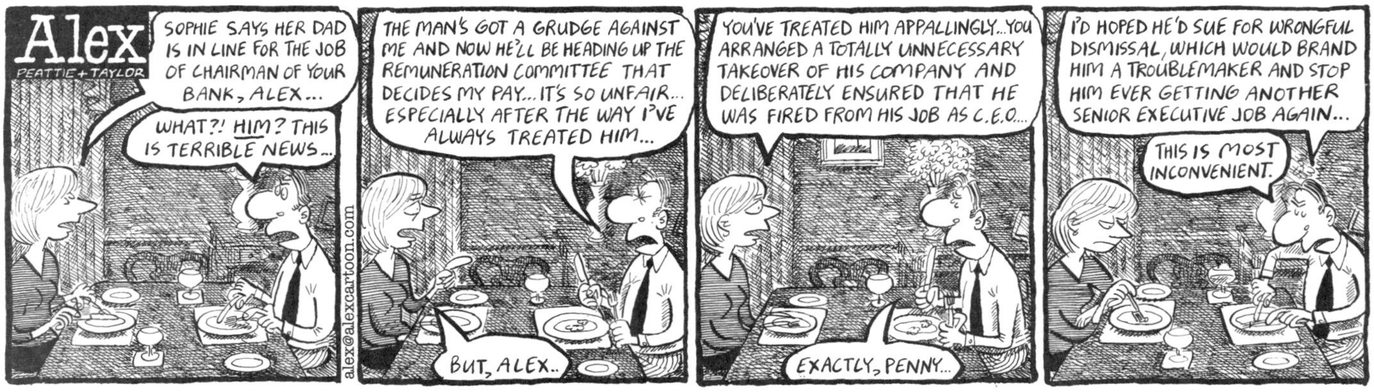
Alex
PEATTIE + TAYLOR
SOPHIE SAYS HER DAD IS IN LINE FOR THE JOB OF CHAIRMAN OF YOUR BANK, ALEX...
WHAT?! HIM? THIS IS TERRIBLE NEWS...
alex@alexcartoon.com
THE MAN'S GOT A GRUDGE AGAINST ME AND NOW HE'LL BE HEADING UP THE REMUNERATION COMMITTEE THAT DECIDES MY PAY... IT'S SO UNFAIR... ESPECIALLY AFTER THE WAY I'VE ALWAYS TREATED HIM...
BUT, ALEX..
YOU'VE TREATED HIM APPALLINGLY... YOU ARRANGED A TOTALLY UNNECESSARY TAKEOVER OF HIS COMPANY AND DELIBERATELY ENSURED THAT HE WAS FIRED FROM HIS JOB AS C.E.O....
EXACTLY, PENNY...
I'D HOPED HE'D SUE FOR WRONGFUL DISMISSAL, WHICH WOULD BRAND HIM A TROUBLEMAKER AND STOP HIM EVER GETTING ANOTHER SENIOR EXECUTIVE JOB AGAIN...
THIS IS MOST INCONVENIENT.

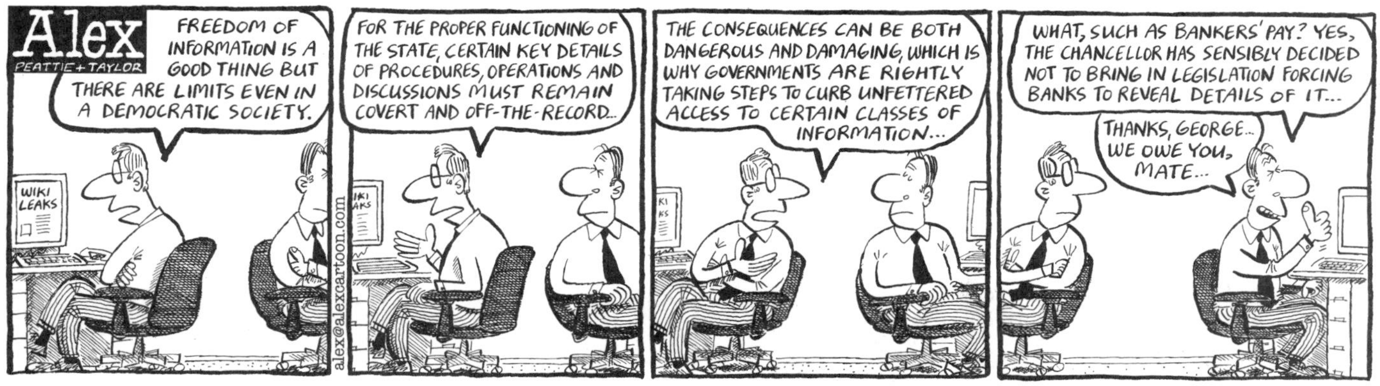

Alex
PEATTIE+TAYLOR
FREEDOM OF INFORMATION IS A GOOD THING BUT THERE ARE LIMITS EVEN IN A DEMOCRATIC SOCIETY.
WIKI LEAKS
alex@alexcartoon.com
FOR THE PROPER FUNCTIONING OF THE STATE, CERTAIN KEY DETAILS OF PROCEDURES, OPERATIONS AND DISCUSSIONS MUST REMAIN COVERT AND OFF-THE-RECORD...
THE CONSEQUENCES CAN BE BOTH DANGEROUS AND DAMAGING, WHICH IS WHY GOVERNMENTS ARE RIGHTLY TAKING STEPS TO CURB UNFETTERED ACCESS TO CERTAIN CLASSES OF INFORMATION...
WHAT, SUCH AS BANKERS' PAY? YES, THE CHANCELLOR HAS SENSIBLY DECIDED NOT TO BRING IN LEGISLATION FORCING BANKS TO REVEAL DETAILS OF IT...
THANKS, GEORGE... WE OWE YOU, MATE...

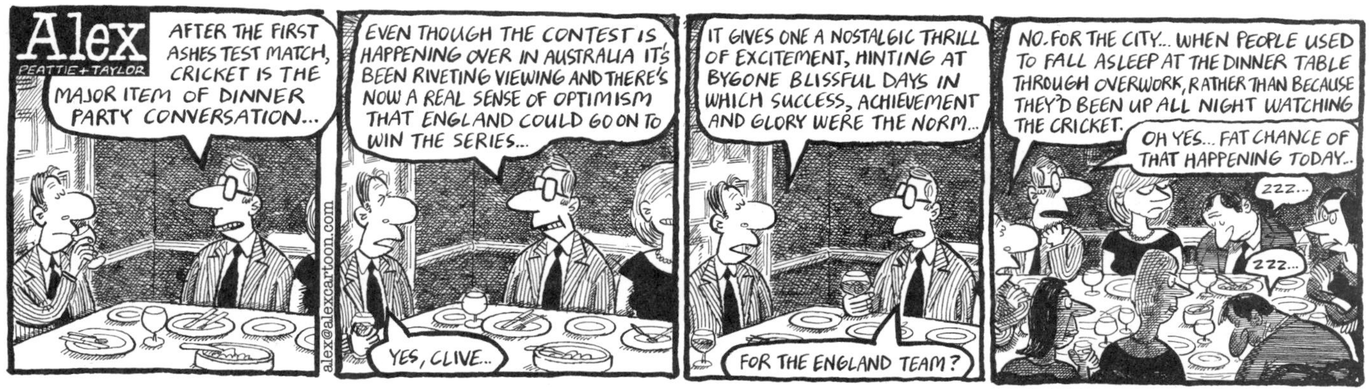

Alex
PEATTIE+TAYLOR
AFTER THE FIRST ASHES TEST MATCH, CRICKET IS THE MAJOR ITEM OF DINNER PARTY CONVERSATION...
alex@alexcartoon.com
EVEN THOUGH THE CONTEST IS HAPPENING OVER IN AUSTRALIA IT'S BEEN RIVETING VIEWING AND THERE'S NOW A REAL SENSE OF OPTIMISM THAT ENGLAND COULD GO ON TO WIN THE SERIES...
YES, CLIVE...
IT GIVES ONE A NOSTALGIC THRILL OF EXCITEMENT, HINTING AT BYGONE BLISSFUL DAYS IN WHICH SUCCESS, ACHIEVEMENT AND GLORY WERE THE NORM...
FOR THE ENGLAND TEAM?
NO. FOR THE CITY... WHEN PEOPLE USED TO FALL ASLEEP AT THE DINNER TABLE THROUGH OVERWORK, RATHER THAN BECAUSE THEY'D BEEN UP ALL NIGHT WATCHING THE CRICKET.
OH YES... FAT CHANCE OF THAT HAPPENING TODAY...
ZZZ...
ZZZ...

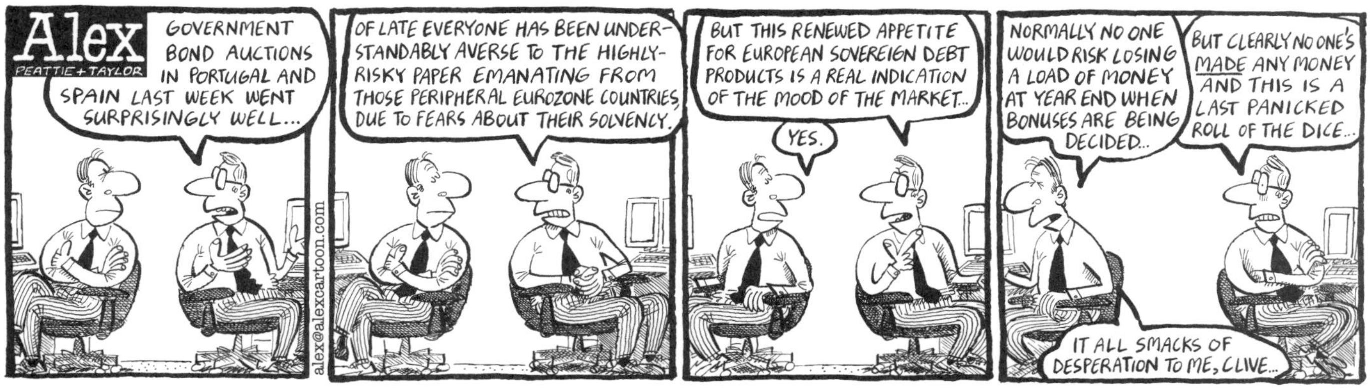

Alex
PEATTIE+TAYLOR
GOVERNMENT BOND AUCTIONS IN PORTUGAL AND SPAIN LAST WEEK WENT SURPRISINGLY WELL...
alex@alexcartoon.com
OF LATE EVERYONE HAS BEEN UNDERSTANDABLY AVERSE TO THE HIGHLY-RISKY PAPER EMANATING FROM THOSE PERIPHERAL EUROZONE COUNTRIES, DUE TO FEARS ABOUT THEIR SOLVENCY.
BUT THIS RENEWED APPETITE FOR EUROPEAN SOVEREIGN DEBT PRODUCTS IS A REAL INDICATION OF THE MOOD OF THE MARKET...
YES.
NORMALLY NO ONE WOULD RISK LOSING A LOAD OF MONEY AT YEAR END WHEN BONUSES ARE BEING DECIDED...
BUT CLEARLY NO ONE'S MADE ANY MONEY AND THIS IS A LAST PANICKED ROLL OF THE DICE...
IT ALL SMACKS OF DESPERATION TO ME, CLIVE...

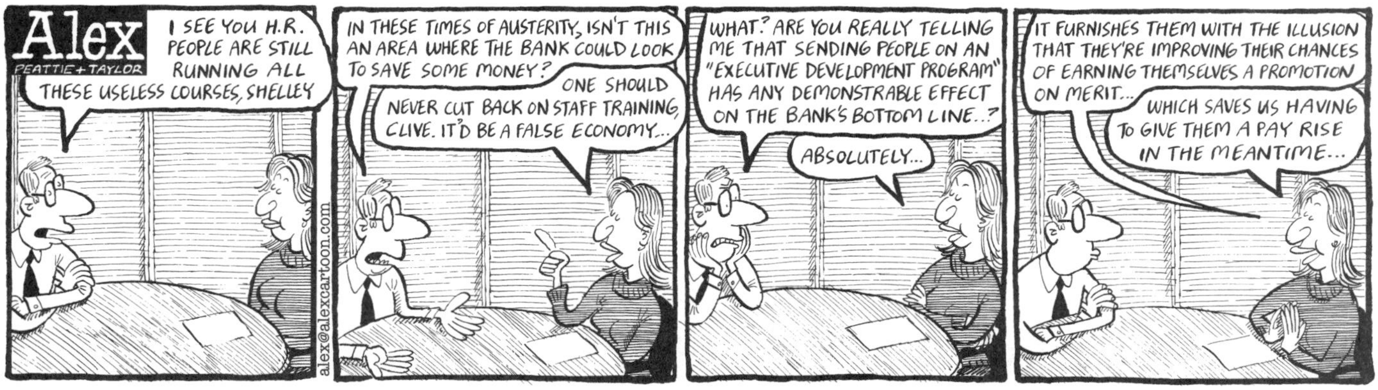

Alex
PEATTIE+TAYLOR
I SEE YOU H.R. PEOPLE ARE STILL RUNNING ALL THESE USELESS COURSES, SHELLEY
alex@alexcartoon.com
IN THESE TIMES OF AUSTERITY, ISN'T THIS AN AREA WHERE THE BANK COULD LOOK TO SAVE SOME MONEY?
ONE SHOULD NEVER CUT BACK ON STAFF TRAINING, CLIVE. IT'D BE A FALSE ECONOMY...
WHAT? ARE YOU REALLY TELLING ME THAT SENDING PEOPLE ON AN "EXECUTIVE DEVELOPMENT PROGRAM" HAS ANY DEMONSTRABLE EFFECT ON THE BANK'S BOTTOM LINE...?
ABSOLUTELY...
IT FURNISHES THEM WITH THE ILLUSION THAT THEY'RE IMPROVING THEIR CHANCES OF EARNING THEMSELVES A PROMOTION ON MERIT...
WHICH SAVES US HAVING TO GIVE THEM A PAY RISE IN THE MEANTIME...

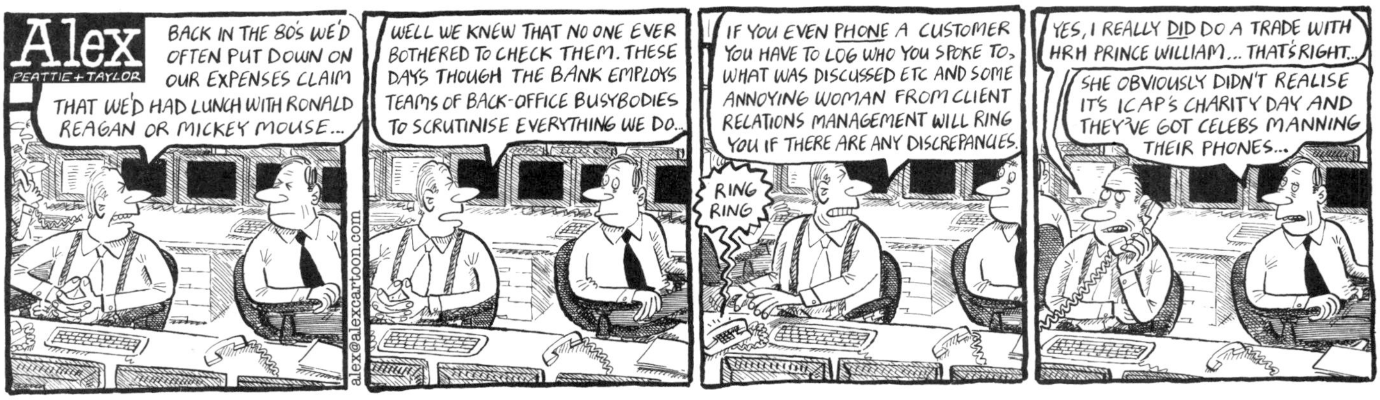
Alex
PEATTIE + TAYLOR
BACK IN THE 80's WE'D OFTEN PUT DOWN ON OUR EXPENSES CLAIM THAT WE'D HAD LUNCH WITH RONALD REAGAN OR MICKEY MOUSE...
alex@alexcartoon.com
WELL WE KNEW THAT NO ONE EVER BOTHERED TO CHECK THEM. THESE DAYS THOUGH THE BANK EMPLOYS TEAMS OF BACK-OFFICE BUSYBODIES TO SCRUTINISE EVERYTHING WE DO...
IF YOU EVEN PHONE A CUSTOMER YOU HAVE TO LOG WHO YOU SPOKE TO, WHAT WAS DISCUSSED ETC AND SOME ANNOYING WOMAN FROM CLIENT RELATIONS MANAGEMENT WILL RING YOU IF THERE ARE ANY DISCREPANCIES.
RING RING
YES, I REALLY DID DO A TRADE WITH HRH PRINCE WILLIAM... THAT'S RIGHT...
SHE OBVIOUSLY DIDN'T REALISE IT'S ICAP'S CHARITY DAY AND THEY'VE GOT CELEBS MANNING THEIR PHONES...

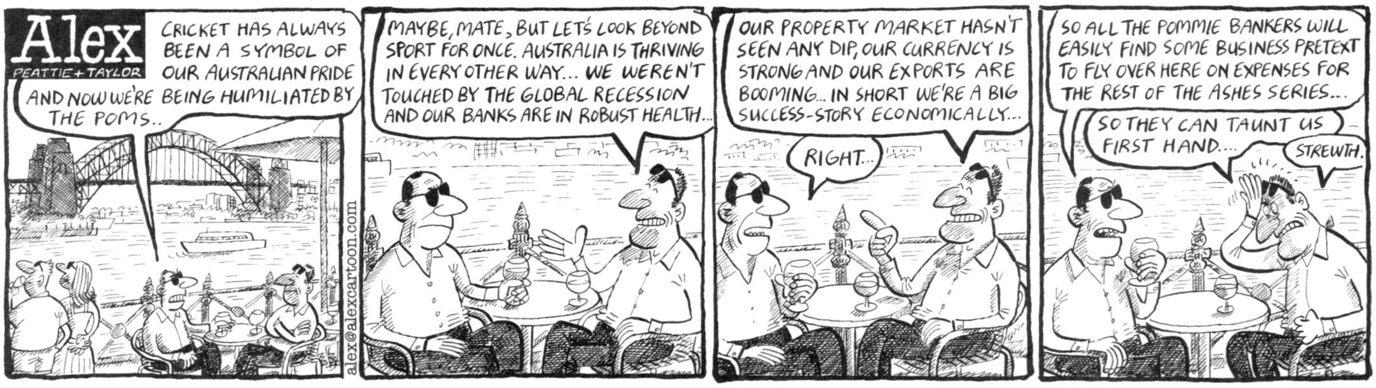
Alex
PEATTIE + TAYLOR
CRICKET HAS ALWAYS BEEN A SYMBOL OF OUR AUSTRALIAN PRIDE AND NOW WE'RE BEING HUMILIATED BY THE POMS..
alex@alexcartoon.com
MAYBE, MATE, BUT LET'S LOOK BEYOND SPORT FOR ONCE. AUSTRALIA IS THRIVING IN EVERY OTHER WAY... WE WEREN'T TOUCHED BY THE GLOBAL RECESSION AND OUR BANKS ARE IN ROBUST HEALTH...
OUR PROPERTY MARKET HASN'T SEEN ANY DIP, OUR CURRENCY IS STRONG AND OUR EXPORTS ARE BOOMING... IN SHORT WE'RE A BIG SUCCESS-STORY ECONOMICALLY...
RIGHT...
SO ALL THE POMMIE BANKERS WILL EASILY FIND SOME BUSINESS PRETEXT TO FLY OVER HERE ON EXPENSES FOR THE REST OF THE ASHES SERIES...
SO THEY CAN TAUNT US FIRST HAND....
STREWTH.

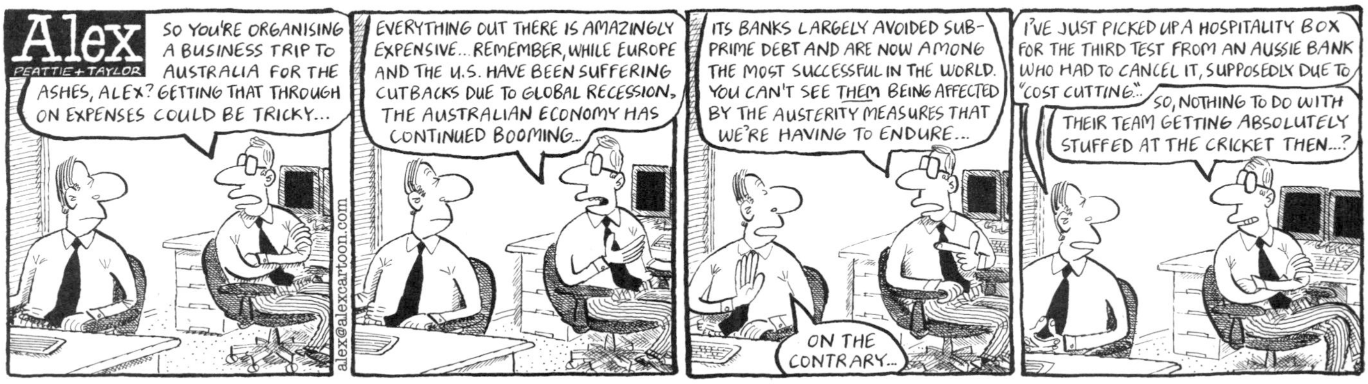
Alex
PEATTIE + TAYLOR
SO YOU'RE ORGANISING A BUSINESS TRIP TO AUSTRALIA FOR THE ASHES, ALEX? GETTING THAT THROUGH ON EXPENSES COULD BE TRICKY...
alex@alexcartoon.com
EVERYTHING OUT THERE IS AMAZINGLY EXPENSIVE... REMEMBER, WHILE EUROPE AND THE U.S. HAVE BEEN SUFFERING CUTBACKS DUE TO GLOBAL RECESSION, THE AUSTRALIAN ECONOMY HAS CONTINUED BOOMING...
ITS BANKS LARGELY AVOIDED SUB-PRIME DEBT AND ARE NOW AMONG THE MOST SUCCESSFUL IN THE WORLD. YOU CAN'T SEE THEM BEING AFFECTED BY THE AUSTERITY MEASURES THAT WE'RE HAVING TO ENDURE...
ON THE CONTRARY...
I'VE JUST PICKED UP A HOSPITALITY BOX FOR THE THIRD TEST FROM AN AUSSIE BANK WHO HAD TO CANCEL IT, SUPPOSEDLY DUE TO "COST CUTTING."
SO, NOTHING TO DO WITH THEIR TEAM GETTING ABSOLUTELY STUFFED AT THE CRICKET THEN...?

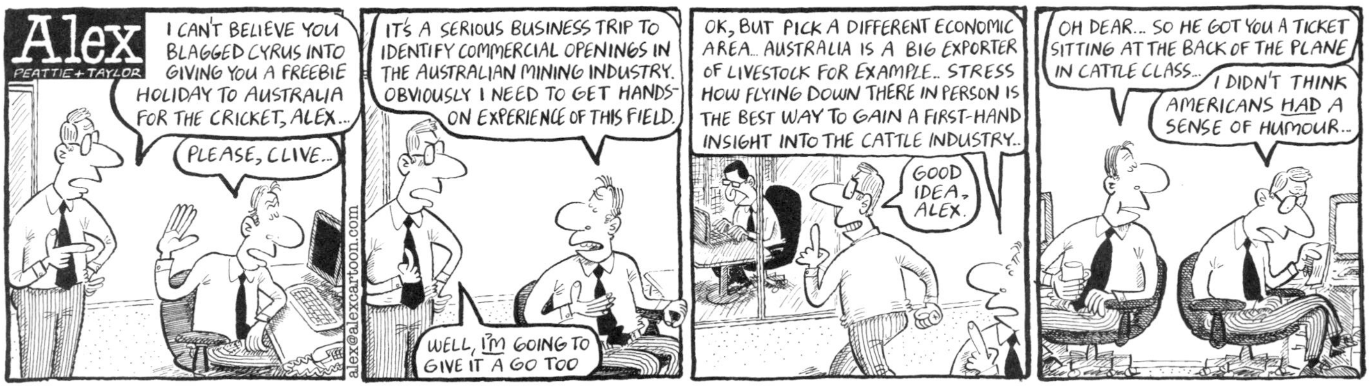
Alex
PEATTIE + TAYLOR
I CAN'T BELIEVE YOU BLAGGED CYRUS INTO GIVING YOU A FREEBIE HOLIDAY TO AUSTRALIA FOR THE CRICKET, ALEX...
PLEASE, CLIVE...
alex@alexcartoon.com
IT'S A SERIOUS BUSINESS TRIP TO IDENTIFY COMMERCIAL OPENINGS IN THE AUSTRALIAN MINING INDUSTRY. OBVIOUSLY I NEED TO GET HANDS-ON EXPERIENCE OF THIS FIELD.
WELL, I'M GOING TO GIVE IT A GO TOO
OK, BUT PICK A DIFFERENT ECONOMIC AREA... AUSTRALIA IS A BIG EXPORTER OF LIVESTOCK FOR EXAMPLE.. STRESS HOW FLYING DOWN THERE IN PERSON IS THE BEST WAY TO GAIN A FIRST-HAND INSIGHT INTO THE CATTLE INDUSTRY..
GOOD IDEA, ALEX.
OH DEAR... SO HE GOT YOU A TICKET SITTING AT THE BACK OF THE PLANE IN CATTLE CLASS...
I DIDN'T THINK AMERICANS HAD A SENSE OF HUMOUR...

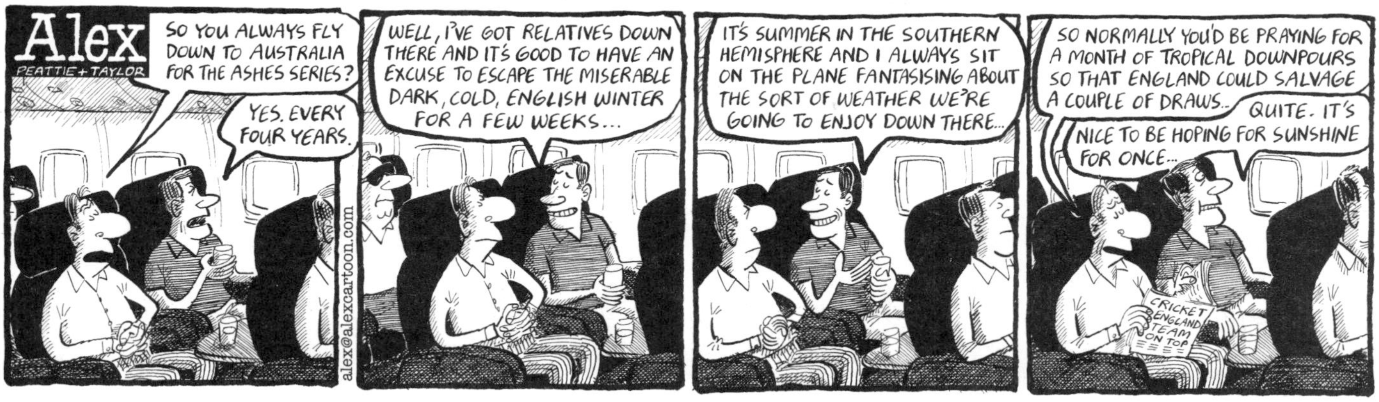
Alex
PEATTIE + TAYLOR
SO YOU ALWAYS FLY DOWN TO AUSTRALIA FOR THE ASHES SERIES?
YES. EVERY FOUR YEARS.
WELL, I'VE GOT RELATIVES DOWN THERE AND IT'S GOOD TO HAVE AN EXCUSE TO ESCAPE THE MISERABLE DARK, COLD, ENGLISH WINTER FOR A FEW WEEKS...
IT'S SUMMER IN THE SOUTHERN HEMISPHERE AND I ALWAYS SIT ON THE PLANE FANTASISING ABOUT THE SORT OF WEATHER WE'RE GOING TO ENJOY DOWN THERE...
SO NORMALLY YOU'D BE PRAYING FOR A MONTH OF TROPICAL DOWNPOURS SO THAT ENGLAND COULD SALVAGE A COUPLE OF DRAWS...
QUITE. IT'S NICE TO BE HOPING FOR SUNSHINE FOR ONCE...
CRICKET ENGLAND TEAM ON TOP
alex@alexcartoon.com

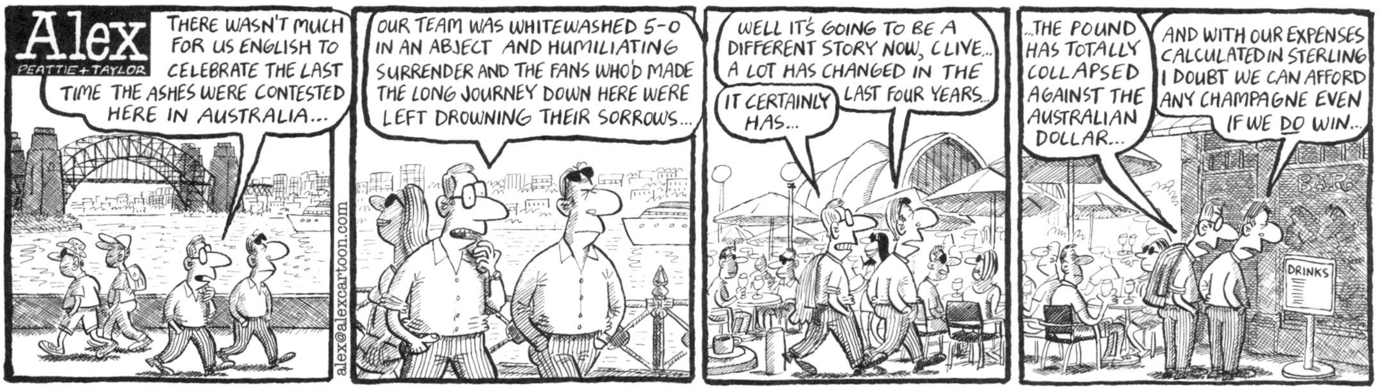
Alex
PEATTIE + TAYLOR
THERE WASN'T MUCH FOR US ENGLISH TO CELEBRATE THE LAST TIME THE ASHES WERE CONTESTED HERE IN AUSTRALIA...
OUR TEAM WAS WHITEWASHED 5-0 IN AN ABJECT AND HUMILIATING SURRENDER AND THE FANS WHO'D MADE THE LONG JOURNEY DOWN HERE WERE LEFT DROWNING THEIR SORROWS...
WELL IT'S GOING TO BE A DIFFERENT STORY NOW, CLIVE... A LOT HAS CHANGED IN THE LAST FOUR YEARS...
IT CERTAINLY HAS...
...THE POUND HAS TOTALLY COLLAPSED AGAINST THE AUSTRALIAN DOLLAR...
AND WITH OUR EXPENSES CALCULATED IN STERLING I DOUBT WE CAN AFFORD ANY CHAMPAGNE EVEN IF WE DO WIN...
BAR
DRINKS
alex@alexcartoon.com

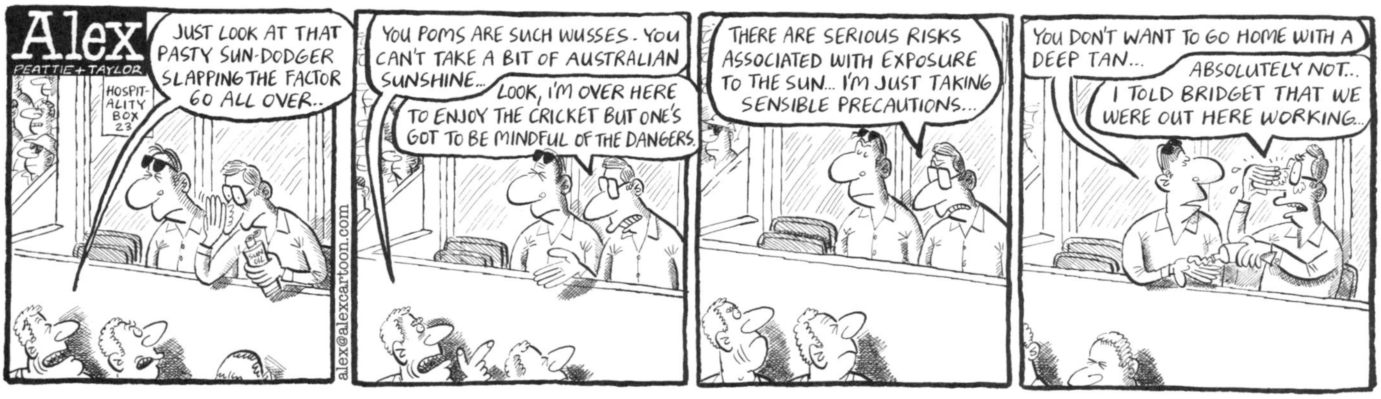
Alex
PEATTIE + TAYLOR
JUST LOOK AT THAT PASTY SUN-DODGER SLAPPING THE FACTOR 60 ALL OVER...
HOSPIT-ALITY BOX 23
YOU POMS ARE SUCH WUSSES. YOU CAN'T TAKE A BIT OF AUSTRALIAN SUNSHINE...
LOOK, I'M OVER HERE TO ENJOY THE CRICKET BUT ONE'S GOT TO BE MINDFUL OF THE DANGERS.
THERE ARE SERIOUS RISKS ASSOCIATED WITH EXPOSURE TO THE SUN... I'M JUST TAKING SENSIBLE PRECAUTIONS...
YOU DON'T WANT TO GO HOME WITH A DEEP TAN...
ABSOLUTELY NOT... I TOLD BRIDGET THAT WE WERE OUT HERE WORKING...
alex@alexcartoon.com

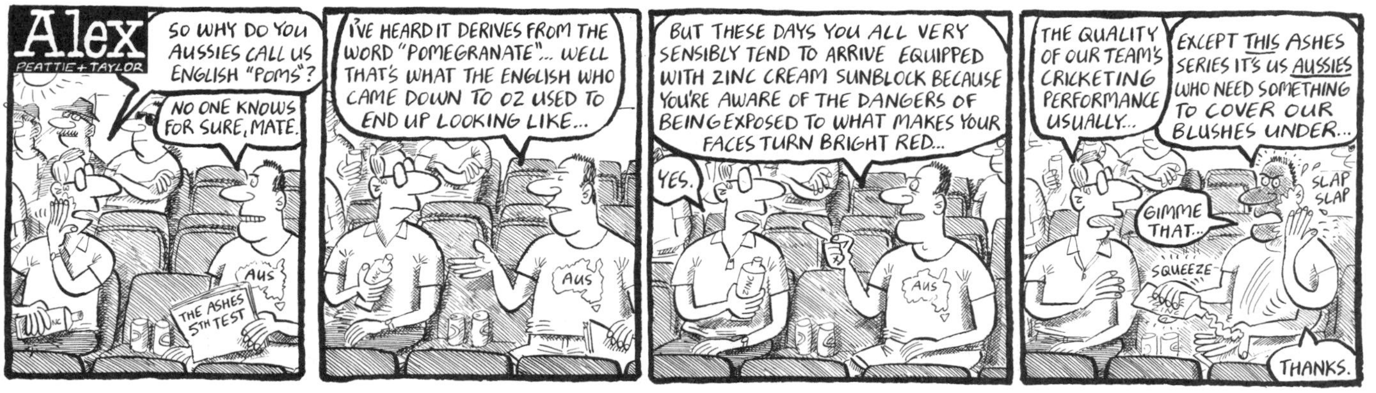
Alex
PEATTIE + TAYLOR
SO WHY DO YOU AUSSIES CALL US ENGLISH "POMS"?
NO ONE KNOWS FOR SURE, MATE.
THE ASHES 5TH TEST
AUS
I'VE HEARD IT DERIVES FROM THE WORD "POMEGRANATE"... WELL THAT'S WHAT THE ENGLISH WHO CAME DOWN TO OZ USED TO END UP LOOKING LIKE...
BUT THESE DAYS YOU ALL VERY SENSIBLY TEND TO ARRIVE EQUIPPED WITH ZINC CREAM SUNBLOCK BECAUSE YOU'RE AWARE OF THE DANGERS OF BEING EXPOSED TO WHAT MAKES YOUR FACES TURN BRIGHT RED...
YES.
ZINC
THE QUALITY OF OUR TEAM'S CRICKETING PERFORMANCE USUALLY...
EXCEPT THIS ASHES SERIES IT'S US AUSSIES WHO NEED SOMETHING TO COVER OUR BLUSHES UNDER...
SLAP SLAP
GIMME THAT...
SQUEEZE
THANKS.

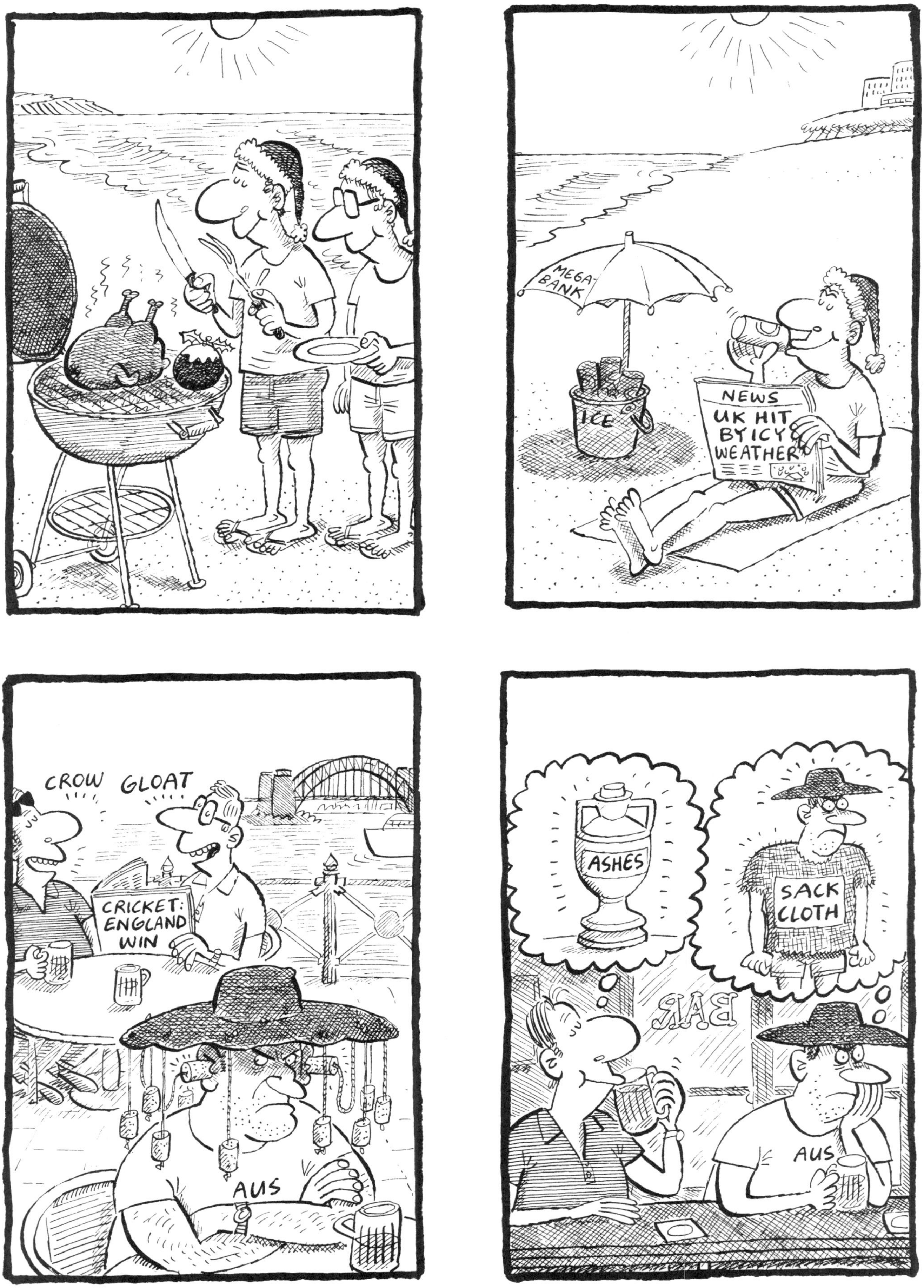

MEGA-BANK
ICE
NEWS
UK HIT BY ICY WEATHER
CROW
GLOAT
CRICKET: ENGLAND WIN
AUS
ASHES
SACK CLOTH
BAR
AUS

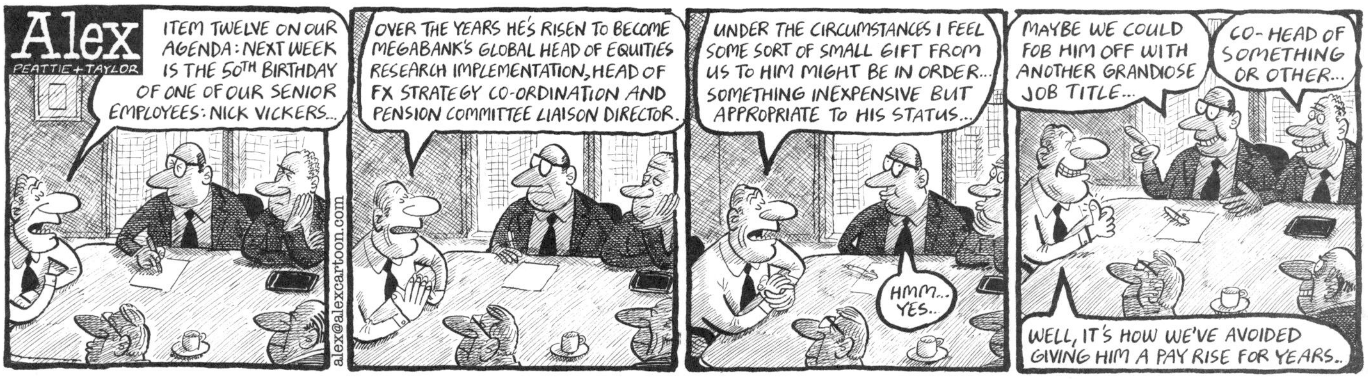
Alex
PEATTIE + TAYLOR
ITEM TWELVE ON OUR AGENDA: NEXT WEEK IS THE 50TH BIRTHDAY OF ONE OF OUR SENIOR EMPLOYEES: NICK VICKERS...
alex@alexcartoon.com
OVER THE YEARS HE'S RISEN TO BECOME MEGABANK'S GLOBAL HEAD OF EQUITIES RESEARCH IMPLEMENTATION, HEAD OF FX STRATEGY CO-ORDINATION AND PENSION COMMITTEE LIAISON DIRECTOR.
UNDER THE CIRCUMSTANCES I FEEL SOME SORT OF SMALL GIFT FROM US TO HIM MIGHT BE IN ORDER... SOMETHING INEXPENSIVE BUT APPROPRIATE TO HIS STATUS...
HMM... YES...
MAYBE WE COULD FOB HIM OFF WITH ANOTHER GRANDIOSE JOB TITLE...
CO-HEAD OF SOMETHING OR OTHER...
WELL, IT'S HOW WE'VE AVOIDED GIVING HIM A PAY RISE FOR YEARS..

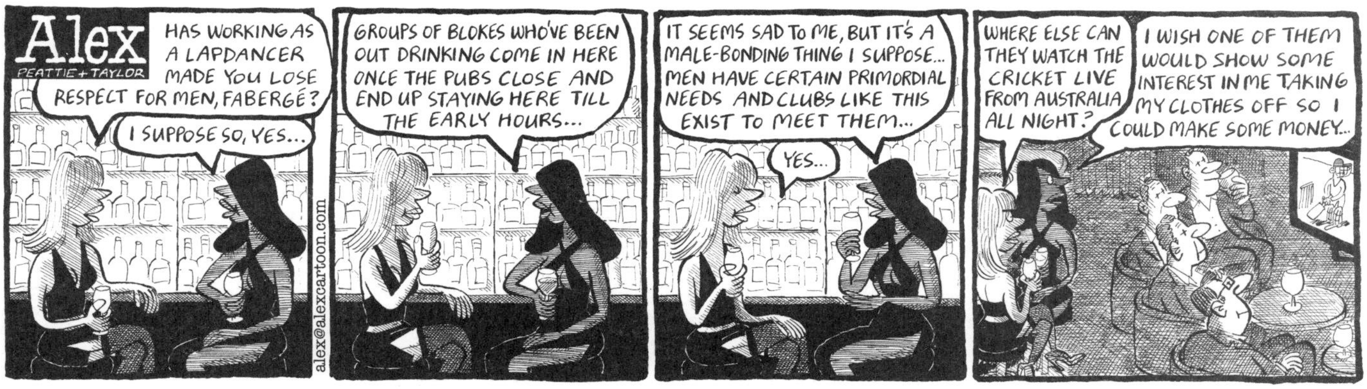
Alex
PEATTIE + TAYLOR
HAS WORKING AS A LAPDANCER MADE YOU LOSE RESPECT FOR MEN, FABERGÉ?
I SUPPOSE SO, YES...
alex@alexcartoon.com
GROUPS OF BLOKES WHO'VE BEEN OUT DRINKING COME IN HERE ONCE THE PUBS CLOSE AND END UP STAYING HERE TILL THE EARLY HOURS...
IT SEEMS SAD TO ME, BUT IT'S A MALE-BONDING THING I SUPPOSE... MEN HAVE CERTAIN PRIMORDIAL NEEDS AND CLUBS LIKE THIS EXIST TO MEET THEM...
YES...
WHERE ELSE CAN THEY WATCH THE CRICKET LIVE FROM AUSTRALIA ALL NIGHT?
I WISH ONE OF THEM WOULD SHOW SOME INTEREST IN ME TAKING MY CLOTHES OFF SO I COULD MAKE SOME MONEY...

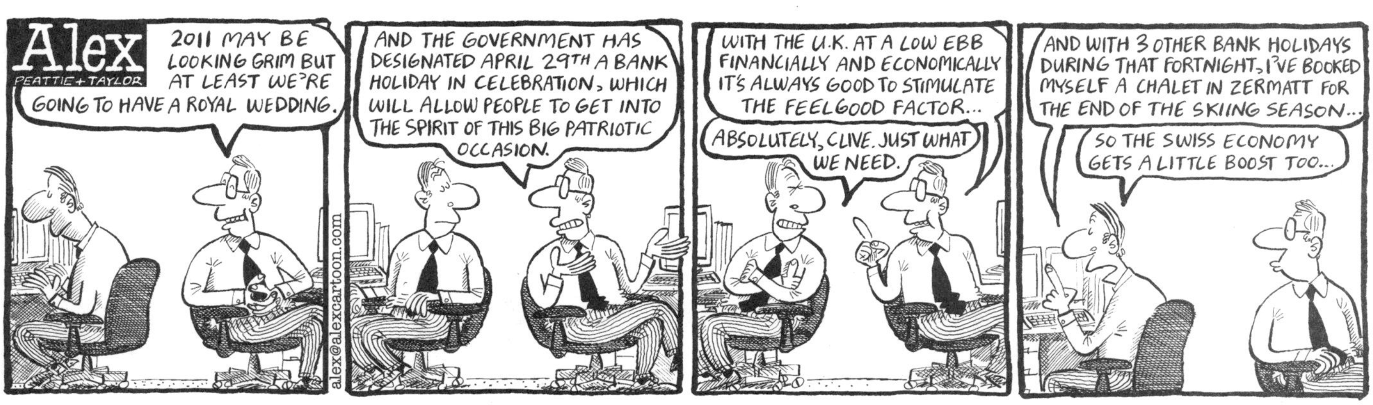
Alex
PEATTIE + TAYLOR
2011 MAY BE LOOKING GRIM BUT AT LEAST WE'RE GOING TO HAVE A ROYAL WEDDING.
alex@alexcartoon.com
AND THE GOVERNMENT HAS DESIGNATED APRIL 29TH A BANK HOLIDAY IN CELEBRATION, WHICH WILL ALLOW PEOPLE TO GET INTO THE SPIRIT OF THIS BIG PATRIOTIC OCCASION.
WITH THE U.K. AT A LOW EBB FINANCIALLY AND ECONOMICALLY IT'S ALWAYS GOOD TO STIMULATE THE FEELGOOD FACTOR...
ABSOLUTELY, CLIVE. JUST WHAT WE NEED.
AND WITH 3 OTHER BANK HOLIDAYS DURING THAT FORTNIGHT, I'VE BOOKED MYSELF A CHALET IN ZERMATT FOR THE END OF THE SKIING SEASON...
SO THE SWISS ECONOMY GETS A LITTLE BOOST TOO...

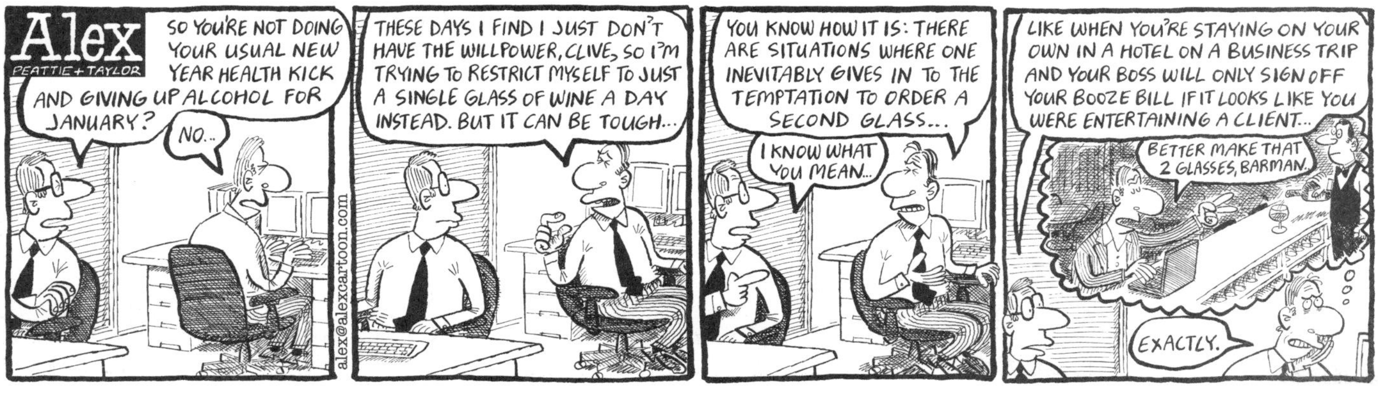
Alex
PEATTIE + TAYLOR
SO YOU'RE NOT DOING YOUR USUAL NEW YEAR HEALTH KICK AND GIVING UP ALCOHOL FOR JANUARY?
NO..
alex@alexcartoon.com
THESE DAYS I FIND I JUST DON'T HAVE THE WILLPOWER, CLIVE, SO I'M TRYING TO RESTRICT MYSELF TO JUST A SINGLE GLASS OF WINE A DAY INSTEAD. BUT IT CAN BE TOUGH...
YOU KNOW HOW IT IS: THERE ARE SITUATIONS WHERE ONE INEVITABLY GIVES IN TO THE TEMPTATION TO ORDER A SECOND GLASS...
I KNOW WHAT YOU MEAN...
LIKE WHEN YOU'RE STAYING ON YOUR OWN IN A HOTEL ON A BUSINESS TRIP AND YOUR BOSS WILL ONLY SIGN OFF YOUR BOOZE BILL IF IT LOOKS LIKE YOU WERE ENTERTAINING A CLIENT...
BETTER MAKE THAT 2 GLASSES, BARMAN.
EXACTLY.

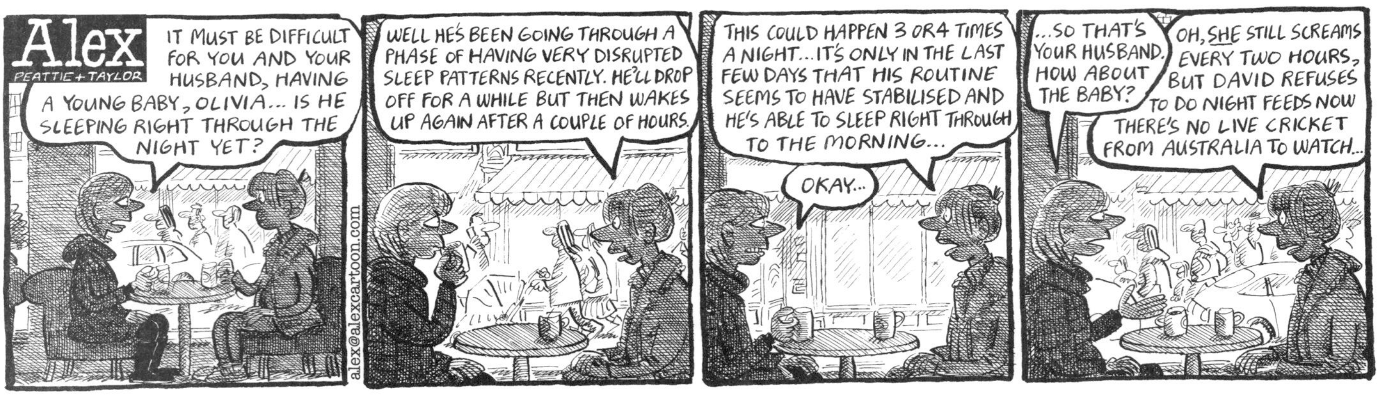
Alex
PEATTIE + TAYLOR
IT MUST BE DIFFICULT FOR YOU AND YOUR HUSBAND, HAVING A YOUNG BABY, OLIVIA... IS HE SLEEPING RIGHT THROUGH THE NIGHT YET?
WELL HE'S BEEN GOING THROUGH A PHASE OF HAVING VERY DISRUPTED SLEEP PATTERNS RECENTLY. HE'LL DROP OFF FOR A WHILE BUT THEN WAKES UP AGAIN AFTER A COUPLE OF HOURS.
THIS COULD HAPPEN 3 OR 4 TIMES A NIGHT... IT'S ONLY IN THE LAST FEW DAYS THAT HIS ROUTINE SEEMS TO HAVE STABILISED AND HE'S ABLE TO SLEEP RIGHT THROUGH TO THE MORNING...
OKAY...
...SO THAT'S YOUR HUSBAND. HOW ABOUT THE BABY?
OH, SHE STILL SCREAMS EVERY TWO HOURS, BUT DAVID REFUSES TO DO NIGHT FEEDS NOW THERE'S NO LIVE CRICKET FROM AUSTRALIA TO WATCH...
alex@alexcartoon.com

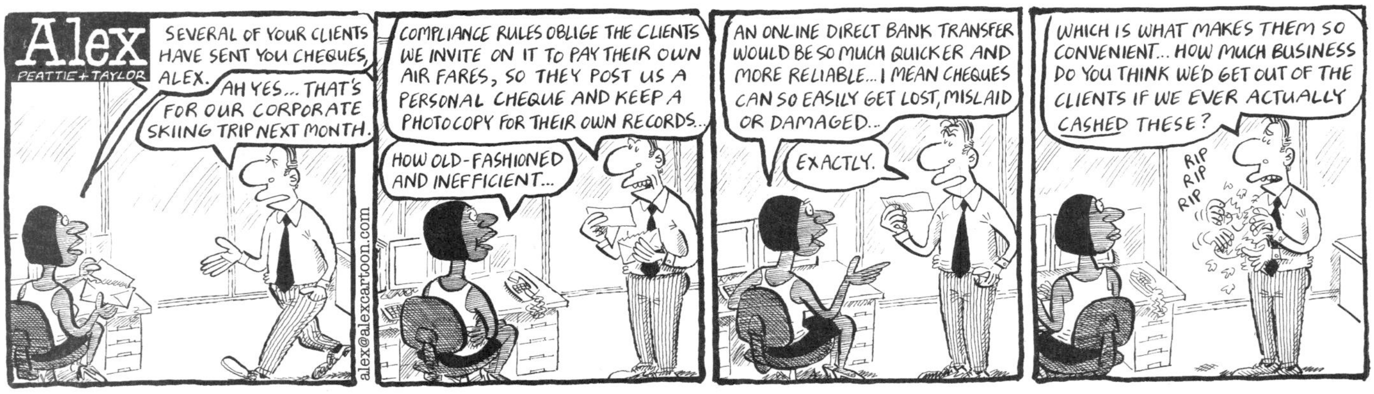
Alex
PEATTIE + TAYLOR
SEVERAL OF YOUR CLIENTS HAVE SENT YOU CHEQUES, ALEX.
AH YES... THAT'S FOR OUR CORPORATE SKIING TRIP NEXT MONTH.
COMPLIANCE RULES OBLIGE THE CLIENTS WE INVITE ON IT TO PAY THEIR OWN AIR FARES, SO THEY POST US A PERSONAL CHEQUE AND KEEP A PHOTOCOPY FOR THEIR OWN RECORDS...
HOW OLD-FASHIONED AND INEFFICIENT...
AN ONLINE DIRECT BANK TRANSFER WOULD BE SO MUCH QUICKER AND MORE RELIABLE... I MEAN CHEQUES CAN SO EASILY GET LOST, MISLAID OR DAMAGED...
EXACTLY.
WHICH IS WHAT MAKES THEM SO CONVENIENT... HOW MUCH BUSINESS DO YOU THINK WE'D GET OUT OF THE CLIENTS IF WE EVER ACTUALLY CASHED THESE?
RIP RIP RIP
alex@alexcartoon.com

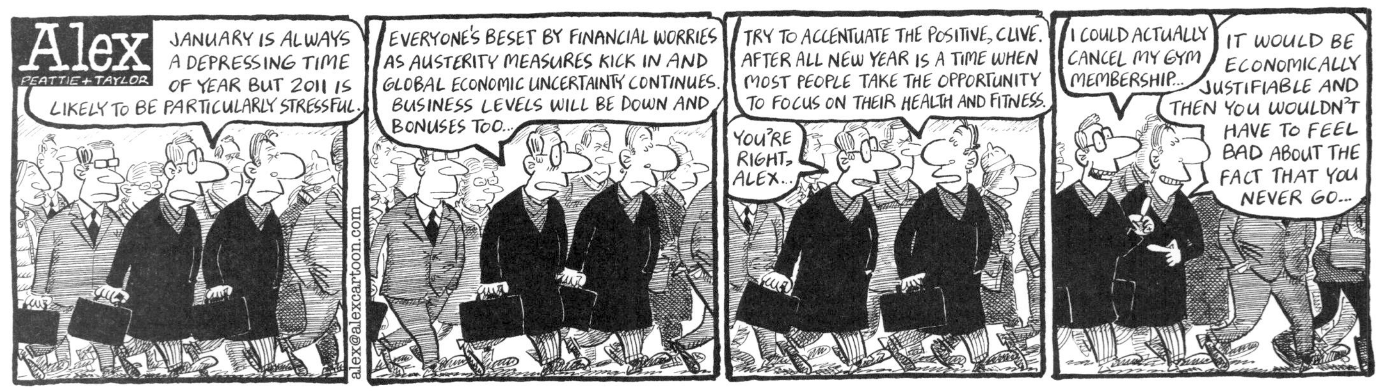
Alex
PEATTIE + TAYLOR
JANUARY IS ALWAYS A DEPRESSING TIME OF YEAR BUT 2011 IS LIKELY TO BE PARTICULARLY STRESSFUL.
EVERYONE'S BESET BY FINANCIAL WORRIES AS AUSTERITY MEASURES KICK IN AND GLOBAL ECONOMIC UNCERTAINTY CONTINUES. BUSINESS LEVELS WILL BE DOWN AND BONUSES TOO...
TRY TO ACCENTUATE THE POSITIVE, CLIVE. AFTER ALL NEW YEAR IS A TIME WHEN MOST PEOPLE TAKE THE OPPORTUNITY TO FOCUS ON THEIR HEALTH AND FITNESS.
YOU'RE RIGHT, ALEX...
I COULD ACTUALLY CANCEL MY GYM MEMBERSHIP...
IT WOULD BE ECONOMICALLY JUSTIFIABLE AND THEN YOU WOULDN'T HAVE TO FEEL BAD ABOUT THE FACT THAT YOU NEVER GO...
alex@alexcartoon.com

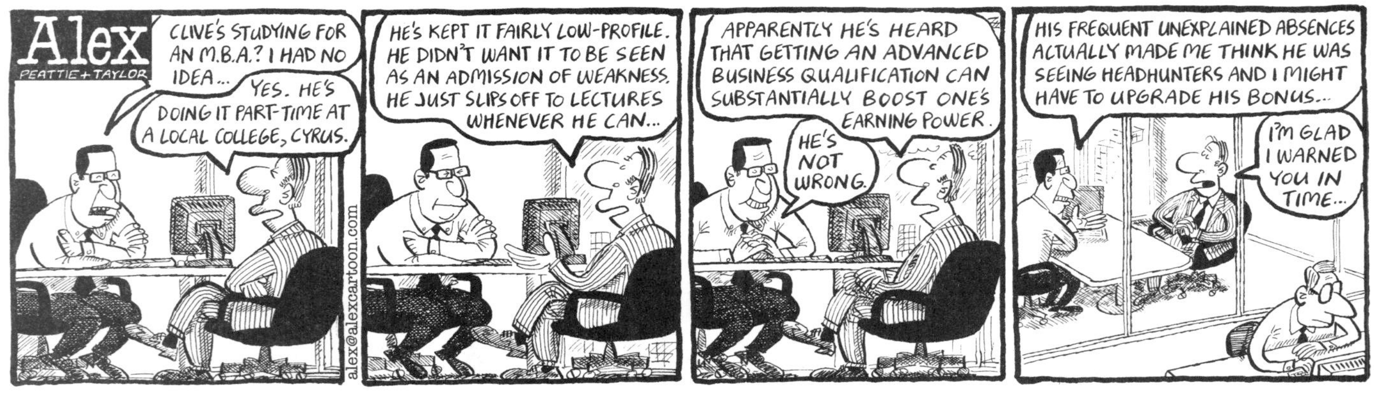
Alex
PEATTIE + TAYLOR
CLIVE'S STUDYING FOR AN M.B.A.? I HAD NO IDEA...
YES. HE'S DOING IT PART-TIME AT A LOCAL COLLEGE, CYRUS.
HE'S KEPT IT FAIRLY LOW-PROFILE. HE DIDN'T WANT IT TO BE SEEN AS AN ADMISSION OF WEAKNESS. HE JUST SLIPS OFF TO LECTURES WHENEVER HE CAN...
APPARENTLY HE'S HEARD THAT GETTING AN ADVANCED BUSINESS QUALIFICATION CAN SUBSTANTIALLY BOOST ONE'S EARNING POWER.
HE'S NOT WRONG.
HIS FREQUENT UNEXPLAINED ABSENCES ACTUALLY MADE ME THINK HE WAS SEEING HEADHUNTERS AND I MIGHT HAVE TO UPGRADE HIS BONUS...
I'M GLAD I WARNED YOU IN TIME...
alex@alexcartoon.com

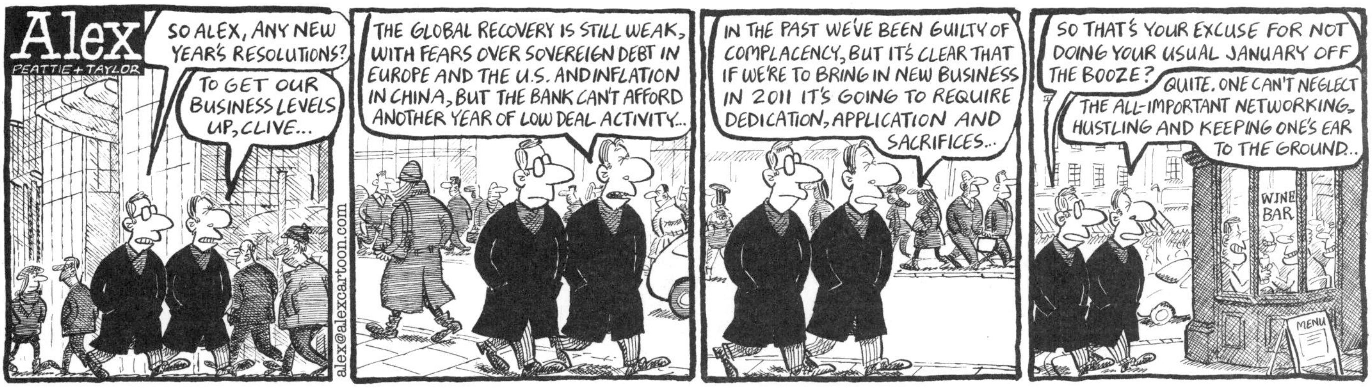
Alex
PEATTIE + TAYLOR
SO ALEX, ANY NEW YEAR'S RESOLUTIONS?
TO GET OUR BUSINESS LEVELS UP, CLIVE...
THE GLOBAL RECOVERY IS STILL WEAK, WITH FEARS OVER SOVEREIGN DEBT IN EUROPE AND THE U.S. AND INFLATION IN CHINA, BUT THE BANK CAN'T AFFORD ANOTHER YEAR OF LOW DEAL ACTIVITY...
alex@alexcartoon.com
IN THE PAST WE'VE BEEN GUILTY OF COMPLACENCY, BUT IT'S CLEAR THAT IF WE'RE TO BRING IN NEW BUSINESS IN 2011 IT'S GOING TO REQUIRE DEDICATION, APPLICATION AND SACRIFICES...
SO THAT'S YOUR EXCUSE FOR NOT DOING YOUR USUAL JANUARY OFF THE BOOZE?
QUITE. ONE CAN'T NEGLECT THE ALL-IMPORTANT NETWORKING, HUSTLING AND KEEPING ONE'S EAR TO THE GROUND...
WINE BAR
MENU

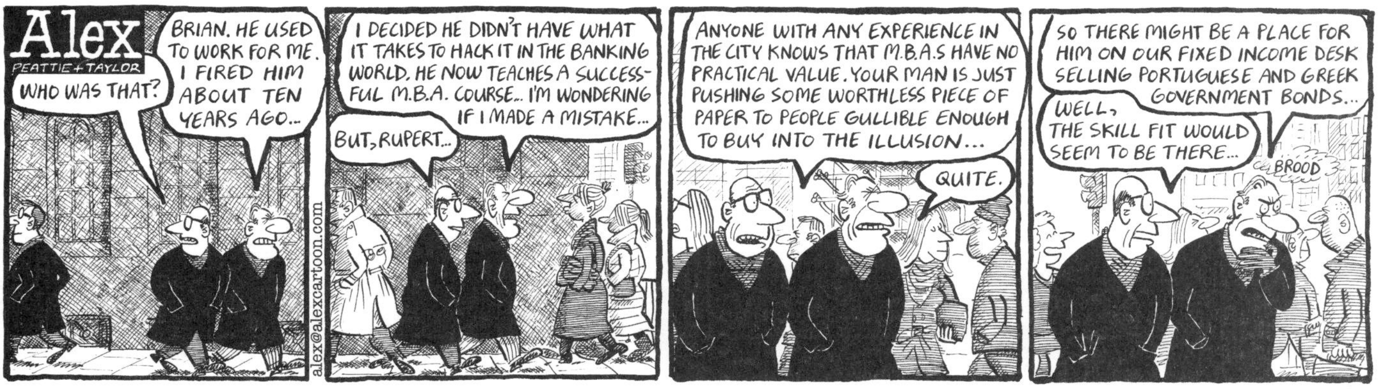
Alex
PEATTIE + TAYLOR
WHO WAS THAT?
BRIAN. HE USED TO WORK FOR ME. I FIRED HIM ABOUT TEN YEARS AGO...
I DECIDED HE DIDN'T HAVE WHAT IT TAKES TO HACK IT IN THE BANKING WORLD. HE NOW TEACHES A SUCCESSFUL M.B.A. COURSE... I'M WONDERING IF I MADE A MISTAKE...
BUT, RUPERT...
alex@alexcartoon.com
ANYONE WITH ANY EXPERIENCE IN THE CITY KNOWS THAT M.B.A.S HAVE NO PRACTICAL VALUE. YOUR MAN IS JUST PUSHING SOME WORTHLESS PIECE OF PAPER TO PEOPLE GULLIBLE ENOUGH TO BUY INTO THE ILLUSION...
QUITE.
SO THERE MIGHT BE A PLACE FOR HIM ON OUR FIXED INCOME DESK SELLING PORTUGUESE AND GREEK GOVERNMENT BONDS...
WELL, THE SKILL FIT WOULD SEEM TO BE THERE...
BROOD

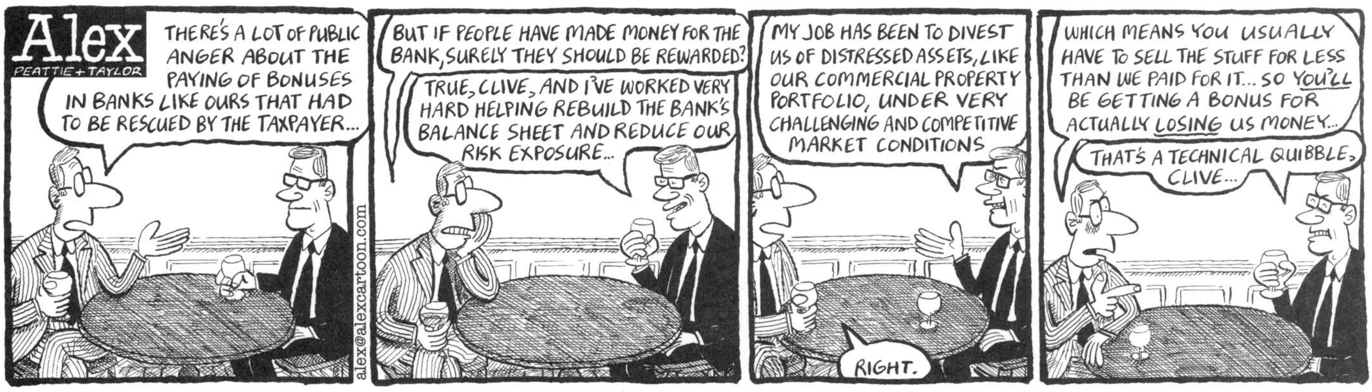
Alex
PEATTIE + TAYLOR
THERE'S A LOT OF PUBLIC ANGER ABOUT THE PAYING OF BONUSES IN BANKS LIKE OURS THAT HAD TO BE RESCUED BY THE TAXPAYER...
BUT IF PEOPLE HAVE MADE MONEY FOR THE BANK, SURELY THEY SHOULD BE REWARDED?
TRUE, CLIVE, AND I'VE WORKED VERY HARD HELPING REBUILD THE BANK'S BALANCE SHEET AND REDUCE OUR RISK EXPOSURE...
alex@alexcartoon.com
MY JOB HAS BEEN TO DIVEST US OF DISTRESSED ASSETS, LIKE OUR COMMERCIAL PROPERTY PORTFOLIO, UNDER VERY CHALLENGING AND COMPETITIVE MARKET CONDITIONS
RIGHT.
WHICH MEANS YOU USUALLY HAVE TO SELL THE STUFF FOR LESS THAN WE PAID FOR IT... SO YOU'LL BE GETTING A BONUS FOR ACTUALLY LOSING US MONEY...
THAT'S A TECHNICAL QUIBBLE, CLIVE...

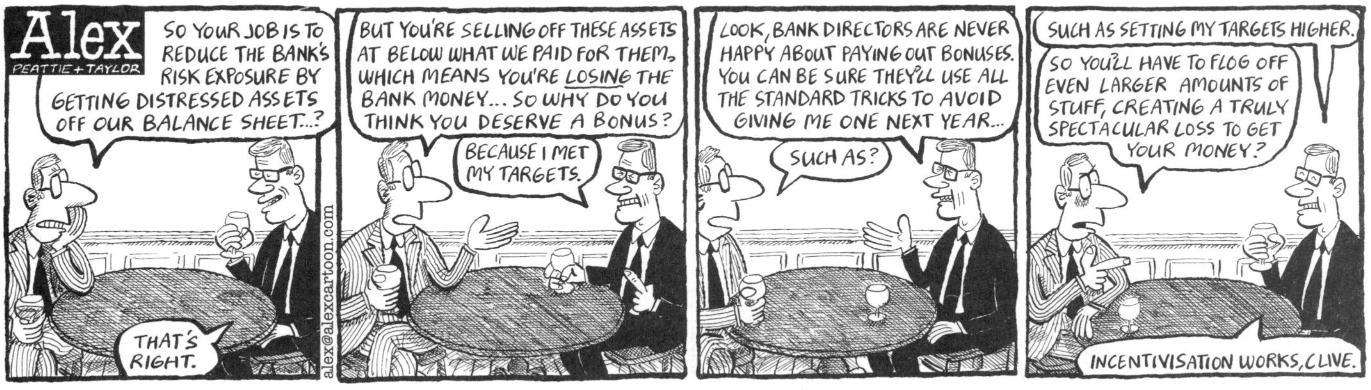
Alex
PEATTIE + TAYLOR
SO YOUR JOB IS TO REDUCE THE BANK'S RISK EXPOSURE BY GETTING DISTRESSED ASSETS OFF OUR BALANCE SHEET...?
THAT'S RIGHT.
BUT YOU'RE SELLING OFF THESE ASSETS AT BELOW WHAT WE PAID FOR THEM, WHICH MEANS YOU'RE LOSING THE BANK MONEY... SO WHY DO YOU THINK YOU DESERVE A BONUS?
BECAUSE I MET MY TARGETS.
alex@alexcartoon.com
LOOK, BANK DIRECTORS ARE NEVER HAPPY ABOUT PAYING OUT BONUSES. YOU CAN BE SURE THEY'LL USE ALL THE STANDARD TRICKS TO AVOID GIVING ME ONE NEXT YEAR...
SUCH AS?
SUCH AS SETTING MY TARGETS HIGHER.
SO YOU'LL HAVE TO FLOG OFF EVEN LARGER AMOUNTS OF STUFF, CREATING A TRULY SPECTACULAR LOSS TO GET YOUR MONEY?
INCENTIVISATION WORKS, CLIVE.

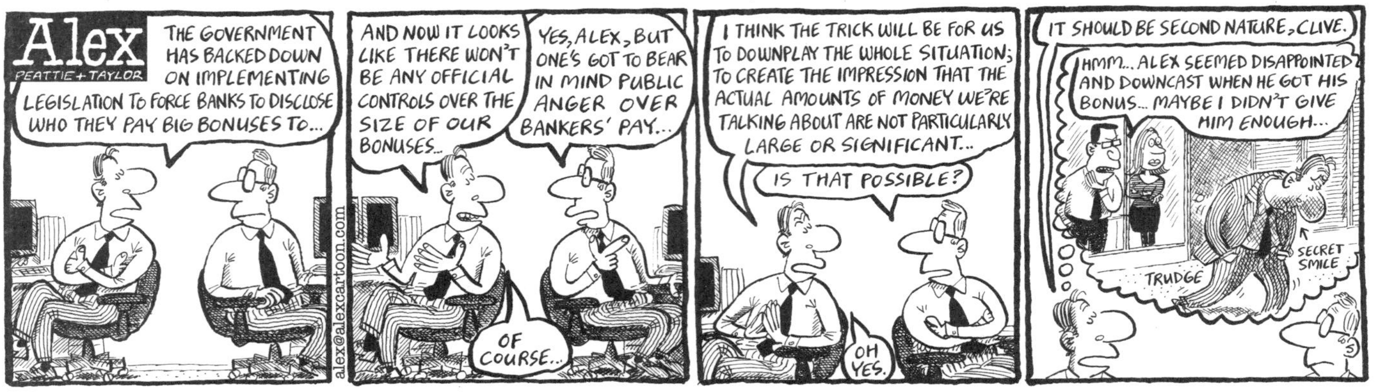
Alex
PEATTIE+TAYLOR
THE GOVERNMENT HAS BACKED DOWN ON IMPLEMENTING LEGISLATION TO FORCE BANKS TO DISCLOSE WHO THEY PAY BIG BONUSES TO...
AND NOW IT LOOKS LIKE THERE WON'T BE ANY OFFICIAL CONTROLS OVER THE SIZE OF OUR BONUSES...
YES, ALEX, BUT ONE'S GOT TO BEAR IN MIND PUBLIC ANGER OVER BANKERS' PAY...
OF COURSE...
alex@alexcartoon.com
I THINK THE TRICK WILL BE FOR US TO DOWNPLAY THE WHOLE SITUATION; TO CREATE THE IMPRESSION THAT THE ACTUAL AMOUNTS OF MONEY WE'RE TALKING ABOUT ARE NOT PARTICULARLY LARGE OR SIGNIFICANT...
IS THAT POSSIBLE?
OH YES.
IT SHOULD BE SECOND NATURE, CLIVE.
HMM... ALEX SEEMED DISAPPOINTED AND DOWNCAST WHEN HE GOT HIS BONUS... MAYBE I DIDN'T GIVE HIM ENOUGH...
SECRET SMILE
TRUDGE

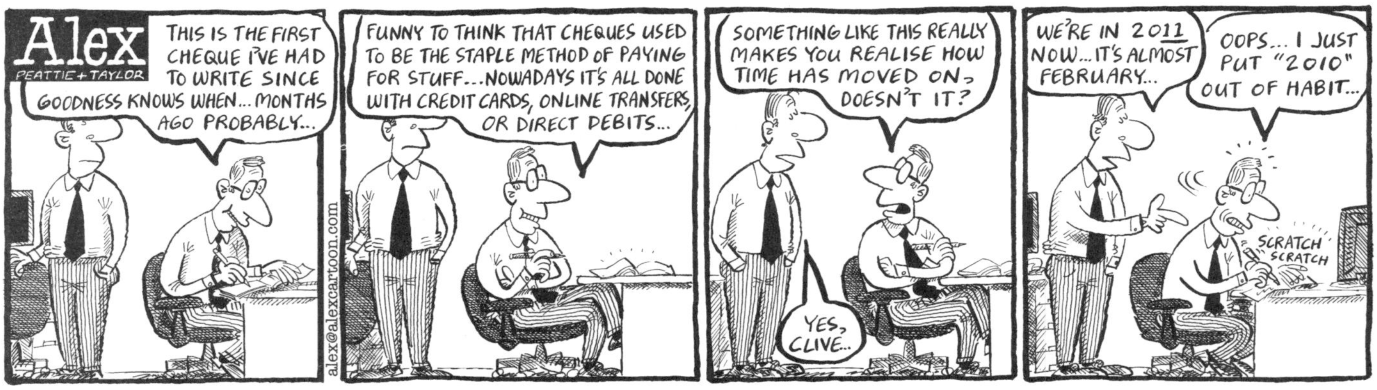
Alex
PEATTIE+TAYLOR
THIS IS THE FIRST CHEQUE I'VE HAD TO WRITE SINCE GOODNESS KNOWS WHEN... MONTHS AGO PROBABLY...
FUNNY TO THINK THAT CHEQUES USED TO BE THE STAPLE METHOD OF PAYING FOR STUFF... NOWADAYS IT'S ALL DONE WITH CREDIT CARDS, ONLINE TRANSFERS, OR DIRECT DEBITS...
alex@alexcartoon.com
SOMETHING LIKE THIS REALLY MAKES YOU REALISE HOW TIME HAS MOVED ON, DOESN'T IT?
YES, CLIVE...
WE'RE IN 2011 NOW... IT'S ALMOST FEBRUARY...
OOPS... I JUST PUT "2010" OUT OF HABIT...
SCRATCH SCRATCH

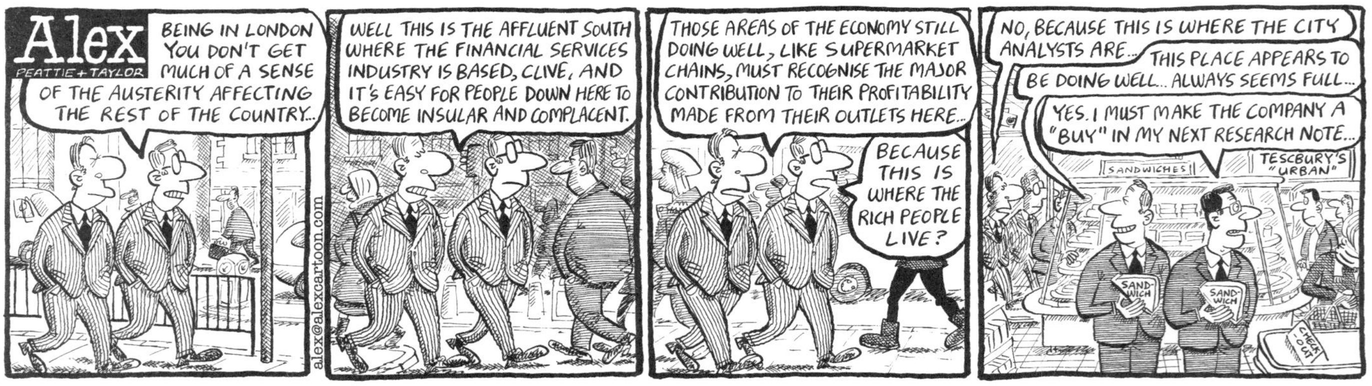
Alex
PEATTIE+TAYLOR
BEING IN LONDON YOU DON'T GET MUCH OF A SENSE OF THE AUSTERITY AFFECTING THE REST OF THE COUNTRY...
WELL THIS IS THE AFFLUENT SOUTH WHERE THE FINANCIAL SERVICES INDUSTRY IS BASED, CLIVE, AND IT'S EASY FOR PEOPLE DOWN HERE TO BECOME INSULAR AND COMPLACENT.
alex@alexcartoon.com
THOSE AREAS OF THE ECONOMY STILL DOING WELL, LIKE SUPERMARKET CHAINS, MUST RECOGNISE THE MAJOR CONTRIBUTION TO THEIR PROFITABILITY MADE FROM THEIR OUTLETS HERE...
BECAUSE THIS IS WHERE THE RICH PEOPLE LIVE?
NO, BECAUSE THIS IS WHERE THE CITY ANALYSTS ARE...
THIS PLACE APPEARS TO BE DOING WELL... ALWAYS SEEMS FULL...
YES. I MUST MAKE THE COMPANY A "BUY" IN MY NEXT RESEARCH NOTE...
SANDWICHES
TESCBURY'S "URBAN"
SAND-WICH
SAND-WICH
CHECK-OUT

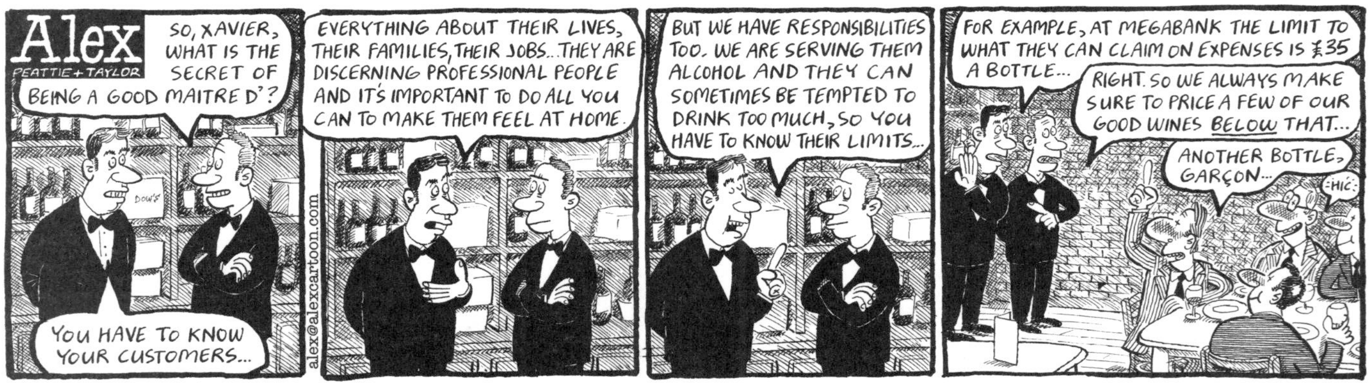
Alex
PEATTIE+TAYLOR
SO, XAVIER, WHAT IS THE SECRET OF BEING A GOOD MAITRE D'?
YOU HAVE TO KNOW YOUR CUSTOMERS...
EVERYTHING ABOUT THEIR LIVES, THEIR FAMILIES, THEIR JOBS... THEY ARE DISCERNING PROFESSIONAL PEOPLE AND IT'S IMPORTANT TO DO ALL YOU CAN TO MAKE THEM FEEL AT HOME
alex@alexcartoon.com
BUT WE HAVE RESPONSIBILITIES TOO. WE ARE SERVING THEM ALCOHOL AND THEY CAN SOMETIMES BE TEMPTED TO DRINK TOO MUCH, SO YOU HAVE TO KNOW THEIR LIMITS...
FOR EXAMPLE, AT MEGABANK THE LIMIT TO WHAT THEY CAN CLAIM ON EXPENSES IS ₤35 A BOTTLE...
RIGHT. SO WE ALWAYS MAKE SURE TO PRICE A FEW OF OUR GOOD WINES BELOW THAT...
ANOTHER BOTTLE, GARÇON...
HIC

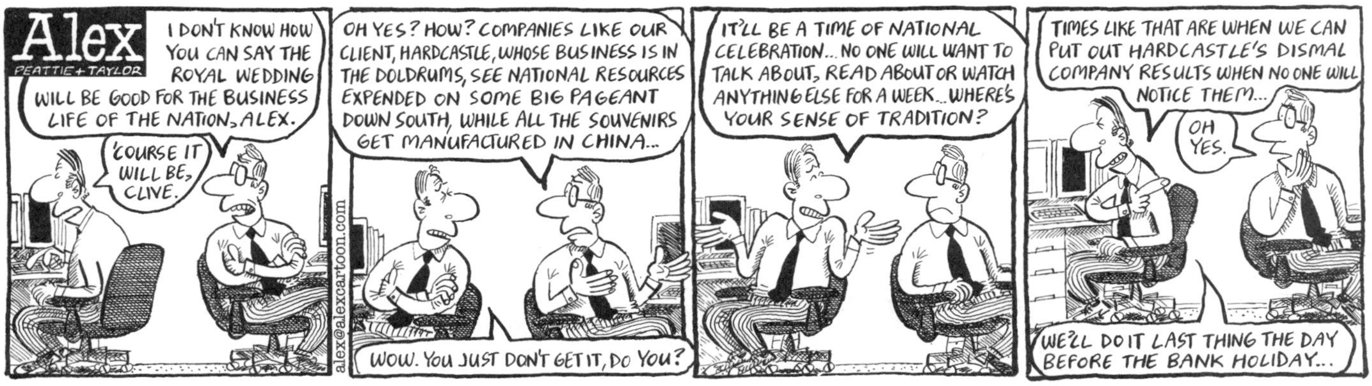
Alex
PEATTIE+TAYLOR
I DON'T KNOW HOW YOU CAN SAY THE ROYAL WEDDING WILL BE GOOD FOR THE BUSINESS LIFE OF THE NATION, ALEX.
'COURSE IT WILL BE, CLIVE.
alex@alexcartoon.com
OH YES? HOW? COMPANIES LIKE OUR CLIENT, HARDCASTLE, WHOSE BUSINESS IS IN THE DOLDRUMS, SEE NATIONAL RESOURCES EXPENDED ON SOME BIG PAGEANT DOWN SOUTH, WHILE ALL THE SOUVENIRS GET MANUFACTURED IN CHINA...
WOW. YOU JUST DON'T GET IT, DO YOU?
IT'LL BE A TIME OF NATIONAL CELEBRATION... NO ONE WILL WANT TO TALK ABOUT, READ ABOUT OR WATCH ANYTHING ELSE FOR A WEEK... WHERE'S YOUR SENSE OF TRADITION?
TIMES LIKE THAT ARE WHEN WE CAN PUT OUT HARDCASTLE'S DISMAL COMPANY RESULTS WHEN NO ONE WILL NOTICE THEM...
OH YES.
WE'LL DO IT LAST THING THE DAY BEFORE THE BANK HOLIDAY...

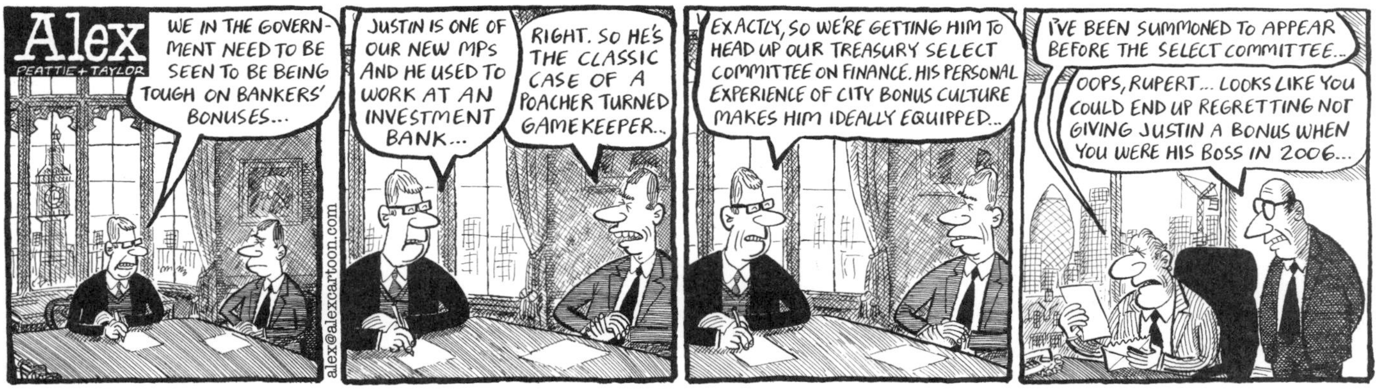
Alex
PEATTIE+TAYLOR
WE IN THE GOVERNMENT NEED TO BE SEEN TO BE BEING TOUGH ON BANKERS' BONUSES...
alex@alexcartoon.com
JUSTIN IS ONE OF OUR NEW MPs AND HE USED TO WORK AT AN INVESTMENT BANK...
RIGHT. SO HE'S THE CLASSIC CASE OF A POACHER TURNED GAMEKEEPER...
EXACTLY, SO WE'RE GETTING HIM TO HEAD UP OUR TREASURY SELECT COMMITTEE ON FINANCE. HIS PERSONAL EXPERIENCE OF CITY BONUS CULTURE MAKES HIM IDEALLY EQUIPPED...
I'VE BEEN SUMMONED TO APPEAR BEFORE THE SELECT COMMITTEE...
OOPS, RUPERT... LOOKS LIKE YOU COULD END UP REGRETTING NOT GIVING JUSTIN A BONUS WHEN YOU WERE HIS BOSS IN 2006...

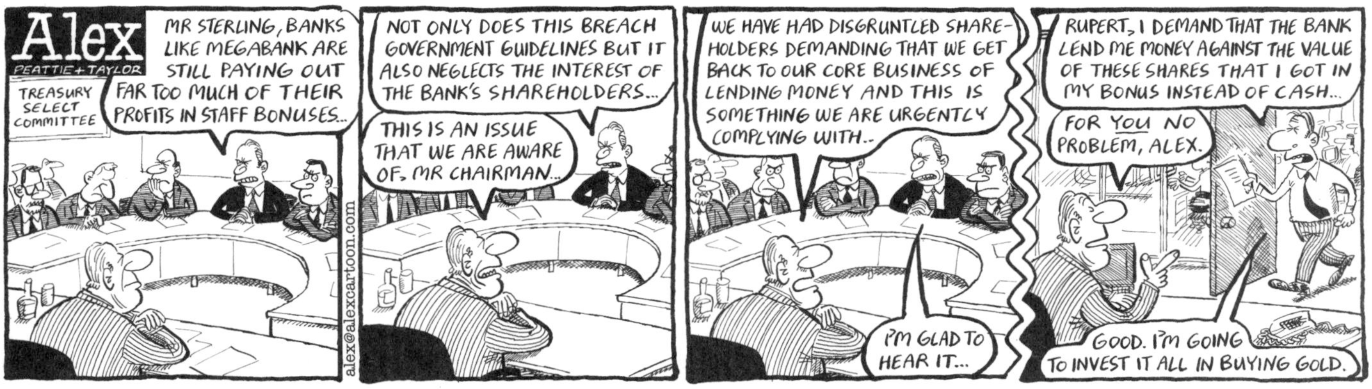
Alex
PEATTIE+TAYLOR
TREASURY SELECT COMMITTEE
MR STERLING, BANKS LIKE MEGABANK ARE STILL PAYING OUT FAR TOO MUCH OF THEIR PROFITS IN STAFF BONUSES...
alex@alexcartoon.com
NOT ONLY DOES THIS BREACH GOVERNMENT GUIDELINES BUT IT ALSO NEGLECTS THE INTEREST OF THE BANK'S SHAREHOLDERS...
THIS IS AN ISSUE THAT WE ARE AWARE OF, MR CHAIRMAN...
WE HAVE HAD DISGRUNTLED SHAREHOLDERS DEMANDING THAT WE GET BACK TO OUR CORE BUSINESS OF LENDING MONEY AND THIS IS SOMETHING WE ARE URGENTLY COMPLYING WITH...
I'M GLAD TO HEAR IT...
RUPERT, I DEMAND THAT THE BANK LEND ME MONEY AGAINST THE VALUE OF THESE SHARES THAT I GOT IN MY BONUS INSTEAD OF CASH...
FOR YOU NO PROBLEM, ALEX.
GOOD. I'M GOING TO INVEST IT ALL IN BUYING GOLD.

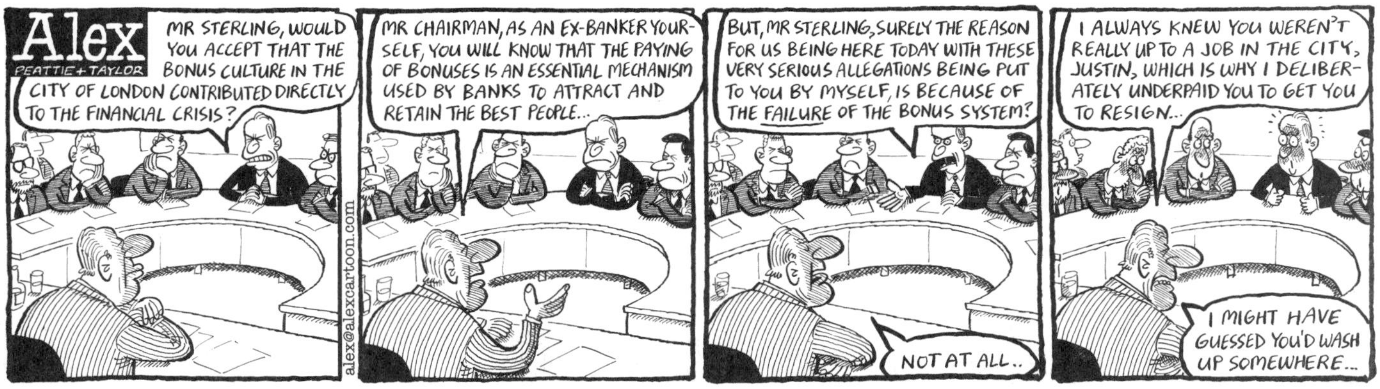
Alex
PEATTIE+TAYLOR
MR STERLING, WOULD YOU ACCEPT THAT THE BONUS CULTURE IN THE CITY OF LONDON CONTRIBUTED DIRECTLY TO THE FINANCIAL CRISIS?
alex@alexcartoon.com
MR CHAIRMAN, AS AN EX-BANKER YOURSELF, YOU WILL KNOW THAT THE PAYING OF BONUSES IS AN ESSENTIAL MECHANISM USED BY BANKS TO ATTRACT AND RETAIN THE BEST PEOPLE...
BUT, MR STERLING, SURELY THE REASON FOR US BEING HERE TODAY WITH THESE VERY SERIOUS ALLEGATIONS BEING PUT TO YOU BY MYSELF, IS BECAUSE OF THE FAILURE OF THE BONUS SYSTEM?
NOT AT ALL..
I ALWAYS KNEW YOU WEREN'T REALLY UP TO A JOB IN THE CITY, JUSTIN, WHICH IS WHY I DELIBERATELY UNDERPAID YOU TO GET YOU TO RESIGN...
I MIGHT HAVE GUESSED YOU'D WASH UP SOMEWHERE...

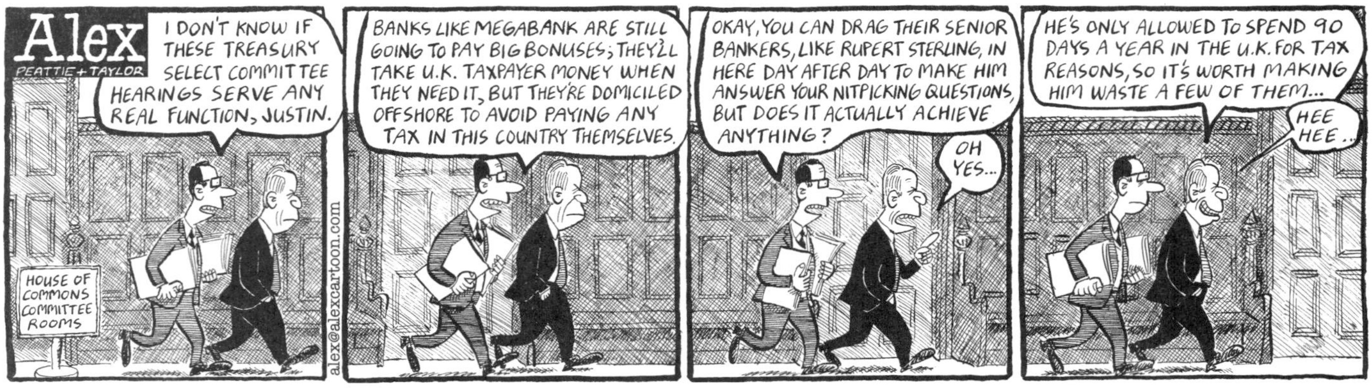
Alex
PEATTIE + TAYLOR
I DON'T KNOW IF THESE TREASURY SELECT COMMITTEE HEARINGS SERVE ANY REAL FUNCTION, JUSTIN.
HOUSE OF COMMONS COMMITTEE ROOMS
BANKS LIKE MEGABANK ARE STILL GOING TO PAY BIG BONUSES; THEY'LL TAKE U.K. TAXPAYER MONEY WHEN THEY NEED IT, BUT THEY'RE DOMICILED OFFSHORE TO AVOID PAYING ANY TAX IN THIS COUNTRY THEMSELVES.
alex@alexcartoon.com
OKAY, YOU CAN DRAG THEIR SENIOR BANKERS, LIKE RUPERT STERLING, IN HERE DAY AFTER DAY TO MAKE HIM ANSWER YOUR NITPICKING QUESTIONS, BUT DOES IT ACTUALLY ACHIEVE ANYTHING?
OH YES...
HE'S ONLY ALLOWED TO SPEND 90 DAYS A YEAR IN THE U.K. FOR TAX REASONS, SO IT'S WORTH MAKING HIM WASTE A FEW OF THEM...
HEE HEE...

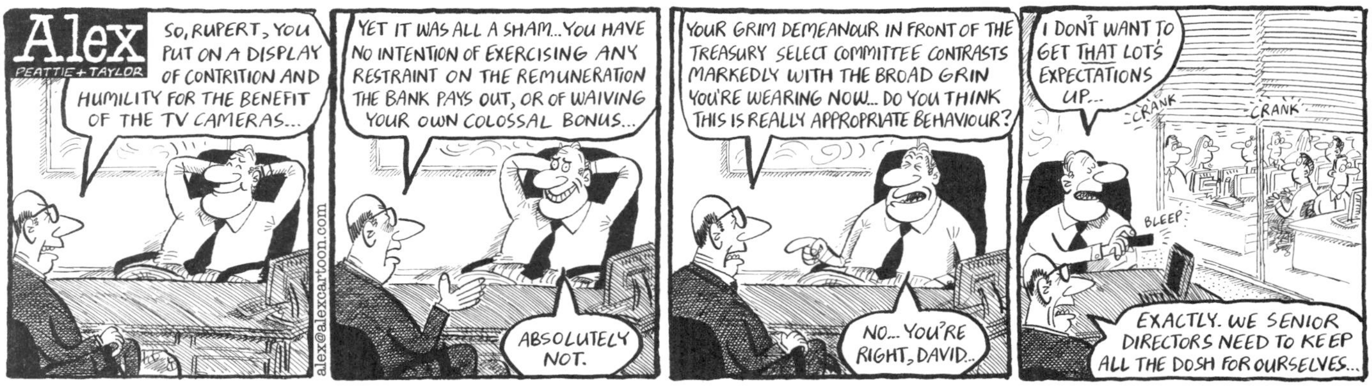
Alex
PEATTIE + TAYLOR
SO, RUPERT, YOU PUT ON A DISPLAY OF CONTRITION AND HUMILITY FOR THE BENEFIT OF THE TV CAMERAS...
YET IT WAS ALL A SHAM... YOU HAVE NO INTENTION OF EXERCISING ANY RESTRAINT ON THE REMUNERATION THE BANK PAYS OUT, OR OF WAIVING YOUR OWN COLOSSAL BONUS...
ABSOLUTELY NOT.
alex@alexcartoon.com
YOUR GRIM DEMEANOUR IN FRONT OF THE TREASURY SELECT COMMITTEE CONTRASTS MARKEDLY WITH THE BROAD GRIN YOU'RE WEARING NOW... DO YOU THINK THIS IS REALLY APPROPRIATE BEHAVIOUR?
NO... YOU'RE RIGHT, DAVID...
I DON'T WANT TO GET THAT LOT'S EXPECTATIONS UP...
CRANK
CRANK
BLEEP
EXACTLY. WE SENIOR DIRECTORS NEED TO KEEP ALL THE DOSH FOR OURSELVES...

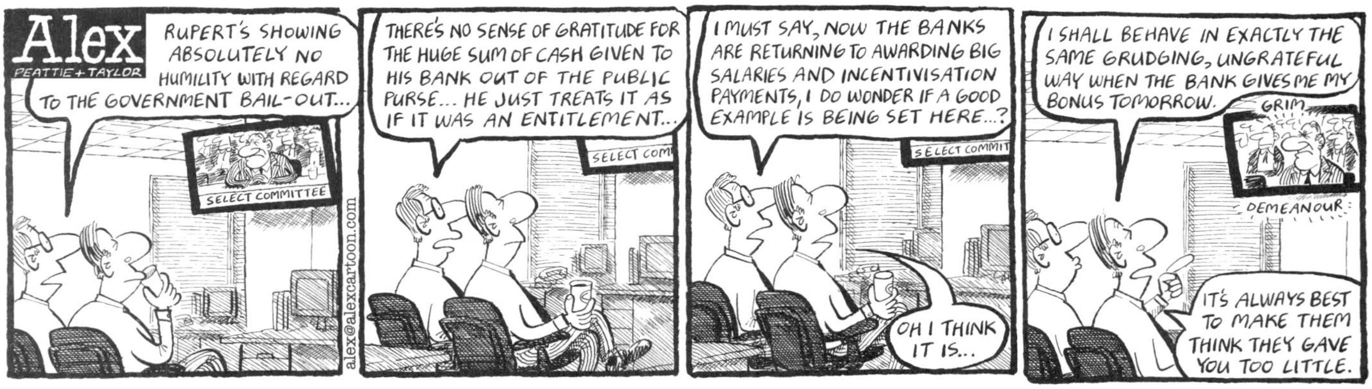
Alex
PEATTIE + TAYLOR
RUPERT'S SHOWING ABSOLUTELY NO HUMILITY WITH REGARD TO THE GOVERNMENT BAIL-OUT...
SELECT COMMITTEE
THERE'S NO SENSE OF GRATITUDE FOR THE HUGE SUM OF CASH GIVEN TO HIS BANK OUT OF THE PUBLIC PURSE... HE JUST TREATS IT AS IF IT WAS AN ENTITLEMENT...
SELECT COMM
alex@alexcartoon.com
I MUST SAY, NOW THE BANKS ARE RETURNING TO AWARDING BIG SALARIES AND INCENTIVISATION PAYMENTS, I DO WONDER IF A GOOD EXAMPLE IS BEING SET HERE...?
SELECT COMMIT
OH I THINK IT IS...
I SHALL BEHAVE IN EXACTLY THE SAME GRUDGING, UNGRATEFUL WAY WHEN THE BANK GIVES ME MY BONUS TOMORROW.
GRIM
DEMEANOUR
IT'S ALWAYS BEST TO MAKE THEM THINK THEY GAVE YOU TOO LITTLE.

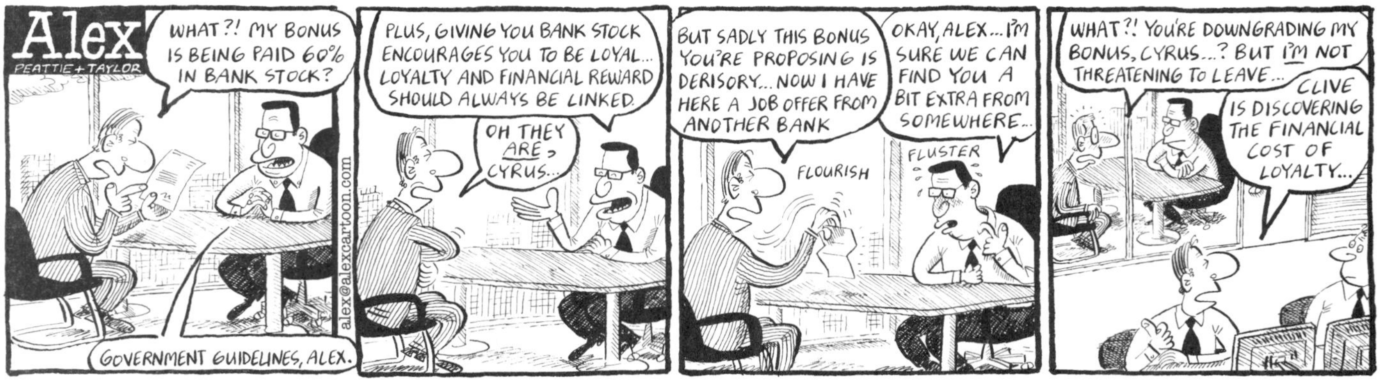
Alex
PEATTIE + TAYLOR
WHAT?! MY BONUS IS BEING PAID 60% IN BANK STOCK?
GOVERNMENT GUIDELINES, ALEX.
PLUS, GIVING YOU BANK STOCK ENCOURAGES YOU TO BE LOYAL... LOYALTY AND FINANCIAL REWARD SHOULD ALWAYS BE LINKED.
OH THEY ARE, CYRUS...
alex@alexcartoon.com
BUT SADLY THIS BONUS YOU'RE PROPOSING IS DERISORY... NOW I HAVE HERE A JOB OFFER FROM ANOTHER BANK
OKAY, ALEX... I'M SURE WE CAN FIND YOU A BIT EXTRA FROM SOMEWHERE...
FLOURISH
FLUSTER
WHAT?! YOU'RE DOWNGRADING MY BONUS, CYRUS...? BUT I'M NOT THREATENING TO LEAVE...
CLIVE IS DISCOVERING THE FINANCIAL COST OF LOYALTY...

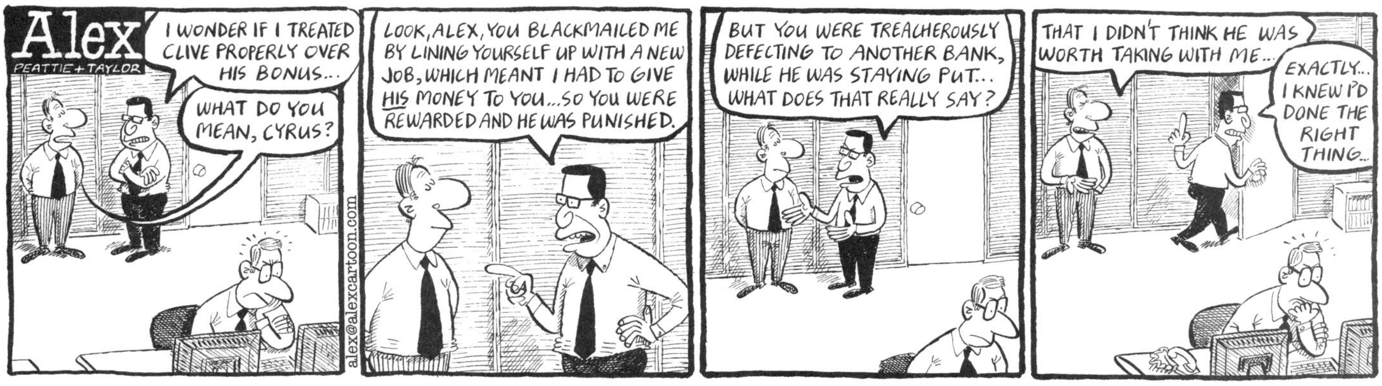
Alex
PEATTIE + TAYLOR
I WONDER IF I TREATED CLIVE PROPERLY OVER HIS BONUS...
WHAT DO YOU MEAN, CYRUS?
alex@alexcartoon.com
LOOK, ALEX, YOU BLACKMAILED ME BY LINING YOURSELF UP WITH A NEW JOB, WHICH MEANT I HAD TO GIVE HIS MONEY TO YOU...SO YOU WERE REWARDED AND HE WAS PUNISHED.
BUT YOU WERE TREACHEROUSLY DEFECTING TO ANOTHER BANK, WHILE HE WAS STAYING PUT... WHAT DOES THAT REALLY SAY?
THAT I DIDN'T THINK HE WAS WORTH TAKING WITH ME...
EXACTLY... I KNEW I'D DONE THE RIGHT THING...

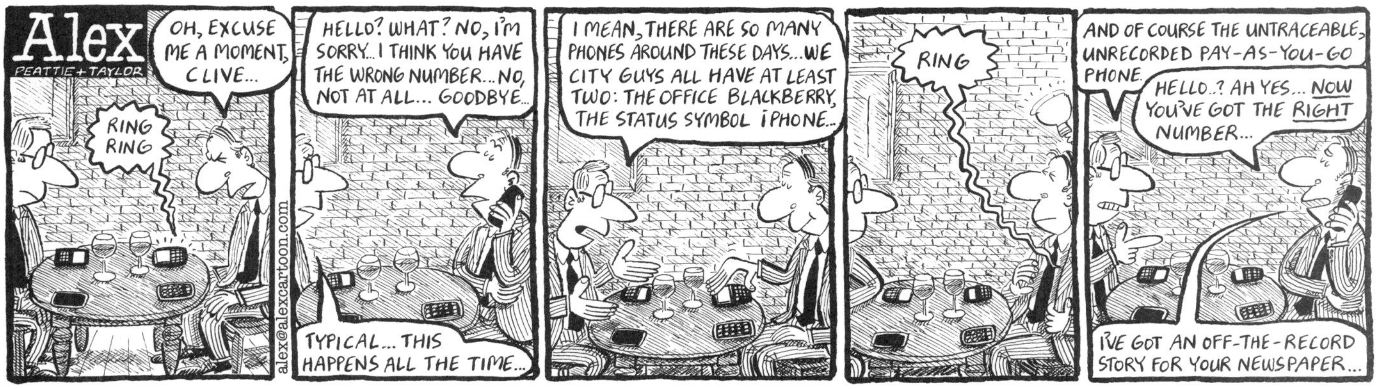
Alex
PEATTIE + TAYLOR
OH, EXCUSE ME A MOMENT, CLIVE...
RING RING
alex@alexcartoon.com
HELLO? WHAT? NO, I'M SORRY... I THINK YOU HAVE THE WRONG NUMBER... NO, NOT AT ALL... GOODBYE...
TYPICAL... THIS HAPPENS ALL THE TIME...
I MEAN, THERE ARE SO MANY PHONES AROUND THESE DAYS... WE CITY GUYS ALL HAVE AT LEAST TWO: THE OFFICE BLACKBERRY, THE STATUS SYMBOL iPHONE...
RING
AND OF COURSE THE UNTRACEABLE, UNRECORDED PAY-AS-YOU-GO PHONE.
HELLO..? AH YES... NOW YOU'VE GOT THE RIGHT NUMBER...
I'VE GOT AN OFF-THE-RECORD STORY FOR YOUR NEWSPAPER...

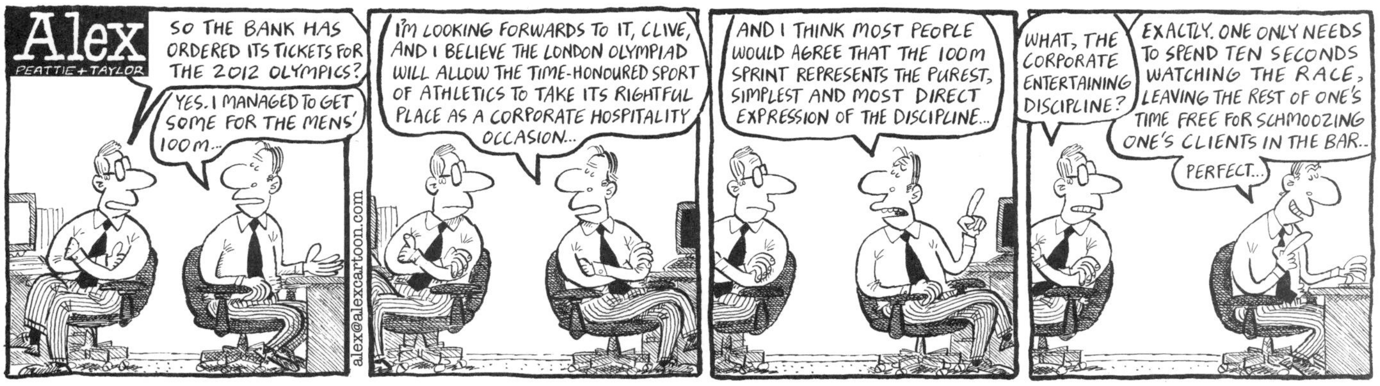
Alex
PEATTIE + TAYLOR
SO THE BANK HAS ORDERED ITS TICKETS FOR THE 2012 OLYMPICS?
YES. I MANAGED TO GET SOME FOR THE MENS' 100m...
alex@alexcartoon.com
I'M LOOKING FORWARDS TO IT, CLIVE, AND I BELIEVE THE LONDON OLYMPIAD WILL ALLOW THE TIME-HONOURED SPORT OF ATHLETICS TO TAKE ITS RIGHTFUL PLACE AS A CORPORATE HOSPITALITY OCCASION...
AND I THINK MOST PEOPLE WOULD AGREE THAT THE 100m SPRINT REPRESENTS THE PUREST, SIMPLEST AND MOST DIRECT EXPRESSION OF THE DISCIPLINE...
WHAT, THE CORPORATE ENTERTAINING DISCIPLINE?
EXACTLY. ONE ONLY NEEDS TO SPEND TEN SECONDS WATCHING THE RACE, LEAVING THE REST OF ONE'S TIME FREE FOR SCHMOOZING ONE'S CLIENTS IN THE BAR...
PERFECT...

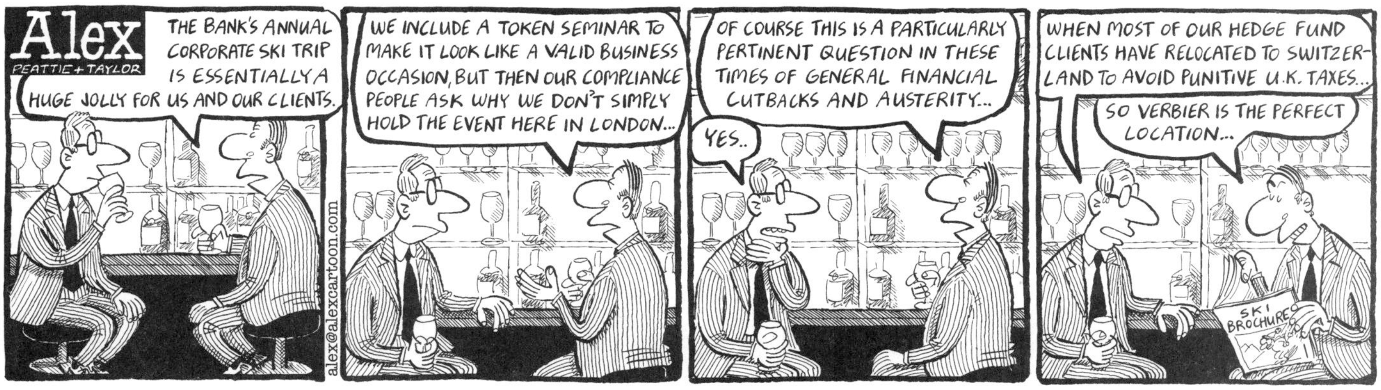
Alex
PEATTIE + TAYLOR
THE BANK'S ANNUAL CORPORATE SKI TRIP IS ESSENTIALLY A HUGE JOLLY FOR US AND OUR CLIENTS.
alex@alexcartoon.com
WE INCLUDE A TOKEN SEMINAR TO MAKE IT LOOK LIKE A VALID BUSINESS OCCASION, BUT THEN OUR COMPLIANCE PEOPLE ASK WHY WE DON'T SIMPLY HOLD THE EVENT HERE IN LONDON...
OF COURSE THIS IS A PARTICULARLY PERTINENT QUESTION IN THESE TIMES OF GENERAL FINANCIAL CUTBACKS AND AUSTERITY...
YES..
WHEN MOST OF OUR HEDGE FUND CLIENTS HAVE RELOCATED TO SWITZERLAND TO AVOID PUNITIVE U.K. TAXES...
SO VERBIER IS THE PERFECT LOCATION...
SKI BROCHURES

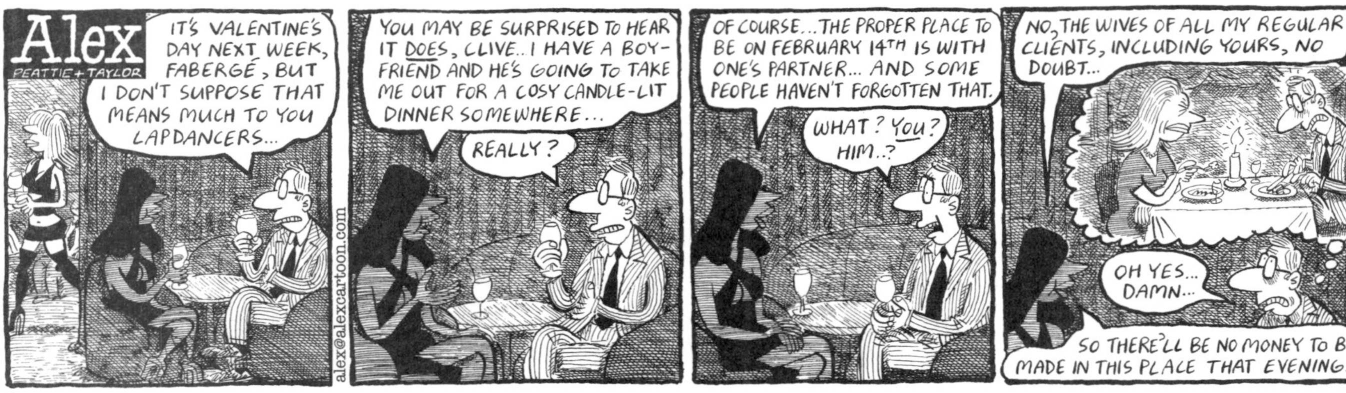
Alex
PEATTIE + TAYLOR
IT'S VALENTINE'S DAY NEXT WEEK, FABERGÉ, BUT I DON'T SUPPOSE THAT MEANS MUCH TO YOU LAPDANCERS...
YOU MAY BE SURPRISED TO HEAR IT DOES, CLIVE.. I HAVE A BOY-FRIEND AND HE'S GOING TO TAKE ME OUT FOR A COSY CANDLE-LIT DINNER SOMEWHERE...
REALLY?
alex@alexcartoon.com
OF COURSE... THE PROPER PLACE TO BE ON FEBRUARY 14TH IS WITH ONE'S PARTNER... AND SOME PEOPLE HAVEN'T FORGOTTEN THAT.
WHAT? YOU? HIM..?
NO, THE WIVES OF ALL MY REGULAR CLIENTS, INCLUDING YOURS, NO DOUBT...
OH YES... DAMN...
SO THERE'LL BE NO MONEY TO BE MADE IN THIS PLACE THAT EVENING...

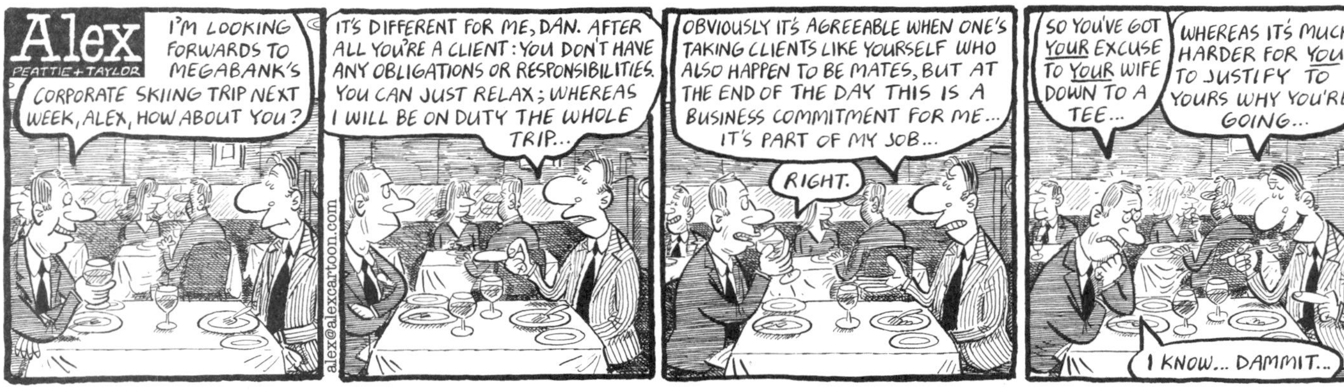
Alex
PEATTIE + TAYLOR
I'M LOOKING FORWARDS TO MEGABANK'S CORPORATE SKIING TRIP NEXT WEEK, ALEX, HOW ABOUT YOU?
IT'S DIFFERENT FOR ME, DAN. AFTER ALL YOU'RE A CLIENT: YOU DON'T HAVE ANY OBLIGATIONS OR RESPONSIBILITIES. YOU CAN JUST RELAX; WHEREAS I WILL BE ON DUTY THE WHOLE TRIP...
alex@alexcartoon.com
OBVIOUSLY IT'S AGREEABLE WHEN ONE'S TAKING CLIENTS LIKE YOURSELF WHO ALSO HAPPEN TO BE MATES, BUT AT THE END OF THE DAY THIS IS A BUSINESS COMMITMENT FOR ME... IT'S PART OF MY JOB...
RIGHT.
SO YOU'VE GOT YOUR EXCUSE TO YOUR WIFE DOWN TO A TEE...
WHEREAS IT'S MUCH HARDER FOR YOU TO JUSTIFY TO YOURS WHY YOU'RE GOING...
I KNOW... DAMMIT...

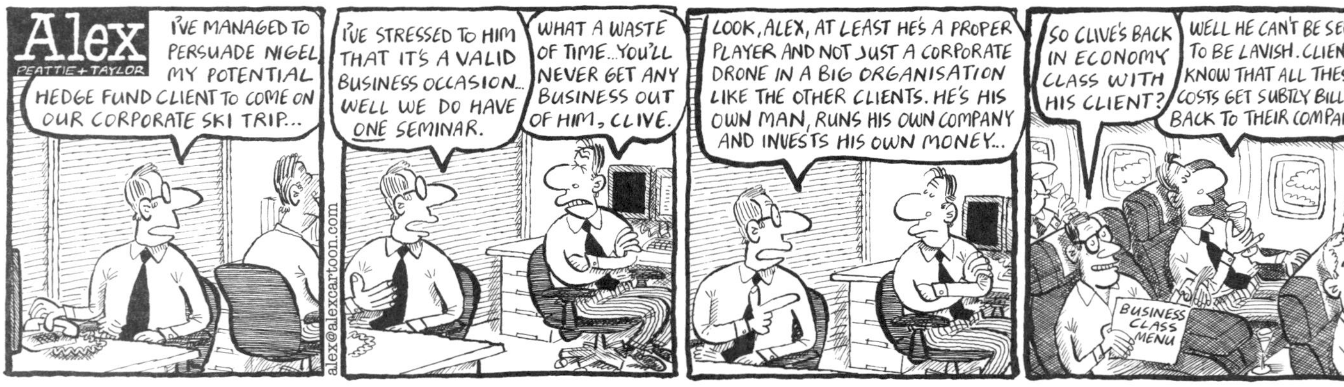
Alex
PEATTIE + TAYLOR
I'VE MANAGED TO PERSUADE NIGEL, MY POTENTIAL HEDGE FUND CLIENT TO COME ON OUR CORPORATE SKI TRIP...
alex@alexcartoon.com
I'VE STRESSED TO HIM THAT IT'S A VALID BUSINESS OCCASION... WELL WE DO HAVE ONE SEMINAR.
WHAT A WASTE OF TIME...YOU'LL NEVER GET ANY BUSINESS OUT OF HIM, CLIVE.
LOOK, ALEX, AT LEAST HE'S A PROPER PLAYER AND NOT JUST A CORPORATE DRONE IN A BIG ORGANISATION LIKE THE OTHER CLIENTS. HE'S HIS OWN MAN, RUNS HIS OWN COMPANY AND INVESTS HIS OWN MONEY...
SO CLIVE'S BACK IN ECONOMY CLASS WITH HIS CLIENT?
WELL HE CAN'T BE SEEN TO BE LAVISH. CLIENTS KNOW THAT ALL THESE COSTS GET SUBTLY BILLED BACK TO THEIR COMPANY.
BUSINESS CLASS MENU

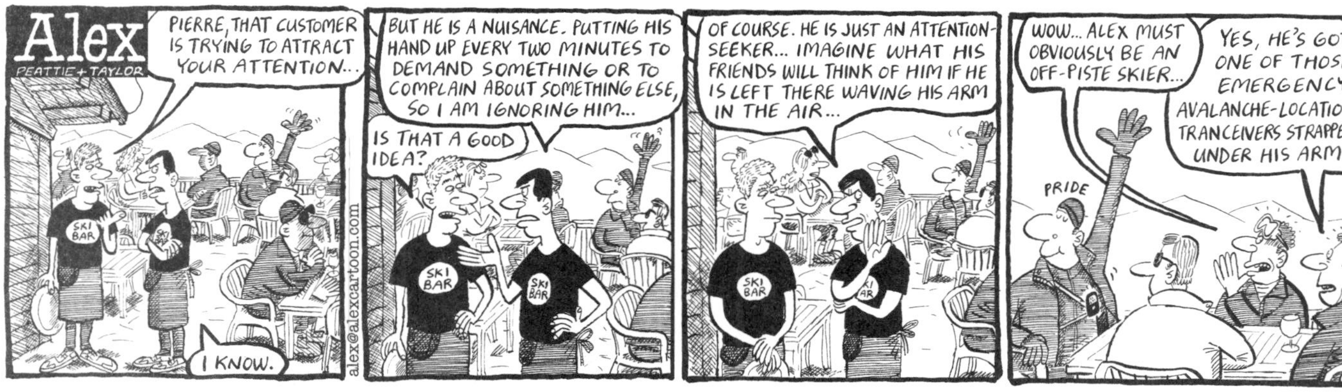
Alex
PEATTIE + TAYLOR
PIERRE, THAT CUSTOMER IS TRYING TO ATTRACT YOUR ATTENTION...
SKI BAR
I KNOW.
alex@alexcartoon.com
BUT HE IS A NUISANCE. PUTTING HIS HAND UP EVERY TWO MINUTES TO DEMAND SOMETHING OR TO COMPLAIN ABOUT SOMETHING ELSE, SO I AM IGNORING HIM...
IS THAT A GOOD IDEA?
OF COURSE. HE IS JUST AN ATTENTION-SEEKER... IMAGINE WHAT HIS FRIENDS WILL THINK OF HIM IF HE IS LEFT THERE WAVING HIS ARM IN THE AIR...
WOW... ALEX MUST OBVIOUSLY BE AN OFF-PISTE SKIER...
YES, HE'S GOT ONE OF THOSE EMERGENCY AVALANCHE-LOCATION TRANCEIVERS STRAPPED UNDER HIS ARM...
PRIDE

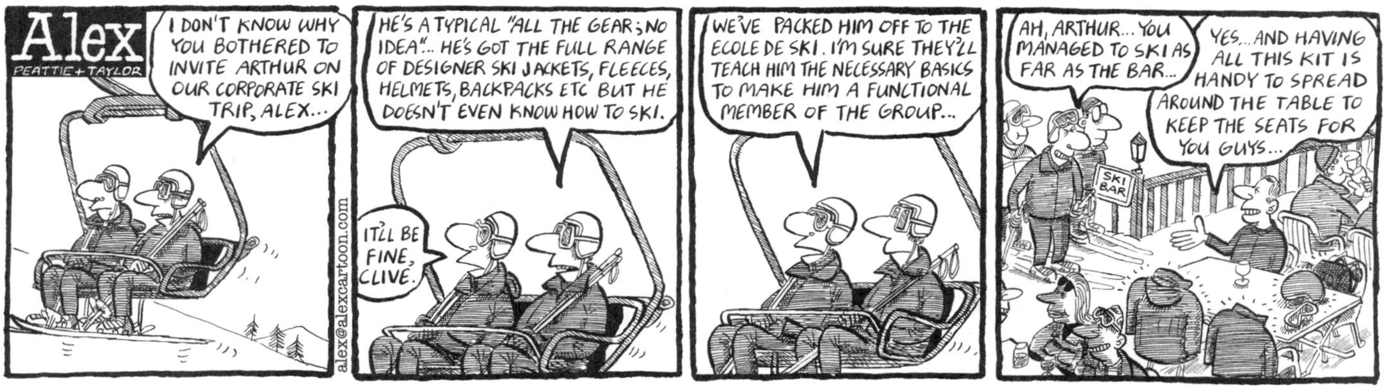
Alex
PEATTIE + TAYLOR
I DON'T KNOW WHY YOU BOTHERED TO INVITE ARTHUR ON OUR CORPORATE SKI TRIP, ALEX...
HE'S A TYPICAL "ALL THE GEAR; NO IDEA"... HE'S GOT THE FULL RANGE OF DESIGNER SKI JACKETS, FLEECES, HELMETS, BACKPACKS ETC BUT HE DOESN'T EVEN KNOW HOW TO SKI.
IT'LL BE FINE, CLIVE.
WE'VE PACKED HIM OFF TO THE ECOLE DE SKI. I'M SURE THEY'LL TEACH HIM THE NECESSARY BASICS TO MAKE HIM A FUNCTIONAL MEMBER OF THE GROUP...
AH, ARTHUR... YOU MANAGED TO SKI AS FAR AS THE BAR...
YES... AND HAVING ALL THIS KIT IS HANDY TO SPREAD AROUND THE TABLE TO KEEP THE SEATS FOR YOU GUYS...
SKI BAR
alex@alexcartoon.com

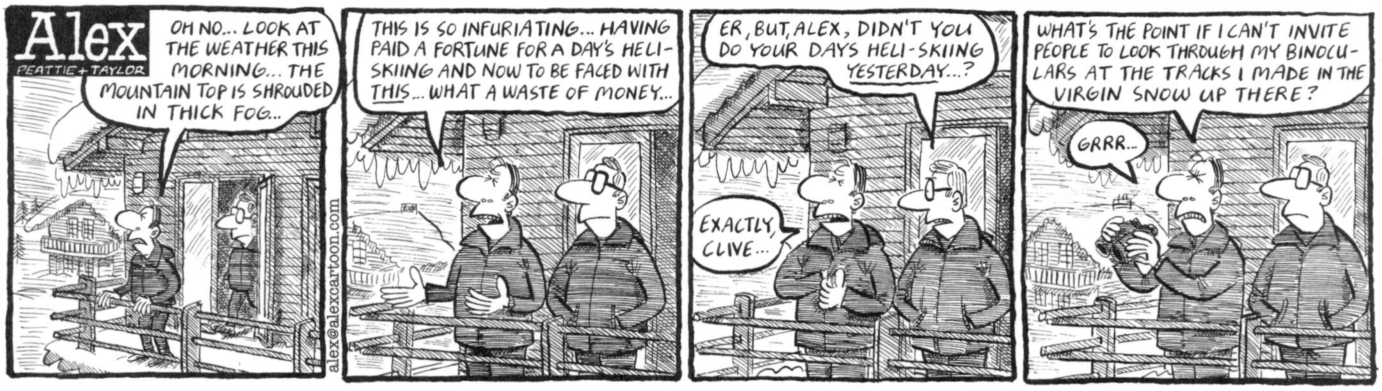
Alex
PEATTIE + TAYLOR
OH NO... LOOK AT THE WEATHER THIS MORNING... THE MOUNTAIN TOP IS SHROUDED IN THICK FOG...
THIS IS SO INFURIATING... HAVING PAID A FORTUNE FOR A DAY'S HELI-SKIING AND NOW TO BE FACED WITH THIS... WHAT A WASTE OF MONEY...
ER, BUT, ALEX, DIDN'T YOU DO YOUR DAYS HELI-SKIING YESTERDAY...?
EXACTLY, CLIVE...
WHAT'S THE POINT IF I CAN'T INVITE PEOPLE TO LOOK THROUGH MY BINOCULARS AT THE TRACKS I MADE IN THE VIRGIN SNOW UP THERE?
GRRR...
alex@alexcartoon.com

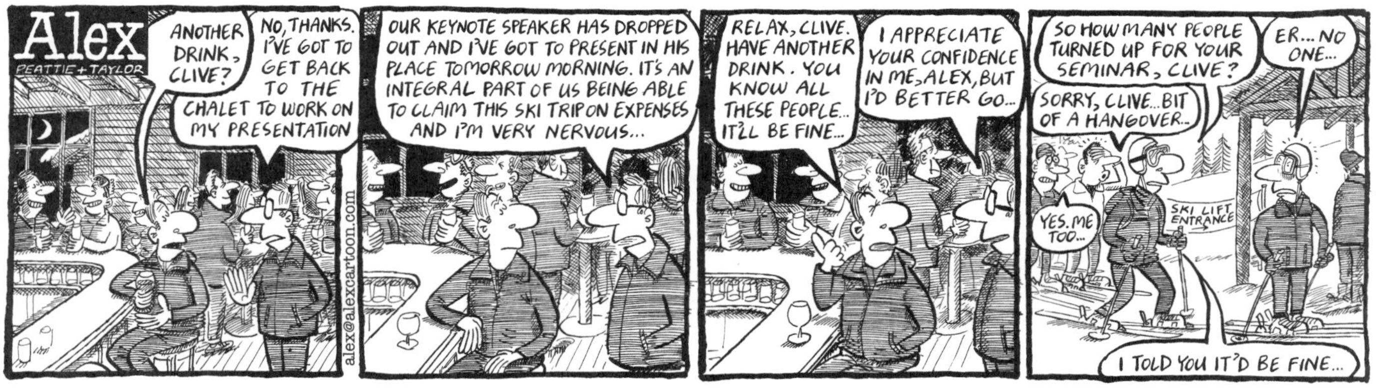
Alex
PEATTIE + TAYLOR
ANOTHER DRINK, CLIVE?
NO, THANKS. I'VE GOT TO GET BACK TO THE CHALET TO WORK ON MY PRESENTATION
OUR KEYNOTE SPEAKER HAS DROPPED OUT AND I'VE GOT TO PRESENT IN HIS PLACE TOMORROW MORNING. IT'S AN INTEGRAL PART OF US BEING ABLE TO CLAIM THIS SKI TRIP ON EXPENSES AND I'M VERY NERVOUS...
RELAX, CLIVE. HAVE ANOTHER DRINK. YOU KNOW ALL THESE PEOPLE... IT'LL BE FINE...
I APPRECIATE YOUR CONFIDENCE IN ME, ALEX, BUT I'D BETTER GO...
SO HOW MANY PEOPLE TURNED UP FOR YOUR SEMINAR, CLIVE?
ER... NO ONE...
SORRY, CLIVE... BIT OF A HANGOVER...
YES. ME TOO...
SKI LIFT ENTRANCE
I TOLD YOU IT'D BE FINE...
alex@alexcartoon.com

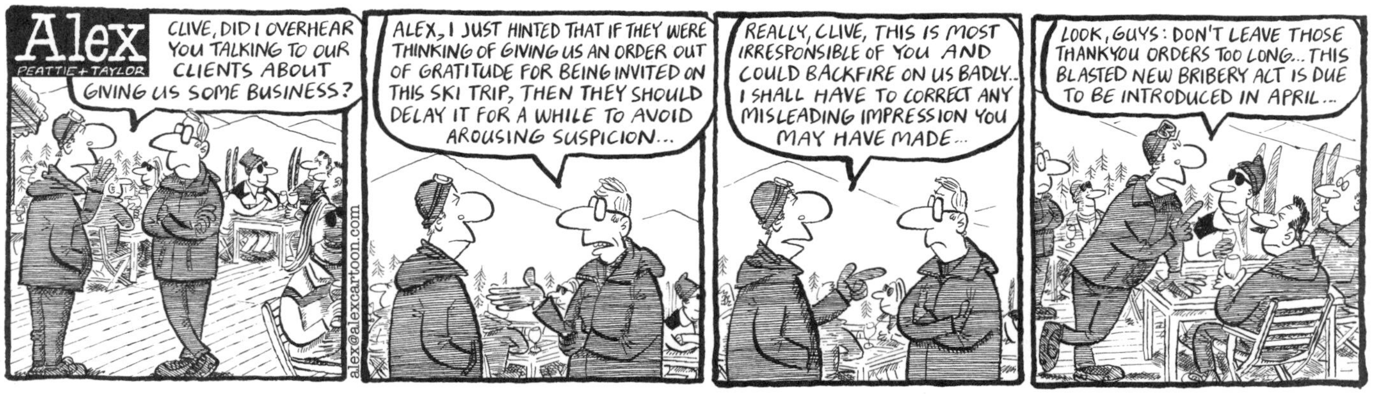
Alex
PEATTIE + TAYLOR
CLIVE, DID I OVERHEAR YOU TALKING TO OUR CLIENTS ABOUT GIVING US SOME BUSINESS?
ALEX, I JUST HINTED THAT IF THEY WERE THINKING OF GIVING US AN ORDER OUT OF GRATITUDE FOR BEING INVITED ON THIS SKI TRIP, THEN THEY SHOULD DELAY IT FOR A WHILE TO AVOID AROUSING SUSPICION...
REALLY, CLIVE, THIS IS MOST IRRESPONSIBLE OF YOU AND COULD BACKFIRE ON US BADLY... I SHALL HAVE TO CORRECT ANY MISLEADING IMPRESSION YOU MAY HAVE MADE...
LOOK, GUYS: DON'T LEAVE THOSE THANKYOU ORDERS TOO LONG... THIS BLASTED NEW BRIBERY ACT IS DUE TO BE INTRODUCED IN APRIL...
alex@alexcartoon.com

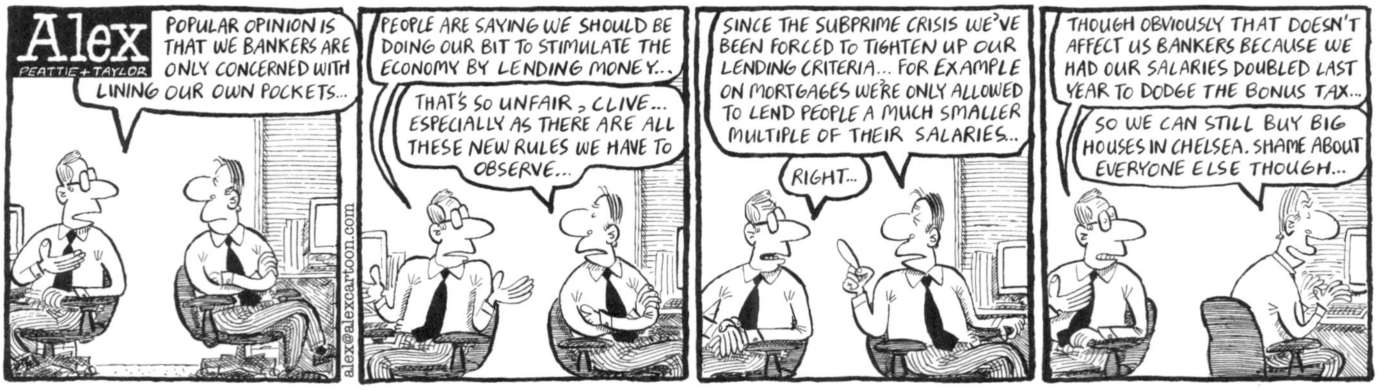
Alex
PEATTIE + TAYLOR
POPULAR OPINION IS THAT WE BANKERS ARE ONLY CONCERNED WITH LINING OUR OWN POCKETS...
alex@alexcartoon.com
PEOPLE ARE SAYING WE SHOULD BE DOING OUR BIT TO STIMULATE THE ECONOMY BY LENDING MONEY...
THAT'S SO UNFAIR, CLIVE... ESPECIALLY AS THERE ARE ALL THESE NEW RULES WE HAVE TO OBSERVE...
SINCE THE SUBPRIME CRISIS WE'VE BEEN FORCED TO TIGHTEN UP OUR LENDING CRITERIA... FOR EXAMPLE ON MORTGAGES WE'RE ONLY ALLOWED TO LEND PEOPLE A MUCH SMALLER MULTIPLE OF THEIR SALARIES...
RIGHT...
THOUGH OBVIOUSLY THAT DOESN'T AFFECT US BANKERS BECAUSE WE HAD OUR SALARIES DOUBLED LAST YEAR TO DODGE THE BONUS TAX...
SO WE CAN STILL BUY BIG HOUSES IN CHELSEA. SHAME ABOUT EVERYONE ELSE THOUGH...

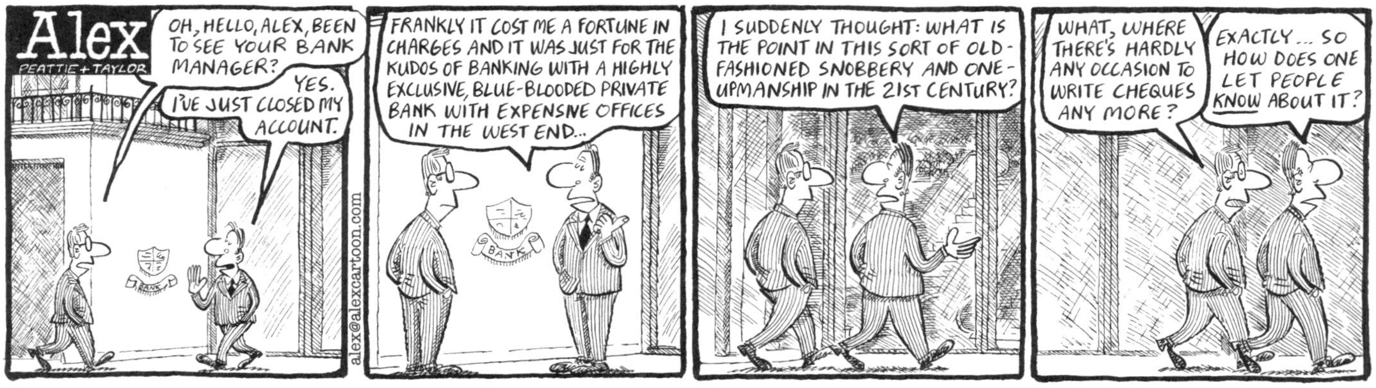
Alex
PEATTIE + TAYLOR
OH, HELLO, ALEX, BEEN TO SEE YOUR BANK MANAGER?
YES. I'VE JUST CLOSED MY ACCOUNT.
alex@alexcartoon.com
FRANKLY IT COST ME A FORTUNE IN CHARGES AND IT WAS JUST FOR THE KUDOS OF BANKING WITH A HIGHLY EXCLUSIVE, BLUE-BLOODED PRIVATE BANK WITH EXPENSIVE OFFICES IN THE WEST END...
BANK
I SUDDENLY THOUGHT: WHAT IS THE POINT IN THIS SORT OF OLD-FASHIONED SNOBBERY AND ONE-UPMANSHIP IN THE 21ST CENTURY?
WHAT, WHERE THERE'S HARDLY ANY OCCASION TO WRITE CHEQUES ANY MORE?
EXACTLY... SO HOW DOES ONE LET PEOPLE KNOW ABOUT IT?

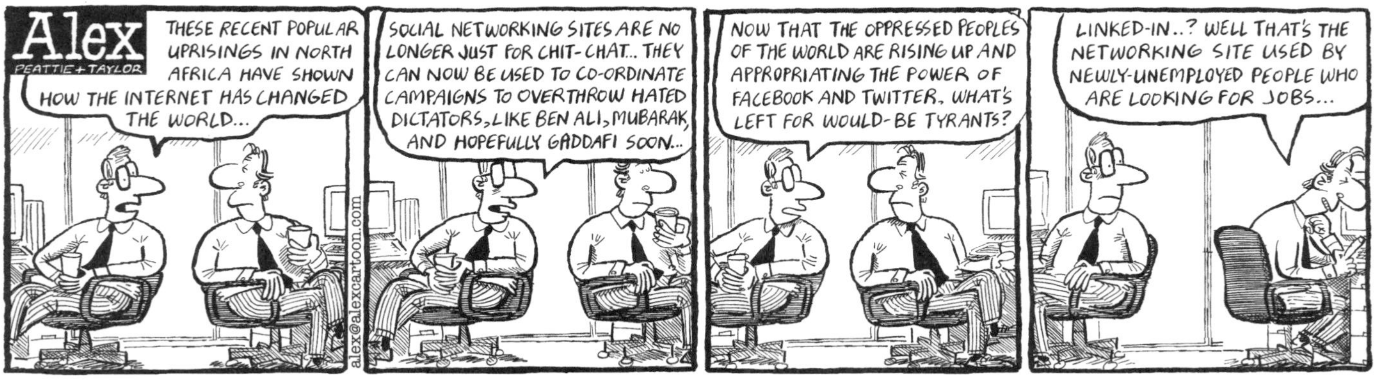
Alex
PEATTIE + TAYLOR
THESE RECENT POPULAR UPRISINGS IN NORTH AFRICA HAVE SHOWN HOW THE INTERNET HAS CHANGED THE WORLD...
alex@alexcartoon.com
SOCIAL NETWORKING SITES ARE NO LONGER JUST FOR CHIT-CHAT... THEY CAN NOW BE USED TO CO-ORDINATE CAMPAIGNS TO OVERTHROW HATED DICTATORS, LIKE BEN ALI, MUBARAK, AND HOPEFULLY GADDAFI SOON...
NOW THAT THE OPPRESSED PEOPLES OF THE WORLD ARE RISING UP AND APPROPRIATING THE POWER OF FACEBOOK AND TWITTER, WHAT'S LEFT FOR WOULD-BE TYRANTS?
LINKED-IN..? WELL THAT'S THE NETWORKING SITE USED BY NEWLY-UNEMPLOYED PEOPLE WHO ARE LOOKING FOR JOBS...

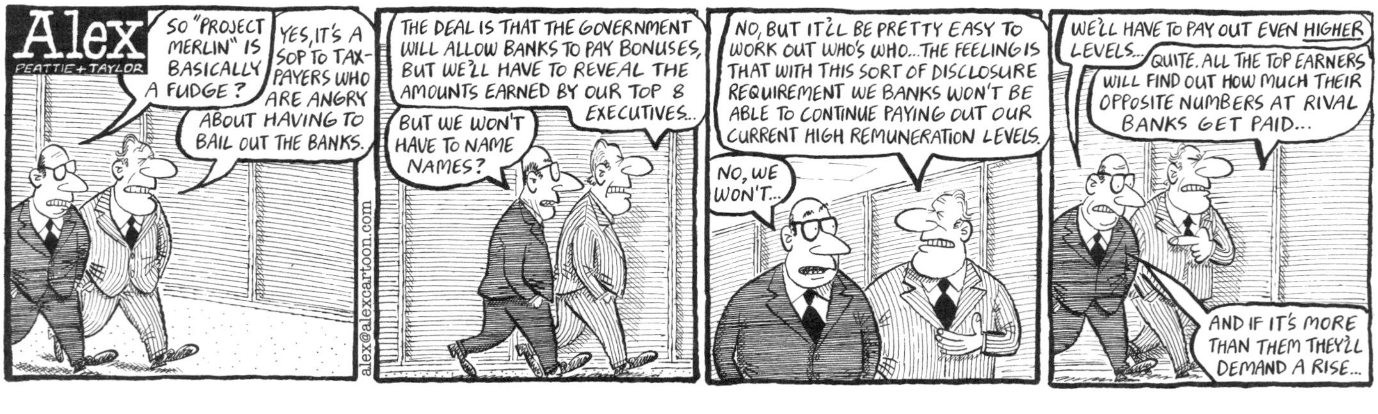
Alex
PEATTIE + TAYLOR
SO "PROJECT MERLIN" IS BASICALLY A FUDGE?
YES, IT'S A SOP TO TAX-PAYERS WHO ARE ANGRY ABOUT HAVING TO BAIL OUT THE BANKS.
alex@alexcartoon.com
THE DEAL IS THAT THE GOVERNMENT WILL ALLOW BANKS TO PAY BONUSES, BUT WE'LL HAVE TO REVEAL THE AMOUNTS EARNED BY OUR TOP 8 EXECUTIVES...
BUT WE WON'T HAVE TO NAME NAMES?
NO, BUT IT'LL BE PRETTY EASY TO WORK OUT WHO'S WHO... THE FEELING IS THAT WITH THIS SORT OF DISCLOSURE REQUIREMENT WE BANKS WON'T BE ABLE TO CONTINUE PAYING OUT OUR CURRENT HIGH REMUNERATION LEVELS.
NO, WE WON'T...
WE'LL HAVE TO PAY OUT EVEN HIGHER LEVELS...
QUITE. ALL THE TOP EARNERS WILL FIND OUT HOW MUCH THEIR OPPOSITE NUMBERS AT RIVAL BANKS GET PAID...
AND IF IT'S MORE THAN THEM THEY'LL DEMAND A RISE...

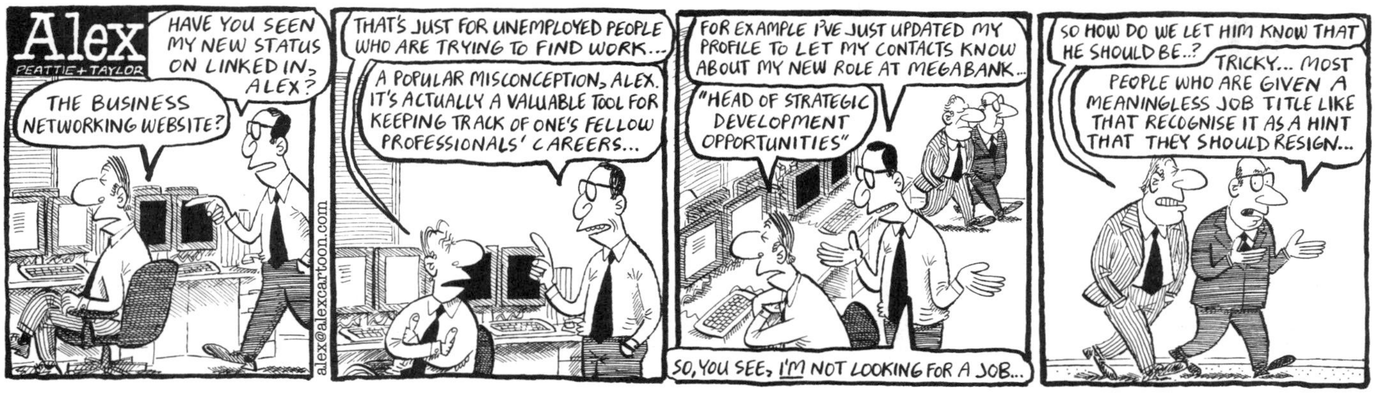
Alex
PEATTIE + TAYLOR
HAVE YOU SEEN MY NEW STATUS ON LINKEDIN, ALEX?
THE BUSINESS NETWORKING WEBSITE?
THAT'S JUST FOR UNEMPLOYED PEOPLE WHO ARE TRYING TO FIND WORK...
A POPULAR MISCONCEPTION, ALEX. IT'S ACTUALLY A VALUABLE TOOL FOR KEEPING TRACK OF ONE'S FELLOW PROFESSIONALS' CAREERS...
FOR EXAMPLE I'VE JUST UPDATED MY PROFILE TO LET MY CONTACTS KNOW ABOUT MY NEW ROLE AT MEGABANK...
"HEAD OF STRATEGIC DEVELOPMENT OPPORTUNITIES"
SO, YOU SEE, I'M NOT LOOKING FOR A JOB...
SO HOW DO WE LET HIM KNOW THAT HE SHOULD BE..?
TRICKY... MOST PEOPLE WHO ARE GIVEN A MEANINGLESS JOB TITLE LIKE THAT RECOGNISE IT AS A HINT THAT THEY SHOULD RESIGN...
alex@alexcartoon.com

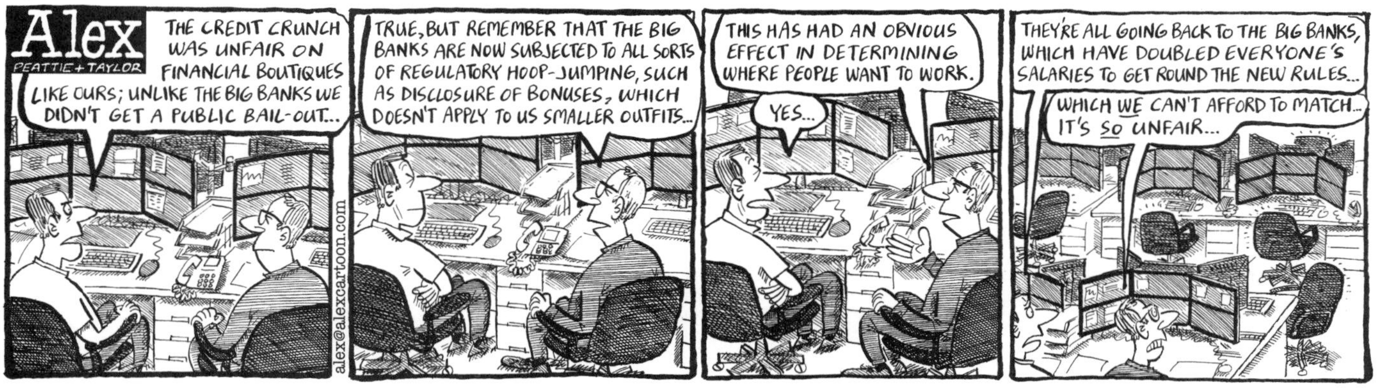
Alex
PEATTIE + TAYLOR
THE CREDIT CRUNCH WAS UNFAIR ON FINANCIAL BOUTIQUES LIKE OURS; UNLIKE THE BIG BANKS WE DIDN'T GET A PUBLIC BAIL-OUT...
TRUE, BUT REMEMBER THAT THE BIG BANKS ARE NOW SUBJECTED TO ALL SORTS OF REGULATORY HOOP-JUMPING, SUCH AS DISCLOSURE OF BONUSES, WHICH DOESN'T APPLY TO US SMALLER OUTFITS...
THIS HAS HAD AN OBVIOUS EFFECT IN DETERMINING WHERE PEOPLE WANT TO WORK.
YES...
THEY'RE ALL GOING BACK TO THE BIG BANKS, WHICH HAVE DOUBLED EVERYONE'S SALARIES TO GET ROUND THE NEW RULES...
WHICH WE CAN'T AFFORD TO MATCH... IT'S SO UNFAIR...
alex@alexcartoon.com

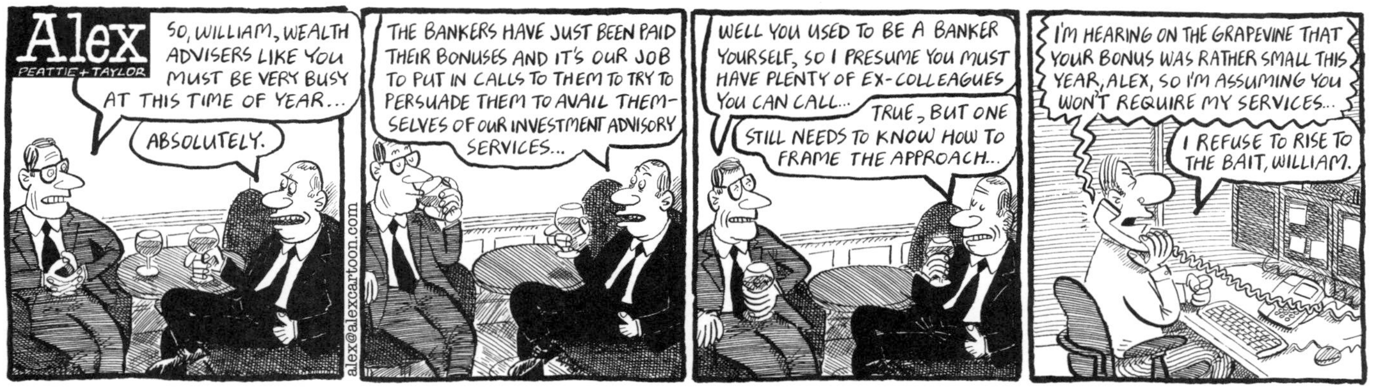
Alex
PEATTIE + TAYLOR
SO, WILLIAM, WEALTH ADVISERS LIKE YOU MUST BE VERY BUSY AT THIS TIME OF YEAR...
ABSOLUTELY.
THE BANKERS HAVE JUST BEEN PAID THEIR BONUSES AND IT'S OUR JOB TO PUT IN CALLS TO THEM TO TRY TO PERSUADE THEM TO AVAIL THEMSELVES OF OUR INVESTMENT ADVISORY SERVICES...
WELL YOU USED TO BE A BANKER YOURSELF, SO I PRESUME YOU MUST HAVE PLENTY OF EX-COLLEAGUES YOU CAN CALL...
TRUE, BUT ONE STILL NEEDS TO KNOW HOW TO FRAME THE APPROACH...
I'M HEARING ON THE GRAPEVINE THAT YOUR BONUS WAS RATHER SMALL THIS YEAR, ALEX, SO I'M ASSUMING YOU WON'T REQUIRE MY SERVICES...
I REFUSE TO RISE TO THE BAIT, WILLIAM.
alex@alexcartoon.com

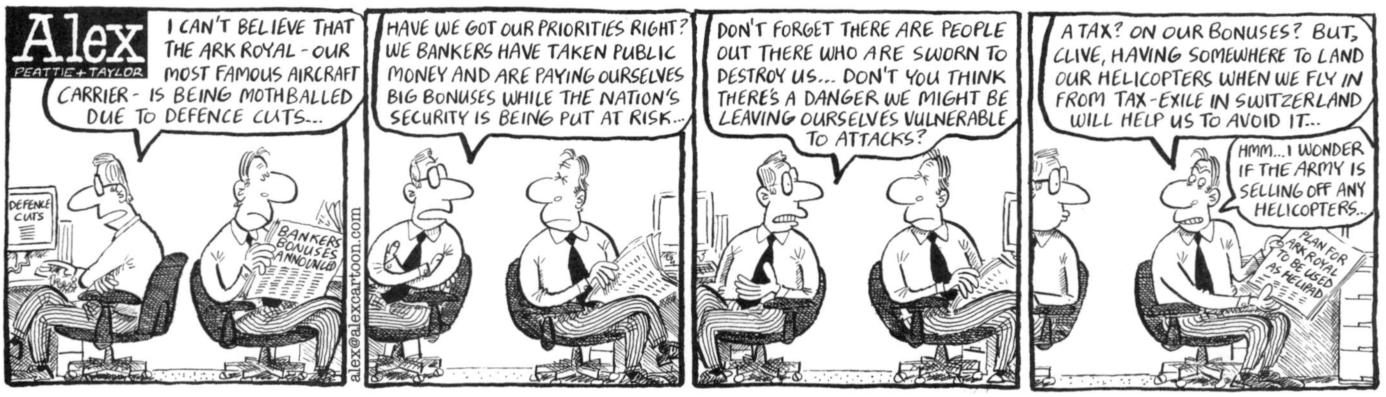
Alex
PEATTIE + TAYLOR
I CAN'T BELIEVE THAT THE ARK ROYAL - OUR MOST FAMOUS AIRCRAFT CARRIER - IS BEING MOTHBALLED DUE TO DEFENCE CUTS...
DEFENCE CUTS
BANKERS BONUSES ANNOUNCED
HAVE WE GOT OUR PRIORITIES RIGHT? WE BANKERS HAVE TAKEN PUBLIC MONEY AND ARE PAYING OURSELVES BIG BONUSES WHILE THE NATION'S SECURITY IS BEING PUT AT RISK...
DON'T FORGET THERE ARE PEOPLE OUT THERE WHO ARE SWORN TO DESTROY US... DON'T YOU THINK THERE'S A DANGER WE MIGHT BE LEAVING OURSELVES VULNERABLE TO ATTACKS?
A TAX? ON OUR BONUSES? BUT, CLIVE, HAVING SOMEWHERE TO LAND OUR HELICOPTERS WHEN WE FLY IN FROM TAX-EXILE IN SWITZERLAND WILL HELP US TO AVOID IT...
HMM... I WONDER IF THE ARMY IS SELLING OFF ANY HELICOPTERS...
PLAN FOR ARK ROYAL TO BE USED AS HELIPAD
alex@alexcartoon.com

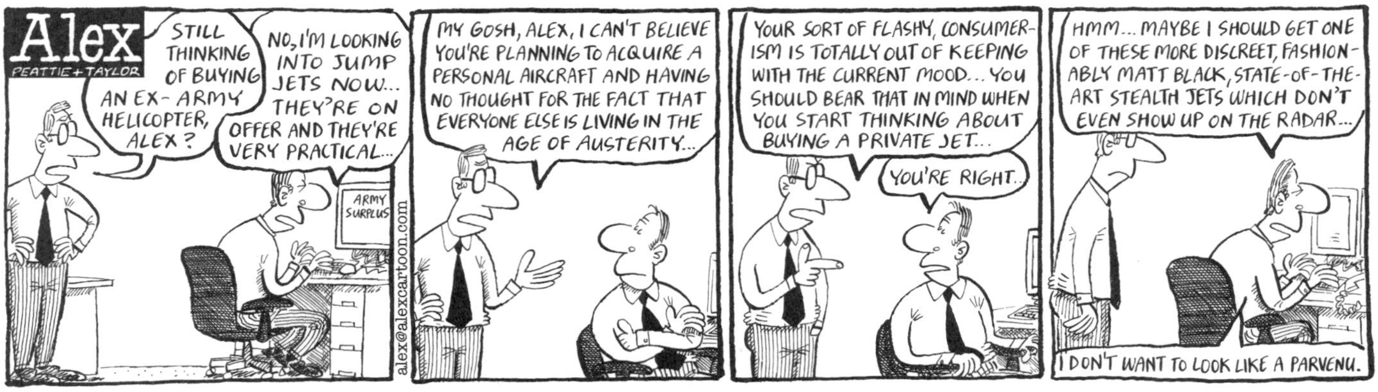
Alex
PEATTIE + TAYLOR
STILL THINKING OF BUYING AN EX-ARMY HELICOPTER, ALEX?
NO, I'M LOOKING INTO JUMP JETS NOW... THEY'RE ON OFFER AND THEY'RE VERY PRACTICAL...
ARMY SURPLUS
alex@alexcartoon.com
MY GOSH, ALEX, I CAN'T BELIEVE YOU'RE PLANNING TO ACQUIRE A PERSONAL AIRCRAFT AND HAVING NO THOUGHT FOR THE FACT THAT EVERYONE ELSE IS LIVING IN THE AGE OF AUSTERITY...
YOUR SORT OF FLASHY, CONSUMERISM IS TOTALLY OUT OF KEEPING WITH THE CURRENT MOOD... YOU SHOULD BEAR THAT IN MIND WHEN YOU START THINKING ABOUT BUYING A PRIVATE JET...
YOU'RE RIGHT...
HMM... MAYBE I SHOULD GET ONE OF THESE MORE DISCREET, FASHIONABLY MATT BLACK, STATE-OF-THE-ART STEALTH JETS WHICH DON'T EVEN SHOW UP ON THE RADAR...
I DON'T WANT TO LOOK LIKE A PARVENU.

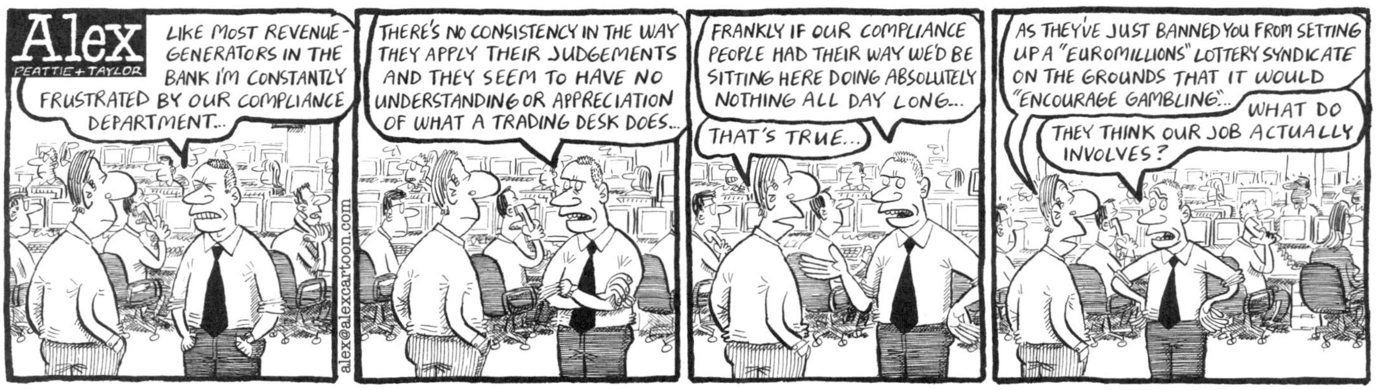
Alex
PEATTIE + TAYLOR
LIKE MOST REVENUE-GENERATORS IN THE BANK I'M CONSTANTLY FRUSTRATED BY OUR COMPLIANCE DEPARTMENT...
alex@alexcartoon.com
THERE'S NO CONSISTENCY IN THE WAY THEY APPLY THEIR JUDGEMENTS AND THEY SEEM TO HAVE NO UNDERSTANDING OR APPRECIATION OF WHAT A TRADING DESK DOES...
FRANKLY IF OUR COMPLIANCE PEOPLE HAD THEIR WAY WE'D BE SITTING HERE DOING ABSOLUTELY NOTHING ALL DAY LONG...
THAT'S TRUE...
AS THEY'VE JUST BANNED YOU FROM SETTING UP A "EUROMILLIONS" LOTTERY SYNDICATE ON THE GROUNDS THAT IT WOULD "ENCOURAGE GAMBLING"...
WHAT DO THEY THINK OUR JOB ACTUALLY INVOLVES?

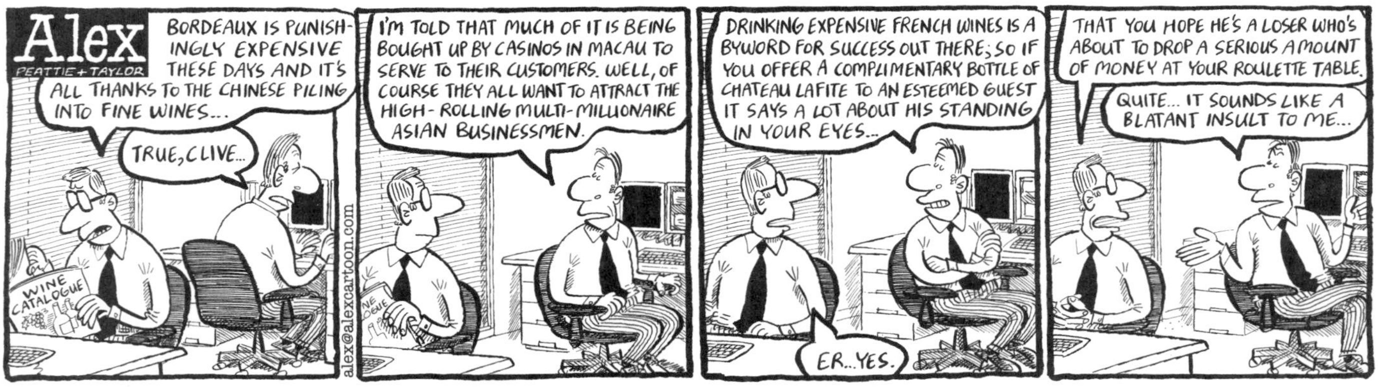
Alex
PEATTIE + TAYLOR
BORDEAUX IS PUNISHINGLY EXPENSIVE THESE DAYS AND IT'S ALL THANKS TO THE CHINESE PILING INTO FINE WINES...
TRUE, CLIVE...
WINE CATALOGUE
alex@alexcartoon.com
I'M TOLD THAT MUCH OF IT IS BEING BOUGHT UP BY CASINOS IN MACAU TO SERVE TO THEIR CUSTOMERS. WELL, OF COURSE THEY ALL WANT TO ATTRACT THE HIGH-ROLLING MULTI-MILLIONAIRE ASIAN BUSINESSMEN.
DRINKING EXPENSIVE FRENCH WINES IS A BYWORD FOR SUCCESS OUT THERE; SO IF YOU OFFER A COMPLIMENTARY BOTTLE OF CHATEAU LAFITE TO AN ESTEEMED GUEST IT SAYS A LOT ABOUT HIS STANDING IN YOUR EYES...
ER... YES.
THAT YOU HOPE HE'S A LOSER WHO'S ABOUT TO DROP A SERIOUS AMOUNT OF MONEY AT YOUR ROULETTE TABLE.
QUITE... IT SOUNDS LIKE A BLATANT INSULT TO ME...

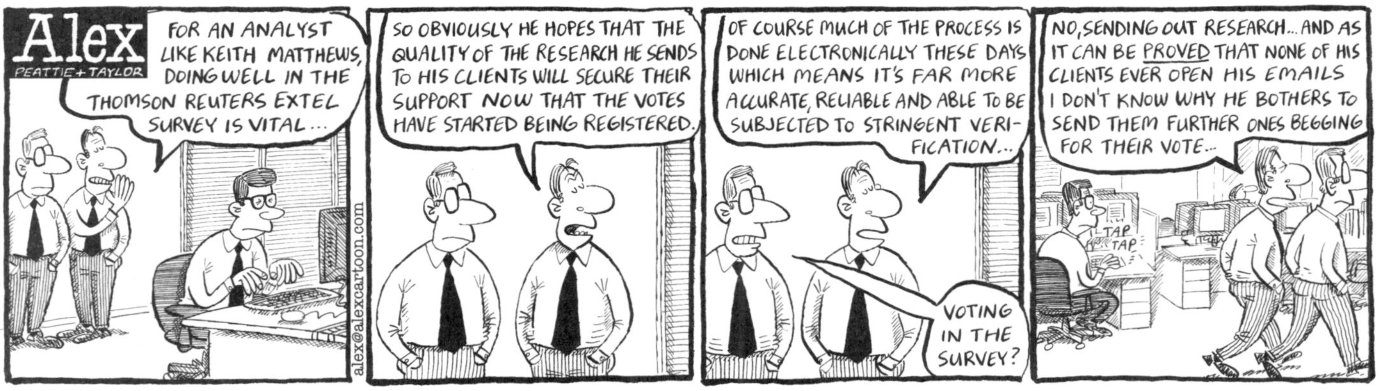
Alex
PEATTIE + TAYLOR
FOR AN ANALYST LIKE KEITH MATTHEWS, DOING WELL IN THE THOMSON REUTERS EXTEL SURVEY IS VITAL...
alex@alexcartoon.com
SO OBVIOUSLY HE HOPES THAT THE QUALITY OF THE RESEARCH HE SENDS TO HIS CLIENTS WILL SECURE THEIR SUPPORT NOW THAT THE VOTES HAVE STARTED BEING REGISTERED.
OF COURSE MUCH OF THE PROCESS IS DONE ELECTRONICALLY THESE DAYS WHICH MEANS IT'S FAR MORE ACCURATE, RELIABLE AND ABLE TO BE SUBJECTED TO STRINGENT VERIFICATION...
VOTING IN THE SURVEY?
NO, SENDING OUT RESEARCH... AND AS IT CAN BE PROVED THAT NONE OF HIS CLIENTS EVER OPEN HIS EMAILS I DON'T KNOW WHY HE BOTHERS TO SEND THEM FURTHER ONES BEGGING FOR THEIR VOTE...
TAP TAP

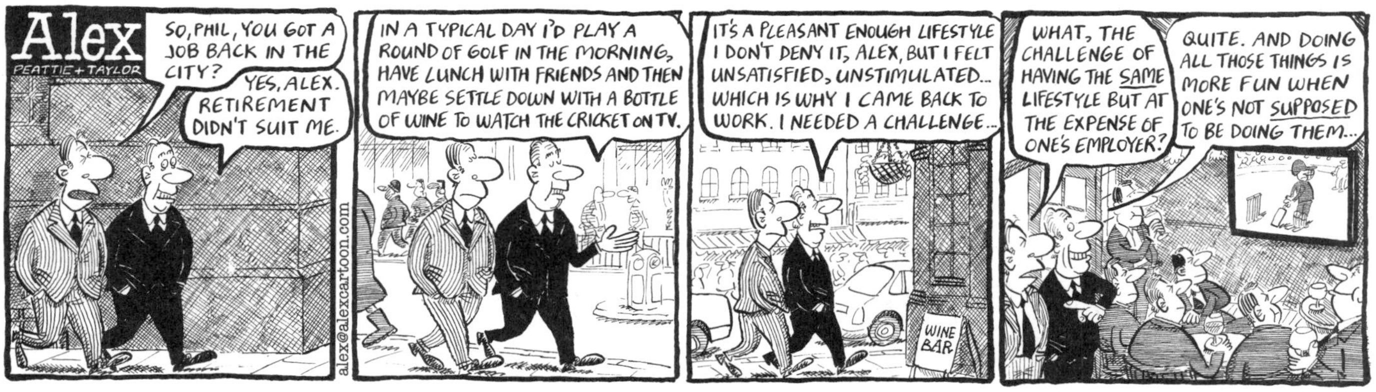

Alex
PEATTIE + TAYLOR
SO, PHIL, YOU GOT A JOB BACK IN THE CITY?
YES, ALEX. RETIREMENT DIDN'T SUIT ME.
alex@alexcartoon.com
IN A TYPICAL DAY I'D PLAY A ROUND OF GOLF IN THE MORNING, HAVE LUNCH WITH FRIENDS AND THEN MAYBE SETTLE DOWN WITH A BOTTLE OF WINE TO WATCH THE CRICKET ON TV.
IT'S A PLEASANT ENOUGH LIFESTYLE I DON'T DENY IT, ALEX, BUT I FELT UNSATISFIED, UNSTIMULATED... WHICH IS WHY I CAME BACK TO WORK. I NEEDED A CHALLENGE...
WINE BAR
WHAT, THE CHALLENGE OF HAVING THE SAME LIFESTYLE BUT AT THE EXPENSE OF ONE'S EMPLOYER?
QUITE. AND DOING ALL THOSE THINGS IS MORE FUN WHEN ONE'S NOT SUPPOSED TO BE DOING THEM...

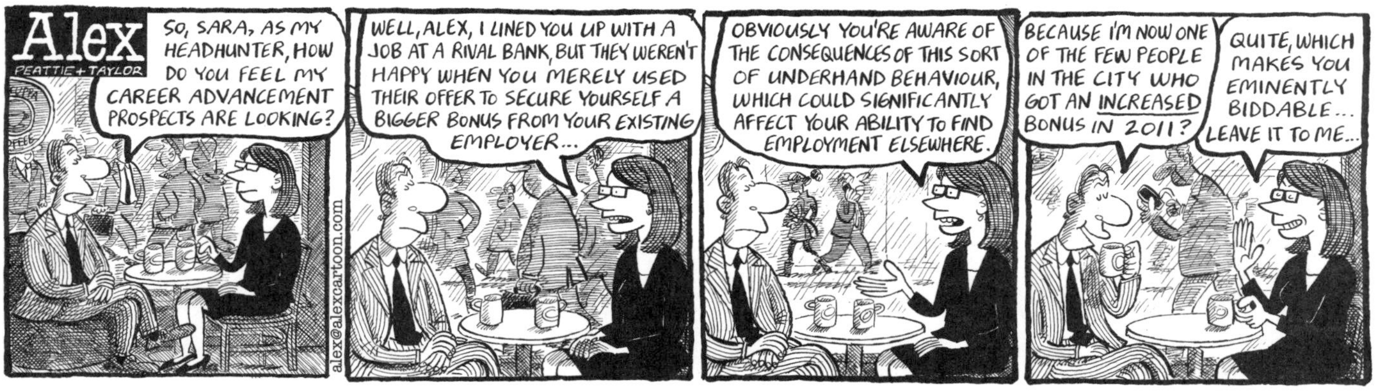

Alex
PEATTIE + TAYLOR
SO, SARA, AS MY HEADHUNTER, HOW DO YOU FEEL MY CAREER ADVANCEMENT PROSPECTS ARE LOOKING?
alex@alexcartoon.com
WELL, ALEX, I LINED YOU UP WITH A JOB AT A RIVAL BANK, BUT THEY WEREN'T HAPPY WHEN YOU MERELY USED THEIR OFFER TO SECURE YOURSELF A BIGGER BONUS FROM YOUR EXISTING EMPLOYER...
OBVIOUSLY YOU'RE AWARE OF THE CONSEQUENCES OF THIS SORT OF UNDERHAND BEHAVIOUR, WHICH COULD SIGNIFICANTLY AFFECT YOUR ABILITY TO FIND EMPLOYMENT ELSEWHERE.
BECAUSE I'M NOW ONE OF THE FEW PEOPLE IN THE CITY WHO GOT AN INCREASED BONUS IN 2011?
QUITE, WHICH MAKES YOU EMINENTLY BIDDABLE... LEAVE IT TO ME...

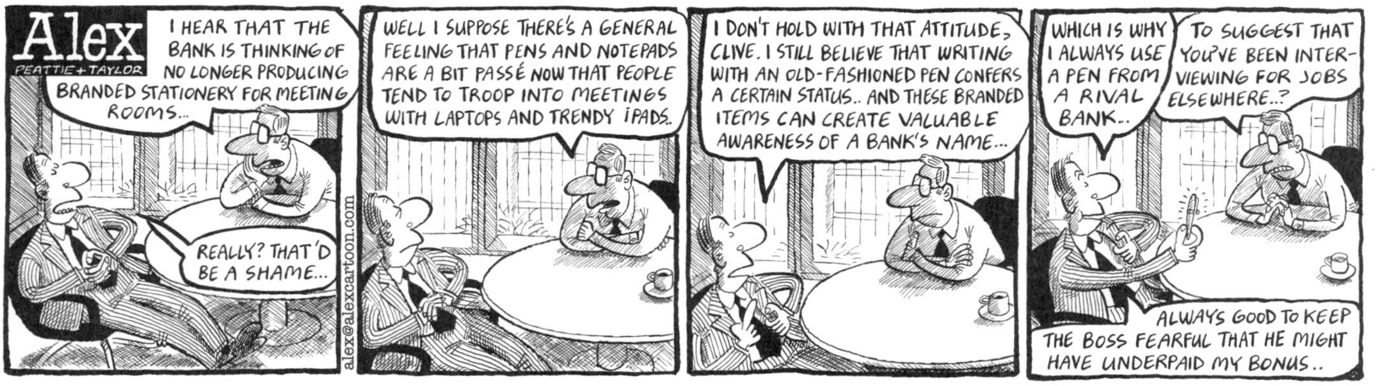

Alex
PEATTIE + TAYLOR
I HEAR THAT THE BANK IS THINKING OF NO LONGER PRODUCING BRANDED STATIONERY FOR MEETING ROOMS...
REALLY? THAT'D BE A SHAME...
alex@alexcartoon.com
WELL I SUPPOSE THERE'S A GENERAL FEELING THAT PENS AND NOTEPADS ARE A BIT PASSÉ NOW THAT PEOPLE TEND TO TROOP INTO MEETINGS WITH LAPTOPS AND TRENDY iPADS.
I DON'T HOLD WITH THAT ATTITUDE, CLIVE. I STILL BELIEVE THAT WRITING WITH AN OLD-FASHIONED PEN CONFERS A CERTAIN STATUS.. AND THESE BRANDED ITEMS CAN CREATE VALUABLE AWARENESS OF A BANK'S NAME...
WHICH IS WHY I ALWAYS USE A PEN FROM A RIVAL BANK..
TO SUGGEST THAT YOU'VE BEEN INTERVIEWING FOR JOBS ELSEWHERE..?
ALWAYS GOOD TO KEEP THE BOSS FEARFUL THAT HE MIGHT HAVE UNDERPAID MY BONUS..

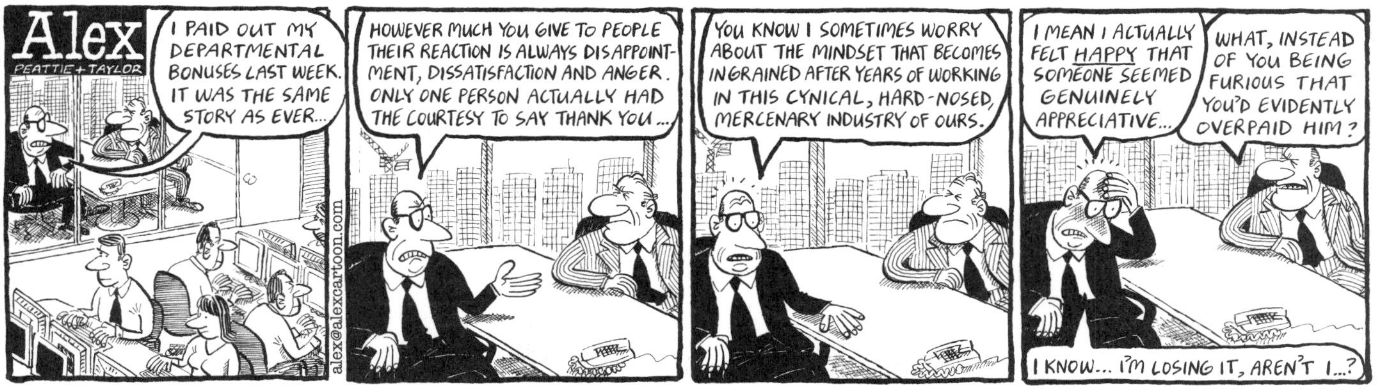

Alex
PEATTIE + TAYLOR
I PAID OUT MY DEPARTMENTAL BONUSES LAST WEEK. IT WAS THE SAME STORY AS EVER...
alex@alexcartoon.com
HOWEVER MUCH YOU GIVE TO PEOPLE THEIR REACTION IS ALWAYS DISAPPOINTMENT, DISSATISFACTION AND ANGER. ONLY ONE PERSON ACTUALLY HAD THE COURTESY TO SAY THANK YOU...
YOU KNOW I SOMETIMES WORRY ABOUT THE MINDSET THAT BECOMES INGRAINED AFTER YEARS OF WORKING IN THIS CYNICAL, HARD-NOSED, MERCENARY INDUSTRY OF OURS.
I MEAN I ACTUALLY FELT HAPPY THAT SOMEONE SEEMED GENUINELY APPRECIATIVE...
WHAT, INSTEAD OF YOU BEING FURIOUS THAT YOU'D EVIDENTLY OVERPAID HIM?
I KNOW... I'M LOSING IT, AREN'T I...?

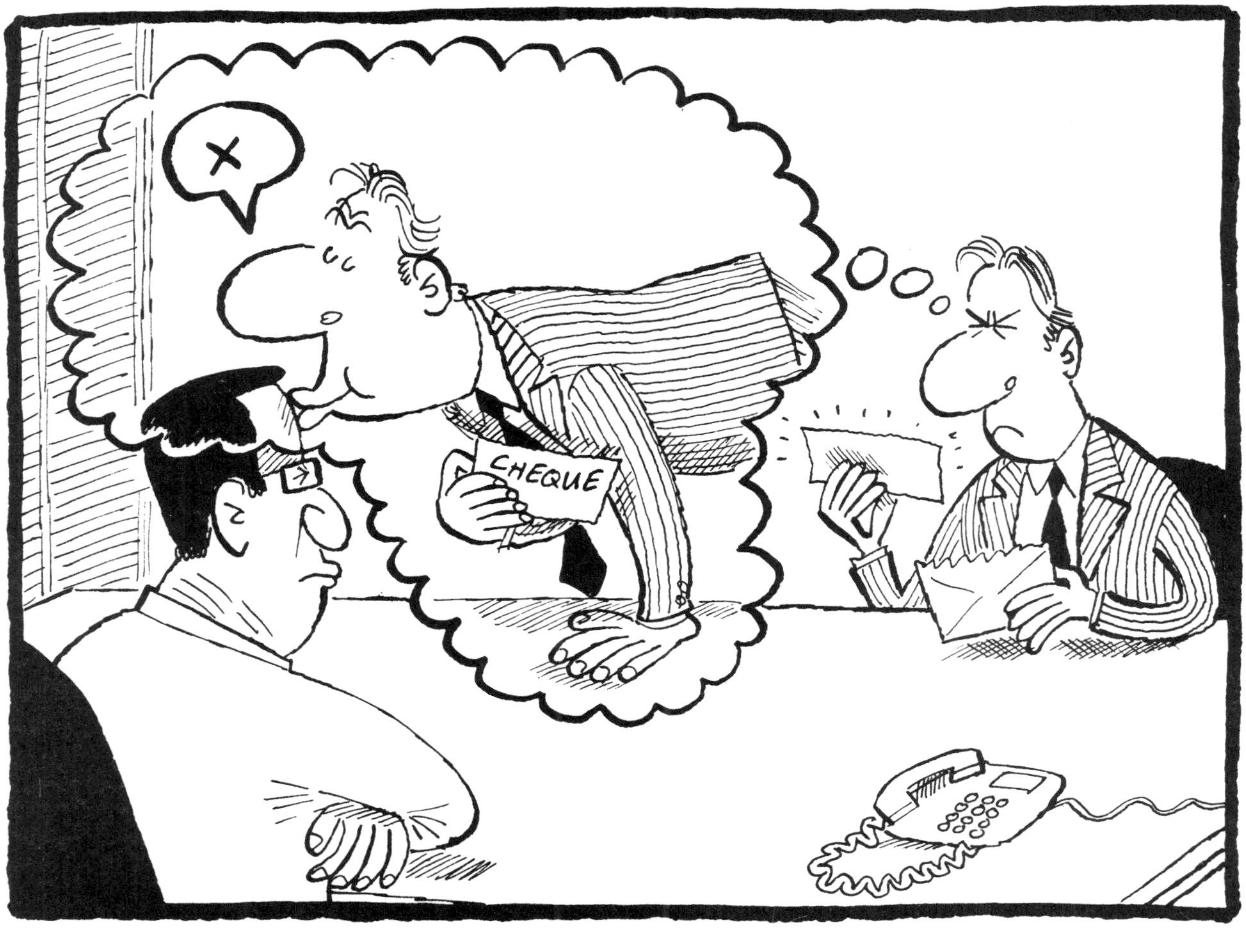
CHEQUE

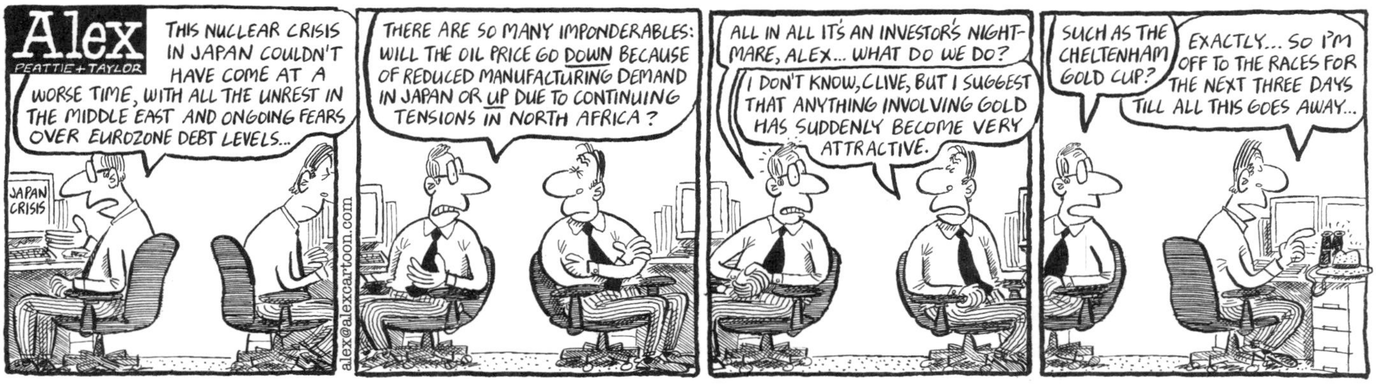
Alex
PEATTIE + TAYLOR
THIS NUCLEAR CRISIS IN JAPAN COULDN'T HAVE COME AT A WORSE TIME, WITH ALL THE UNREST IN THE MIDDLE EAST AND ONGOING FEARS OVER EUROZONE DEBT LEVELS...
JAPAN CRISIS
alex@alexcartoon.com
THERE ARE SO MANY IMPONDERABLES: WILL THE OIL PRICE GO DOWN BECAUSE OF REDUCED MANUFACTURING DEMAND IN JAPAN OR UP DUE TO CONTINUING TENSIONS IN NORTH AFRICA?
ALL IN ALL IT'S AN INVESTOR'S NIGHTMARE, ALEX... WHAT DO WE DO?
I DON'T KNOW, CLIVE, BUT I SUGGEST THAT ANYTHING INVOLVING GOLD HAS SUDDENLY BECOME VERY ATTRACTIVE.
SUCH AS THE CHELTENHAM GOLD CUP?
EXACTLY... SO I'M OFF TO THE RACES FOR THE NEXT THREE DAYS TILL ALL THIS GOES AWAY...

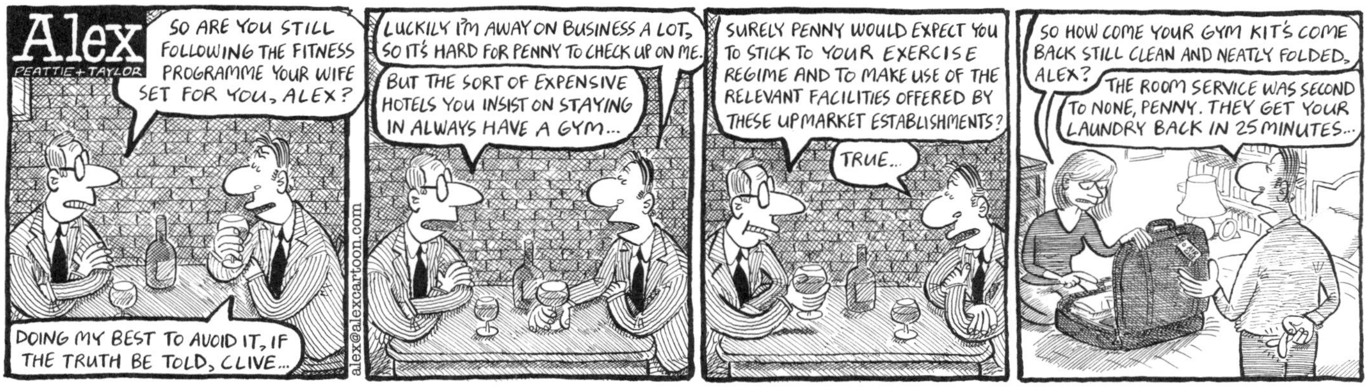
Alex
PEATTIE + TAYLOR
SO ARE YOU STILL FOLLOWING THE FITNESS PROGRAMME YOUR WIFE SET FOR YOU, ALEX?
DOING MY BEST TO AVOID IT, IF THE TRUTH BE TOLD, CLIVE...
alex@alexcartoon.com
LUCKILY I'M AWAY ON BUSINESS A LOT, SO IT'S HARD FOR PENNY TO CHECK UP ON ME.
BUT THE SORT OF EXPENSIVE HOTELS YOU INSIST ON STAYING IN ALWAYS HAVE A GYM...
SURELY PENNY WOULD EXPECT YOU TO STICK TO YOUR EXERCISE REGIME AND TO MAKE USE OF THE RELEVANT FACILITIES OFFERED BY THESE UPMARKET ESTABLISHMENTS?
TRUE...
SO HOW COME YOUR GYM KIT'S COME BACK STILL CLEAN AND NEATLY FOLDED, ALEX?
THE ROOM SERVICE WAS SECOND TO NONE, PENNY. THEY GET YOUR LAUNDRY BACK IN 25 MINUTES...

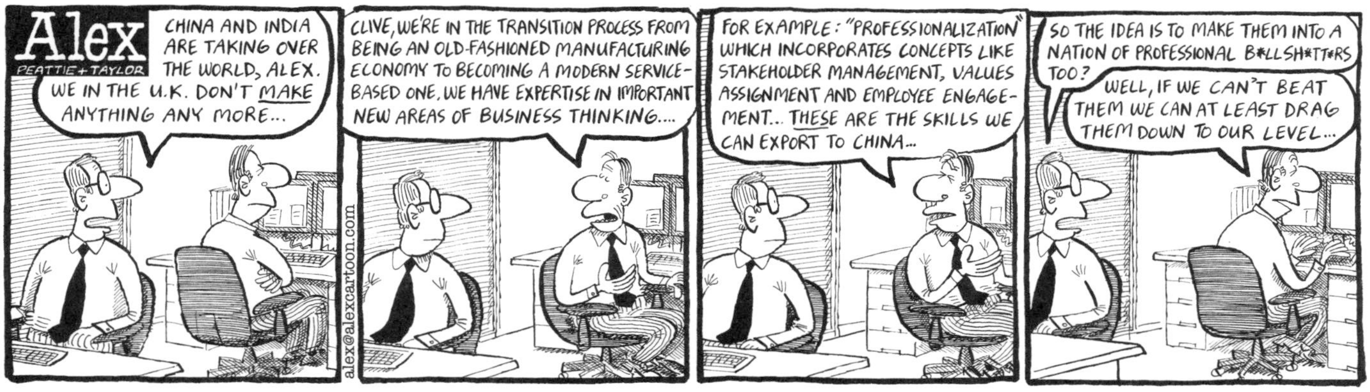
Alex
PEATTIE + TAYLOR
CHINA AND INDIA ARE TAKING OVER THE WORLD, ALEX. WE IN THE U.K. DON'T MAKE ANYTHING ANY MORE...
alex@alexcartoon.com
CLIVE, WE'RE IN THE TRANSITION PROCESS FROM BEING AN OLD-FASHIONED MANUFACTURING ECONOMY TO BECOMING A MODERN SERVICE-BASED ONE. WE HAVE EXPERTISE IN IMPORTANT NEW AREAS OF BUSINESS THINKING....
FOR EXAMPLE: "PROFESSIONALIZATION" WHICH INCORPORATES CONCEPTS LIKE STAKEHOLDER MANAGEMENT, VALUES ASSIGNMENT AND EMPLOYEE ENGAGEMENT... THESE ARE THE SKILLS WE CAN EXPORT TO CHINA...
SO THE IDEA IS TO MAKE THEM INTO A NATION OF PROFESSIONAL B*LLSH*TT*RS TOO?
WELL, IF WE CAN'T BEAT THEM WE CAN AT LEAST DRAG THEM DOWN TO OUR LEVEL...

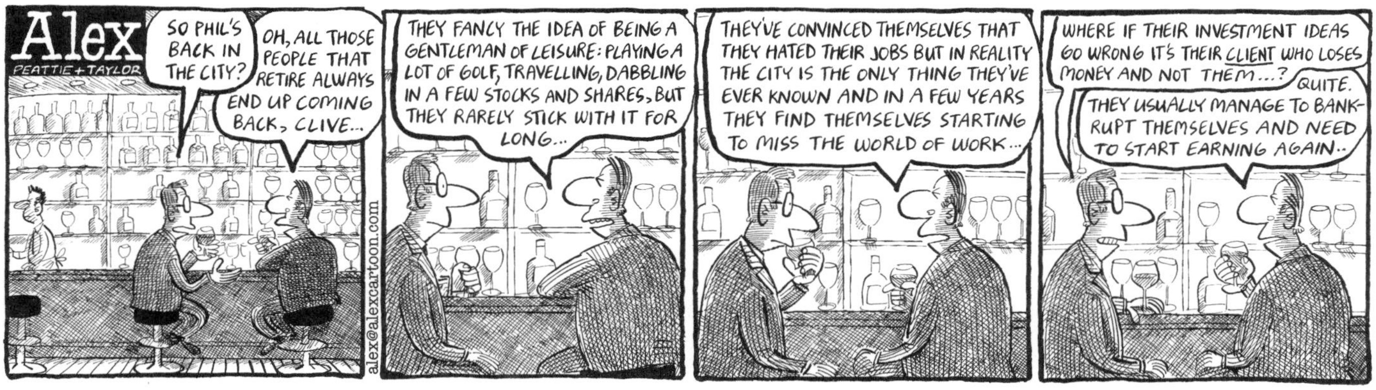
Alex
PEATTIE + TAYLOR
SO PHIL'S BACK IN THE CITY?
OH, ALL THOSE PEOPLE THAT RETIRE ALWAYS END UP COMING BACK, CLIVE...
alex@alexcartoon.com
THEY FANCY THE IDEA OF BEING A GENTLEMAN OF LEISURE: PLAYING A LOT OF GOLF, TRAVELLING, DABBLING IN A FEW STOCKS AND SHARES, BUT THEY RARELY STICK WITH IT FOR LONG...
THEY'VE CONVINCED THEMSELVES THAT THEY HATED THEIR JOBS BUT IN REALITY THE CITY IS THE ONLY THING THEY'VE EVER KNOWN AND IN A FEW YEARS THEY FIND THEMSELVES STARTING TO MISS THE WORLD OF WORK...
WHERE IF THEIR INVESTMENT IDEAS GO WRONG IT'S THEIR CLIENT WHO LOSES MONEY AND NOT THEM...?
QUITE. THEY USUALLY MANAGE TO BANKRUPT THEMSELVES AND NEED TO START EARNING AGAIN..

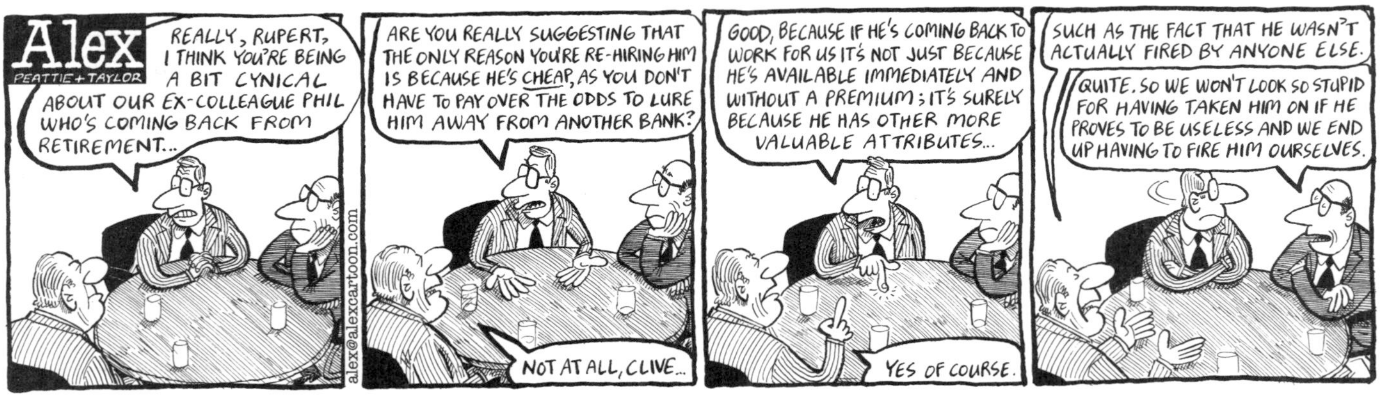
Alex
PEATTIE + TAYLOR
REALLY, RUPERT, I THINK YOU'RE BEING A BIT CYNICAL ABOUT OUR EX-COLLEAGUE PHIL WHO'S COMING BACK FROM RETIREMENT...
ARE YOU REALLY SUGGESTING THAT THE ONLY REASON YOU'RE RE-HIRING HIM IS BECAUSE HE'S CHEAP, AS YOU DON'T HAVE TO PAY OVER THE ODDS TO LURE HIM AWAY FROM ANOTHER BANK?
NOT AT ALL, CLIVE...
GOOD, BECAUSE IF HE'S COMING BACK TO WORK FOR US IT'S NOT JUST BECAUSE HE'S AVAILABLE IMMEDIATELY AND WITHOUT A PREMIUM; IT'S SURELY BECAUSE HE HAS OTHER MORE VALUABLE ATTRIBUTES...
YES OF COURSE.
SUCH AS THE FACT THAT HE WASN'T ACTUALLY FIRED BY ANYONE ELSE.
QUITE. SO WE WON'T LOOK SO STUPID FOR HAVING TAKEN HIM ON IF HE PROVES TO BE USELESS AND WE END UP HAVING TO FIRE HIM OURSELVES.
alex@alexcartoon.com

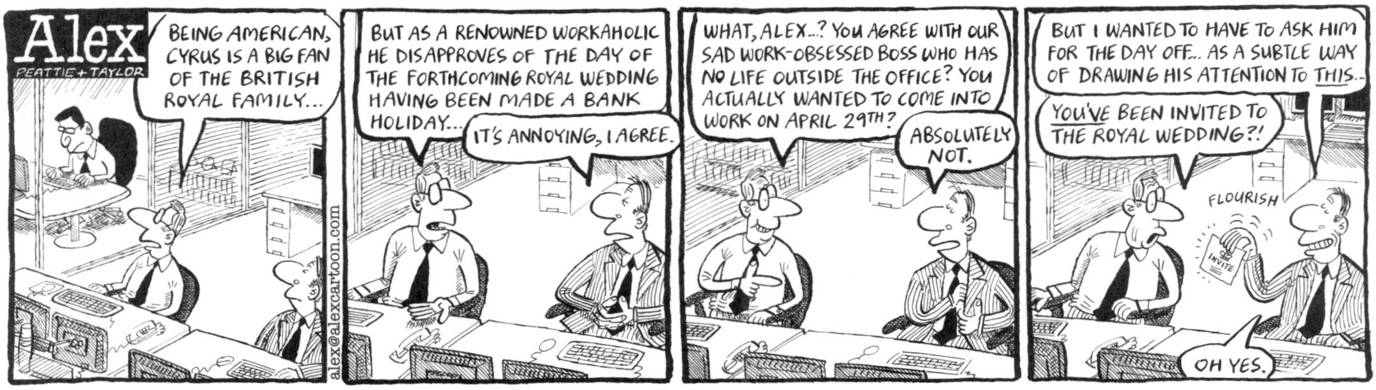
Alex
PEATTIE + TAYLOR
BEING AMERICAN, CYRUS IS A BIG FAN OF THE BRITISH ROYAL FAMILY...
BUT AS A RENOWNED WORKAHOLIC HE DISAPPROVES OF THE DAY OF THE FORTHCOMING ROYAL WEDDING HAVING BEEN MADE A BANK HOLIDAY...
IT'S ANNOYING, I AGREE.
WHAT, ALEX...? YOU AGREE WITH OUR SAD WORK-OBSESSED BOSS WHO HAS NO LIFE OUTSIDE THE OFFICE? YOU ACTUALLY WANTED TO COME INTO WORK ON APRIL 29TH?
ABSOLUTELY NOT.
BUT I WANTED TO HAVE TO ASK HIM FOR THE DAY OFF... AS A SUBTLE WAY OF DRAWING HIS ATTENTION TO THIS...
YOU'VE BEEN INVITED TO THE ROYAL WEDDING?!
FLOURISH
INVITE
OH YES.
alex@alexcartoon.com

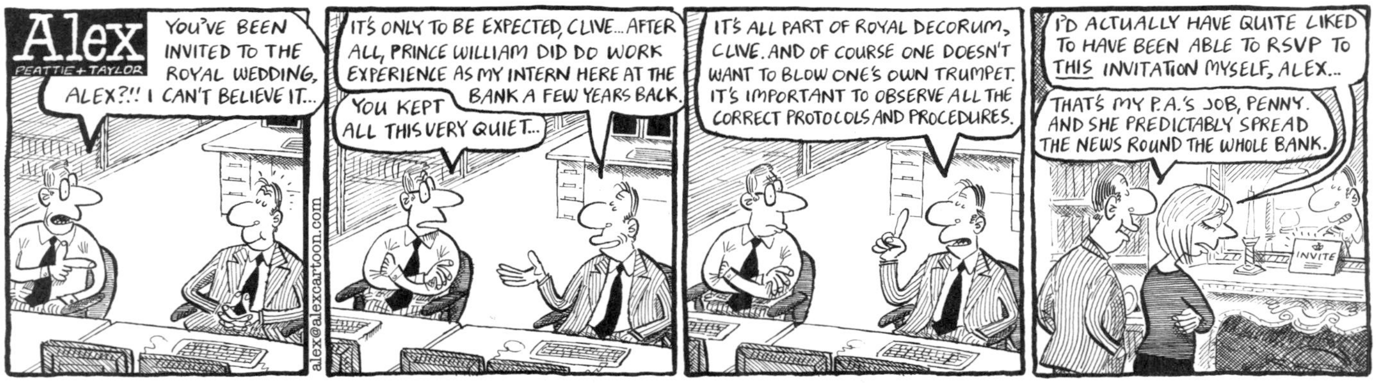
Alex
PEATTIE + TAYLOR
YOU'VE BEEN INVITED TO THE ROYAL WEDDING, ALEX?!! I CAN'T BELIEVE IT...
IT'S ONLY TO BE EXPECTED, CLIVE... AFTER ALL, PRINCE WILLIAM DID DO WORK EXPERIENCE AS MY INTERN HERE AT THE BANK A FEW YEARS BACK.
YOU KEPT ALL THIS VERY QUIET...
IT'S ALL PART OF ROYAL DECORUM, CLIVE. AND OF COURSE ONE DOESN'T WANT TO BLOW ONE'S OWN TRUMPET. IT'S IMPORTANT TO OBSERVE ALL THE CORRECT PROTOCOLS AND PROCEDURES.
I'D ACTUALLY HAVE QUITE LIKED TO HAVE BEEN ABLE TO RSVP TO THIS INVITATION MYSELF, ALEX...
THAT'S MY P.A.'S JOB, PENNY. AND SHE PREDICTABLY SPREAD THE NEWS ROUND THE WHOLE BANK.
INVITE
alex@alexcartoon.com

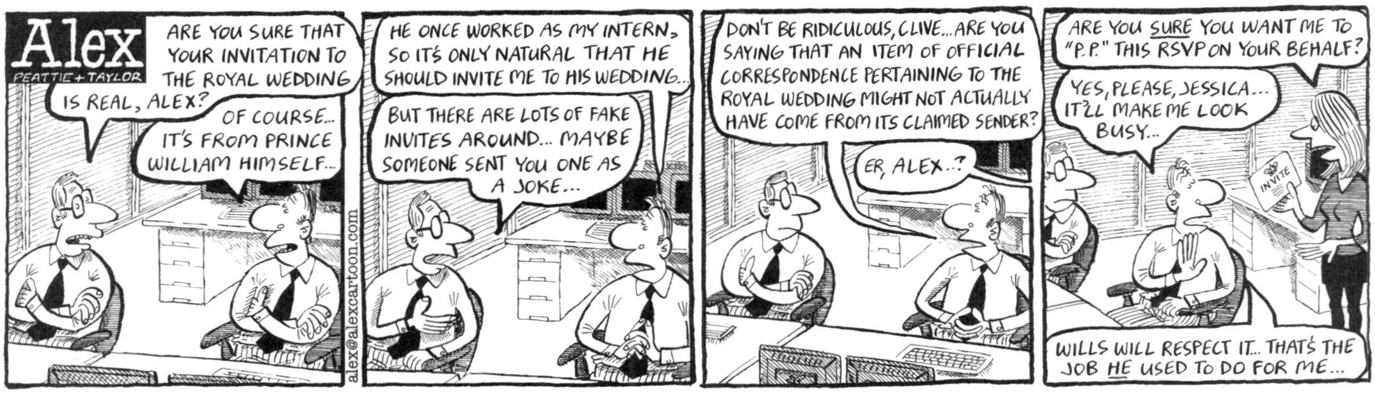
Alex
PEATTIE + TAYLOR
ARE YOU SURE THAT YOUR INVITATION TO THE ROYAL WEDDING IS REAL, ALEX?
OF COURSE... IT'S FROM PRINCE WILLIAM HIMSELF...
HE ONCE WORKED AS MY INTERN, SO IT'S ONLY NATURAL THAT HE SHOULD INVITE ME TO HIS WEDDING...
BUT THERE ARE LOTS OF FAKE INVITES AROUND... MAYBE SOMEONE SENT YOU ONE AS A JOKE...
DON'T BE RIDICULOUS, CLIVE... ARE YOU SAYING THAT AN ITEM OF OFFICIAL CORRESPONDENCE PERTAINING TO THE ROYAL WEDDING MIGHT NOT ACTUALLY HAVE COME FROM ITS CLAIMED SENDER?
ER, ALEX..?
ARE YOU SURE YOU WANT ME TO "P.P." THIS RSVP ON YOUR BEHALF?
YES, PLEASE, JESSICA... IT'LL MAKE ME LOOK BUSY...
INVITE
WILLS WILL RESPECT IT... THAT'S THE JOB HE USED TO DO FOR ME...
alex@alexcartoon.com

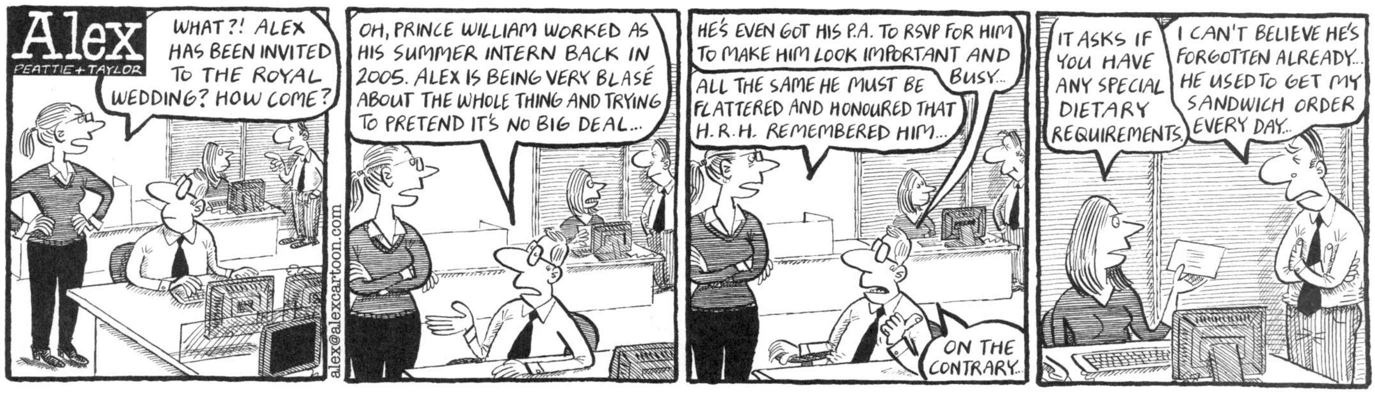
Alex
PEATTIE+TAYLOR
WHAT?! ALEX HAS BEEN INVITED TO THE ROYAL WEDDING? HOW COME?
OH, PRINCE WILLIAM WORKED AS HIS SUMMER INTERN BACK IN 2005. ALEX IS BEING VERY BLASÉ ABOUT THE WHOLE THING AND TRYING TO PRETEND IT'S NO BIG DEAL...
alex@alexcartoon.com
HE'S EVEN GOT HIS P.A. TO RSVP FOR HIM TO MAKE HIM LOOK IMPORTANT AND BUSY...
ALL THE SAME HE MUST BE FLATTERED AND HONOURED THAT H.R.H. REMEMBERED HIM...
ON THE CONTRARY...
IT ASKS IF YOU HAVE ANY SPECIAL DIETARY REQUIREMENTS.
I CAN'T BELIEVE HE'S FORGOTTEN ALREADY... HE USED TO GET MY SANDWICH ORDER EVERY DAY...

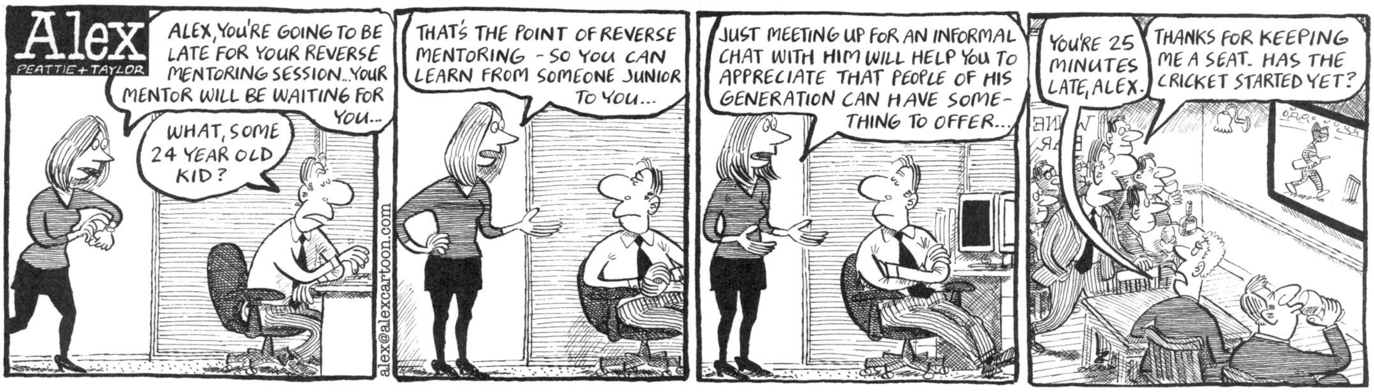
Alex
PEATTIE+TAYLOR
ALEX, YOU'RE GOING TO BE LATE FOR YOUR REVERSE MENTORING SESSION... YOUR MENTOR WILL BE WAITING FOR YOU...
WHAT, SOME 24 YEAR OLD KID?
THAT'S THE POINT OF REVERSE MENTORING - SO YOU CAN LEARN FROM SOMEONE JUNIOR TO YOU...
alex@alexcartoon.com
JUST MEETING UP FOR AN INFORMAL CHAT WITH HIM WILL HELP YOU TO APPRECIATE THAT PEOPLE OF HIS GENERATION CAN HAVE SOMETHING TO OFFER...
YOU'RE 25 MINUTES LATE, ALEX.
THANKS FOR KEEPING ME A SEAT. HAS THE CRICKET STARTED YET?

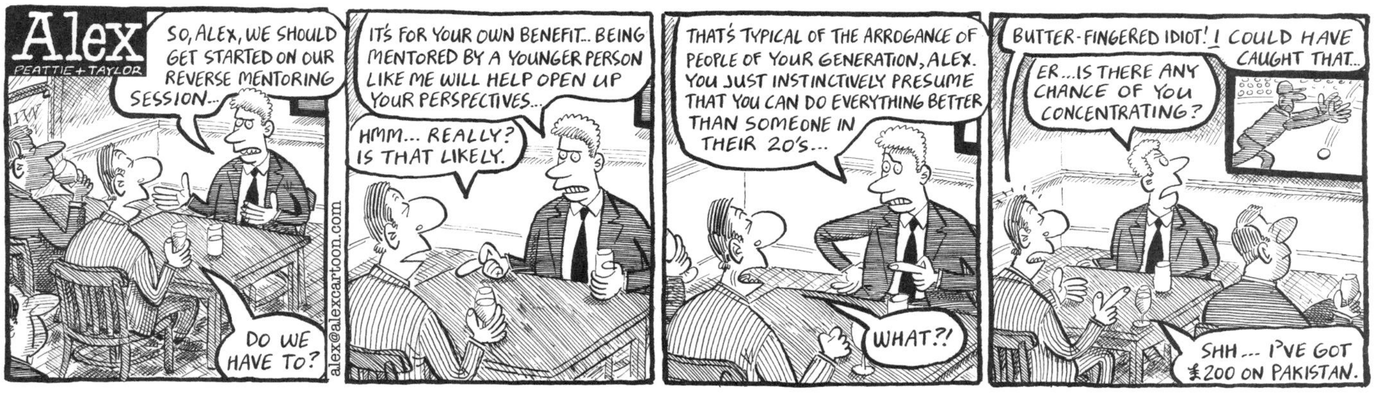
Alex
PEATTIE+TAYLOR
SO, ALEX, WE SHOULD GET STARTED ON OUR REVERSE MENTORING SESSION...
DO WE HAVE TO?
alex@alexcartoon.com
IT'S FOR YOUR OWN BENEFIT... BEING MENTORED BY A YOUNGER PERSON LIKE ME WILL HELP OPEN UP YOUR PERSPECTIVES...
HMM... REALLY? IS THAT LIKELY.
THAT'S TYPICAL OF THE ARROGANCE OF PEOPLE OF YOUR GENERATION, ALEX. YOU JUST INSTINCTIVELY PRESUME THAT YOU CAN DO EVERYTHING BETTER THAN SOMEONE IN THEIR 20'S...
WHAT?!
BUTTER-FINGERED IDIOT! I COULD HAVE CAUGHT THAT...
ER... IS THERE ANY CHANCE OF YOU CONCENTRATING?
SHH... I'VE GOT £200 ON PAKISTAN.

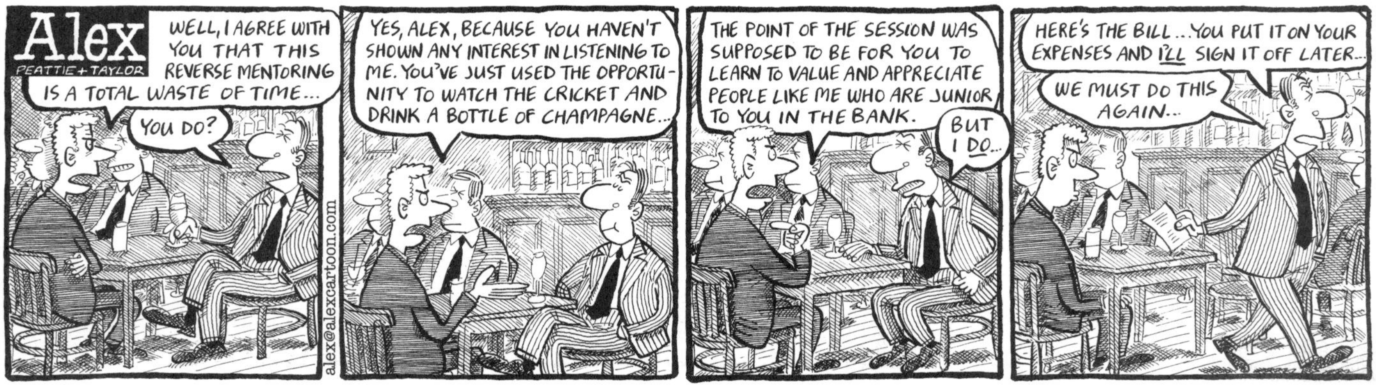
Alex
PEATTIE+TAYLOR
WELL, I AGREE WITH YOU THAT THIS REVERSE MENTORING IS A TOTAL WASTE OF TIME...
YOU DO?
alex@alexcartoon.com
YES, ALEX, BECAUSE YOU HAVEN'T SHOWN ANY INTEREST IN LISTENING TO ME. YOU'VE JUST USED THE OPPORTUNITY TO WATCH THE CRICKET AND DRINK A BOTTLE OF CHAMPAGNE...
THE POINT OF THE SESSION WAS SUPPOSED TO BE FOR YOU TO LEARN TO VALUE AND APPRECIATE PEOPLE LIKE ME WHO ARE JUNIOR TO YOU IN THE BANK.
BUT I DO...
HERE'S THE BILL... YOU PUT IT ON YOUR EXPENSES AND I'LL SIGN IT OFF LATER...
WE MUST DO THIS AGAIN...

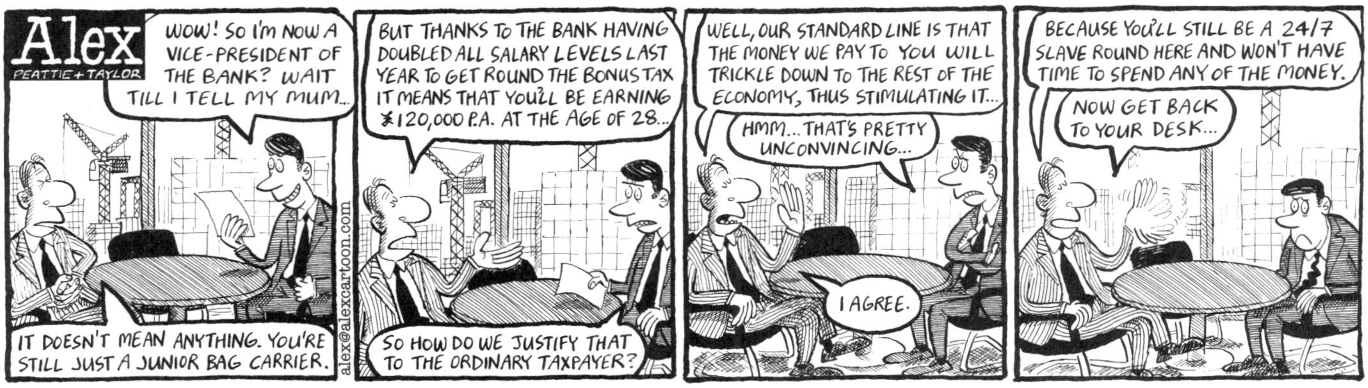
Alex
PEATTIE + TAYLOR
WOW! SO I'M NOW A VICE-PRESIDENT OF THE BANK? WAIT TILL I TELL MY MUM...
IT DOESN'T MEAN ANYTHING. YOU'RE STILL JUST A JUNIOR BAG CARRIER.
BUT THANKS TO THE BANK HAVING DOUBLED ALL SALARY LEVELS LAST YEAR TO GET ROUND THE BONUS TAX IT MEANS THAT YOU'LL BE EARNING ¥120,000 P.A. AT THE AGE OF 28...
SO HOW DO WE JUSTIFY THAT TO THE ORDINARY TAXPAYER?
alex@alexcartoon.com
WELL, OUR STANDARD LINE IS THAT THE MONEY WE PAY TO YOU WILL TRICKLE DOWN TO THE REST OF THE ECONOMY, THUS STIMULATING IT...
HMM... THAT'S PRETTY UNCONVINCING...
I AGREE.
BECAUSE YOU'LL STILL BE A 24/7 SLAVE ROUND HERE AND WON'T HAVE TIME TO SPEND ANY OF THE MONEY.
NOW GET BACK TO YOUR DESK...

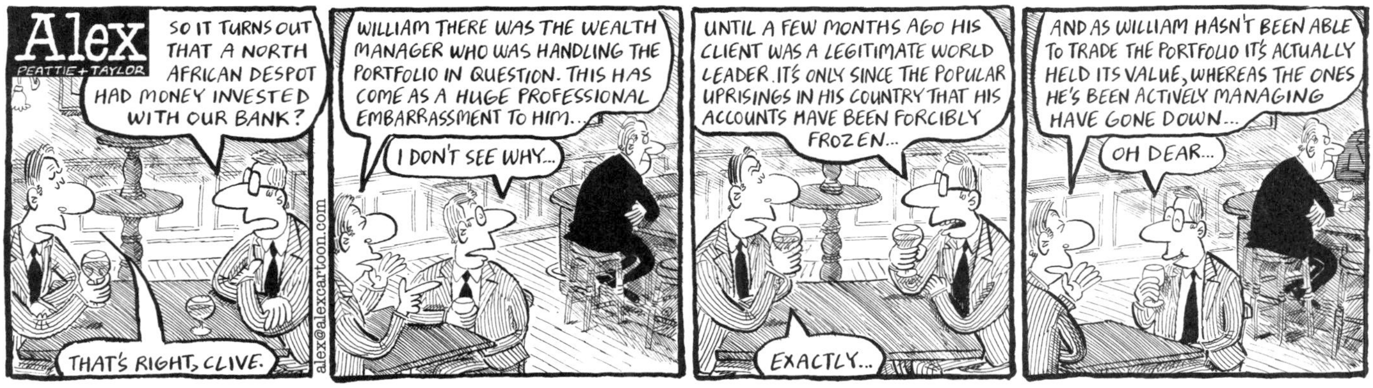
Alex
PEATTIE + TAYLOR
SO IT TURNS OUT THAT A NORTH AFRICAN DESPOT HAD MONEY INVESTED WITH OUR BANK?
THAT'S RIGHT, CLIVE.
alex@alexcartoon.com
WILLIAM THERE WAS THE WEALTH MANAGER WHO WAS HANDLING THE PORTFOLIO IN QUESTION. THIS HAS COME AS A HUGE PROFESSIONAL EMBARRASSMENT TO HIM...
I DON'T SEE WHY...
UNTIL A FEW MONTHS AGO HIS CLIENT WAS A LEGITIMATE WORLD LEADER. IT'S ONLY SINCE THE POPULAR UPRISINGS IN HIS COUNTRY THAT HIS ACCOUNTS HAVE BEEN FORCIBLY FROZEN...
EXACTLY...
AND AS WILLIAM HASN'T BEEN ABLE TO TRADE THE PORTFOLIO IT'S ACTUALLY HELD ITS VALUE, WHEREAS THE ONES HE'S BEEN ACTIVELY MANAGING HAVE GONE DOWN...
OH DEAR...

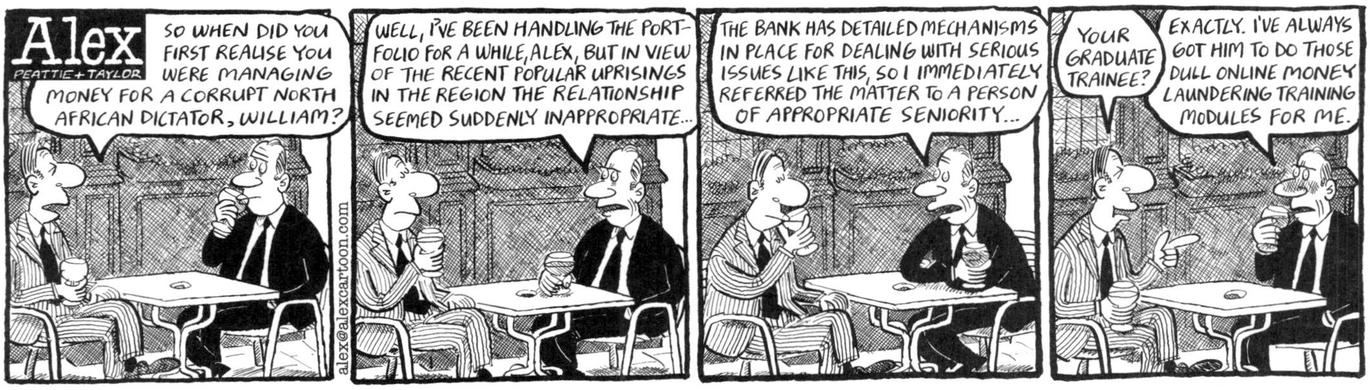
Alex
PEATTIE + TAYLOR
SO WHEN DID YOU FIRST REALISE YOU WERE MANAGING MONEY FOR A CORRUPT NORTH AFRICAN DICTATOR, WILLIAM?
alex@alexcartoon.com
WELL, I'VE BEEN HANDLING THE PORTFOLIO FOR A WHILE, ALEX, BUT IN VIEW OF THE RECENT POPULAR UPRISINGS IN THE REGION THE RELATIONSHIP SEEMED SUDDENLY INAPPROPRIATE...
THE BANK HAS DETAILED MECHANISMS IN PLACE FOR DEALING WITH SERIOUS ISSUES LIKE THIS, SO I IMMEDIATELY REFERRED THE MATTER TO A PERSON OF APPROPRIATE SENIORITY...
YOUR GRADUATE TRAINEE?
EXACTLY. I'VE ALWAYS GOT HIM TO DO THOSE DULL ONLINE MONEY LAUNDERING TRAINING MODULES FOR ME.

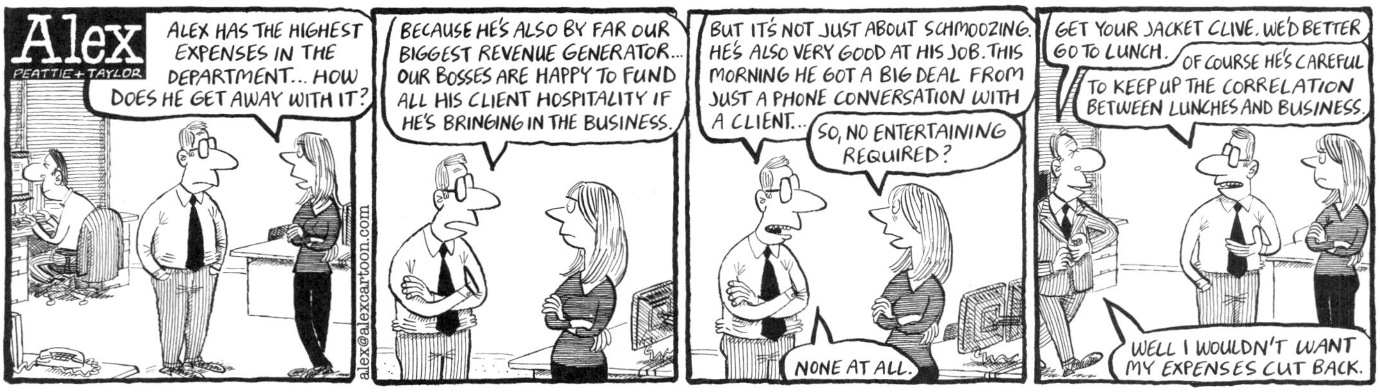
Alex
PEATTIE + TAYLOR
ALEX HAS THE HIGHEST EXPENSES IN THE DEPARTMENT... HOW DOES HE GET AWAY WITH IT?
alex@alexcartoon.com
BECAUSE HE'S ALSO BY FAR OUR BIGGEST REVENUE GENERATOR... OUR BOSSES ARE HAPPY TO FUND ALL HIS CLIENT HOSPITALITY IF HE'S BRINGING IN THE BUSINESS.
BUT IT'S NOT JUST ABOUT SCHMOOZING. HE'S ALSO VERY GOOD AT HIS JOB. THIS MORNING HE GOT A BIG DEAL FROM JUST A PHONE CONVERSATION WITH A CLIENT...
SO, NO ENTERTAINING REQUIRED?
NONE AT ALL.
GET YOUR JACKET CLIVE. WE'D BETTER GO TO LUNCH.
OF COURSE HE'S CAREFUL TO KEEP UP THE CORRELATION BETWEEN LUNCHES AND BUSINESS.
WELL I WOULDN'T WANT MY EXPENSES CUT BACK.

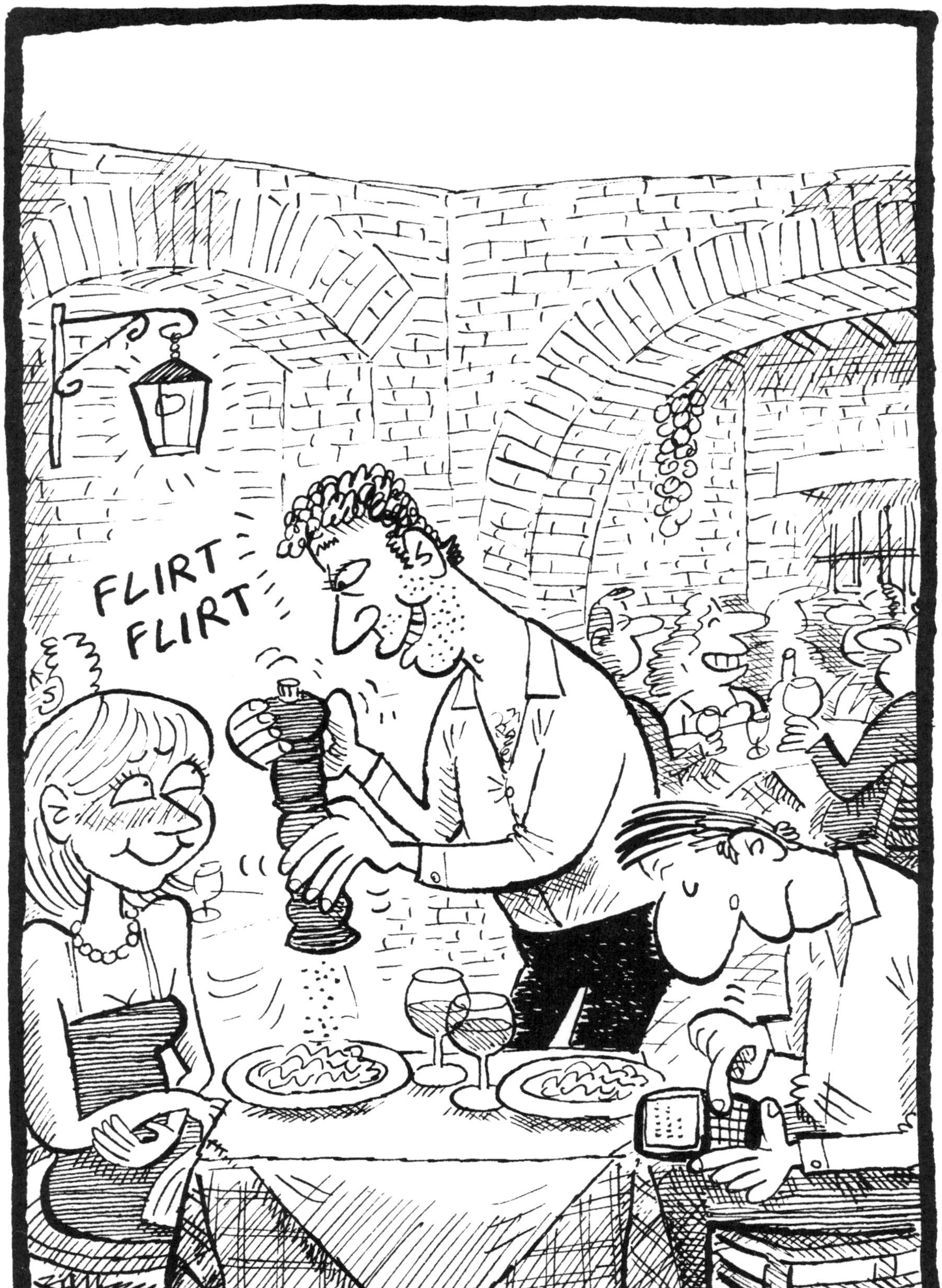
FLIRT
FLIRT

ALEX WENT ON HOLIDAY TO ITALY...

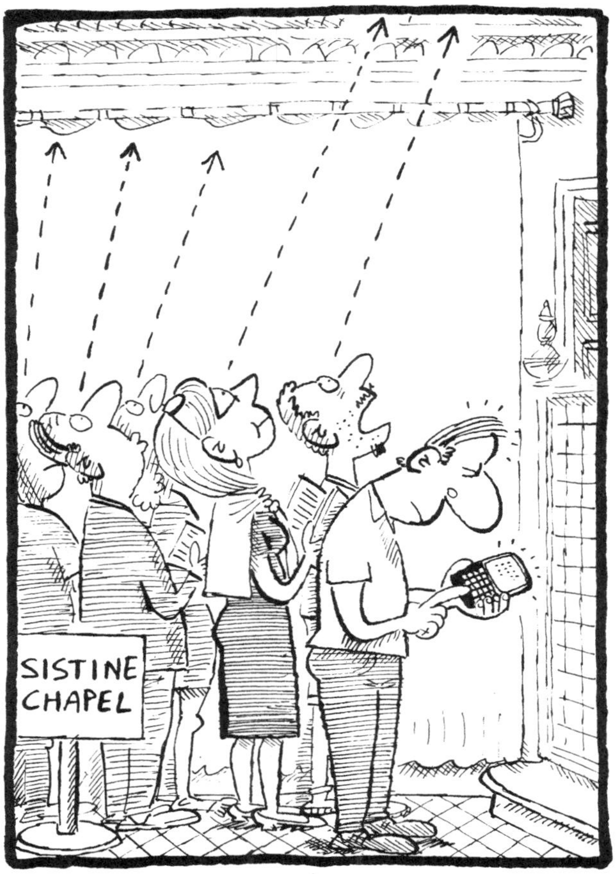
SISTINE
CHAPEL

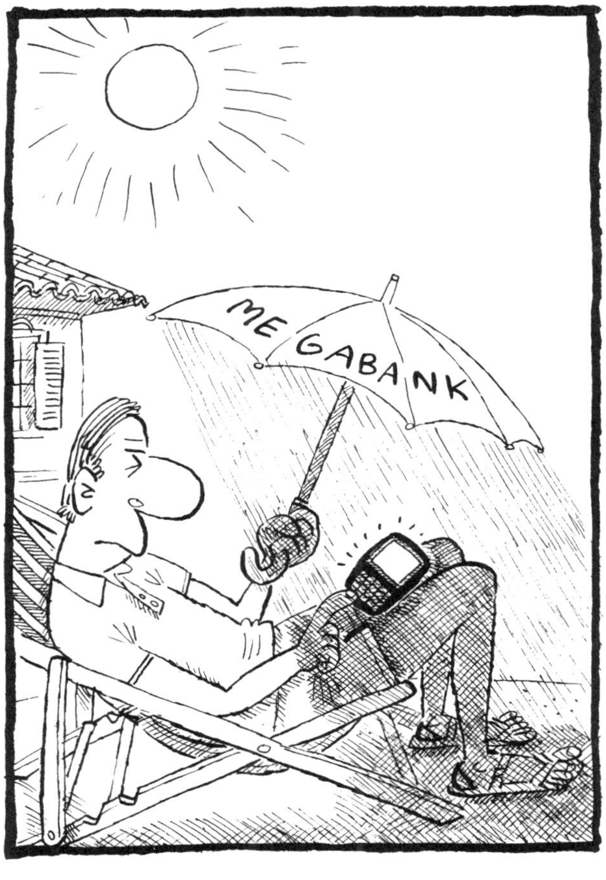
MEGABANK

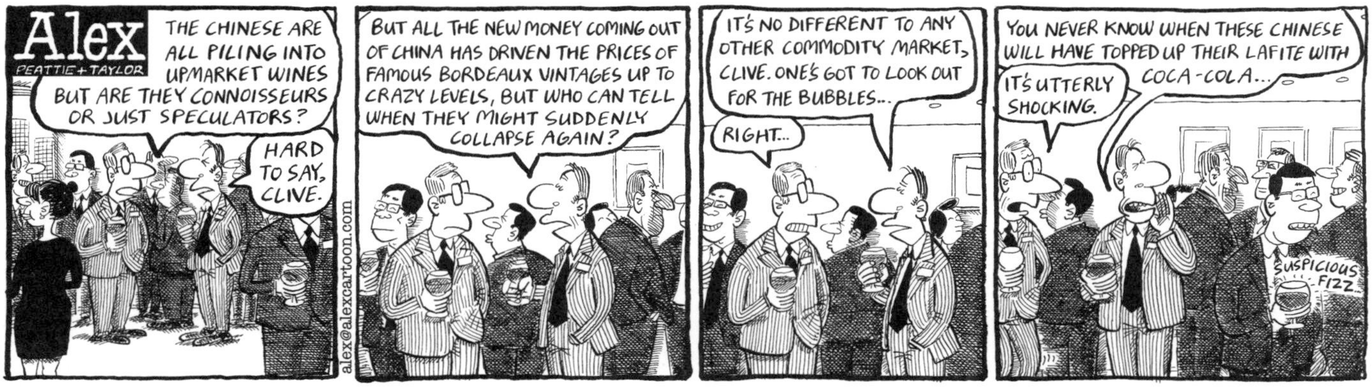
Alex
PEATTIE + TAYLOR
THE CHINESE ARE ALL PILING INTO UPMARKET WINES BUT ARE THEY CONNOISSEURS OR JUST SPECULATORS?
HARD TO SAY, CLIVE.
alex@alexcartoon.com
BUT ALL THE NEW MONEY COMING OUT OF CHINA HAS DRIVEN THE PRICES OF FAMOUS BORDEAUX VINTAGES UP TO CRAZY LEVELS, BUT WHO CAN TELL WHEN THEY MIGHT SUDDENLY COLLAPSE AGAIN?
IT'S NO DIFFERENT TO ANY OTHER COMMODITY MARKET, CLIVE. ONE'S GOT TO LOOK OUT FOR THE BUBBLES...
RIGHT...
YOU NEVER KNOW WHEN THESE CHINESE WILL HAVE TOPPED UP THEIR LAFITE WITH COCA-COLA...
IT'S UTTERLY SHOCKING.
SUSPICIOUS FIZZ

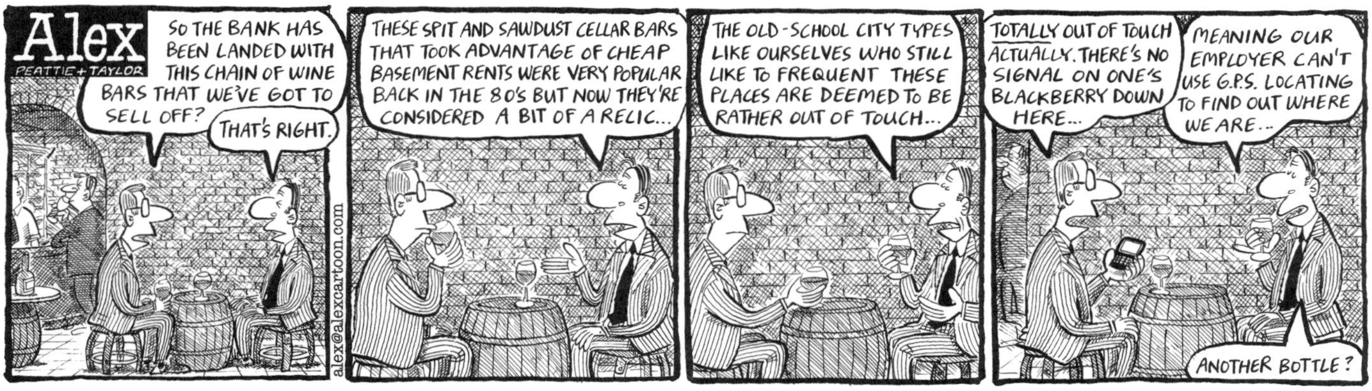
Alex
PEATTIE + TAYLOR
SO THE BANK HAS BEEN LANDED WITH THIS CHAIN OF WINE BARS THAT WE'VE GOT TO SELL OFF?
THAT'S RIGHT.
alex@alexcartoon.com
THESE SPIT AND SAWDUST CELLAR BARS THAT TOOK ADVANTAGE OF CHEAP BASEMENT RENTS WERE VERY POPULAR BACK IN THE 80'S BUT NOW THEY'RE CONSIDERED A BIT OF A RELIC...
THE OLD-SCHOOL CITY TYPES LIKE OURSELVES WHO STILL LIKE TO FREQUENT THESE PLACES ARE DEEMED TO BE RATHER OUT OF TOUCH...
TOTALLY OUT OF TOUCH ACTUALLY. THERE'S NO SIGNAL ON ONE'S BLACKBERRY DOWN HERE...
MEANING OUR EMPLOYER CAN'T USE G.P.S. LOCATING TO FIND OUT WHERE WE ARE...
ANOTHER BOTTLE?

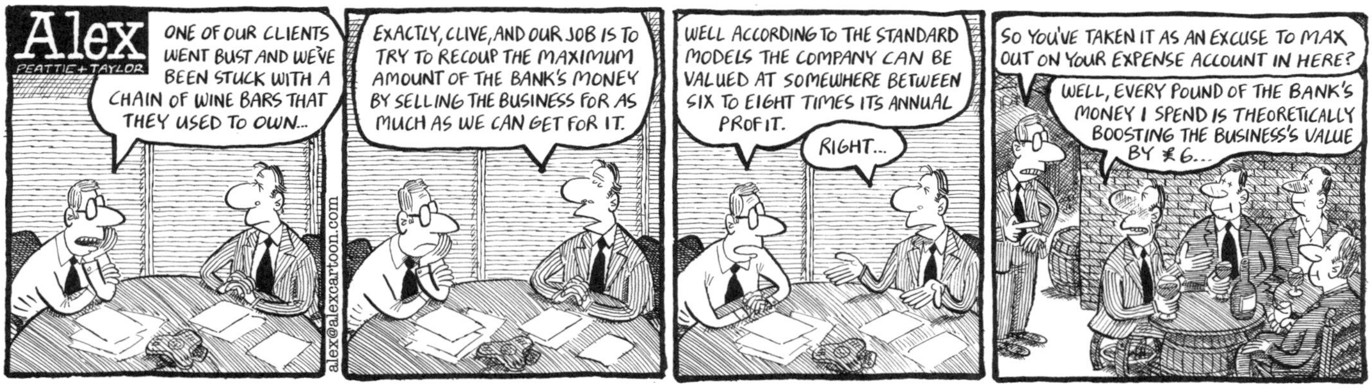
Alex
PEATTIE + TAYLOR
ONE OF OUR CLIENTS WENT BUST AND WE'VE BEEN STUCK WITH A CHAIN OF WINE BARS THAT THEY USED TO OWN...
alex@alexcartoon.com
EXACTLY, CLIVE, AND OUR JOB IS TO TRY TO RECOUP THE MAXIMUM AMOUNT OF THE BANK'S MONEY BY SELLING THE BUSINESS FOR AS MUCH AS WE CAN GET FOR IT.
WELL ACCORDING TO THE STANDARD MODELS THE COMPANY CAN BE VALUED AT SOMEWHERE BETWEEN SIX TO EIGHT TIMES ITS ANNUAL PROFIT.
RIGHT...
SO YOU'VE TAKEN IT AS AN EXCUSE TO MAX OUT ON YOUR EXPENSE ACCOUNT IN HERE?
WELL, EVERY POUND OF THE BANK'S MONEY I SPEND IS THEORETICALLY BOOSTING THE BUSINESS'S VALUE BY £6...

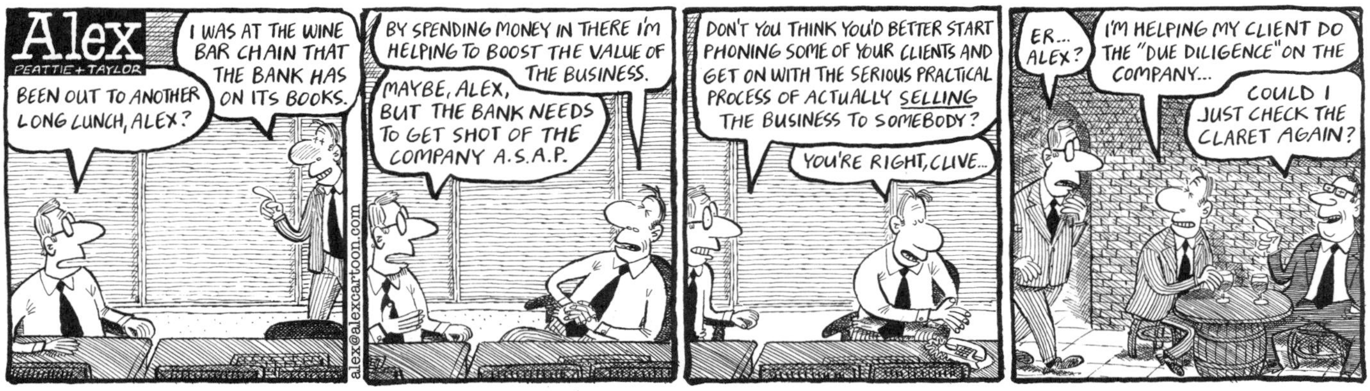
Alex
PEATTIE + TAYLOR
BEEN OUT TO ANOTHER LONG LUNCH, ALEX?
I WAS AT THE WINE BAR CHAIN THAT THE BANK HAS ON ITS BOOKS.
alex@alexcartoon.com
BY SPENDING MONEY IN THERE I'M HELPING TO BOOST THE VALUE OF THE BUSINESS.
MAYBE, ALEX, BUT THE BANK NEEDS TO GET SHOT OF THE COMPANY A.S.A.P.
DON'T YOU THINK YOU'D BETTER START PHONING SOME OF YOUR CLIENTS AND GET ON WITH THE SERIOUS PRACTICAL PROCESS OF ACTUALLY SELLING THE BUSINESS TO SOMEBODY?
YOU'RE RIGHT, CLIVE...
ER... ALEX?
I'M HELPING MY CLIENT DO THE "DUE DILIGENCE" ON THE COMPANY...
COULD I JUST CHECK THE CLARET AGAIN?

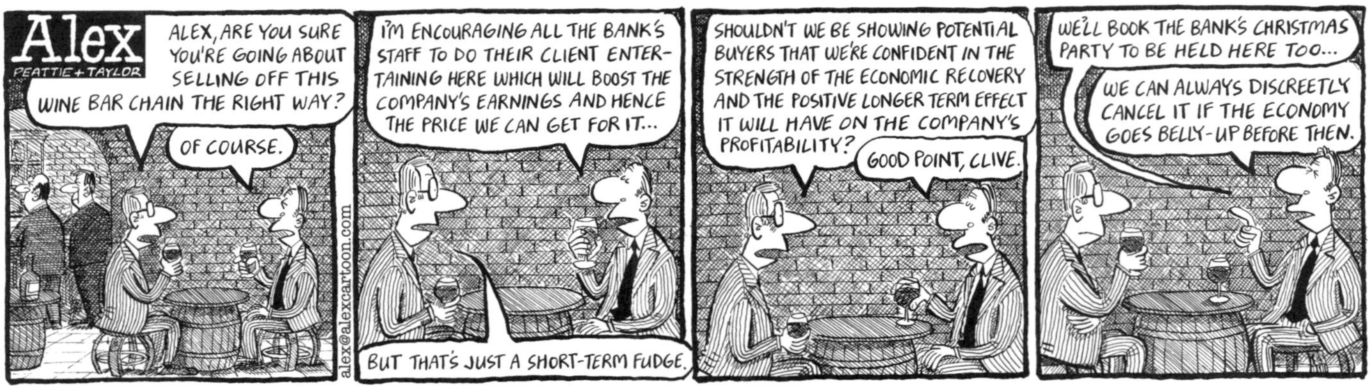

Alex
PEATTIE+TAYLOR
ALEX, ARE YOU SURE YOU'RE GOING ABOUT SELLING OFF THIS WINE BAR CHAIN THE RIGHT WAY?
OF COURSE.
alex@alexcartoon.com
I'M ENCOURAGING ALL THE BANK'S STAFF TO DO THEIR CLIENT ENTERTAINING HERE WHICH WILL BOOST THE COMPANY'S EARNINGS AND HENCE THE PRICE WE CAN GET FOR IT...
BUT THAT'S JUST A SHORT-TERM FUDGE.
SHOULDN'T WE BE SHOWING POTENTIAL BUYERS THAT WE'RE CONFIDENT IN THE STRENGTH OF THE ECONOMIC RECOVERY AND THE POSITIVE LONGER TERM EFFECT IT WILL HAVE ON THE COMPANY'S PROFITABILITY?
GOOD POINT, CLIVE.
WE'LL BOOK THE BANK'S CHRISTMAS PARTY TO BE HELD HERE TOO...
WE CAN ALWAYS DISCREETLY CANCEL IT IF THE ECONOMY GOES BELLY-UP BEFORE THEN.

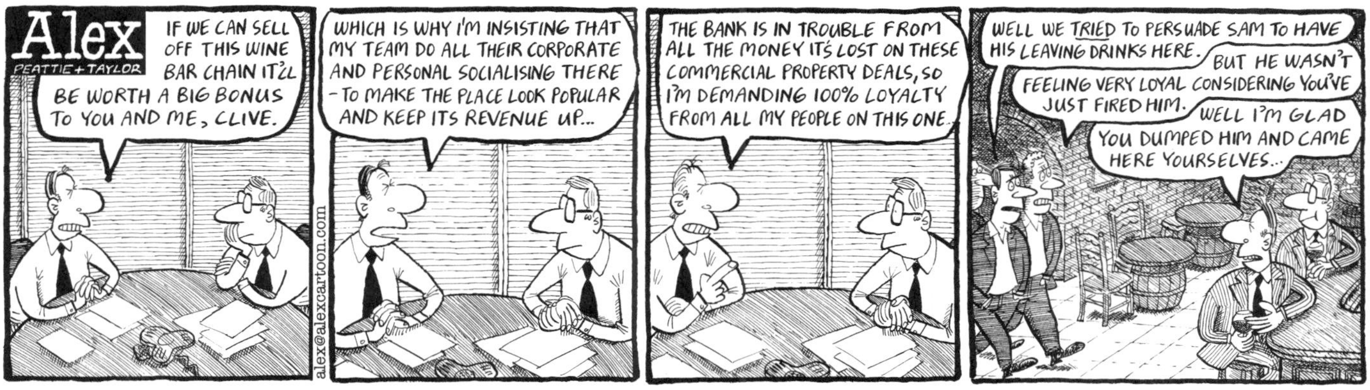

Alex
PEATTIE+TAYLOR
IF WE CAN SELL OFF THIS WINE BAR CHAIN IT'LL BE WORTH A BIG BONUS TO YOU AND ME, CLIVE.
alex@alexcartoon.com
WHICH IS WHY I'M INSISTING THAT MY TEAM DO ALL THEIR CORPORATE AND PERSONAL SOCIALISING THERE - TO MAKE THE PLACE LOOK POPULAR AND KEEP ITS REVENUE UP...
THE BANK IS IN TROUBLE FROM ALL THE MONEY IT'S LOST ON THESE COMMERCIAL PROPERTY DEALS, SO I'M DEMANDING 100% LOYALTY FROM ALL MY PEOPLE ON THIS ONE.
WELL WE TRIED TO PERSUADE SAM TO HAVE HIS LEAVING DRINKS HERE.
BUT HE WASN'T FEELING VERY LOYAL CONSIDERING YOU'VE JUST FIRED HIM.
WELL I'M GLAD YOU DUMPED HIM AND CAME HERE YOURSELVES...

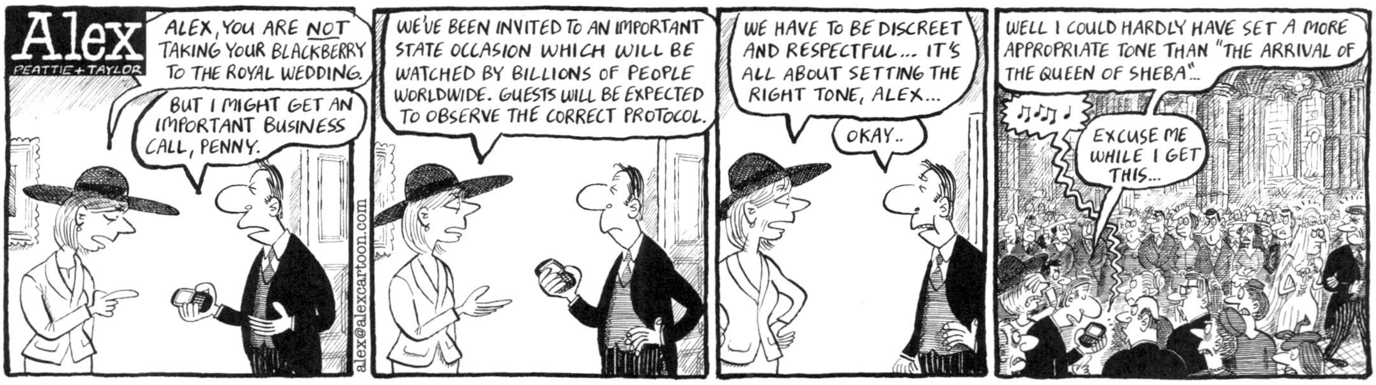

Alex
PEATTIE+TAYLOR
ALEX, YOU ARE NOT TAKING YOUR BLACKBERRY TO THE ROYAL WEDDING.
BUT I MIGHT GET AN IMPORTANT BUSINESS CALL, PENNY.
alex@alexcartoon.com
WE'VE BEEN INVITED TO AN IMPORTANT STATE OCCASION WHICH WILL BE WATCHED BY BILLIONS OF PEOPLE WORLDWIDE. GUESTS WILL BE EXPECTED TO OBSERVE THE CORRECT PROTOCOL.
WE HAVE TO BE DISCREET AND RESPECTFUL... IT'S ALL ABOUT SETTING THE RIGHT TONE, ALEX...
OKAY..
WELL I COULD HARDLY HAVE SET A MORE APPROPRIATE TONE THAN "THE ARRIVAL OF THE QUEEN OF SHEBA"...
EXCUSE ME WHILE I GET THIS...

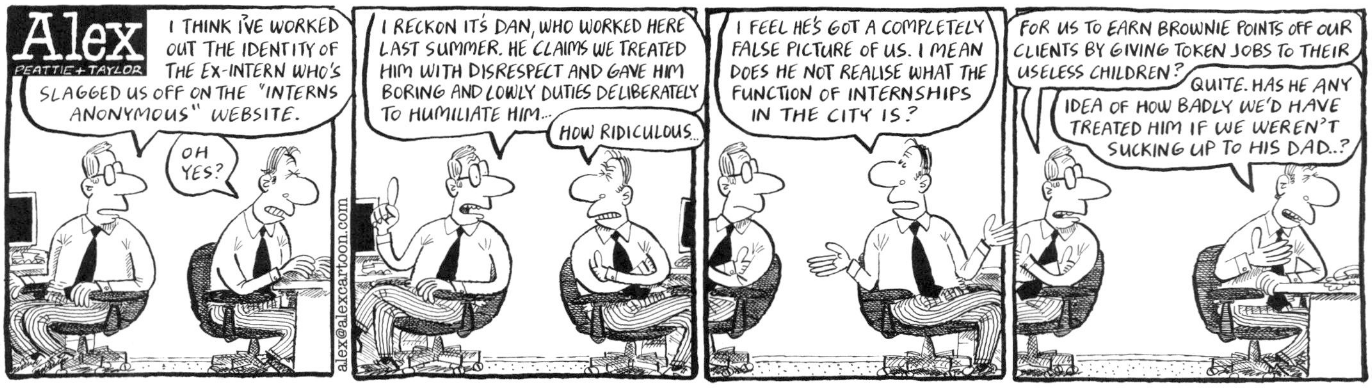

Alex
PEATTIE+TAYLOR
I THINK I'VE WORKED OUT THE IDENTITY OF THE EX-INTERN WHO'S SLAGGED US OFF ON THE "INTERNS ANONYMOUS" WEBSITE.
OH YES?
alex@alexcartoon.com
I RECKON IT'S DAN, WHO WORKED HERE LAST SUMMER. HE CLAIMS WE TREATED HIM WITH DISRESPECT AND GAVE HIM BORING AND LOWLY DUTIES DELIBERATELY TO HUMILIATE HIM...
HOW RIDICULOUS...
I FEEL HE'S GOT A COMPLETELY FALSE PICTURE OF US. I MEAN DOES HE NOT REALISE WHAT THE FUNCTION OF INTERNSHIPS IN THE CITY IS?
FOR US TO EARN BROWNIE POINTS OFF OUR CLIENTS BY GIVING TOKEN JOBS TO THEIR USELESS CHILDREN?
QUITE. HAS HE ANY IDEA OF HOW BADLY WE'D HAVE TREATED HIM IF WE WEREN'T SUCKING UP TO HIS DAD..?

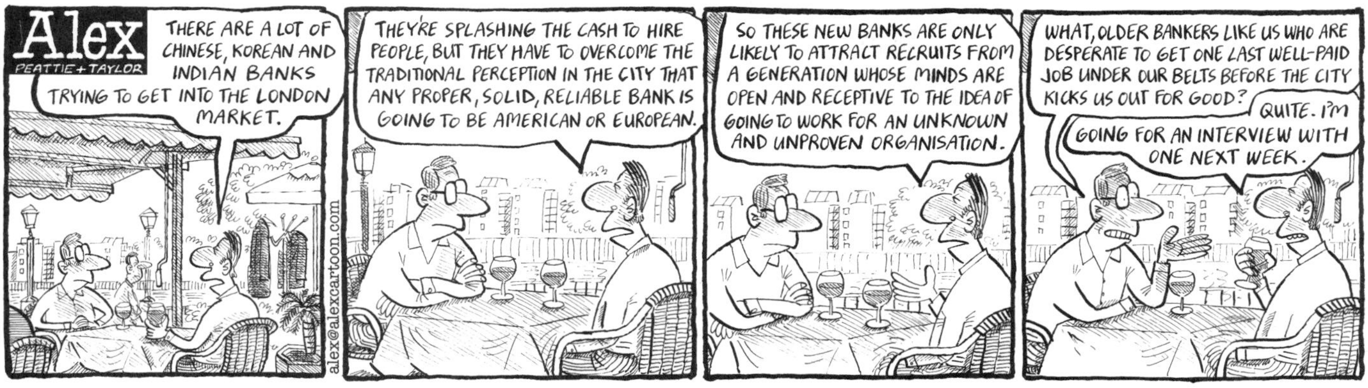
Alex
PEATTIE+TAYLOR
THERE ARE A LOT OF CHINESE, KOREAN AND INDIAN BANKS TRYING TO GET INTO THE LONDON MARKET.
alex@alexcartoon.com
THEY'RE SPLASHING THE CASH TO HIRE PEOPLE, BUT THEY HAVE TO OVERCOME THE TRADITIONAL PERCEPTION IN THE CITY THAT ANY PROPER, SOLID, RELIABLE BANK IS GOING TO BE AMERICAN OR EUROPEAN.
SO THESE NEW BANKS ARE ONLY LIKELY TO ATTRACT RECRUITS FROM A GENERATION WHOSE MINDS ARE OPEN AND RECEPTIVE TO THE IDEA OF GOING TO WORK FOR AN UNKNOWN AND UNPROVEN ORGANISATION.
WHAT, OLDER BANKERS LIKE US WHO ARE DESPERATE TO GET ONE LAST WELL-PAID JOB UNDER OUR BELTS BEFORE THE CITY KICKS US OUT FOR GOOD?
QUITE. I'M GOING FOR AN INTERVIEW WITH ONE NEXT WEEK.

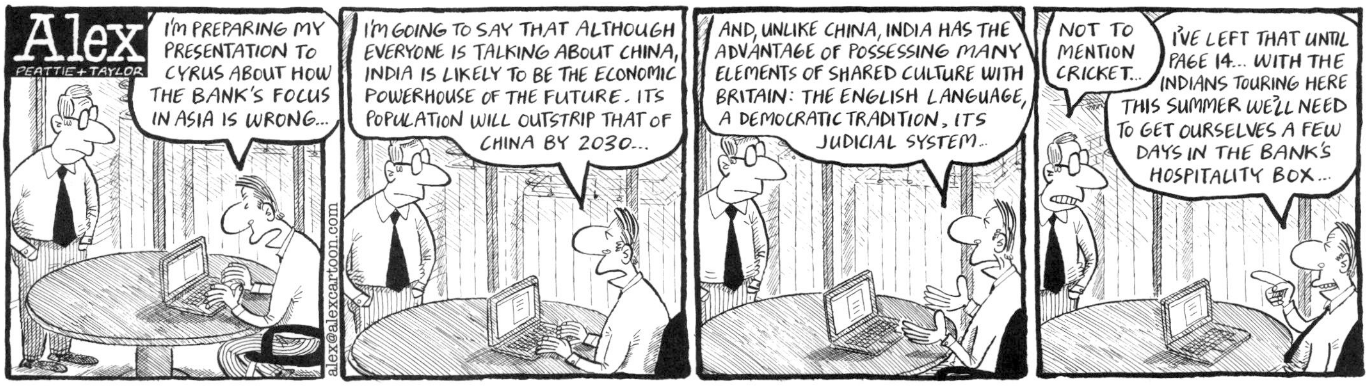
Alex
PEATTIE+TAYLOR
I'M PREPARING MY PRESENTATION TO CYRUS ABOUT HOW THE BANK'S FOCUS IN ASIA IS WRONG...
alex@alexcartoon.com
I'M GOING TO SAY THAT ALTHOUGH EVERYONE IS TALKING ABOUT CHINA, INDIA IS LIKELY TO BE THE ECONOMIC POWERHOUSE OF THE FUTURE. ITS POPULATION WILL OUTSTRIP THAT OF CHINA BY 2030...
AND, UNLIKE CHINA, INDIA HAS THE ADVANTAGE OF POSSESSING MANY ELEMENTS OF SHARED CULTURE WITH BRITAIN: THE ENGLISH LANGUAGE, A DEMOCRATIC TRADITION, ITS JUDICIAL SYSTEM...
NOT TO MENTION CRICKET...
I'VE LEFT THAT UNTIL PAGE 14... WITH THE INDIANS TOURING HERE THIS SUMMER WE'LL NEED TO GET OURSELVES A FEW DAYS IN THE BANK'S HOSPITALITY BOX...

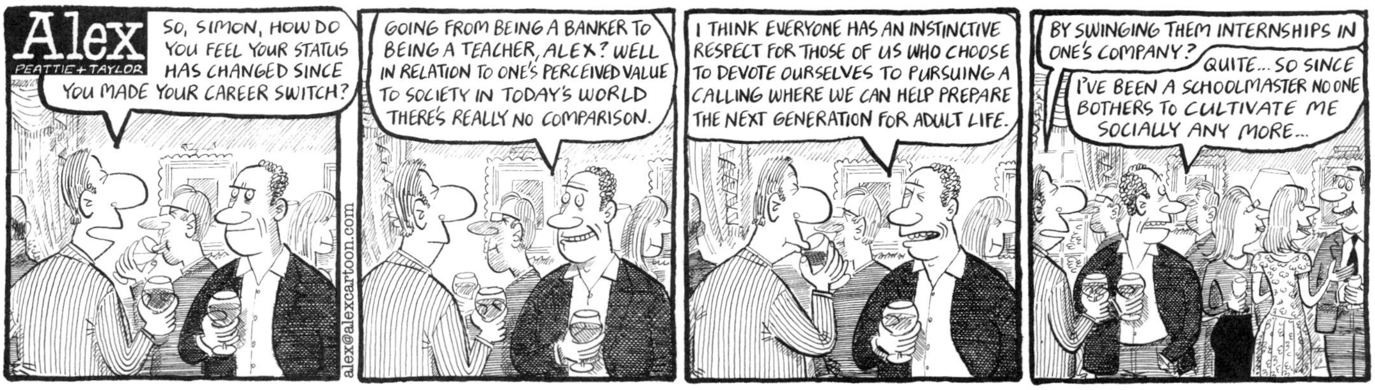
Alex
PEATTIE+TAYLOR
SO, SIMON, HOW DO YOU FEEL YOUR STATUS HAS CHANGED SINCE YOU MADE YOUR CAREER SWITCH?
alex@alexcartoon.com
GOING FROM BEING A BANKER TO BEING A TEACHER, ALEX? WELL IN RELATION TO ONE'S PERCEIVED VALUE TO SOCIETY IN TODAY'S WORLD THERE'S REALLY NO COMPARISON.
I THINK EVERYONE HAS AN INSTINCTIVE RESPECT FOR THOSE OF US WHO CHOOSE TO DEVOTE OURSELVES TO PURSUING A CALLING WHERE WE CAN HELP PREPARE THE NEXT GENERATION FOR ADULT LIFE.
BY SWINGING THEM INTERNSHIPS IN ONE'S COMPANY?
QUITE... SO SINCE I'VE BEEN A SCHOOLMASTER NO ONE BOTHERS TO CULTIVATE ME SOCIALLY ANY MORE...

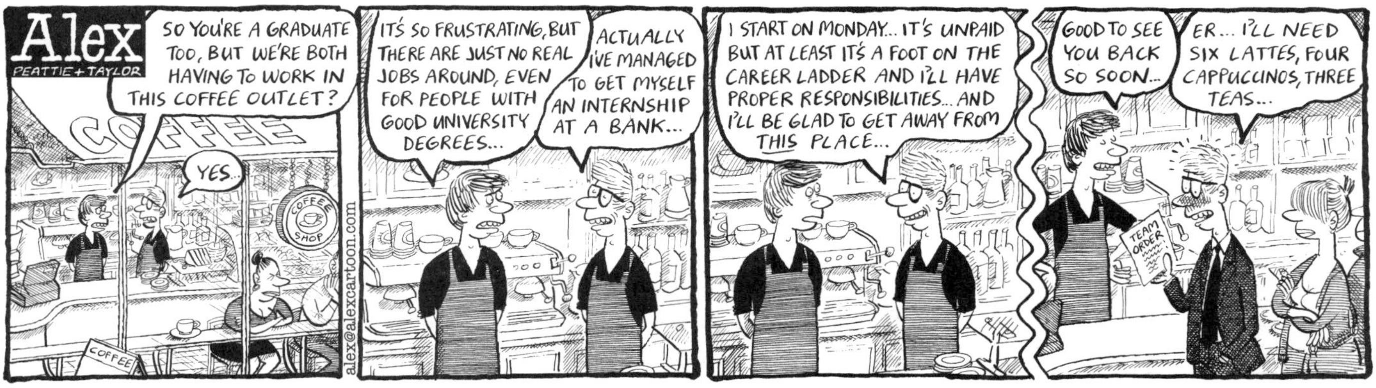
Alex
PEATTIE+TAYLOR
SO YOU'RE A GRADUATE TOO, BUT WE'RE BOTH HAVING TO WORK IN THIS COFFEE OUTLET?
YES.
COFFEE
COFFEE SHOP
COFFEE
alex@alexcartoon.com
IT'S SO FRUSTRATING, BUT THERE ARE JUST NO REAL JOBS AROUND, EVEN FOR PEOPLE WITH GOOD UNIVERSITY DEGREES...
ACTUALLY I'VE MANAGED TO GET MYSELF AN INTERNSHIP AT A BANK...
I START ON MONDAY... IT'S UNPAID BUT AT LEAST IT'S A FOOT ON THE CAREER LADDER AND I'LL HAVE PROPER RESPONSIBILITIES... AND I'LL BE GLAD TO GET AWAY FROM THIS PLACE...
GOOD TO SEE YOU BACK SO SOON...
TEAM ORDER
ER... I'LL NEED SIX LATTES, FOUR CAPPUCCINOS, THREE TEAS...

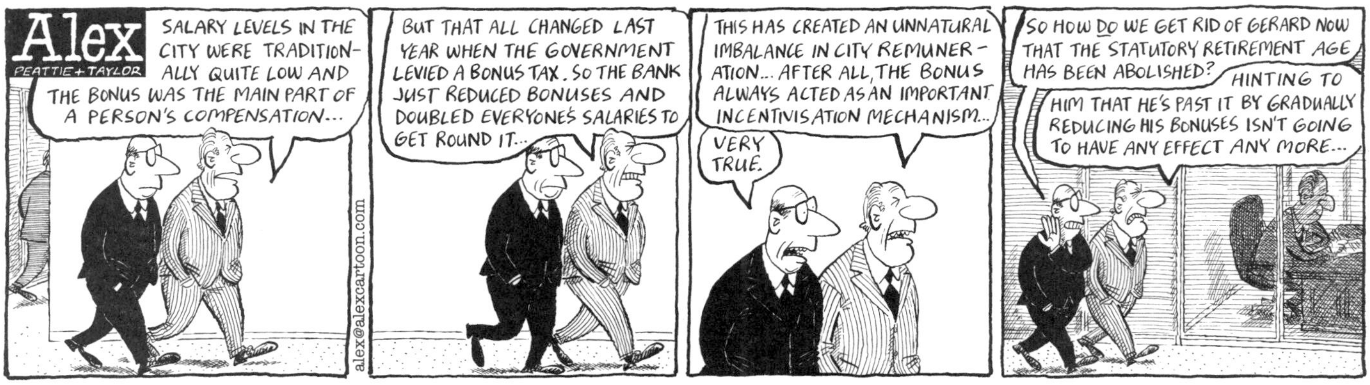
Alex
PEATTIE+TAYLOR
SALARY LEVELS IN THE CITY WERE TRADITIONALLY QUITE LOW AND THE BONUS WAS THE MAIN PART OF A PERSON'S COMPENSATION...
alex@alexcartoon.com
BUT THAT ALL CHANGED LAST YEAR WHEN THE GOVERNMENT LEVIED A BONUS TAX. SO THE BANK JUST REDUCED BONUSES AND DOUBLED EVERYONE'S SALARIES TO GET ROUND IT...
THIS HAS CREATED AN UNNATURAL IMBALANCE IN CITY REMUNERATION... AFTER ALL, THE BONUS ALWAYS ACTED AS AN IMPORTANT INCENTIVISATION MECHANISM...
VERY TRUE.
SO HOW DO WE GET RID OF GERARD NOW THAT THE STATUTORY RETIREMENT AGE HAS BEEN ABOLISHED?
HINTING TO HIM THAT HE'S PAST IT BY GRADUALLY REDUCING HIS BONUSES ISN'T GOING TO HAVE ANY EFFECT ANY MORE...

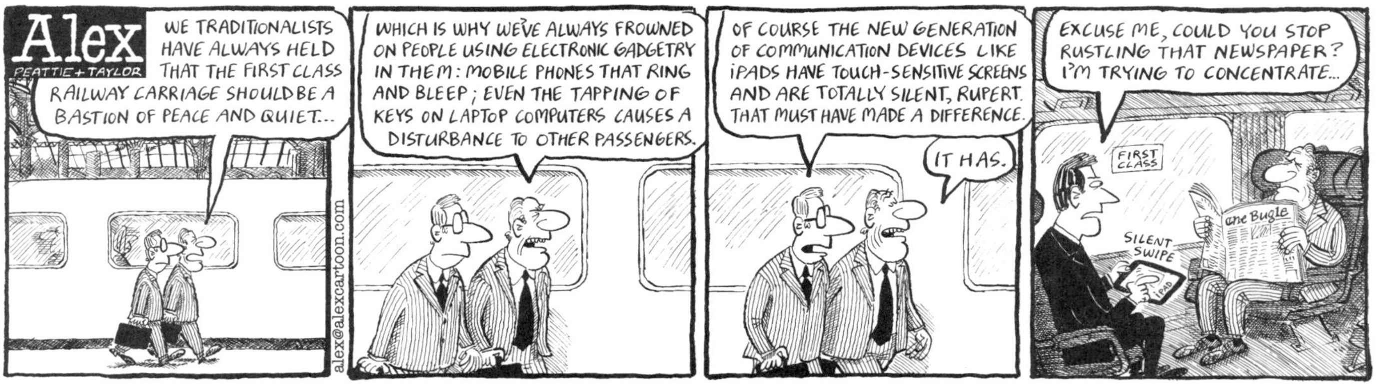
Alex
PEATTIE+TAYLOR
WE TRADITIONALISTS HAVE ALWAYS HELD THAT THE FIRST CLASS RAILWAY CARRIAGE SHOULD BE A BASTION OF PEACE AND QUIET...
alex@alexcartoon.com
WHICH IS WHY WE'VE ALWAYS FROWNED ON PEOPLE USING ELECTRONIC GADGETRY IN THEM: MOBILE PHONES THAT RING AND BLEEP; EVEN THE TAPPING OF KEYS ON LAPTOP COMPUTERS CAUSES A DISTURBANCE TO OTHER PASSENGERS.
OF COURSE THE NEW GENERATION OF COMMUNICATION DEVICES LIKE iPADS HAVE TOUCH-SENSITIVE SCREENS AND ARE TOTALLY SILENT, RUPERT. THAT MUST HAVE MADE A DIFFERENCE.
IT HAS.
EXCUSE ME, COULD YOU STOP RUSTLING THAT NEWSPAPER? I'M TRYING TO CONCENTRATE...
FIRST CLASS
SILENT SWIPE
iPAD
The Bugle

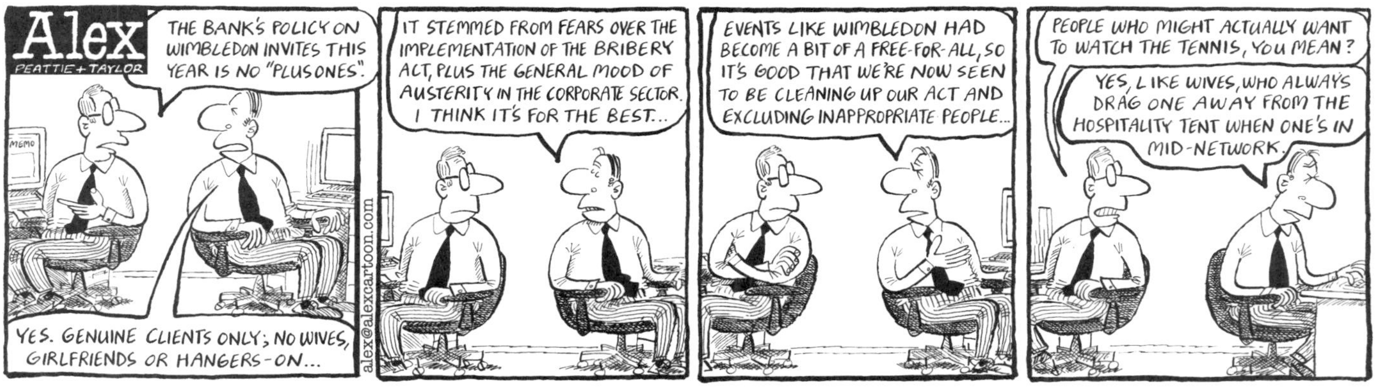
Alex
PEATTIE+TAYLOR
THE BANK'S POLICY ON WIMBLEDON INVITES THIS YEAR IS NO "PLUS ONES".
MEMO
YES. GENUINE CLIENTS ONLY; NO WIVES, GIRLFRIENDS OR HANGERS-ON...
alex@alexcartoon.com
IT STEMMED FROM FEARS OVER THE IMPLEMENTATION OF THE BRIBERY ACT, PLUS THE GENERAL MOOD OF AUSTERITY IN THE CORPORATE SECTOR. I THINK IT'S FOR THE BEST...
EVENTS LIKE WIMBLEDON HAD BECOME A BIT OF A FREE-FOR-ALL, SO IT'S GOOD THAT WE'RE NOW SEEN TO BE CLEANING UP OUR ACT AND EXCLUDING INAPPROPRIATE PEOPLE...
PEOPLE WHO MIGHT ACTUALLY WANT TO WATCH THE TENNIS, YOU MEAN?
YES, LIKE WIVES, WHO ALWAYS DRAG ONE AWAY FROM THE HOSPITALITY TENT WHEN ONE'S IN MID-NETWORK.

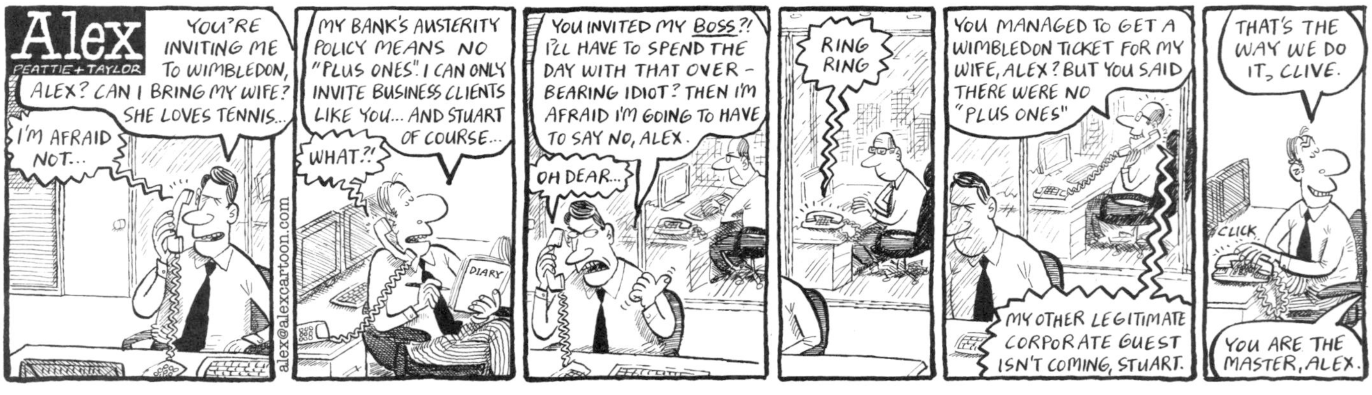
Alex
PEATTIE+TAYLOR
YOU'RE INVITING ME TO WIMBLEDON, ALEX? CAN I BRING MY WIFE? SHE LOVES TENNIS...
I'M AFRAID NOT...
alex@alexcartoon.com
MY BANK'S AUSTERITY POLICY MEANS NO "PLUS ONES". I CAN ONLY INVITE BUSINESS CLIENTS LIKE YOU... AND STUART OF COURSE...
WHAT?!
DIARY
YOU INVITED MY BOSS?! I'LL HAVE TO SPEND THE DAY WITH THAT OVERBEARING IDIOT? THEN I'M AFRAID I'M GOING TO HAVE TO SAY NO, ALEX.
OH DEAR...
RING RING
YOU MANAGED TO GET A WIMBLEDON TICKET FOR MY WIFE, ALEX? BUT YOU SAID THERE WERE NO "PLUS ONES"
MY OTHER LEGITIMATE CORPORATE GUEST ISN'T COMING, STUART.
THAT'S THE WAY WE DO IT, CLIVE.
CLICK
YOU ARE THE MASTER, ALEX.

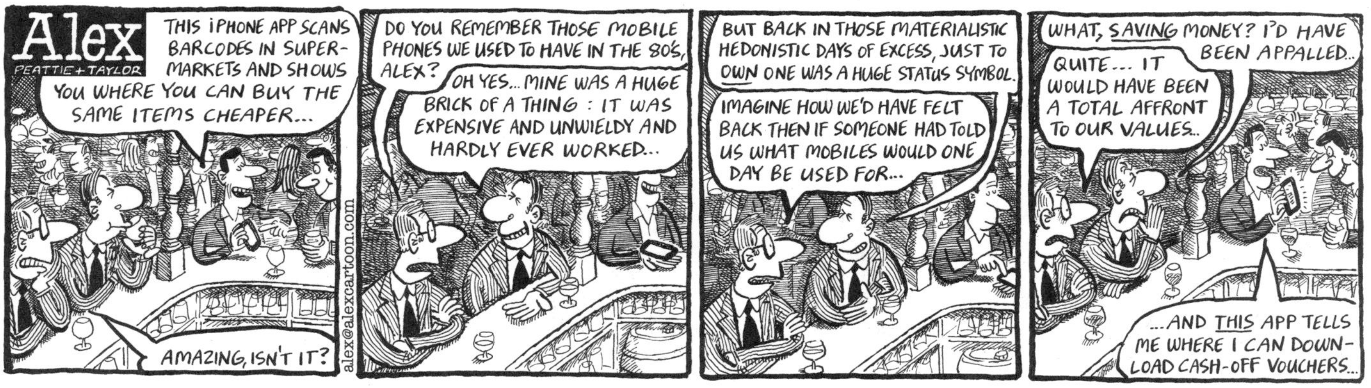
Alex
PEATTIE + TAYLOR
THIS iPHONE APP SCANS BARCODES IN SUPER-MARKETS AND SHOWS YOU WHERE YOU CAN BUY THE SAME ITEMS CHEAPER...
AMAZING, ISN'T IT?
DO YOU REMEMBER THOSE MOBILE PHONES WE USED TO HAVE IN THE 80's, ALEX?
OH YES... MINE WAS A HUGE BRICK OF A THING : IT WAS EXPENSIVE AND UNWIELDY AND HARDLY EVER WORKED...
alex@alexcartoon.com
BUT BACK IN THOSE MATERIALISTIC HEDONISTIC DAYS OF EXCESS, JUST TO OWN ONE WAS A HUGE STATUS SYMBOL.
IMAGINE HOW WE'D HAVE FELT BACK THEN IF SOMEONE HAD TOLD US WHAT MOBILES WOULD ONE DAY BE USED FOR...
WHAT, SAVING MONEY? I'D HAVE BEEN APPALLED..
QUITE... IT WOULD HAVE BEEN A TOTAL AFFRONT TO OUR VALUES..
...AND THIS APP TELLS ME WHERE I CAN DOWN-LOAD CASH-OFF VOUCHERS...

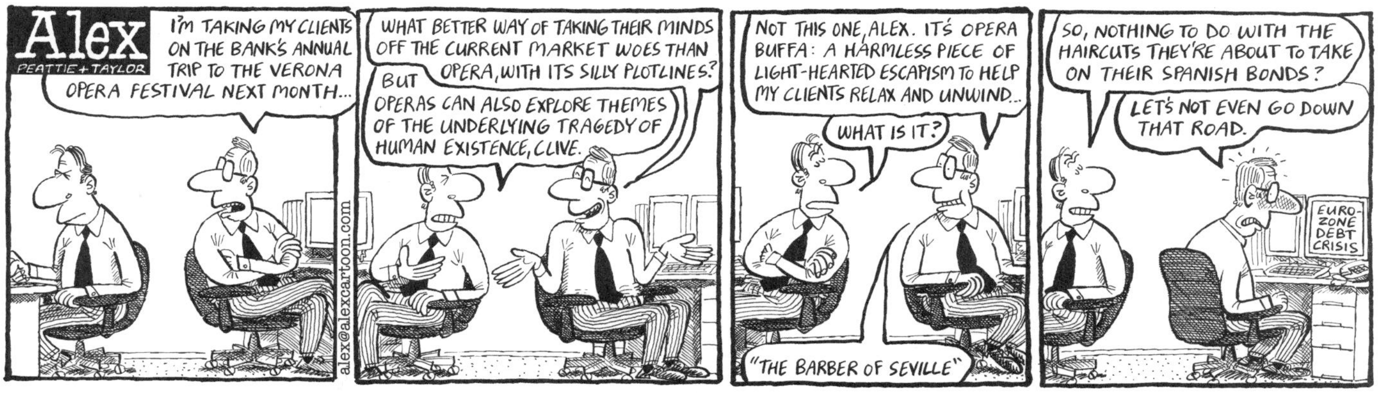
Alex
PEATTIE + TAYLOR
I'M TAKING MY CLIENTS ON THE BANK'S ANNUAL TRIP TO THE VERONA OPERA FESTIVAL NEXT MONTH...
WHAT BETTER WAY OF TAKING THEIR MINDS OFF THE CURRENT MARKET WOES THAN OPERA, WITH ITS SILLY PLOTLINES?
BUT OPERAS CAN ALSO EXPLORE THEMES OF THE UNDERLYING TRAGEDY OF HUMAN EXISTENCE, CLIVE.
alex@alexcartoon.com
NOT THIS ONE, ALEX. IT'S OPERA BUFFA: A HARMLESS PIECE OF LIGHT-HEARTED ESCAPISM TO HELP MY CLIENTS RELAX AND UNWIND...
WHAT IS IT?
"THE BARBER OF SEVILLE"
SO, NOTHING TO DO WITH THE HAIRCUTS THEY'RE ABOUT TO TAKE ON THEIR SPANISH BONDS?
LET'S NOT EVEN GO DOWN THAT ROAD.
EURO-ZONE DEBT CRISIS

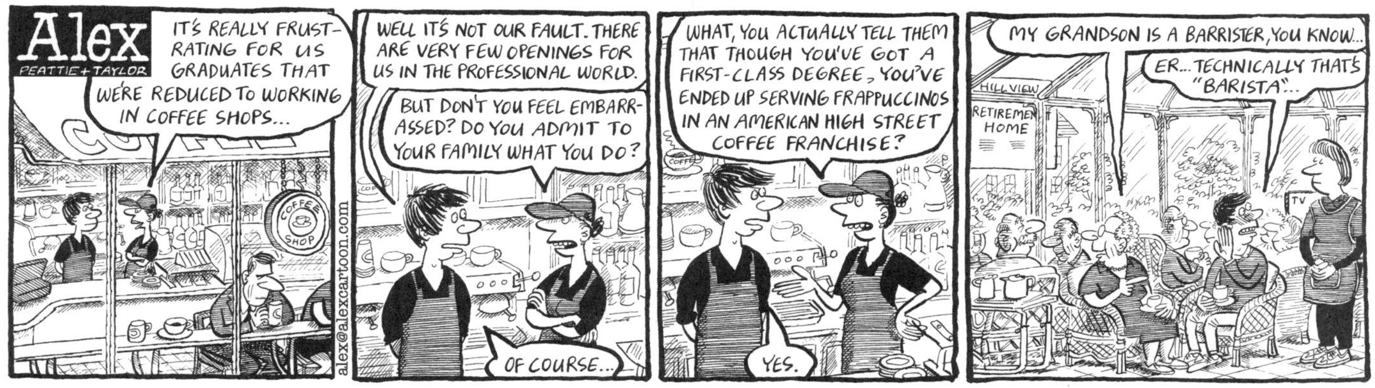
Alex
PEATTIE + TAYLOR
IT'S REALLY FRUST-RATING FOR US GRADUATES THAT WE'RE REDUCED TO WORKING IN COFFEE SHOPS...
COFFEE SHOP
WELL IT'S NOT OUR FAULT. THERE ARE VERY FEW OPENINGS FOR US IN THE PROFESSIONAL WORLD.
BUT DON'T YOU FEEL EMBARR-ASSED? DO YOU ADMIT TO YOUR FAMILY WHAT YOU DO?
OF COURSE...
alex@alexcartoon.com
WHAT, YOU ACTUALLY TELL THEM THAT THOUGH YOU'VE GOT A FIRST-CLASS DEGREE, YOU'VE ENDED UP SERVING FRAPPUCCINOS IN AN AMERICAN HIGH STREET COFFEE FRANCHISE?
YES.
MY GRANDSON IS A BARRISTER, YOU KNOW...
ER... TECHNICALLY THAT'S "BARISTA"...
HILL VIEW RETIREMENT HOME
TV

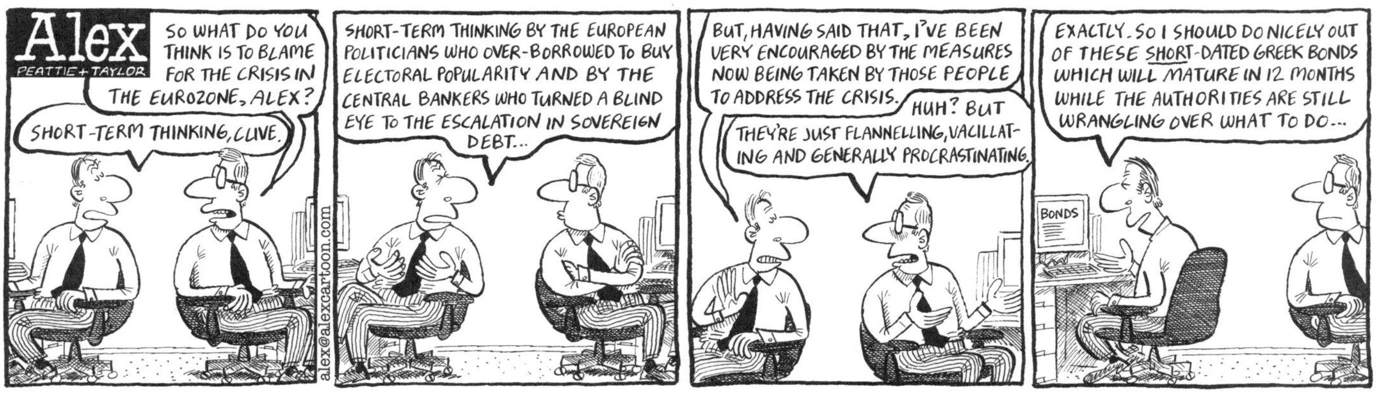
Alex
PEATTIE + TAYLOR
SO WHAT DO YOU THINK IS TO BLAME FOR THE CRISIS IN THE EUROZONE, ALEX?
SHORT-TERM THINKING, CLIVE.
SHORT-TERM THINKING BY THE EUROPEAN POLITICIANS WHO OVER-BORROWED TO BUY ELECTORAL POPULARITY AND BY THE CENTRAL BANKERS WHO TURNED A BLIND EYE TO THE ESCALATION IN SOVEREIGN DEBT...
alex@alexcartoon.com
BUT, HAVING SAID THAT, I'VE BEEN VERY ENCOURAGED BY THE MEASURES NOW BEING TAKEN BY THOSE PEOPLE TO ADDRESS THE CRISIS.
HUH? BUT THEY'RE JUST FLANNELLING, VACILLAT-ING AND GENERALLY PROCRASTINATING.
EXACTLY. SO I SHOULD DO NICELY OUT OF THESE SHORT-DATED GREEK BONDS WHICH WILL MATURE IN 12 MONTHS WHILE THE AUTHORITIES ARE STILL WRANGLING OVER WHAT TO DO...
BONDS

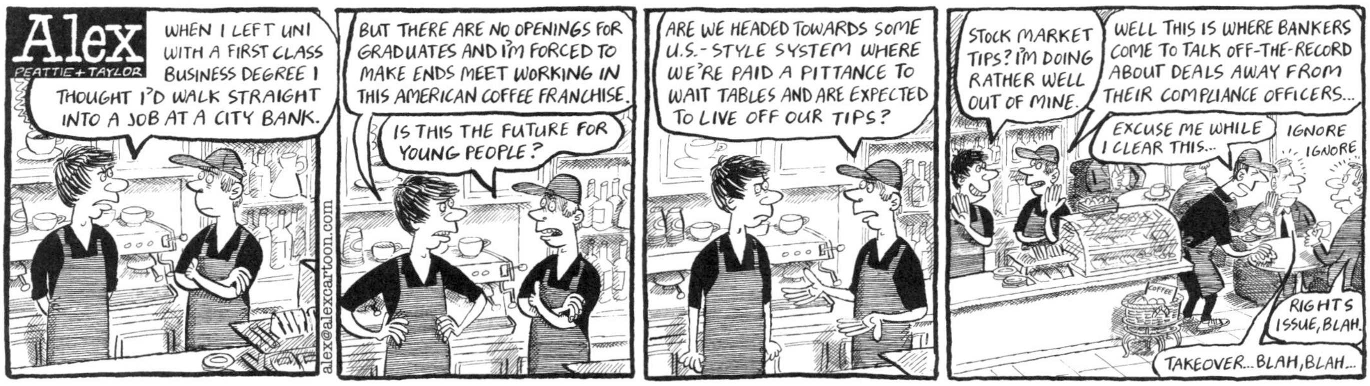
Alex
PEATTIE + TAYLOR
WHEN I LEFT UNI WITH A FIRST CLASS BUSINESS DEGREE I THOUGHT I'D WALK STRAIGHT INTO A JOB AT A CITY BANK.
BUT THERE ARE NO OPENINGS FOR GRADUATES AND I'M FORCED TO MAKE ENDS MEET WORKING IN THIS AMERICAN COFFEE FRANCHISE.
IS THIS THE FUTURE FOR YOUNG PEOPLE?
alex@alexcartoon.com
ARE WE HEADED TOWARDS SOME U.S.-STYLE SYSTEM WHERE WE'RE PAID A PITTANCE TO WAIT TABLES AND ARE EXPECTED TO LIVE OFF OUR TIPS?
STOCK MARKET TIPS? I'M DOING RATHER WELL OUT OF MINE.
WELL THIS IS WHERE BANKERS COME TO TALK OFF-THE-RECORD ABOUT DEALS AWAY FROM THEIR COMPLIANCE OFFICERS...
EXCUSE ME WHILE I CLEAR THIS...
IGNORE IGNORE
RIGHTS ISSUE, BLAH.
TAKEOVER... BLAH, BLAH...

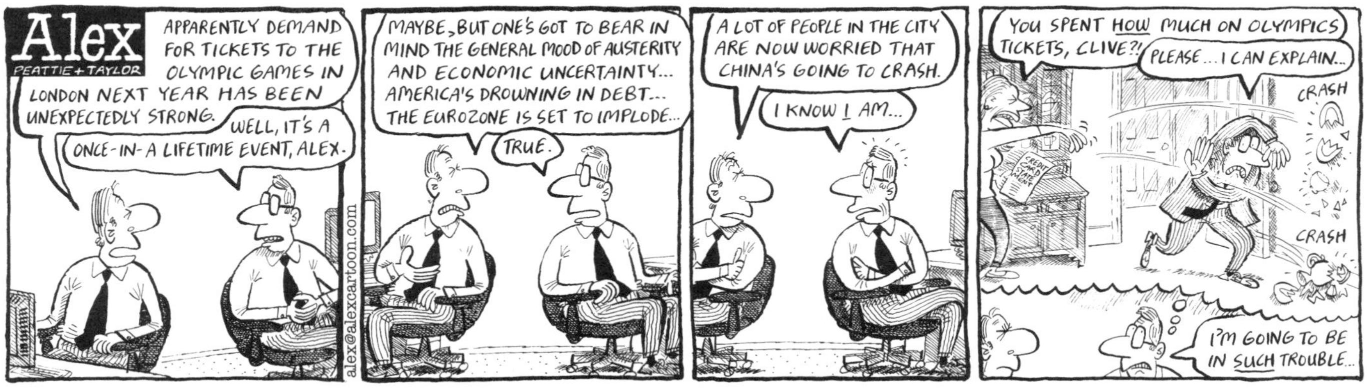
Alex
PEATTIE + TAYLOR
APPARENTLY DEMAND FOR TICKETS TO THE OLYMPIC GAMES IN LONDON NEXT YEAR HAS BEEN UNEXPECTEDLY STRONG.
WELL, IT'S A ONCE-IN-A LIFETIME EVENT, ALEX.
alex@alexcartoon.com
MAYBE, BUT ONE'S GOT TO BEAR IN MIND THE GENERAL MOOD OF AUSTERITY AND ECONOMIC UNCERTAINTY... AMERICA'S DROWNING IN DEBT... THE EUROZONE IS SET TO IMPLODE...
TRUE.
A LOT OF PEOPLE IN THE CITY ARE NOW WORRIED THAT CHINA'S GOING TO CRASH.
I KNOW I AM...
YOU SPENT HOW MUCH ON OLYMPICS TICKETS, CLIVE?!
PLEASE... I CAN EXPLAIN...
CRASH
CRASH
I'M GOING TO BE IN SUCH TROUBLE...

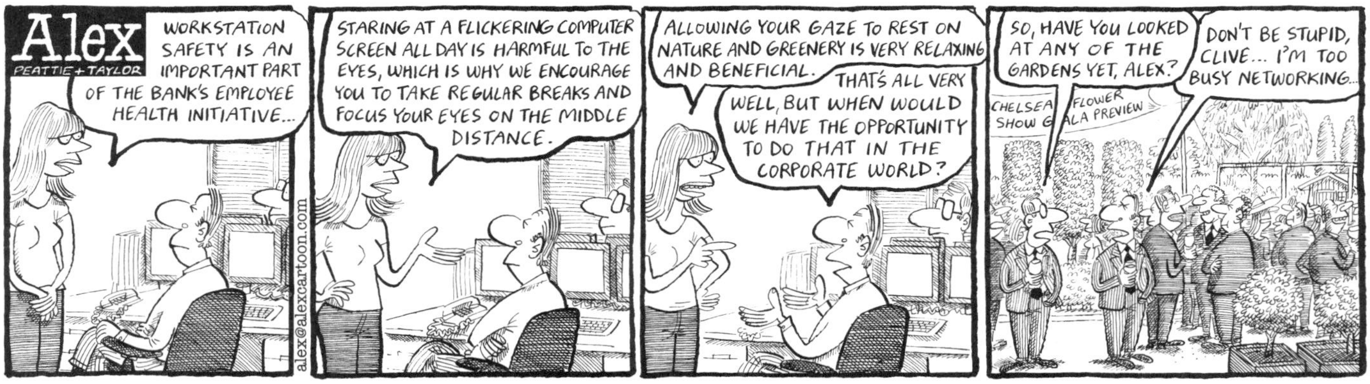
Alex
PEATTIE + TAYLOR
WORKSTATION SAFETY IS AN IMPORTANT PART OF THE BANK'S EMPLOYEE HEALTH INITIATIVE...
alex@alexcartoon.com
STARING AT A FLICKERING COMPUTER SCREEN ALL DAY IS HARMFUL TO THE EYES, WHICH IS WHY WE ENCOURAGE YOU TO TAKE REGULAR BREAKS AND FOCUS YOUR EYES ON THE MIDDLE DISTANCE.
ALLOWING YOUR GAZE TO REST ON NATURE AND GREENERY IS VERY RELAXING AND BENEFICIAL.
THAT'S ALL VERY WELL, BUT WHEN WOULD WE HAVE THE OPPORTUNITY TO DO THAT IN THE CORPORATE WORLD?
SO, HAVE YOU LOOKED AT ANY OF THE GARDENS YET, ALEX?
DON'T BE STUPID, CLIVE... I'M TOO BUSY NETWORKING...
CHELSEA FLOWER SHOW GALA PREVIEW

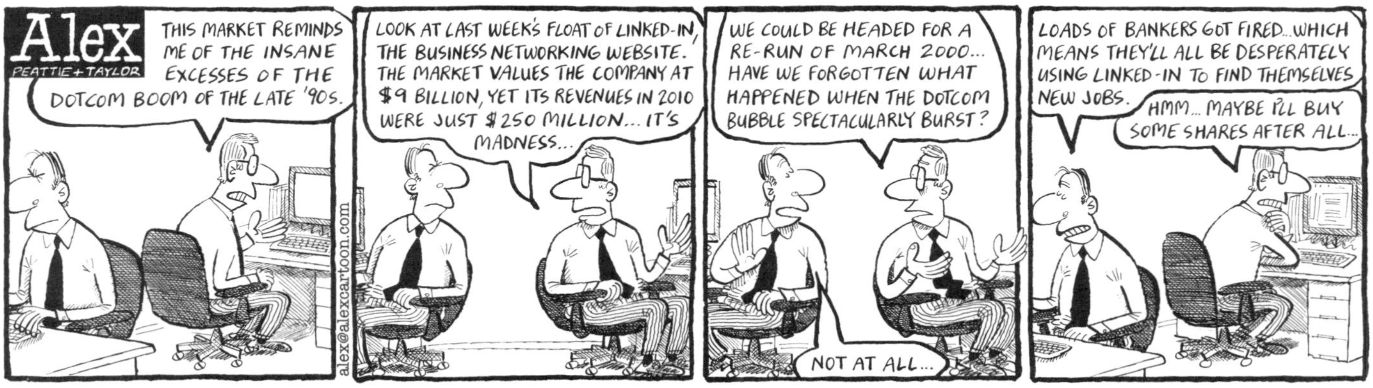
Alex
PEATTIE + TAYLOR
THIS MARKET REMINDS ME OF THE INSANE EXCESSES OF THE DOTCOM BOOM OF THE LATE '90S.
alex@alexcartoon.com
LOOK AT LAST WEEK'S FLOAT OF LINKED-IN, THE BUSINESS NETWORKING WEBSITE. THE MARKET VALUES THE COMPANY AT $9 BILLION, YET ITS REVENUES IN 2010 WERE JUST $250 MILLION... IT'S MADNESS...
WE COULD BE HEADED FOR A RE-RUN OF MARCH 2000... HAVE WE FORGOTTEN WHAT HAPPENED WHEN THE DOTCOM BUBBLE SPECTACULARLY BURST?
NOT AT ALL...
LOADS OF BANKERS GOT FIRED... WHICH MEANS THEY'LL ALL BE DESPERATELY USING LINKED-IN TO FIND THEMSELVES NEW JOBS.
HMM... MAYBE I'LL BUY SOME SHARES AFTER ALL...

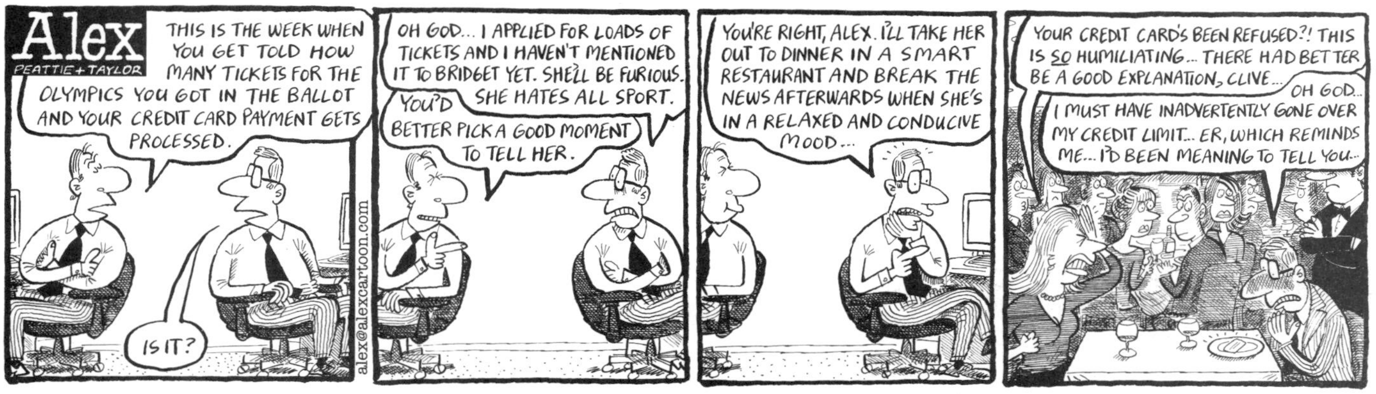
Alex
PEATTIE+TAYLOR
THIS IS THE WEEK WHEN YOU GET TOLD HOW MANY TICKETS FOR THE OLYMPICS YOU GOT IN THE BALLOT AND YOUR CREDIT CARD PAYMENT GETS PROCESSED.
IS IT?
alex@alexcartoon.com
OH GOD... I APPLIED FOR LOADS OF TICKETS AND I HAVEN'T MENTIONED IT TO BRIDGET YET. SHE'LL BE FURIOUS. SHE HATES ALL SPORT.
YOU'D BETTER PICK A GOOD MOMENT TO TELL HER.
YOU'RE RIGHT, ALEX. I'LL TAKE HER OUT TO DINNER IN A SMART RESTAURANT AND BREAK THE NEWS AFTERWARDS WHEN SHE'S IN A RELAXED AND CONDUCIVE MOOD...
YOUR CREDIT CARD'S BEEN REFUSED?! THIS IS SO HUMILIATING... THERE HAD BETTER BE A GOOD EXPLANATION, CLIVE...
OH GOD... I MUST HAVE INADVERTENTLY GONE OVER MY CREDIT LIMIT... ER, WHICH REMINDS ME... I'D BEEN MEANING TO TELL YOU...

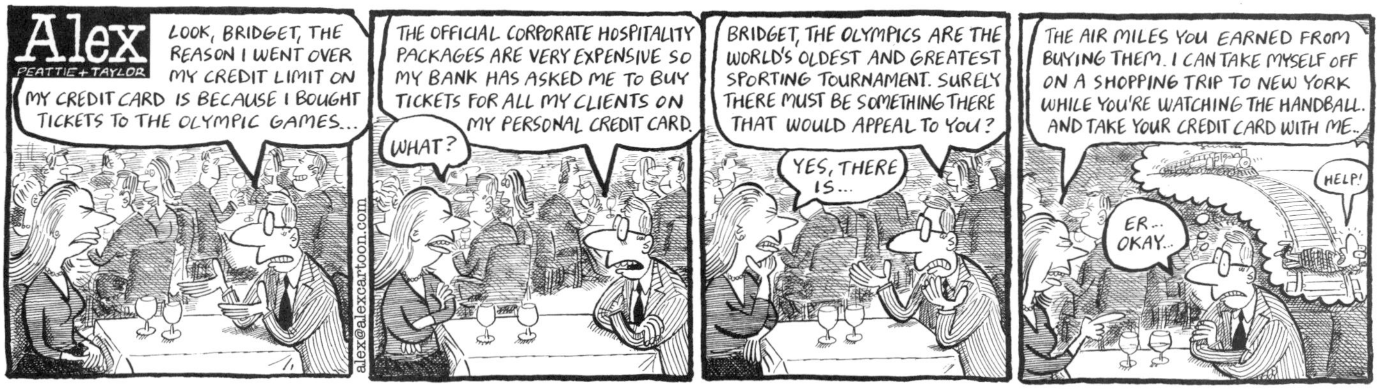
Alex
PEATTIE+TAYLOR
LOOK, BRIDGET, THE REASON I WENT OVER MY CREDIT LIMIT ON MY CREDIT CARD IS BECAUSE I BOUGHT TICKETS TO THE OLYMPIC GAMES...
alex@alexcartoon.com
THE OFFICIAL CORPORATE HOSPITALITY PACKAGES ARE VERY EXPENSIVE SO MY BANK HAS ASKED ME TO BUY TICKETS FOR ALL MY CLIENTS ON MY PERSONAL CREDIT CARD.
WHAT?
BRIDGET, THE OLYMPICS ARE THE WORLD'S OLDEST AND GREATEST SPORTING TOURNAMENT. SURELY THERE MUST BE SOMETHING THERE THAT WOULD APPEAL TO YOU?
YES, THERE IS...
THE AIR MILES YOU EARNED FROM BUYING THEM. I CAN TAKE MYSELF OFF ON A SHOPPING TRIP TO NEW YORK WHILE YOU'RE WATCHING THE HANDBALL. AND TAKE YOUR CREDIT CARD WITH ME...
ER... OKAY...
HELP!

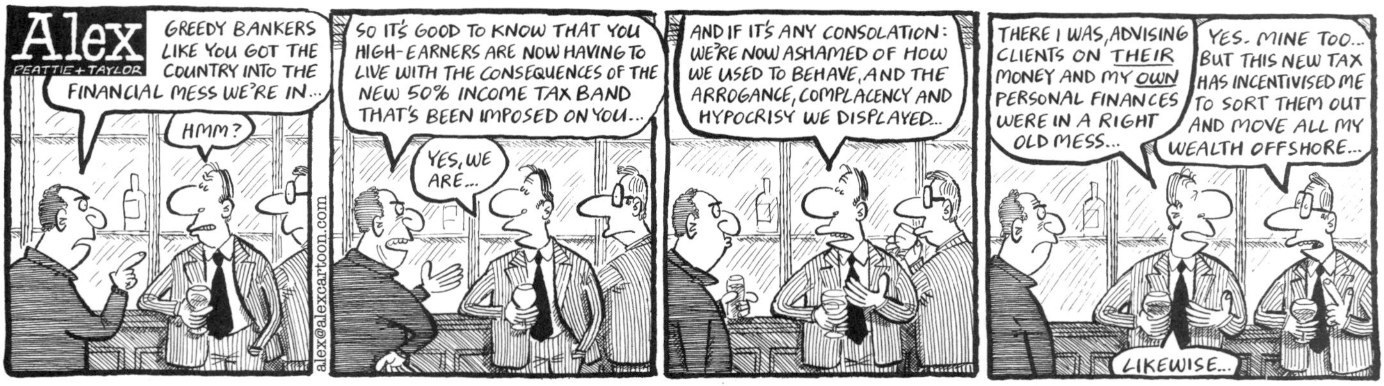
Alex
PEATTIE+TAYLOR
GREEDY BANKERS LIKE YOU GOT THE COUNTRY INTO THE FINANCIAL MESS WE'RE IN...
HMM?
alex@alexcartoon.com
SO IT'S GOOD TO KNOW THAT YOU HIGH-EARNERS ARE NOW HAVING TO LIVE WITH THE CONSEQUENCES OF THE NEW 50% INCOME TAX BAND THAT'S BEEN IMPOSED ON YOU...
YES, WE ARE...
AND IF IT'S ANY CONSOLATION: WE'RE NOW ASHAMED OF HOW WE USED TO BEHAVE, AND THE ARROGANCE, COMPLACENCY AND HYPOCRISY WE DISPLAYED...
THERE I WAS, ADVISING CLIENTS ON THEIR MONEY AND MY OWN PERSONAL FINANCES WERE IN A RIGHT OLD MESS...
YES. MINE TOO... BUT THIS NEW TAX HAS INCENTIVISED ME TO SORT THEM OUT AND MOVE ALL MY WEALTH OFFSHORE...
LIKEWISE...

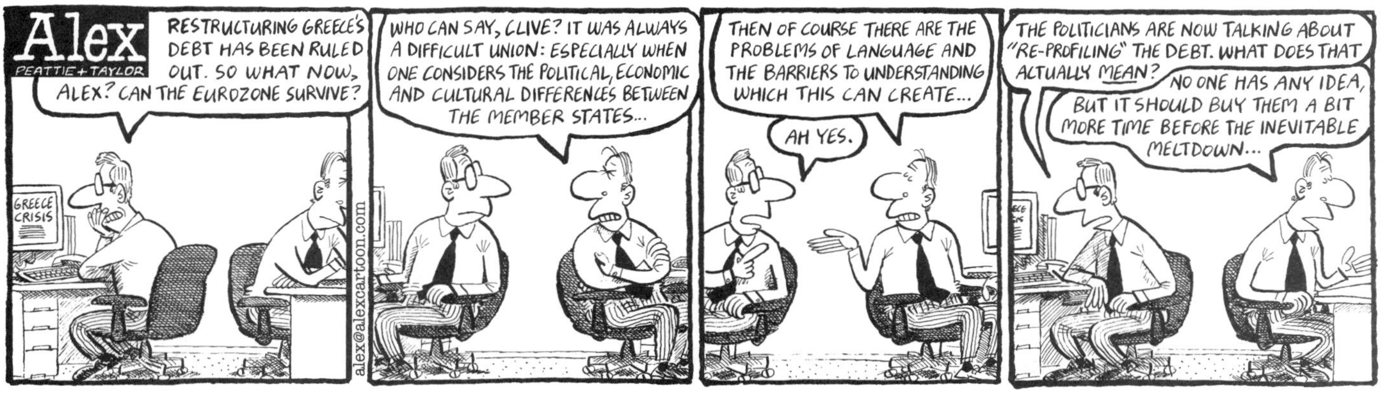
Alex
PEATTIE+TAYLOR
RESTRUCTURING GREECE'S DEBT HAS BEEN RULED OUT. SO WHAT NOW, ALEX? CAN THE EUROZONE SURVIVE?
GREECE CRISIS
alex@alexcartoon.com
WHO CAN SAY, CLIVE? IT WAS ALWAYS A DIFFICULT UNION: ESPECIALLY WHEN ONE CONSIDERS THE POLITICAL, ECONOMIC AND CULTURAL DIFFERENCES BETWEEN THE MEMBER STATES...
THEN OF COURSE THERE ARE THE PROBLEMS OF LANGUAGE AND THE BARRIERS TO UNDERSTANDING WHICH THIS CAN CREATE...
AH YES.
THE POLITICIANS ARE NOW TALKING ABOUT "RE-PROFILING" THE DEBT. WHAT DOES THAT ACTUALLY MEAN?
NO ONE HAS ANY IDEA, BUT IT SHOULD BUY THEM A BIT MORE TIME BEFORE THE INEVITABLE MELTDOWN...

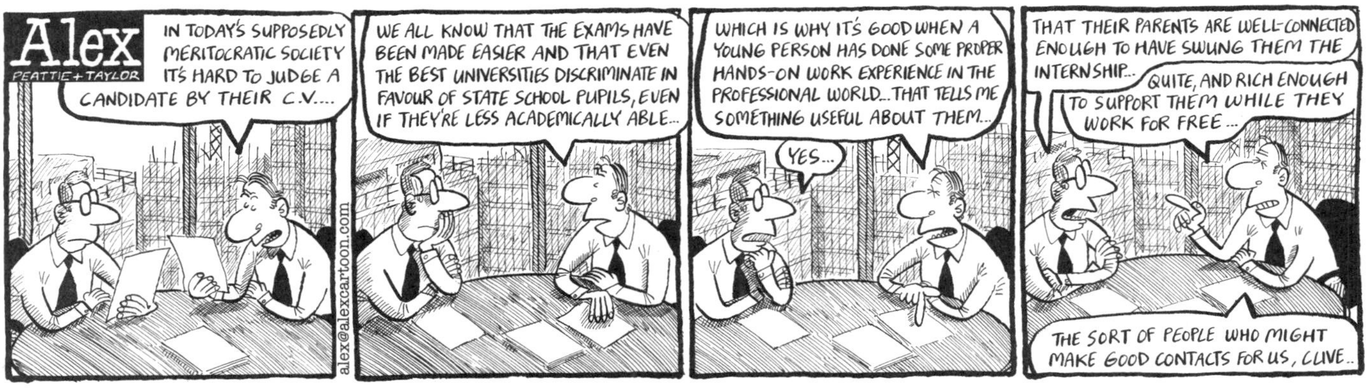
Alex
PEATTIE + TAYLOR
IN TODAY'S SUPPOSEDLY MERITOCRATIC SOCIETY IT'S HARD TO JUDGE A CANDIDATE BY THEIR C.V....
WE ALL KNOW THAT THE EXAMS HAVE BEEN MADE EASIER AND THAT EVEN THE BEST UNIVERSITIES DISCRIMINATE IN FAVOUR OF STATE SCHOOL PUPILS, EVEN IF THEY'RE LESS ACADEMICALLY ABLE...
alex@alexcartoon.com
WHICH IS WHY IT'S GOOD WHEN A YOUNG PERSON HAS DONE SOME PROPER HANDS-ON WORK EXPERIENCE IN THE PROFESSIONAL WORLD... THAT TELLS ME SOMETHING USEFUL ABOUT THEM...
YES...
THAT THEIR PARENTS ARE WELL-CONNECTED ENOUGH TO HAVE SWUNG THEM THE INTERNSHIP...
QUITE, AND RICH ENOUGH TO SUPPORT THEM WHILE THEY WORK FOR FREE...
THE SORT OF PEOPLE WHO MIGHT MAKE GOOD CONTACTS FOR US, CLIVE...

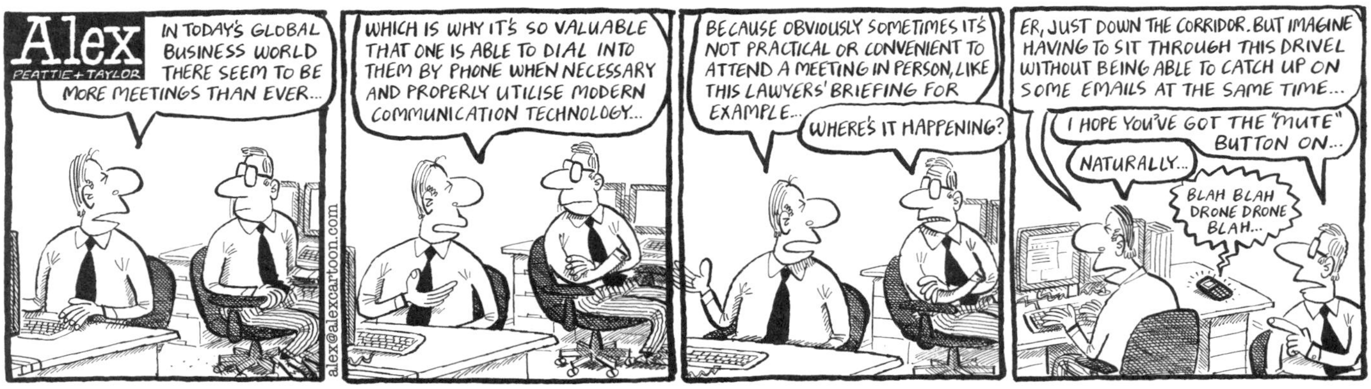
Alex
PEATTIE + TAYLOR
IN TODAY'S GLOBAL BUSINESS WORLD THERE SEEM TO BE MORE MEETINGS THAN EVER...
WHICH IS WHY IT'S SO VALUABLE THAT ONE IS ABLE TO DIAL INTO THEM BY PHONE WHEN NECESSARY AND PROPERLY UTILISE MODERN COMMUNICATION TECHNOLOGY...
alex@alexcartoon.com
BECAUSE OBVIOUSLY SOMETIMES IT'S NOT PRACTICAL OR CONVENIENT TO ATTEND A MEETING IN PERSON, LIKE THIS LAWYERS' BRIEFING FOR EXAMPLE...
WHERE'S IT HAPPENING?
ER, JUST DOWN THE CORRIDOR. BUT IMAGINE HAVING TO SIT THROUGH THIS DRIVEL WITHOUT BEING ABLE TO CATCH UP ON SOME EMAILS AT THE SAME TIME...
I HOPE YOU'VE GOT THE "MUTE" BUTTON ON...
NATURALLY...
BLAH BLAH DRONE DRONE BLAH...

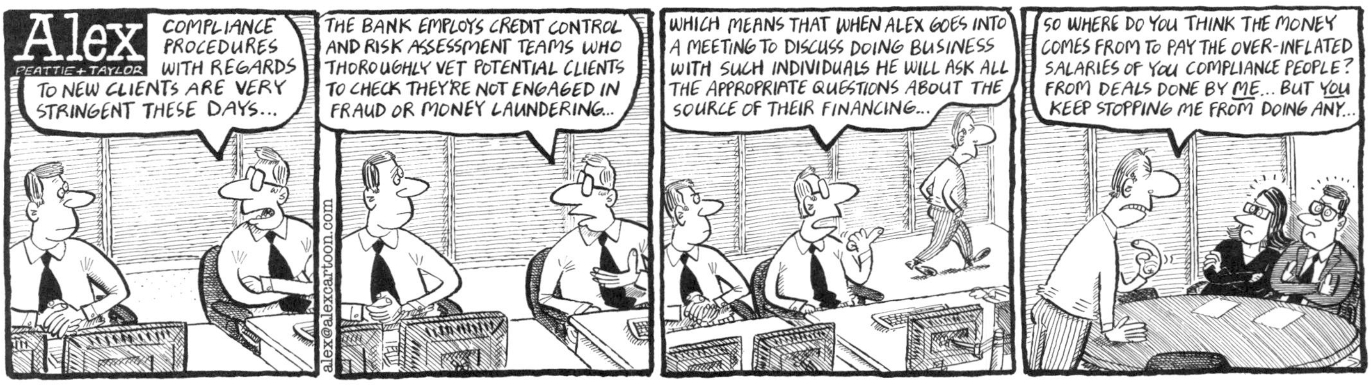
Alex
PEATTIE + TAYLOR
COMPLIANCE PROCEDURES WITH REGARDS TO NEW CLIENTS ARE VERY STRINGENT THESE DAYS...
THE BANK EMPLOYS CREDIT CONTROL AND RISK ASSESSMENT TEAMS WHO THOROUGHLY VET POTENTIAL CLIENTS TO CHECK THEY'RE NOT ENGAGED IN FRAUD OR MONEY LAUNDERING...
alex@alexcartoon.com
WHICH MEANS THAT WHEN ALEX GOES INTO A MEETING TO DISCUSS DOING BUSINESS WITH SUCH INDIVIDUALS HE WILL ASK ALL THE APPROPRIATE QUESTIONS ABOUT THE SOURCE OF THEIR FINANCING...
SO WHERE DO YOU THINK THE MONEY COMES FROM TO PAY THE OVER-INFLATED SALARIES OF YOU COMPLIANCE PEOPLE? FROM DEALS DONE BY ME... BUT YOU KEEP STOPPING ME FROM DOING ANY...

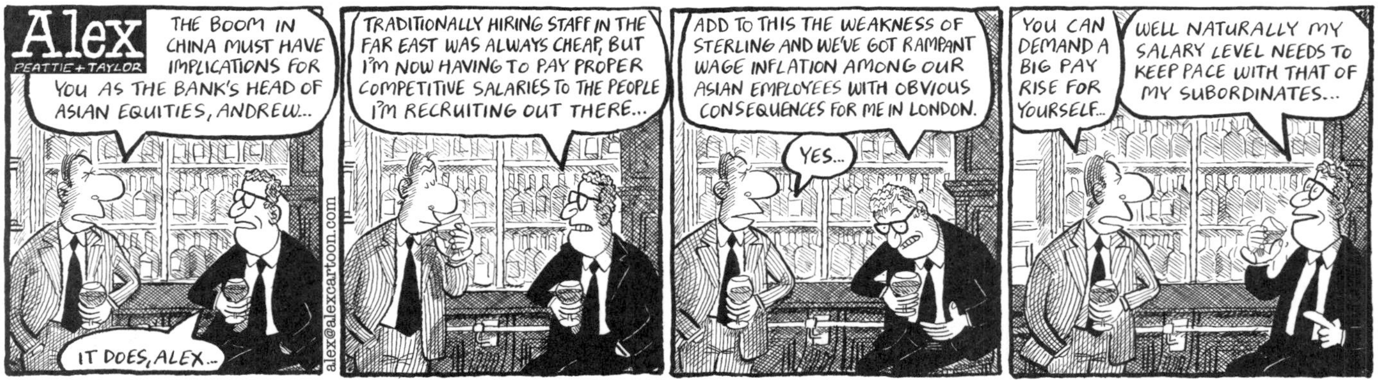
Alex
PEATTIE + TAYLOR
THE BOOM IN CHINA MUST HAVE IMPLICATIONS FOR YOU AS THE BANK'S HEAD OF ASIAN EQUITIES, ANDREW...
IT DOES, ALEX...
TRADITIONALLY HIRING STAFF IN THE FAR EAST WAS ALWAYS CHEAP, BUT I'M NOW HAVING TO PAY PROPER COMPETITIVE SALARIES TO THE PEOPLE I'M RECRUITING OUT THERE...
alex@alexcartoon.com
ADD TO THIS THE WEAKNESS OF STERLING AND WE'VE GOT RAMPANT WAGE INFLATION AMONG OUR ASIAN EMPLOYEES WITH OBVIOUS CONSEQUENCES FOR ME IN LONDON.
YES...
YOU CAN DEMAND A BIG PAY RISE FOR YOURSELF...
WELL NATURALLY MY SALARY LEVEL NEEDS TO KEEP PACE WITH THAT OF MY SUBORDINATES...

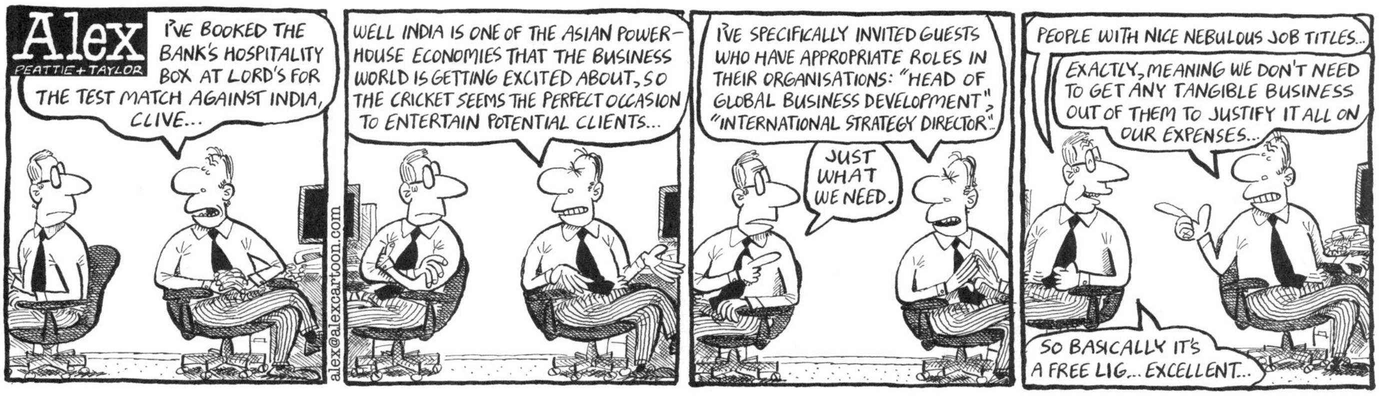
Alex
PEATTIE + TAYLOR
I'VE BOOKED THE BANK'S HOSPITALITY BOX AT LORD'S FOR THE TEST MATCH AGAINST INDIA, CLIVE...
alex@alexcartoon.com
WELL INDIA IS ONE OF THE ASIAN POWER-HOUSE ECONOMIES THAT THE BUSINESS WORLD IS GETTING EXCITED ABOUT, SO THE CRICKET SEEMS THE PERFECT OCCASION TO ENTERTAIN POTENTIAL CLIENTS...
I'VE SPECIFICALLY INVITED GUESTS WHO HAVE APPROPRIATE ROLES IN THEIR ORGANISATIONS: "HEAD OF GLOBAL BUSINESS DEVELOPMENT", "INTERNATIONAL STRATEGY DIRECTOR"
JUST WHAT WE NEED.
PEOPLE WITH NICE NEBULOUS JOB TITLES...
EXACTLY, MEANING WE DON'T NEED TO GET ANY TANGIBLE BUSINESS OUT OF THEM TO JUSTIFY IT ALL ON OUR EXPENSES...
SO BASICALLY IT'S A FREE LIG... EXCELLENT...

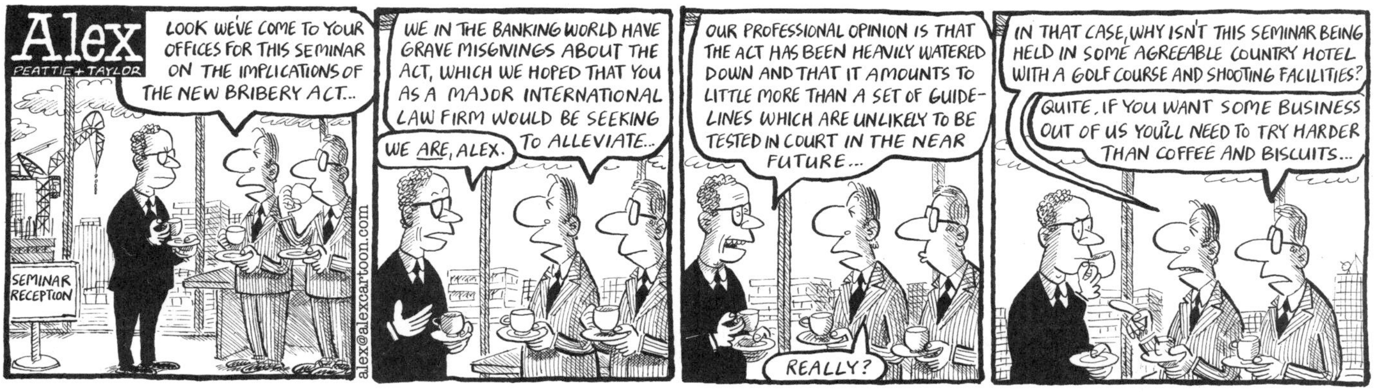
Alex
PEATTIE + TAYLOR
LOOK WE'VE COME TO YOUR OFFICES FOR THIS SEMINAR ON THE IMPLICATIONS OF THE NEW BRIBERY ACT...
SEMINAR RECEPTION
alex@alexcartoon.com
WE IN THE BANKING WORLD HAVE GRAVE MISGIVINGS ABOUT THE ACT, WHICH WE HOPED THAT YOU AS A MAJOR INTERNATIONAL LAW FIRM WOULD BE SEEKING TO ALLEVIATE...
WE ARE, ALEX.
OUR PROFESSIONAL OPINION IS THAT THE ACT HAS BEEN HEAVILY WATERED DOWN AND THAT IT AMOUNTS TO LITTLE MORE THAN A SET OF GUIDE-LINES WHICH ARE UNLIKELY TO BE TESTED IN COURT IN THE NEAR FUTURE...
REALLY?
IN THAT CASE, WHY ISN'T THIS SEMINAR BEING HELD IN SOME AGREEABLE COUNTRY HOTEL WITH A GOLF COURSE AND SHOOTING FACILITIES?
QUITE. IF YOU WANT SOME BUSINESS OUT OF US YOU'LL NEED TO TRY HARDER THAN COFFEE AND BISCUITS...

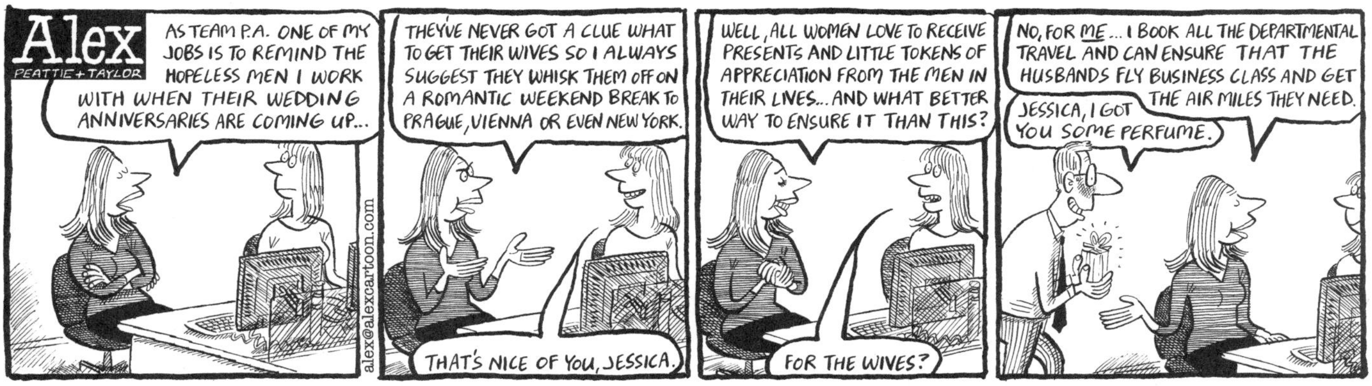
Alex
PEATTIE + TAYLOR
AS TEAM P.A. ONE OF MY JOBS IS TO REMIND THE HOPELESS MEN I WORK WITH WHEN THEIR WEDDING ANNIVERSARIES ARE COMING UP...
alex@alexcartoon.com
THEY'VE NEVER GOT A CLUE WHAT TO GET THEIR WIVES SO I ALWAYS SUGGEST THEY WHISK THEM OFF ON A ROMANTIC WEEKEND BREAK TO PRAGUE, VIENNA OR EVEN NEW YORK.
THAT'S NICE OF YOU, JESSICA.
WELL, ALL WOMEN LOVE TO RECEIVE PRESENTS AND LITTLE TOKENS OF APPRECIATION FROM THE MEN IN THEIR LIVES... AND WHAT BETTER WAY TO ENSURE IT THAN THIS?
FOR THE WIVES?
NO, FOR ME... I BOOK ALL THE DEPARTMENTAL TRAVEL AND CAN ENSURE THAT THE HUSBANDS FLY BUSINESS CLASS AND GET THE AIR MILES THEY NEED.
JESSICA, I GOT YOU SOME PERFUME.

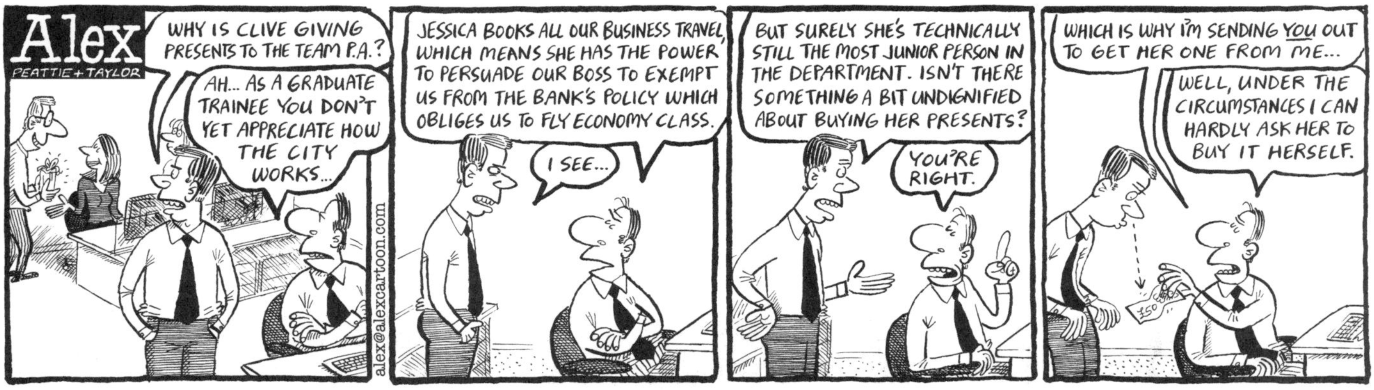
Alex
PEATTIE + TAYLOR
WHY IS CLIVE GIVING PRESENTS TO THE TEAM P.A.?
AH... AS A GRADUATE TRAINEE YOU DON'T YET APPRECIATE HOW THE CITY WORKS...
alex@alexcartoon.com
JESSICA BOOKS ALL OUR BUSINESS TRAVEL, WHICH MEANS SHE HAS THE POWER TO PERSUADE OUR BOSS TO EXEMPT US FROM THE BANK'S POLICY WHICH OBLIGES US TO FLY ECONOMY CLASS.
I SEE...
BUT SURELY SHE'S TECHNICALLY STILL THE MOST JUNIOR PERSON IN THE DEPARTMENT. ISN'T THERE SOMETHING A BIT UNDIGNIFIED ABOUT BUYING HER PRESENTS?
YOU'RE RIGHT.
WHICH IS WHY I'M SENDING YOU OUT TO GET HER ONE FROM ME...
WELL, UNDER THE CIRCUMSTANCES I CAN HARDLY ASK HER TO BUY IT HERSELF.

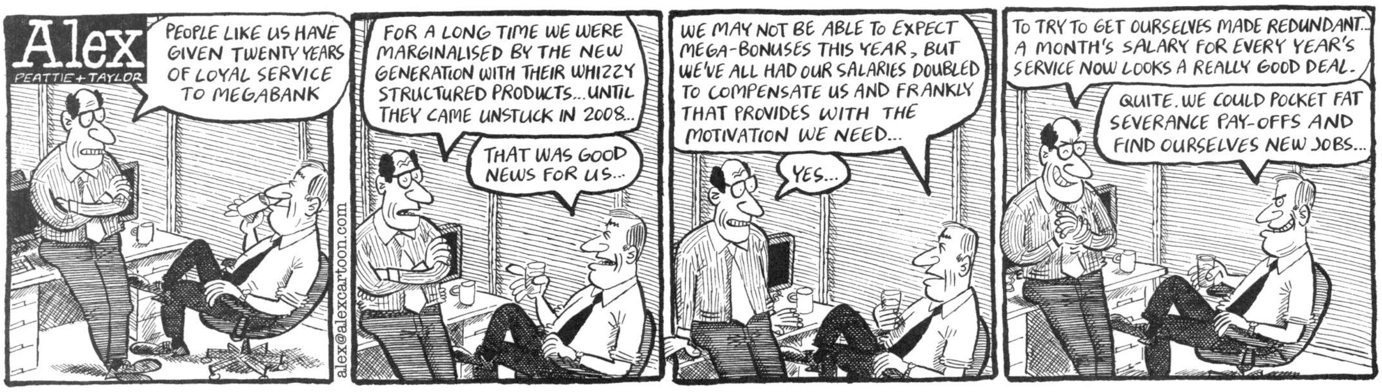
Alex
PEATTIE + TAYLOR
PEOPLE LIKE US HAVE GIVEN TWENTY YEARS OF LOYAL SERVICE TO MEGABANK
FOR A LONG TIME WE WERE MARGINALISED BY THE NEW GENERATION WITH THEIR WHIZZY STRUCTURED PRODUCTS... UNTIL THEY CAME UNSTUCK IN 2008...
THAT WAS GOOD NEWS FOR US...
alex@alexcartoon.com
WE MAY NOT BE ABLE TO EXPECT MEGA-BONUSES THIS YEAR, BUT WE'VE ALL HAD OUR SALARIES DOUBLED TO COMPENSATE US AND FRANKLY THAT PROVIDES WITH THE MOTIVATION WE NEED...
YES...
TO TRY TO GET OURSELVES MADE REDUNDANT... A MONTH'S SALARY FOR EVERY YEAR'S SERVICE NOW LOOKS A REALLY GOOD DEAL.
QUITE. WE COULD POCKET FAT SEVERANCE PAY-OFFS AND FIND OURSELVES NEW JOBS...

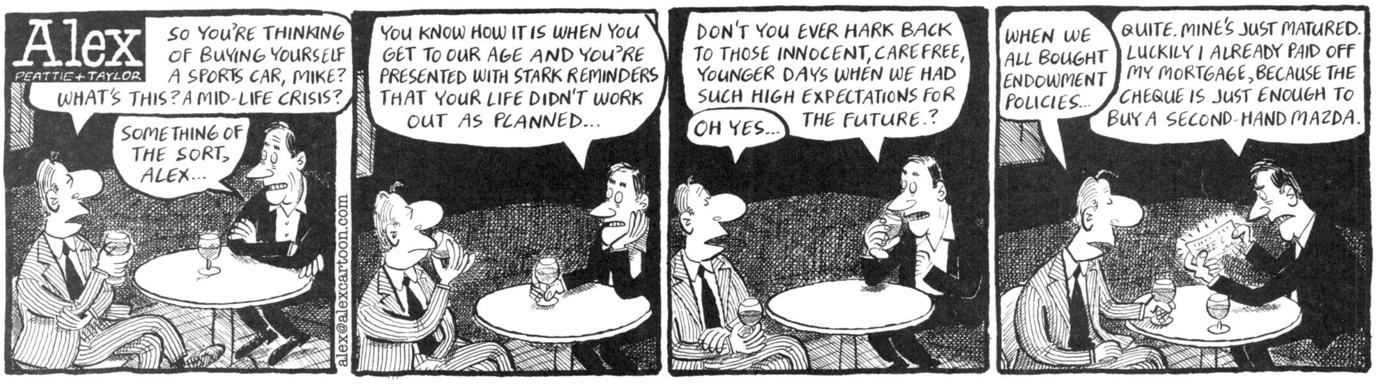
Alex
PEATTIE + TAYLOR
SO YOU'RE THINKING OF BUYING YOURSELF A SPORTS CAR, MIKE? WHAT'S THIS? A MID-LIFE CRISIS?
SOMETHING OF THE SORT, ALEX...
alex@alexcartoon.com
YOU KNOW HOW IT IS WHEN YOU GET TO OUR AGE AND YOU'RE PRESENTED WITH STARK REMINDERS THAT YOUR LIFE DIDN'T WORK OUT AS PLANNED...
DON'T YOU EVER HARK BACK TO THOSE INNOCENT, CAREFREE, YOUNGER DAYS WHEN WE HAD SUCH HIGH EXPECTATIONS FOR THE FUTURE?
OH YES...
WHEN WE ALL BOUGHT ENDOWMENT POLICIES...
QUITE. MINE'S JUST MATURED. LUCKILY I ALREADY PAID OFF MY MORTGAGE, BECAUSE THE CHEQUE IS JUST ENOUGH TO BUY A SECOND-HAND MAZDA.

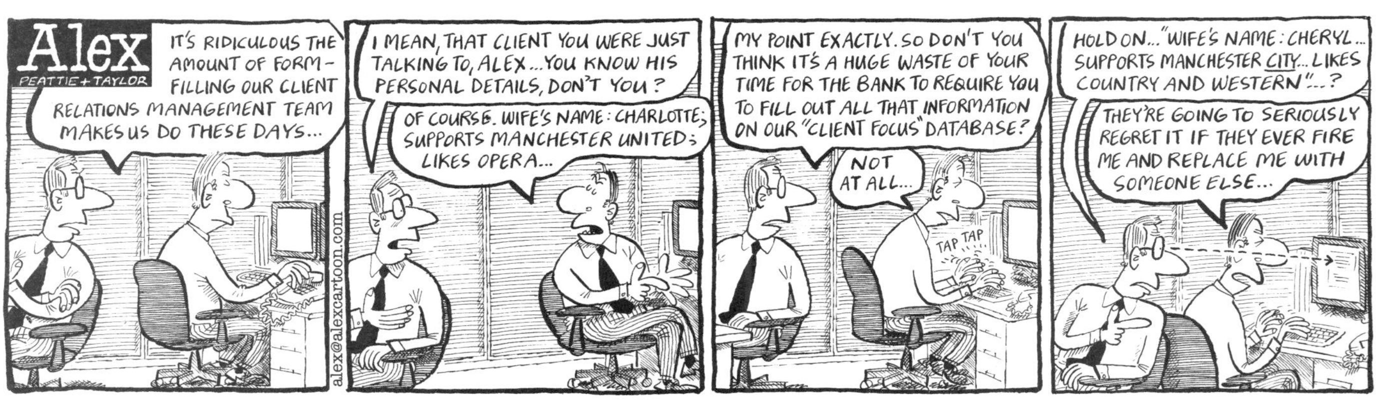
Alex
PEATTIE + TAYLOR
IT'S RIDICULOUS THE AMOUNT OF FORM-FILLING OUR CLIENT RELATIONS MANAGEMENT TEAM MAKES US DO THESE DAYS...
alex@alexcartoon.com
I MEAN, THAT CLIENT YOU WERE JUST TALKING TO, ALEX... YOU KNOW HIS PERSONAL DETAILS, DON'T YOU?
OF COURSE. WIFE'S NAME: CHARLOTTE; SUPPORTS MANCHESTER UNITED; LIKES OPERA...
MY POINT EXACTLY. SO DON'T YOU THINK IT'S A HUGE WASTE OF YOUR TIME FOR THE BANK TO REQUIRE YOU TO FILL OUT ALL THAT INFORMATION ON OUR "CLIENT FOCUS" DATABASE?
NOT AT ALL...
TAP TAP
HOLD ON..."WIFE'S NAME: CHERYL... SUPPORTS MANCHESTER CITY... LIKES COUNTRY AND WESTERN"...?
THEY'RE GOING TO SERIOUSLY REGRET IT IF THEY EVER FIRE ME AND REPLACE ME WITH SOMEONE ELSE...

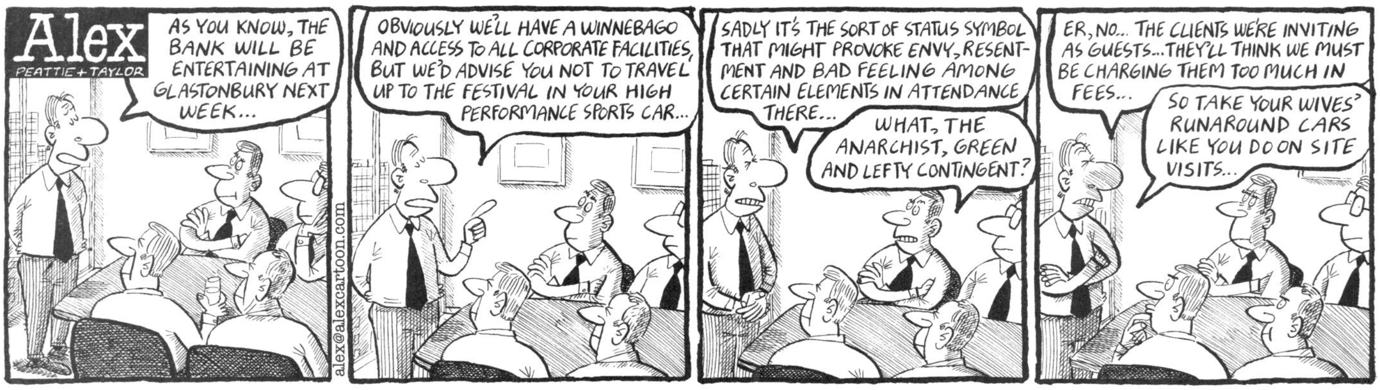
Alex
PEATTIE + TAYLOR
AS YOU KNOW, THE BANK WILL BE ENTERTAINING AT GLASTONBURY NEXT WEEK...
alex@alexcartoon.com
OBVIOUSLY WE'LL HAVE A WINNEBAGO AND ACCESS TO ALL CORPORATE FACILITIES, BUT WE'D ADVISE YOU NOT TO TRAVEL UP TO THE FESTIVAL IN YOUR HIGH PERFORMANCE SPORTS CAR...
SADLY IT'S THE SORT OF STATUS SYMBOL THAT MIGHT PROVOKE ENVY, RESENTMENT AND BAD FEELING AMONG CERTAIN ELEMENTS IN ATTENDANCE THERE...
WHAT, THE ANARCHIST, GREEN AND LEFTY CONTINGENT?
ER, NO... THE CLIENTS WE'RE INVITING AS GUESTS... THEY'LL THINK WE MUST BE CHARGING THEM TOO MUCH IN FEES...
SO TAKE YOUR WIVES' RUNAROUND CARS LIKE YOU DO ON SITE VISITS...

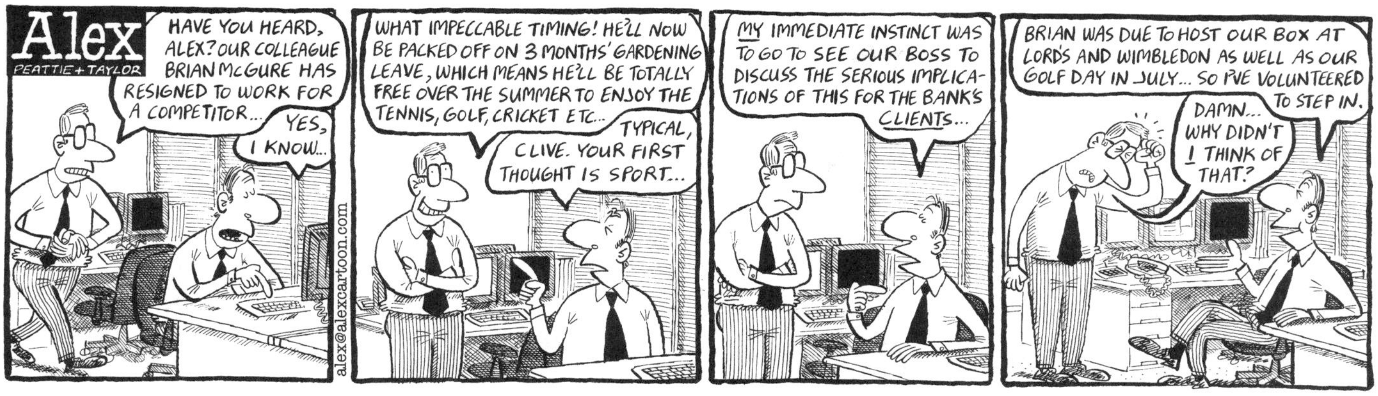
Alex
PEATTIE + TAYLOR
HAVE YOU HEARD, ALEX? OUR COLLEAGUE BRIAN McGURE HAS RESIGNED TO WORK FOR A COMPETITOR...
YES, I KNOW...
alex@alexcartoon.com
WHAT IMPECCABLE TIMING! HE'LL NOW BE PACKED OFF ON 3 MONTHS' GARDENING LEAVE, WHICH MEANS HE'LL BE TOTALLY FREE OVER THE SUMMER TO ENJOY THE TENNIS, GOLF, CRICKET ETC...
TYPICAL, CLIVE. YOUR FIRST THOUGHT IS SPORT...
MY IMMEDIATE INSTINCT WAS TO GO TO SEE OUR BOSS TO DISCUSS THE SERIOUS IMPLICATIONS OF THIS FOR THE BANK'S CLIENTS...
BRIAN WAS DUE TO HOST OUR BOX AT LORD'S AND WIMBLEDON AS WELL AS OUR GOLF DAY IN JULY... SO I'VE VOLUNTEERED TO STEP IN.
DAMN... WHY DIDN'T I THINK OF THAT?

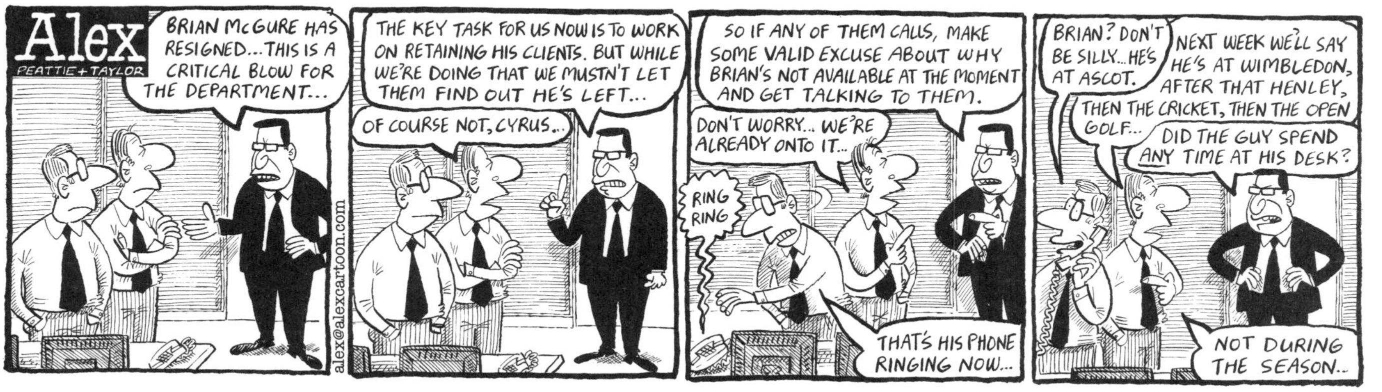
Alex
PEATTIE + TAYLOR
BRIAN McGURE HAS RESIGNED... THIS IS A CRITICAL BLOW FOR THE DEPARTMENT...
alex@alexcartoon.com
THE KEY TASK FOR US NOW IS TO WORK ON RETAINING HIS CLIENTS. BUT WHILE WE'RE DOING THAT WE MUSTN'T LET THEM FIND OUT HE'S LEFT...
OF COURSE NOT, CYRUS...
SO IF ANY OF THEM CALLS, MAKE SOME VALID EXCUSE ABOUT WHY BRIAN'S NOT AVAILABLE AT THE MOMENT AND GET TALKING TO THEM.
DON'T WORRY... WE'RE ALREADY ONTO IT...
RING RING
THAT'S HIS PHONE RINGING NOW...
BRIAN? DON'T BE SILLY... HE'S AT ASCOT.
NEXT WEEK WE'LL SAY HE'S AT WIMBLEDON, AFTER THAT HENLEY, THEN THE CRICKET, THEN THE OPEN GOLF...
DID THE GUY SPEND ANY TIME AT HIS DESK?
NOT DURING THE SEASON...

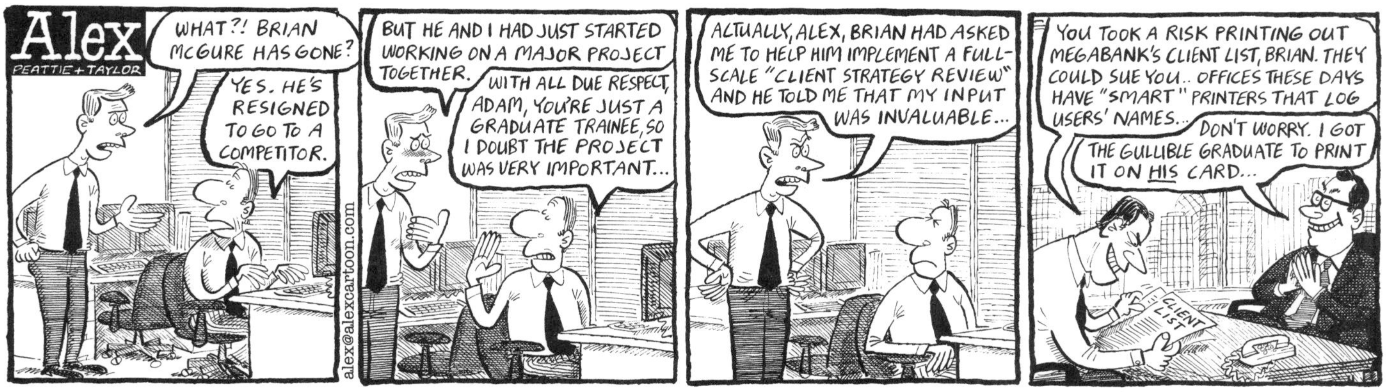
Alex
PEATTIE + TAYLOR
WHAT?! BRIAN McGURE HAS GONE?
YES. HE'S RESIGNED TO GO TO A COMPETITOR.
alex@alexcartoon.com
BUT HE AND I HAD JUST STARTED WORKING ON A MAJOR PROJECT TOGETHER.
WITH ALL DUE RESPECT, ADAM, YOU'RE JUST A GRADUATE TRAINEE, SO I DOUBT THE PROJECT WAS VERY IMPORTANT...
ACTUALLY, ALEX, BRIAN HAD ASKED ME TO HELP HIM IMPLEMENT A FULL-SCALE "CLIENT STRATEGY REVIEW" AND HE TOLD ME THAT MY INPUT WAS INVALUABLE...
YOU TOOK A RISK PRINTING OUT MEGABANK'S CLIENT LIST, BRIAN. THEY COULD SUE YOU.. OFFICES THESE DAYS HAVE "SMART" PRINTERS THAT LOG USERS' NAMES...
DON'T WORRY. I GOT THE GULLIBLE GRADUATE TO PRINT IT ON HIS CARD...
CLIENT LIST

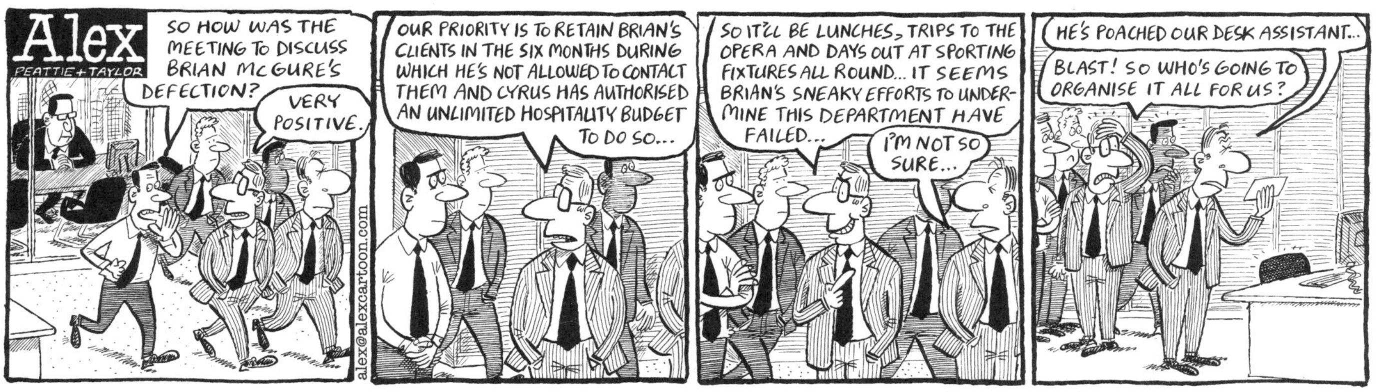
Alex
PEATTIE + TAYLOR
SO HOW WAS THE MEETING TO DISCUSS BRIAN McGURE'S DEFECTION?
VERY POSITIVE.
alex@alexcartoon.com
OUR PRIORITY IS TO RETAIN BRIAN'S CLIENTS IN THE SIX MONTHS DURING WHICH HE'S NOT ALLOWED TO CONTACT THEM AND CYRUS HAS AUTHORISED AN UNLIMITED HOSPITALITY BUDGET TO DO SO...
SO IT'LL BE LUNCHES, TRIPS TO THE OPERA AND DAYS OUT AT SPORTING FIXTURES ALL ROUND... IT SEEMS BRIAN'S SNEAKY EFFORTS TO UNDERMINE THIS DEPARTMENT HAVE FAILED...
I'M NOT SO SURE...
HE'S POACHED OUR DESK ASSISTANT...
BLAST! SO WHO'S GOING TO ORGANISE IT ALL FOR US?

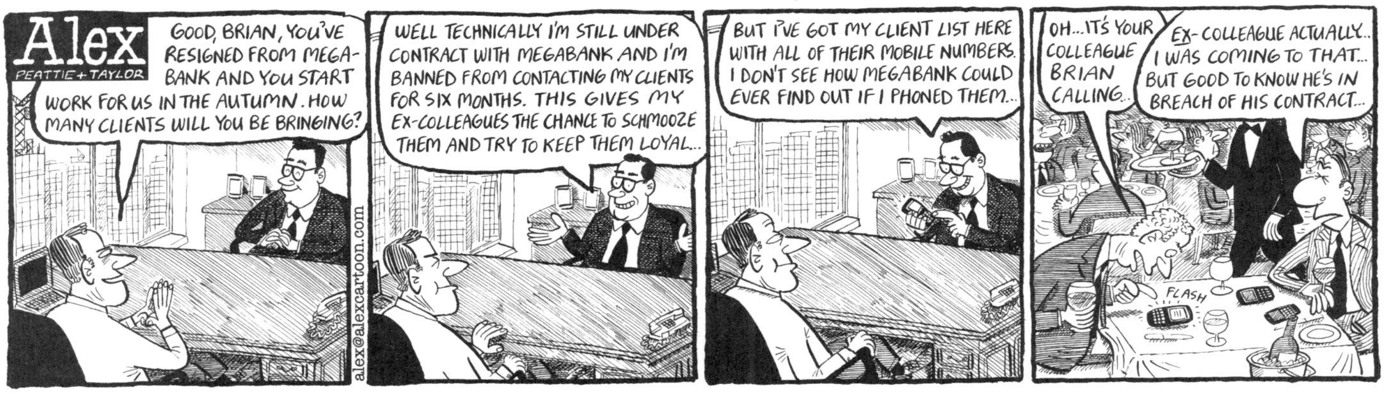
Alex
PEATTIE + TAYLOR
GOOD, BRIAN, YOU'VE RESIGNED FROM MEGA-BANK AND YOU START WORK FOR US IN THE AUTUMN. HOW MANY CLIENTS WILL YOU BE BRINGING?
WELL TECHNICALLY I'M STILL UNDER CONTRACT WITH MEGABANK AND I'M BANNED FROM CONTACTING MY CLIENTS FOR SIX MONTHS. THIS GIVES MY EX-COLLEAGUES THE CHANCE TO SCHMOOZE THEM AND TRY TO KEEP THEM LOYAL...
alex@alexcartoon.com
BUT I'VE GOT MY CLIENT LIST HERE WITH ALL OF THEIR MOBILE NUMBERS. I DON'T SEE HOW MEGABANK COULD EVER FIND OUT IF I PHONED THEM...
OH...IT'S YOUR COLLEAGUE BRIAN CALLING...
EX-COLLEAGUE ACTUALLY... I WAS COMING TO THAT... BUT GOOD TO KNOW HE'S IN BREACH OF HIS CONTRACT...
FLASH

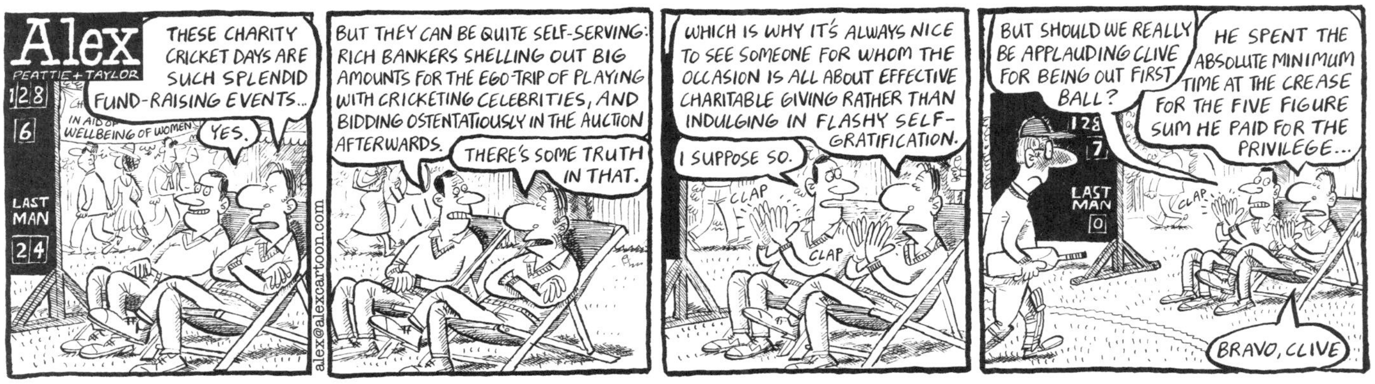
Alex
PEATTIE + TAYLOR
THESE CHARITY CRICKET DAYS ARE SUCH SPLENDID FUND-RAISING EVENTS...
YES.
128
6
LAST MAN
24
WELLBEING OF WOMEN
alex@alexcartoon.com
BUT THEY CAN BE QUITE SELF-SERVING: RICH BANKERS SHELLING OUT BIG AMOUNTS FOR THE EGO-TRIP OF PLAYING WITH CRICKETING CELEBRITIES, AND BIDDING OSTENTATIOUSLY IN THE AUCTION AFTERWARDS.
THERE'S SOME TRUTH IN THAT.
WHICH IS WHY IT'S ALWAYS NICE TO SEE SOMEONE FOR WHOM THE OCCASION IS ALL ABOUT EFFECTIVE CHARITABLE GIVING RATHER THAN INDULGING IN FLASHY SELF-GRATIFICATION.
I SUPPOSE SO.
CLAP
CLAP
BUT SHOULD WE REALLY BE APPLAUDING CLIVE FOR BEING OUT FIRST BALL?
HE SPENT THE ABSOLUTE MINIMUM TIME AT THE CREASE FOR THE FIVE FIGURE SUM HE PAID FOR THE PRIVILEGE...
128
7
LAST MAN
0
CLAP
BRAVO, CLIVE

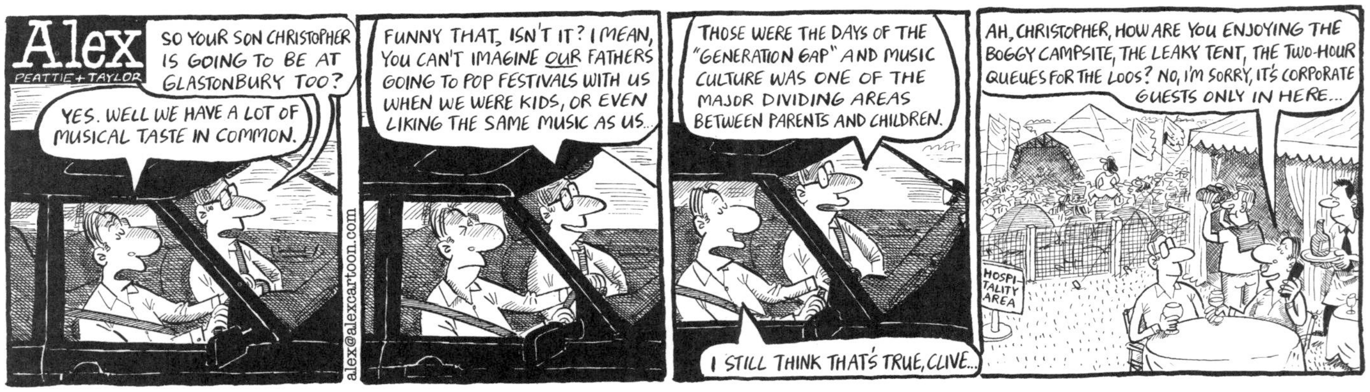
Alex
PEATTIE + TAYLOR
SO YOUR SON CHRISTOPHER IS GOING TO BE AT GLASTONBURY TOO?
YES. WELL WE HAVE A LOT OF MUSICAL TASTE IN COMMON.
alex@alexcartoon.com
FUNNY THAT, ISN'T IT? I MEAN, YOU CAN'T IMAGINE OUR FATHERS GOING TO POP FESTIVALS WITH US WHEN WE WERE KIDS, OR EVEN LIKING THE SAME MUSIC AS US...
THOSE WERE THE DAYS OF THE "GENERATION GAP" AND MUSIC CULTURE WAS ONE OF THE MAJOR DIVIDING AREAS BETWEEN PARENTS AND CHILDREN.
I STILL THINK THAT'S TRUE, CLIVE...
AH, CHRISTOPHER, HOW ARE YOU ENJOYING THE BOGGY CAMPSITE, THE LEAKY TENT, THE TWO-HOUR QUEUES FOR THE LOOS? NO, I'M SORRY, IT'S CORPORATE GUESTS ONLY IN HERE...
HOSPITALITY AREA

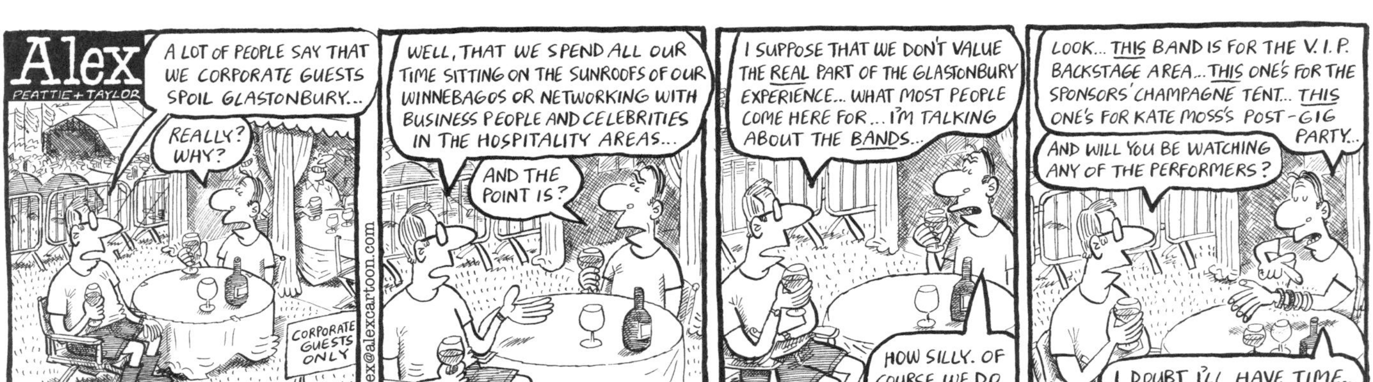
Alex
PEATTIE + TAYLOR
A LOT OF PEOPLE SAY THAT WE CORPORATE GUESTS SPOIL GLASTONBURY...
REALLY? WHY?
CORPORATE GUESTS ONLY
alex@alexcartoon.com
WELL, THAT WE SPEND ALL OUR TIME SITTING ON THE SUNROOFS OF OUR WINNEBAGOS OR NETWORKING WITH BUSINESS PEOPLE AND CELEBRITIES IN THE HOSPITALITY AREAS...
AND THE POINT IS?
I SUPPOSE THAT WE DON'T VALUE THE REAL PART OF THE GLASTONBURY EXPERIENCE... WHAT MOST PEOPLE COME HERE FOR... I'M TALKING ABOUT THE BANDS...
HOW SILLY. OF COURSE WE DO.
LOOK... THIS BAND IS FOR THE V.I.P. BACKSTAGE AREA... THIS ONE'S FOR THE SPONSORS' CHAMPAGNE TENT... THIS ONE'S FOR KATE MOSS'S POST-GIG PARTY...
AND WILL YOU BE WATCHING ANY OF THE PERFORMERS?
I DOUBT I'LL HAVE TIME...

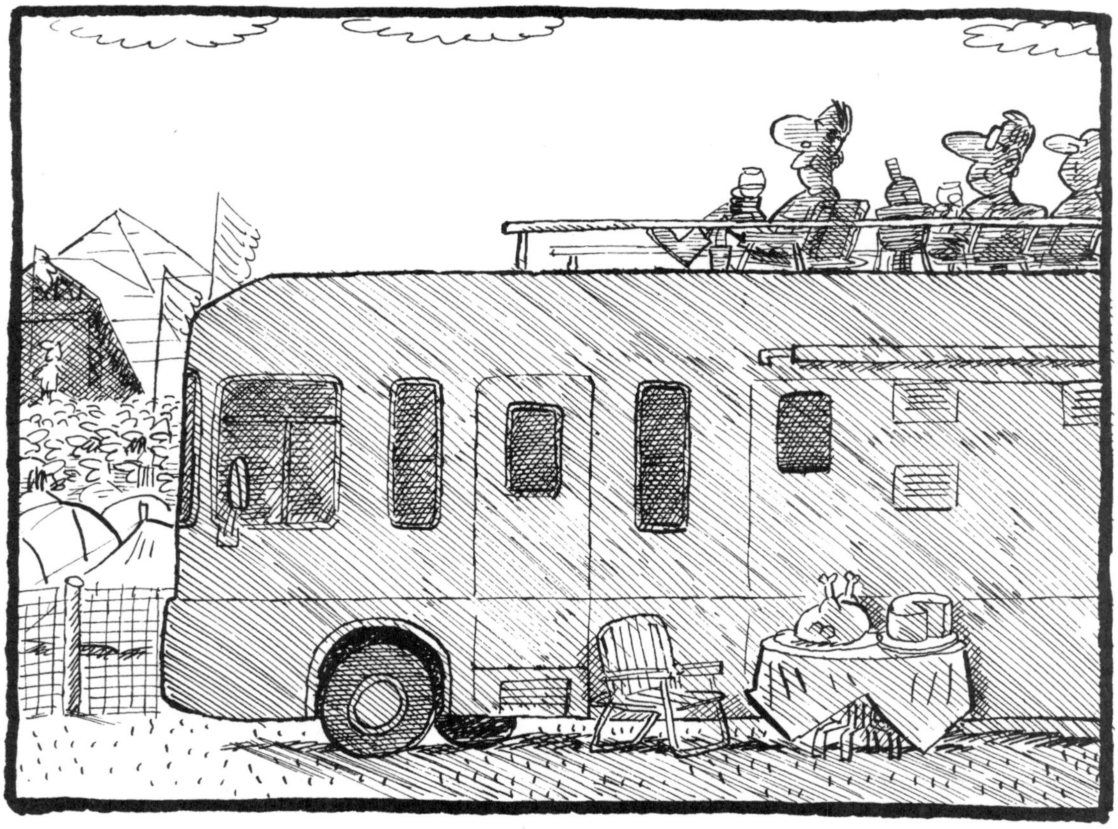

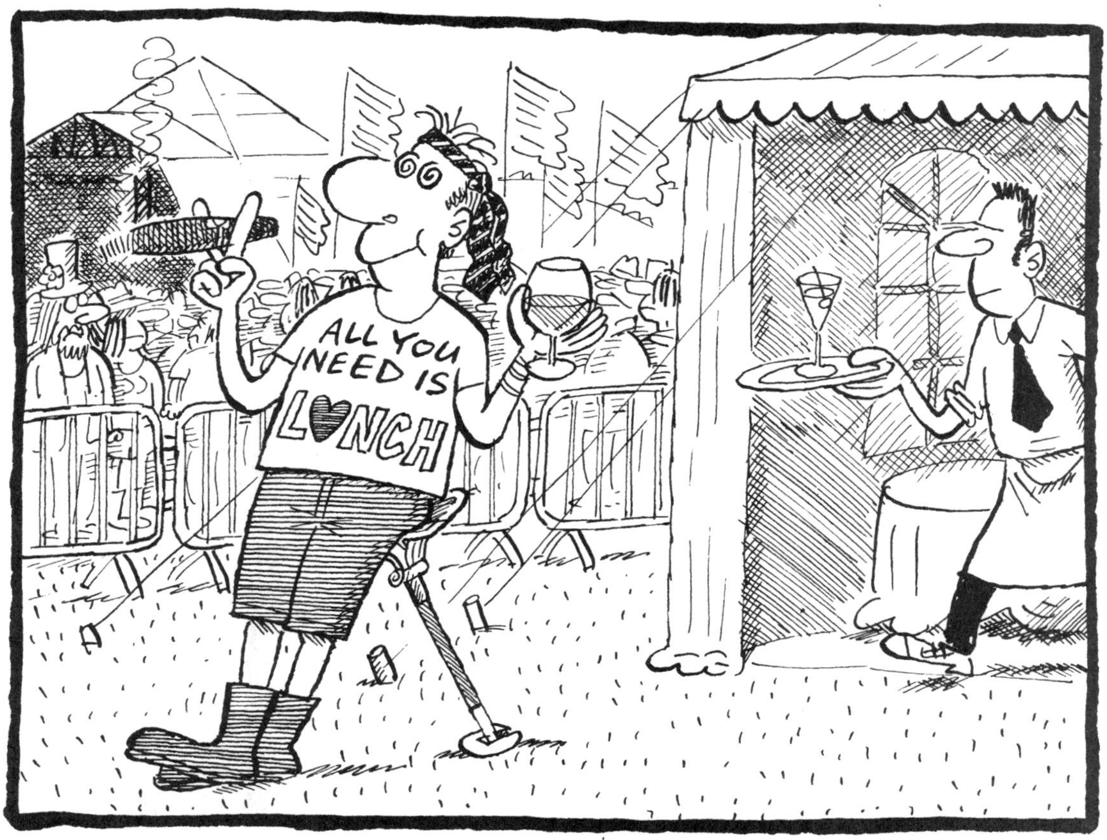
ALL YOU NEED IS L♥NCH

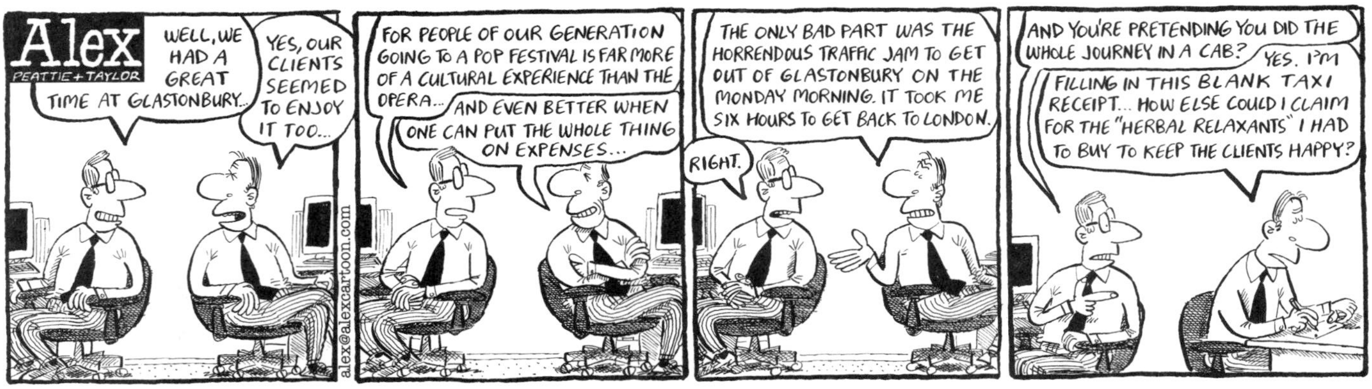

Alex
PEATTIE + TAYLOR
WELL, WE HAD A GREAT TIME AT GLASTONBURY...
YES, OUR CLIENTS SEEMED TO ENJOY IT TOO...
FOR PEOPLE OF OUR GENERATION GOING TO A POP FESTIVAL IS FAR MORE OF A CULTURAL EXPERIENCE THAN THE OPERA...
AND EVEN BETTER WHEN ONE CAN PUT THE WHOLE THING ON EXPENSES...
THE ONLY BAD PART WAS THE HORRENDOUS TRAFFIC JAM TO GET OUT OF GLASTONBURY ON THE MONDAY MORNING. IT TOOK ME SIX HOURS TO GET BACK TO LONDON.
RIGHT.
AND YOU'RE PRETENDING YOU DID THE WHOLE JOURNEY IN A CAB?
YES. I'M FILLING IN THIS BLANK TAXI RECEIPT... HOW ELSE COULD I CLAIM FOR THE "HERBAL RELAXANTS" I HAD TO BUY TO KEEP THE CLIENTS HAPPY?
alex@alexcartoon.com

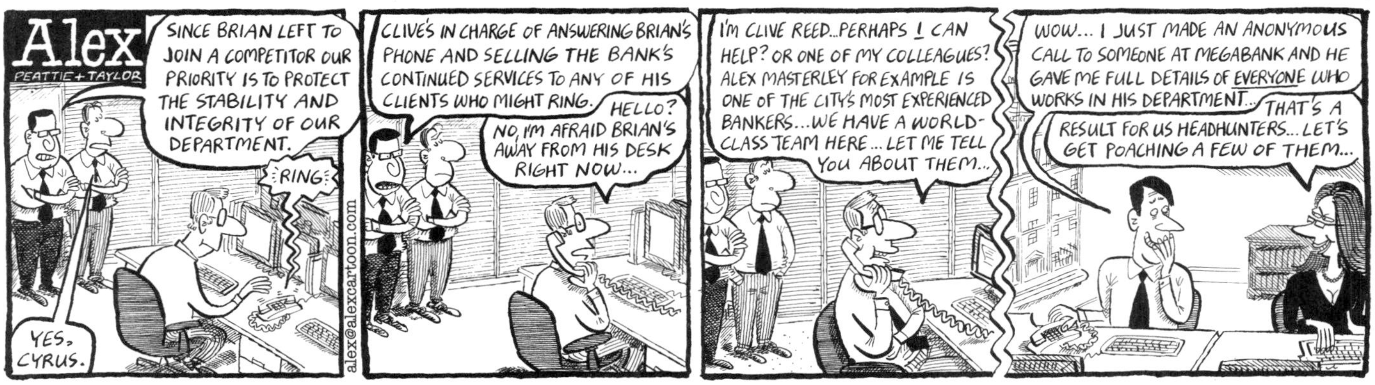

Alex
PEATTIE + TAYLOR
SINCE BRIAN LEFT TO JOIN A COMPETITOR OUR PRIORITY IS TO PROTECT THE STABILITY AND INTEGRITY OF OUR DEPARTMENT.
RING
YES, CYRUS.
CLIVE'S IN CHARGE OF ANSWERING BRIAN'S PHONE AND SELLING THE BANK'S CONTINUED SERVICES TO ANY OF HIS CLIENTS WHO MIGHT RING.
HELLO?
NO, I'M AFRAID BRIAN'S AWAY FROM HIS DESK RIGHT NOW...
I'M CLIVE REED...PERHAPS I CAN HELP? OR ONE OF MY COLLEAGUES? ALEX MASTERLEY FOR EXAMPLE IS ONE OF THE CITY'S MOST EXPERIENCED BANKERS...WE HAVE A WORLD-CLASS TEAM HERE... LET ME TELL YOU ABOUT THEM...
WOW... I JUST MADE AN ANONYMOUS CALL TO SOMEONE AT MEGABANK AND HE GAVE ME FULL DETAILS OF EVERYONE WHO WORKS IN HIS DEPARTMENT...
THAT'S A RESULT FOR US HEADHUNTERS... LET'S GET POACHING A FEW OF THEM...
alex@alexcartoon.com

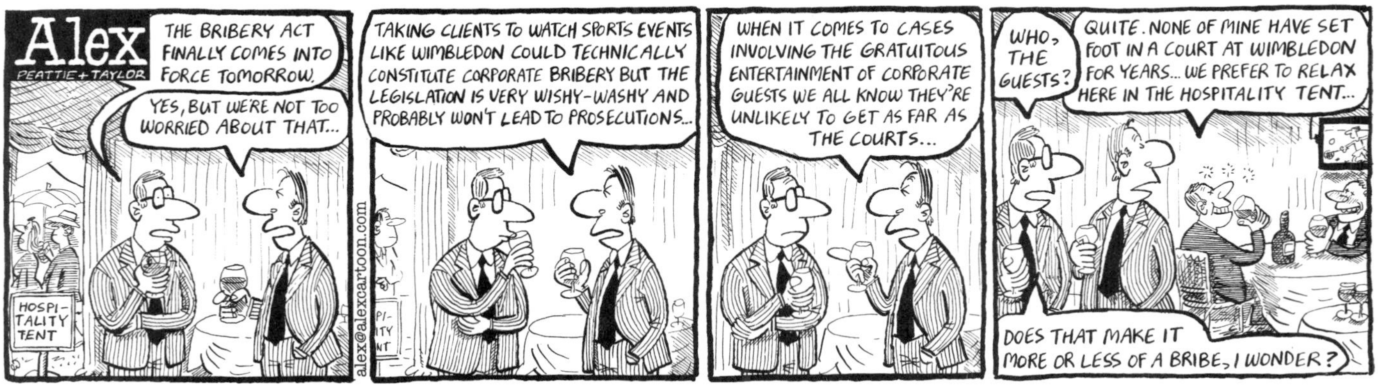

Alex
PEATTIE + TAYLOR
THE BRIBERY ACT FINALLY COMES INTO FORCE TOMORROW.
YES, BUT WE'RE NOT TOO WORRIED ABOUT THAT...
HOSPITALITY TENT
TAKING CLIENTS TO WATCH SPORTS EVENTS LIKE WIMBLEDON COULD TECHNICALLY CONSTITUTE CORPORATE BRIBERY BUT THE LEGISLATION IS VERY WISHY-WASHY AND PROBABLY WON'T LEAD TO PROSECUTIONS...
WHEN IT COMES TO CASES INVOLVING THE GRATUITOUS ENTERTAINMENT OF CORPORATE GUESTS WE ALL KNOW THEY'RE UNLIKELY TO GET AS FAR AS THE COURTS...
WHO, THE GUESTS?
QUITE. NONE OF MINE HAVE SET FOOT IN A COURT AT WIMBLEDON FOR YEARS... WE PREFER TO RELAX HERE IN THE HOSPITALITY TENT...
DOES THAT MAKE IT MORE OR LESS OF A BRIBE, I WONDER?
alex@alexcartoon.com

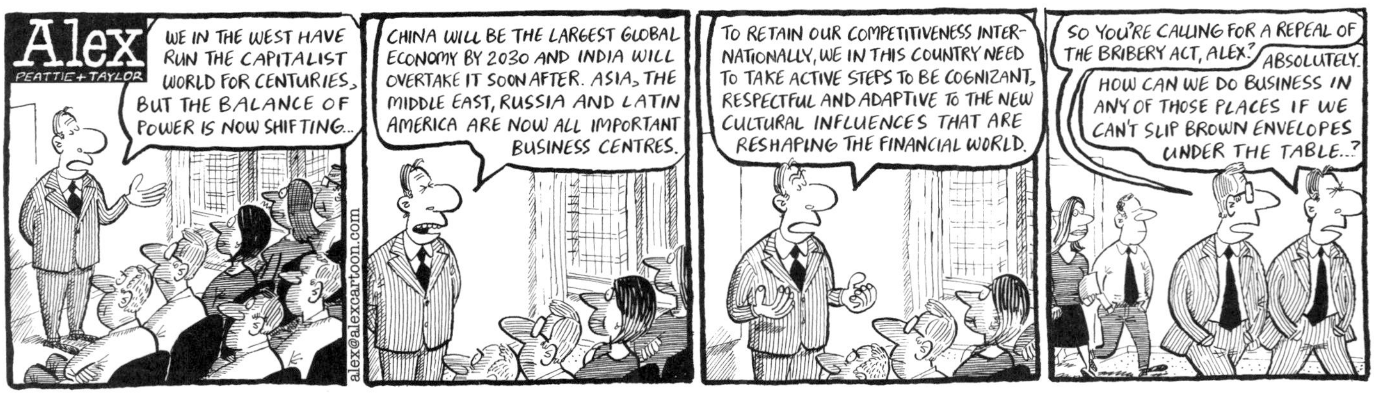

Alex
PEATTIE + TAYLOR
WE IN THE WEST HAVE RUN THE CAPITALIST WORLD FOR CENTURIES, BUT THE BALANCE OF POWER IS NOW SHIFTING...
CHINA WILL BE THE LARGEST GLOBAL ECONOMY BY 2030 AND INDIA WILL OVERTAKE IT SOON AFTER. ASIA, THE MIDDLE EAST, RUSSIA AND LATIN AMERICA ARE NOW ALL IMPORTANT BUSINESS CENTRES.
TO RETAIN OUR COMPETITIVENESS INTERNATIONALLY, WE IN THIS COUNTRY NEED TO TAKE ACTIVE STEPS TO BE COGNIZANT, RESPECTFUL AND ADAPTIVE TO THE NEW CULTURAL INFLUENCES THAT ARE RESHAPING THE FINANCIAL WORLD.
SO YOU'RE CALLING FOR A REPEAL OF THE BRIBERY ACT, ALEX?
ABSOLUTELY.
HOW CAN WE DO BUSINESS IN ANY OF THOSE PLACES IF WE CAN'T SLIP BROWN ENVELOPES UNDER THE TABLE..?
alex@alexcartoon.com

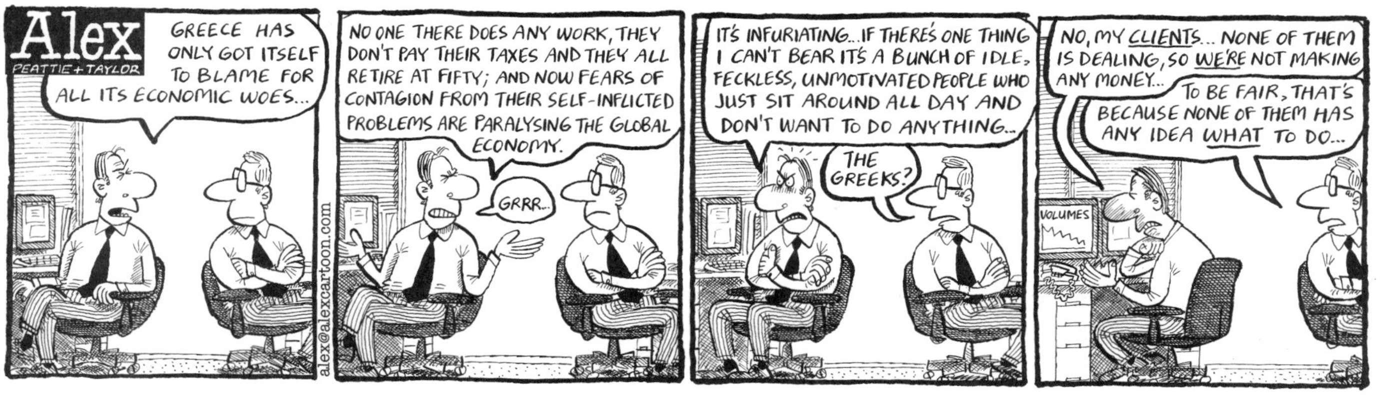
Alex
PEATTIE+TAYLOR
GREECE HAS ONLY GOT ITSELF TO BLAME FOR ALL ITS ECONOMIC WOES...
NO ONE THERE DOES ANY WORK, THEY DON'T PAY THEIR TAXES AND THEY ALL RETIRE AT FIFTY; AND NOW FEARS OF CONTAGION FROM THEIR SELF-INFLICTED PROBLEMS ARE PARALYSING THE GLOBAL ECONOMY.
GRRR...
alex@alexcartoon.com
IT'S INFURIATING... IF THERE'S ONE THING I CAN'T BEAR IT'S A BUNCH OF IDLE, FECKLESS, UNMOTIVATED PEOPLE WHO JUST SIT AROUND ALL DAY AND DON'T WANT TO DO ANYTHING...
THE GREEKS?
NO, MY CLIENTS... NONE OF THEM IS DEALING, SO WE'RE NOT MAKING ANY MONEY...
TO BE FAIR, THAT'S BECAUSE NONE OF THEM HAS ANY IDEA WHAT TO DO...
VOLUMES

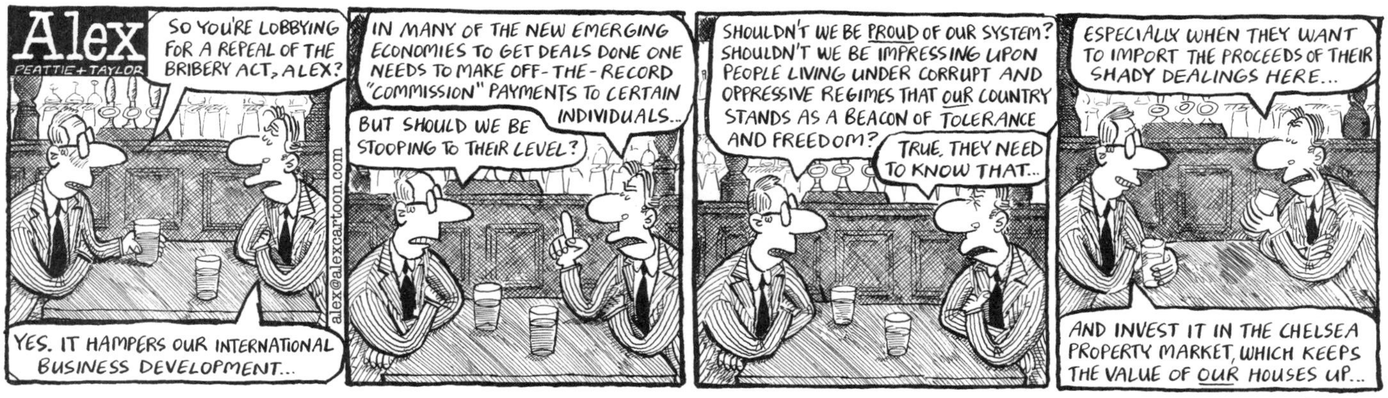
Alex
PEATTIE+TAYLOR
SO YOU'RE LOBBYING FOR A REPEAL OF THE BRIBERY ACT, ALEX?
YES. IT HAMPERS OUR INTERNATIONAL BUSINESS DEVELOPMENT...
alex@alexcartoon.com
IN MANY OF THE NEW EMERGING ECONOMIES TO GET DEALS DONE ONE NEEDS TO MAKE OFF-THE-RECORD "COMMISSION" PAYMENTS TO CERTAIN INDIVIDUALS...
BUT SHOULD WE BE STOOPING TO THEIR LEVEL?
SHOULDN'T WE BE PROUD OF OUR SYSTEM? SHOULDN'T WE BE IMPRESSING UPON PEOPLE LIVING UNDER CORRUPT AND OPPRESSIVE REGIMES THAT OUR COUNTRY STANDS AS A BEACON OF TOLERANCE AND FREEDOM?
TRUE, THEY NEED TO KNOW THAT...
ESPECIALLY WHEN THEY WANT TO IMPORT THE PROCEEDS OF THEIR SHADY DEALINGS HERE...
AND INVEST IT IN THE CHELSEA PROPERTY MARKET, WHICH KEEPS THE VALUE OF OUR HOUSES UP...

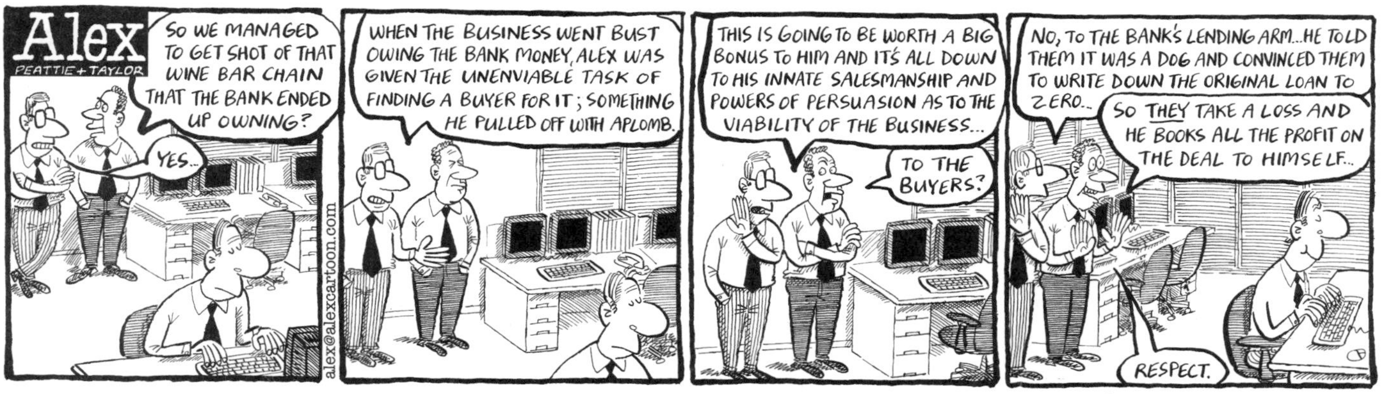
Alex
PEATTIE+TAYLOR
SO WE MANAGED TO GET SHOT OF THAT WINE BAR CHAIN THAT THE BANK ENDED UP OWNING?
YES...
alex@alexcartoon.com
WHEN THE BUSINESS WENT BUST OWING THE BANK MONEY, ALEX WAS GIVEN THE UNENVIABLE TASK OF FINDING A BUYER FOR IT; SOMETHING HE PULLED OFF WITH APLOMB.
THIS IS GOING TO BE WORTH A BIG BONUS TO HIM AND IT'S ALL DOWN TO HIS INNATE SALESMANSHIP AND POWERS OF PERSUASION AS TO THE VIABILITY OF THE BUSINESS...
TO THE BUYERS?
NO, TO THE BANK'S LENDING ARM... HE TOLD THEM IT WAS A DOG AND CONVINCED THEM TO WRITE DOWN THE ORIGINAL LOAN TO ZERO...
SO THEY TAKE A LOSS AND HE BOOKS ALL THE PROFIT ON THE DEAL TO HIMSELF...
RESPECT.

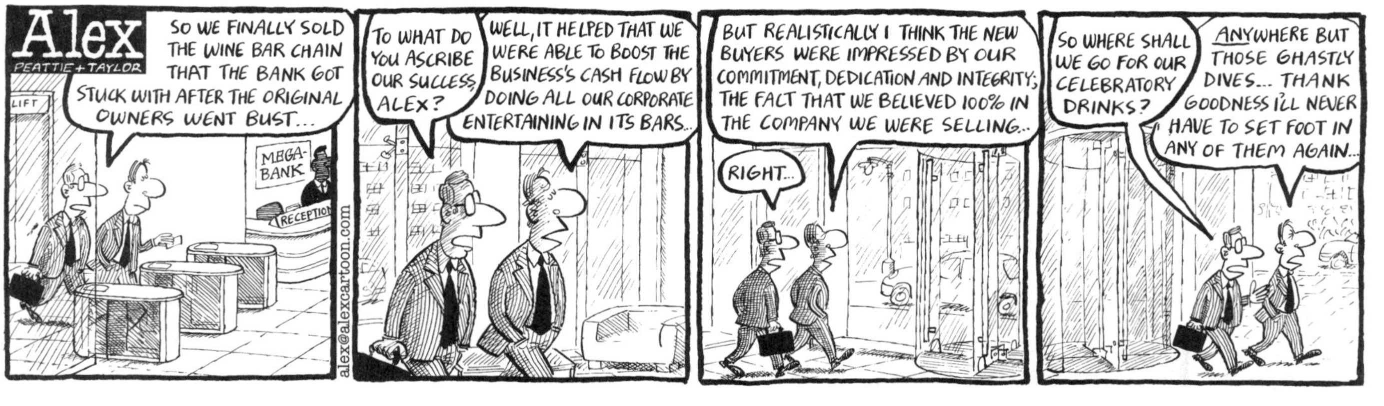
Alex
PEATTIE+TAYLOR
SO WE FINALLY SOLD THE WINE BAR CHAIN THAT THE BANK GOT STUCK WITH AFTER THE ORIGINAL OWNERS WENT BUST...
LIFT
MEGA-BANK
RECEPTION
alex@alexcartoon.com
TO WHAT DO YOU ASCRIBE OUR SUCCESS, ALEX?
WELL, IT HELPED THAT WE WERE ABLE TO BOOST THE BUSINESS'S CASH FLOW BY DOING ALL OUR CORPORATE ENTERTAINING IN ITS BARS...
BUT REALISTICALLY I THINK THE NEW BUYERS WERE IMPRESSED BY OUR COMMITMENT, DEDICATION AND INTEGRITY; THE FACT THAT WE BELIEVED 100% IN THE COMPANY WE WERE SELLING...
RIGHT...
SO WHERE SHALL WE GO FOR OUR CELEBRATORY DRINKS?
ANYWHERE BUT THOSE GHASTLY DIVES... THANK GOODNESS I'LL NEVER HAVE TO SET FOOT IN ANY OF THEM AGAIN...

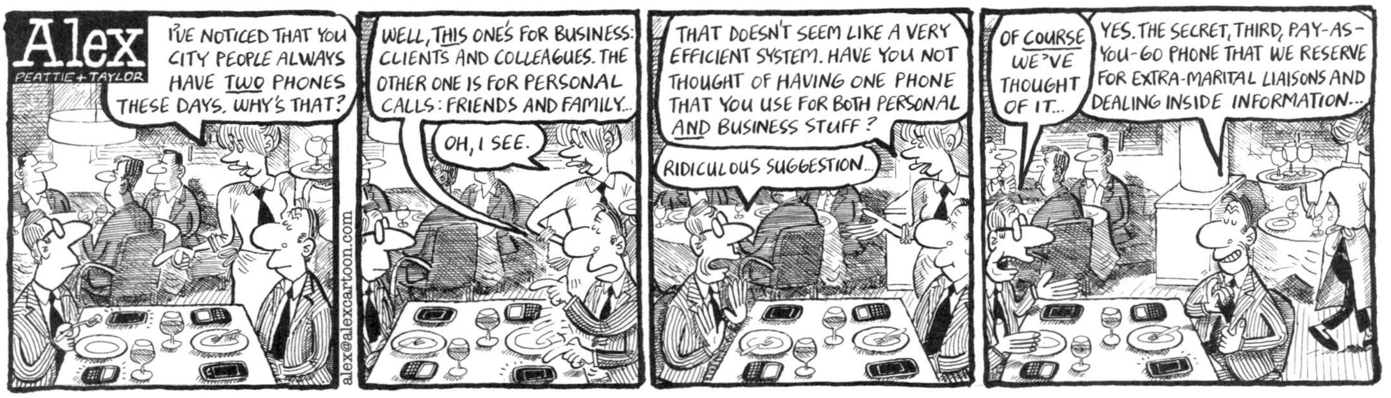
Alex
PEATTIE + TAYLOR
I'VE NOTICED THAT YOU CITY PEOPLE ALWAYS HAVE TWO PHONES THESE DAYS. WHY'S THAT?
WELL, THIS ONE'S FOR BUSINESS: CLIENTS AND COLLEAGUES. THE OTHER ONE IS FOR PERSONAL CALLS: FRIENDS AND FAMILY...
OH, I SEE.
alex@alexcartoon.com
THAT DOESN'T SEEM LIKE A VERY EFFICIENT SYSTEM. HAVE YOU NOT THOUGHT OF HAVING ONE PHONE THAT YOU USE FOR BOTH PERSONAL AND BUSINESS STUFF?
RIDICULOUS SUGGESTION...
OF COURSE WE'VE THOUGHT OF IT...
YES. THE SECRET, THIRD, PAY-AS-YOU-GO PHONE THAT WE RESERVE FOR EXTRA-MARITAL LIAISONS AND DEALING INSIDE INFORMATION...

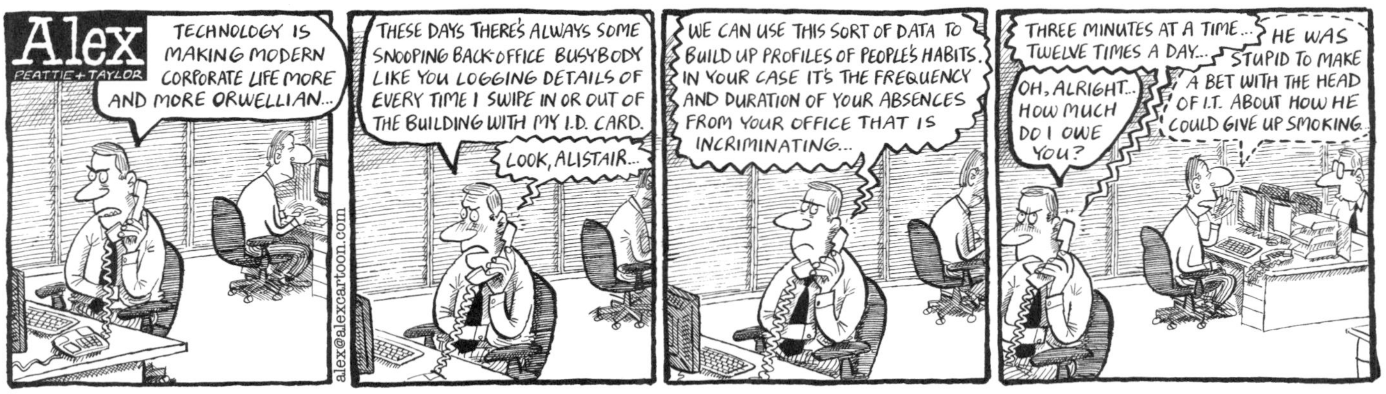
Alex
PEATTIE + TAYLOR
TECHNOLOGY IS MAKING MODERN CORPORATE LIFE MORE AND MORE ORWELLIAN...
alex@alexcartoon.com
THESE DAYS THERE'S ALWAYS SOME SNOOPING BACK OFFICE BUSYBODY LIKE YOU LOGGING DETAILS OF EVERY TIME I SWIPE IN OR OUT OF THE BUILDING WITH MY I.D. CARD.
LOOK, ALISTAIR...
WE CAN USE THIS SORT OF DATA TO BUILD UP PROFILES OF PEOPLE'S HABITS. IN YOUR CASE IT'S THE FREQUENCY AND DURATION OF YOUR ABSENCES FROM YOUR OFFICE THAT IS INCRIMINATING...
THREE MINUTES AT A TIME... TWELVE TIMES A DAY...
OH, ALRIGHT... HOW MUCH DO I OWE YOU?
HE WAS STUPID TO MAKE A BET WITH THE HEAD OF I.T. ABOUT HOW HE COULD GIVE UP SMOKING.

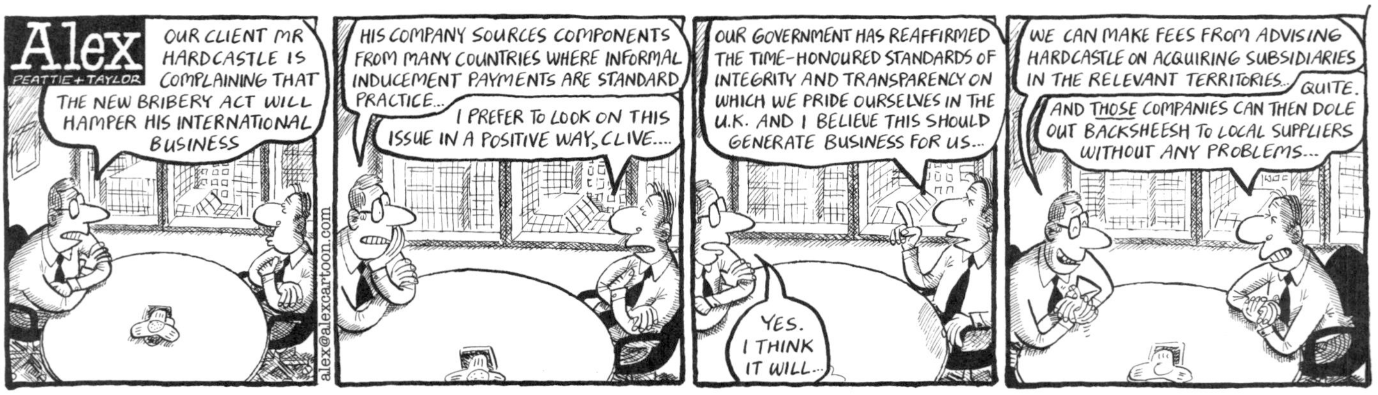
Alex
PEATTIE + TAYLOR
OUR CLIENT MR HARDCASTLE IS COMPLAINING THAT THE NEW BRIBERY ACT WILL HAMPER HIS INTERNATIONAL BUSINESS
alex@alexcartoon.com
HIS COMPANY SOURCES COMPONENTS FROM MANY COUNTRIES WHERE INFORMAL INDUCEMENT PAYMENTS ARE STANDARD PRACTICE...
I PREFER TO LOOK ON THIS ISSUE IN A POSITIVE WAY, CLIVE...
OUR GOVERNMENT HAS REAFFIRMED THE TIME-HONOURED STANDARDS OF INTEGRITY AND TRANSPARENCY ON WHICH WE PRIDE OURSELVES IN THE U.K. AND I BELIEVE THIS SHOULD GENERATE BUSINESS FOR US...
YES. I THINK IT WILL...
WE CAN MAKE FEES FROM ADVISING HARDCASTLE ON ACQUIRING SUBSIDIARIES IN THE RELEVANT TERRITORIES...
QUITE.
AND THOSE COMPANIES CAN THEN DOLE OUT BACKSHEESH TO LOCAL SUPPLIERS WITHOUT ANY PROBLEMS...

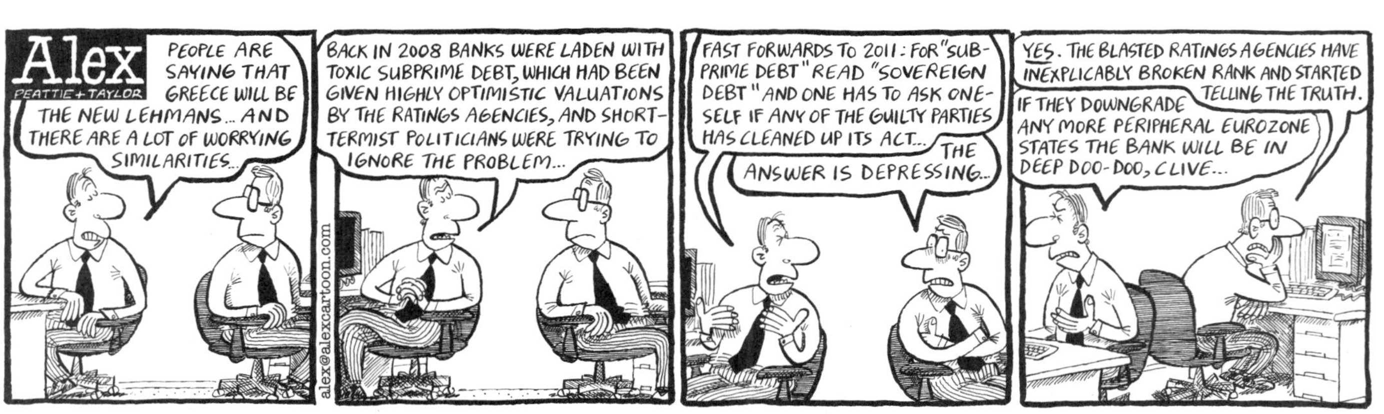
Alex
PEATTIE + TAYLOR
PEOPLE ARE SAYING THAT GREECE WILL BE THE NEW LEHMANS... AND THERE ARE A LOT OF WORRYING SIMILARITIES...
BACK IN 2008 BANKS WERE LADEN WITH TOXIC SUBPRIME DEBT, WHICH HAD BEEN GIVEN HIGHLY OPTIMISTIC VALUATIONS BY THE RATINGS AGENCIES, AND SHORT-TERMIST POLITICIANS WERE TRYING TO IGNORE THE PROBLEM...
alex@alexcartoon.com
FAST FORWARDS TO 2011: FOR "SUB-PRIME DEBT" READ "SOVEREIGN DEBT" AND ONE HAS TO ASK ONE-SELF IF ANY OF THE GUILTY PARTIES HAS CLEANED UP ITS ACT...
THE ANSWER IS DEPRESSING...
YES. THE BLASTED RATINGS AGENCIES HAVE INEXPLICABLY BROKEN RANK AND STARTED TELLING THE TRUTH.
IF THEY DOWNGRADE ANY MORE PERIPHERAL EUROZONE STATES THE BANK WILL BE IN DEEP DOO-DOO, CLIVE...

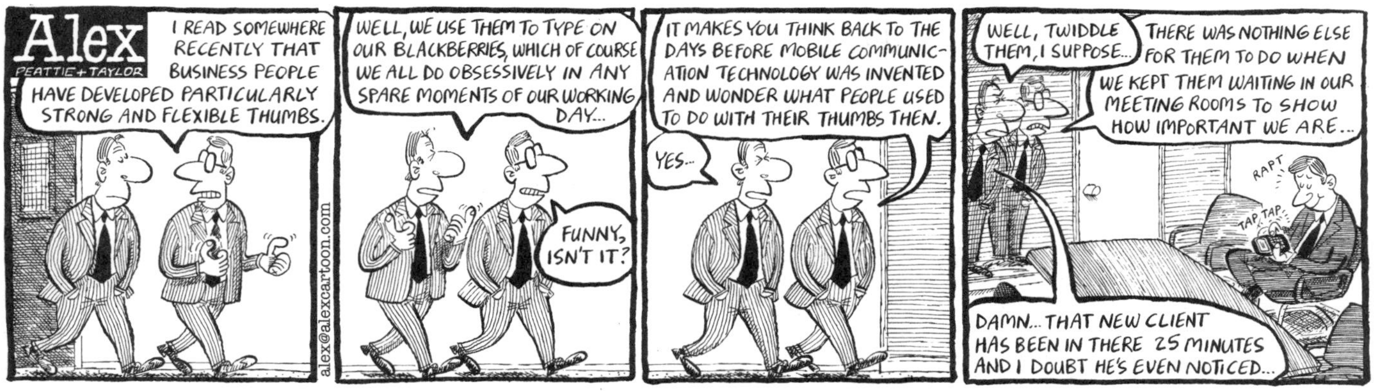
Alex
PEATTIE + TAYLOR
I READ SOMEWHERE RECENTLY THAT BUSINESS PEOPLE HAVE DEVELOPED PARTICULARLY STRONG AND FLEXIBLE THUMBS.
alex@alexcartoon.com
WELL, WE USE THEM TO TYPE ON OUR BLACKBERRIES, WHICH OF COURSE WE ALL DO OBSESSIVELY IN ANY SPARE MOMENTS OF OUR WORKING DAY...
FUNNY, ISN'T IT?
IT MAKES YOU THINK BACK TO THE DAYS BEFORE MOBILE COMMUNICATION TECHNOLOGY WAS INVENTED AND WONDER WHAT PEOPLE USED TO DO WITH THEIR THUMBS THEN.
YES...
WELL, TWIDDLE THEM, I SUPPOSE...
THERE WAS NOTHING ELSE FOR THEM TO DO WHEN WE KEPT THEM WAITING IN OUR MEETING ROOMS TO SHOW HOW IMPORTANT WE ARE...
RAPT
TAP TAP
DAMN... THAT NEW CLIENT HAS BEEN IN THERE 25 MINUTES AND I DOUBT HE'S EVEN NOTICED...

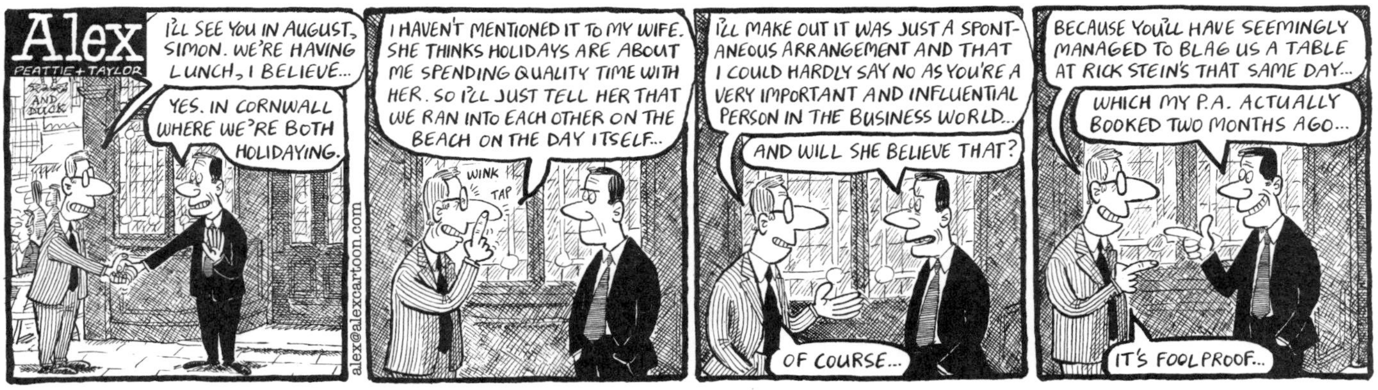
Alex
PEATTIE + TAYLOR
I'LL SEE YOU IN AUGUST, SIMON. WE'RE HAVING LUNCH, I BELIEVE...
YES. IN CORNWALL WHERE WE'RE BOTH HOLIDAYING.
AND DUCK
alex@alexcartoon.com
I HAVEN'T MENTIONED IT TO MY WIFE. SHE THINKS HOLIDAYS ARE ABOUT ME SPENDING QUALITY TIME WITH HER. SO I'LL JUST TELL HER THAT WE RAN INTO EACH OTHER ON THE BEACH ON THE DAY ITSELF...
WINK
TAP
I'LL MAKE OUT IT WAS JUST A SPONTANEOUS ARRANGEMENT AND THAT I COULD HARDLY SAY NO AS YOU'RE A VERY IMPORTANT AND INFLUENTIAL PERSON IN THE BUSINESS WORLD...
AND WILL SHE BELIEVE THAT?
OF COURSE...
BECAUSE YOU'LL HAVE SEEMINGLY MANAGED TO BLAG US A TABLE AT RICK STEIN'S THAT SAME DAY...
WHICH MY P.A. ACTUALLY BOOKED TWO MONTHS AGO...
IT'S FOOLPROOF...

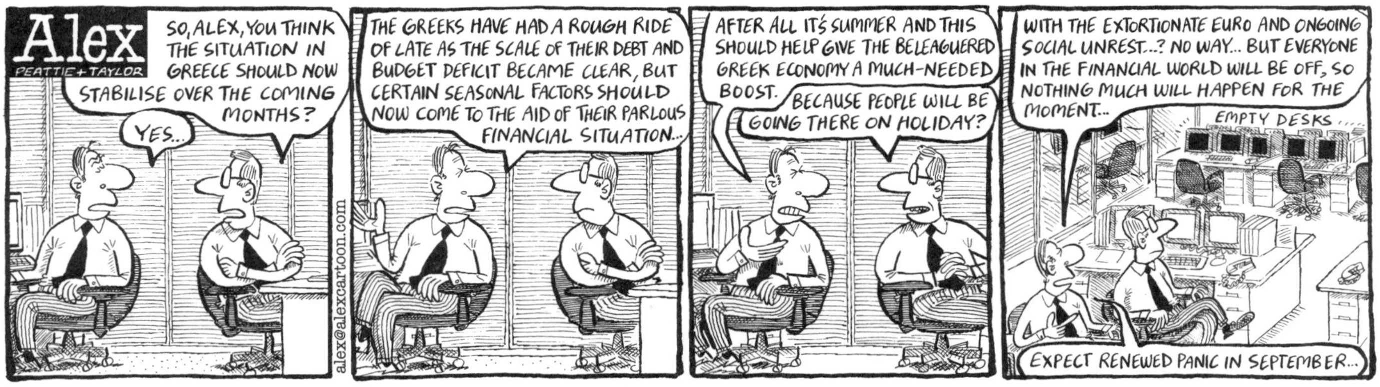
Alex
PEATTIE + TAYLOR
SO, ALEX, YOU THINK THE SITUATION IN GREECE SHOULD NOW STABILISE OVER THE COMING MONTHS?
YES...
alex@alexcartoon.com
THE GREEKS HAVE HAD A ROUGH RIDE OF LATE AS THE SCALE OF THEIR DEBT AND BUDGET DEFICIT BECAME CLEAR, BUT CERTAIN SEASONAL FACTORS SHOULD NOW COME TO THE AID OF THEIR PARLOUS FINANCIAL SITUATION...
AFTER ALL IT'S SUMMER AND THIS SHOULD HELP GIVE THE BELEAGUERED GREEK ECONOMY A MUCH-NEEDED BOOST.
BECAUSE PEOPLE WILL BE GOING THERE ON HOLIDAY?
WITH THE EXTORTIONATE EURO AND ONGOING SOCIAL UNREST...? NO WAY... BUT EVERYONE IN THE FINANCIAL WORLD WILL BE OFF, SO NOTHING MUCH WILL HAPPEN FOR THE MOMENT...
EMPTY DESKS...
EXPECT RENEWED PANIC IN SEPTEMBER...

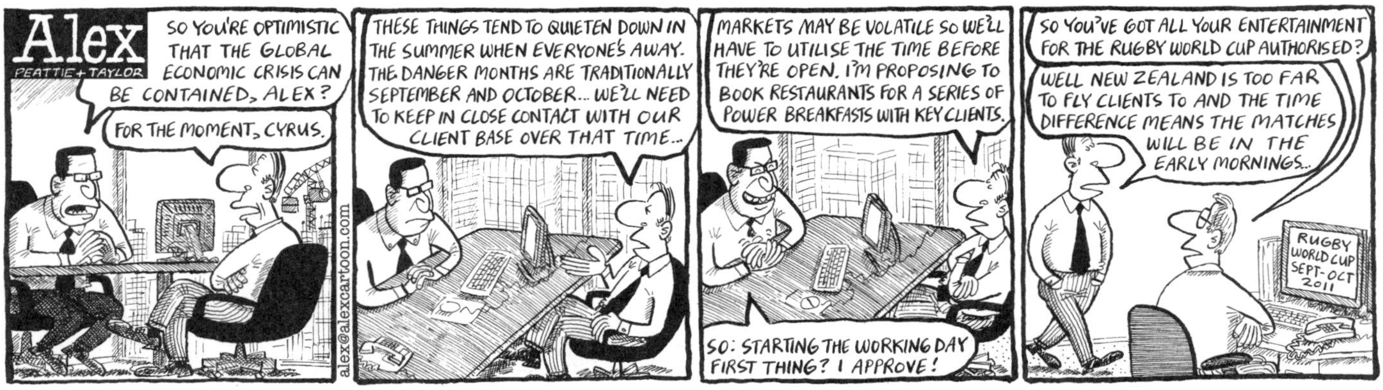
Alex
PEATTIE + TAYLOR
SO YOU'RE OPTIMISTIC THAT THE GLOBAL ECONOMIC CRISIS CAN BE CONTAINED, ALEX?
FOR THE MOMENT, CYRUS.
alex@alexcartoon.com
THESE THINGS TEND TO QUIETEN DOWN IN THE SUMMER WHEN EVERYONE'S AWAY. THE DANGER MONTHS ARE TRADITIONALLY SEPTEMBER AND OCTOBER... WE'LL NEED TO KEEP IN CLOSE CONTACT WITH OUR CLIENT BASE OVER THAT TIME...
MARKETS MAY BE VOLATILE SO WE'LL HAVE TO UTILISE THE TIME BEFORE THEY'RE OPEN. I'M PROPOSING TO BOOK RESTAURANTS FOR A SERIES OF POWER BREAKFASTS WITH KEY CLIENTS.
SO: STARTING THE WORKING DAY FIRST THING? I APPROVE!
SO YOU'VE GOT ALL YOUR ENTERTAINMENT FOR THE RUGBY WORLD CUP AUTHORISED?
WELL NEW ZEALAND IS TOO FAR TO FLY CLIENTS TO AND THE TIME DIFFERENCE MEANS THE MATCHES WILL BE IN THE EARLY MORNINGS...
RUGBY WORLD CUP SEPT-OCT 2011

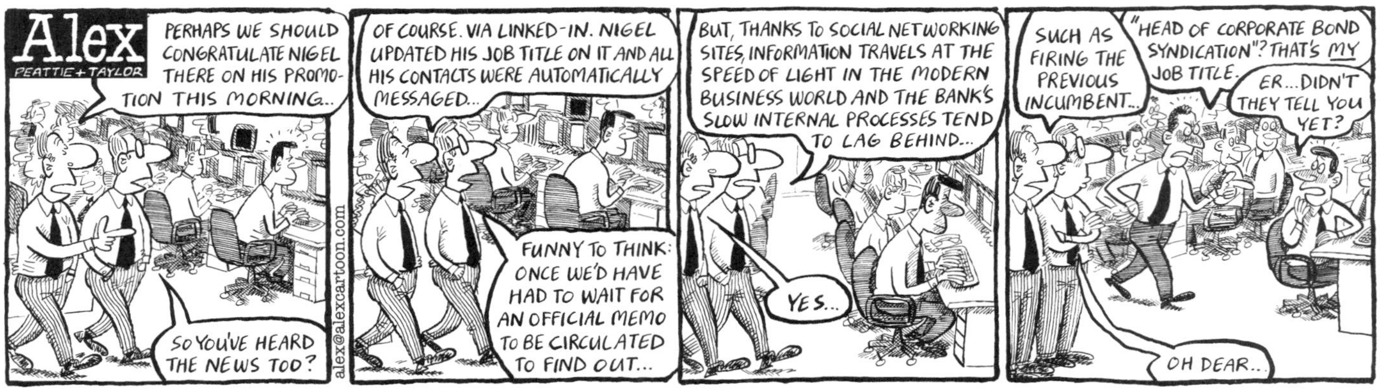
Alex
PEATTIE + TAYLOR
PERHAPS WE SHOULD CONGRATULATE NIGEL THERE ON HIS PROMOTION THIS MORNING...
SO YOU'VE HEARD THE NEWS TOO?
alex@alexcartoon.com
OF COURSE. VIA LINKED-IN. NIGEL UPDATED HIS JOB TITLE ON IT AND ALL HIS CONTACTS WERE AUTOMATICALLY MESSAGED...
FUNNY TO THINK: ONCE WE'D HAVE HAD TO WAIT FOR AN OFFICIAL MEMO TO BE CIRCULATED TO FIND OUT...
BUT, THANKS TO SOCIAL NETWORKING SITES, INFORMATION TRAVELS AT THE SPEED OF LIGHT IN THE MODERN BUSINESS WORLD AND THE BANK'S SLOW INTERNAL PROCESSES TEND TO LAG BEHIND...
YES...
SUCH AS FIRING THE PREVIOUS INCUMBENT...
"HEAD OF CORPORATE BOND SYNDICATION"? THAT'S MY JOB TITLE.
ER...DIDN'T THEY TELL YOU YET?
OH DEAR...

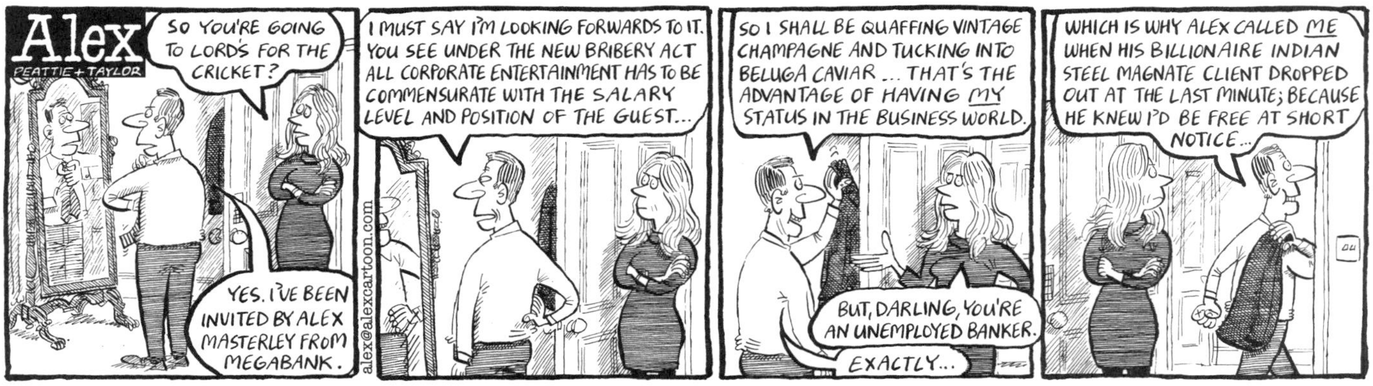
Alex
PEATTIE + TAYLOR
SO YOU'RE GOING TO LORD'S FOR THE CRICKET?
YES. I'VE BEEN INVITED BY ALEX MASTERLEY FROM MEGABANK.
alex@alexcartoon.com
I MUST SAY I'M LOOKING FORWARDS TO IT. YOU SEE UNDER THE NEW BRIBERY ACT ALL CORPORATE ENTERTAINMENT HAS TO BE COMMENSURATE WITH THE SALARY LEVEL AND POSITION OF THE GUEST...
SO I SHALL BE QUAFFING VINTAGE CHAMPAGNE AND TUCKING INTO BELUGA CAVIAR ... THAT'S THE ADVANTAGE OF HAVING MY STATUS IN THE BUSINESS WORLD.
BUT, DARLING, YOU'RE AN UNEMPLOYED BANKER.
EXACTLY...
WHICH IS WHY ALEX CALLED ME WHEN HIS BILLIONAIRE INDIAN STEEL MAGNATE CLIENT DROPPED OUT AT THE LAST MINUTE; BECAUSE HE KNEW I'D BE FREE AT SHORT NOTICE...

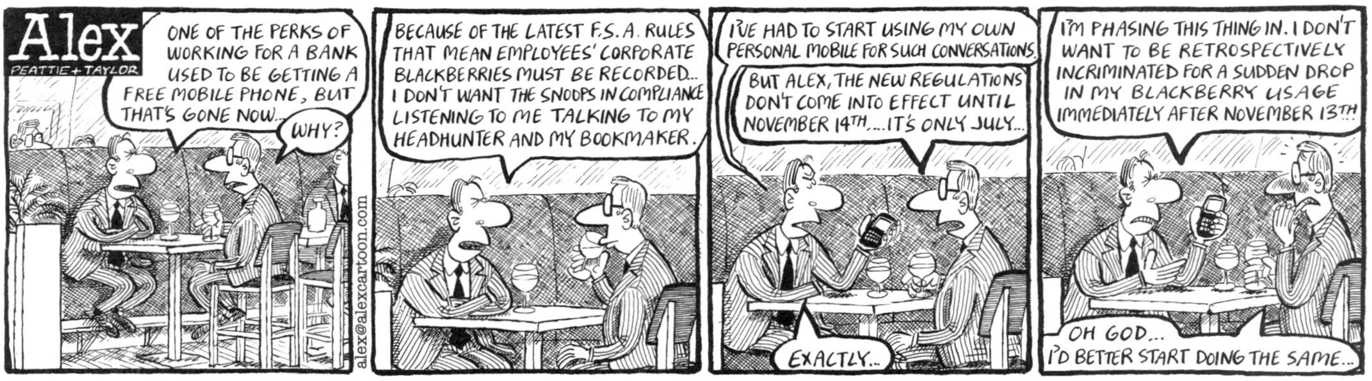
Alex
PEATTIE + TAYLOR
ONE OF THE PERKS OF WORKING FOR A BANK USED TO BE GETTING A FREE MOBILE PHONE, BUT THAT'S GONE NOW...
WHY?
alex@alexcartoon.com
BECAUSE OF THE LATEST F.S.A. RULES THAT MEAN EMPLOYEES' CORPORATE BLACKBERRIES MUST BE RECORDED... I DON'T WANT THE SNOOPS IN COMPLIANCE LISTENING TO ME TALKING TO MY HEADHUNTER AND MY BOOKMAKER.
I'VE HAD TO START USING MY OWN PERSONAL MOBILE FOR SUCH CONVERSATIONS.
BUT ALEX, THE NEW REGULATIONS DON'T COME INTO EFFECT UNTIL NOVEMBER 14TH... IT'S ONLY JULY...
EXACTLY...
I'M PHASING THIS THING IN. I DON'T WANT TO BE RETROSPECTIVELY INCRIMINATED FOR A SUDDEN DROP IN MY BLACKBERRY USAGE IMMEDIATELY AFTER NOVEMBER 13TH
OH GOD... I'D BETTER START DOING THE SAME...

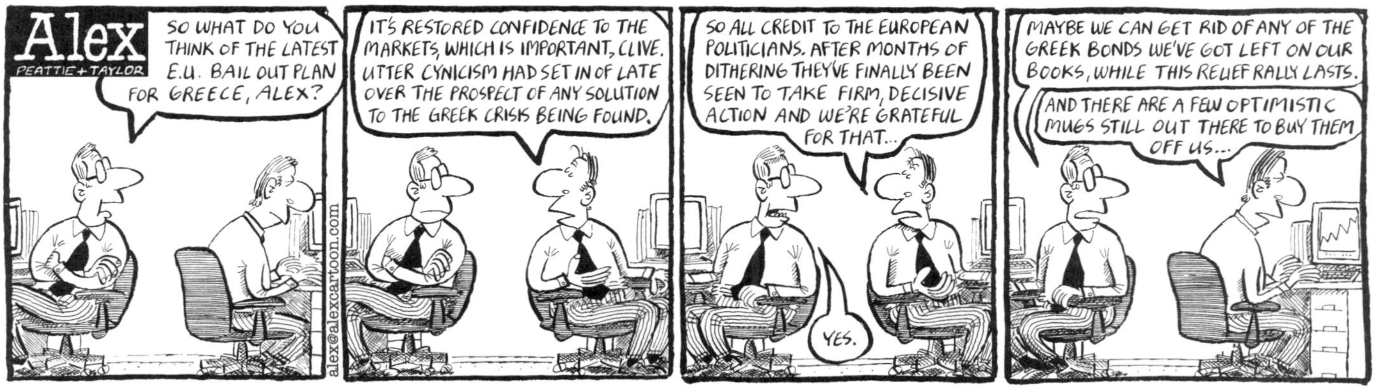
Alex
PEATTIE + TAYLOR
SO WHAT DO YOU THINK OF THE LATEST E.U. BAIL OUT PLAN FOR GREECE, ALEX?
alex@alexcartoon.com
IT'S RESTORED CONFIDENCE TO THE MARKETS, WHICH IS IMPORTANT, CLIVE. UTTER CYNICISM HAD SET IN OF LATE OVER THE PROSPECT OF ANY SOLUTION TO THE GREEK CRISIS BEING FOUND.
SO ALL CREDIT TO THE EUROPEAN POLITICIANS. AFTER MONTHS OF DITHERING THEY'VE FINALLY BEEN SEEN TO TAKE FIRM, DECISIVE ACTION AND WE'RE GRATEFUL FOR THAT...
YES.
MAYBE WE CAN GET RID OF ANY OF THE GREEK BONDS WE'VE GOT LEFT ON OUR BOOKS, WHILE THIS RELIEF RALLY LASTS.
AND THERE ARE A FEW OPTIMISTIC MUGS STILL OUT THERE TO BUY THEM OFF US...

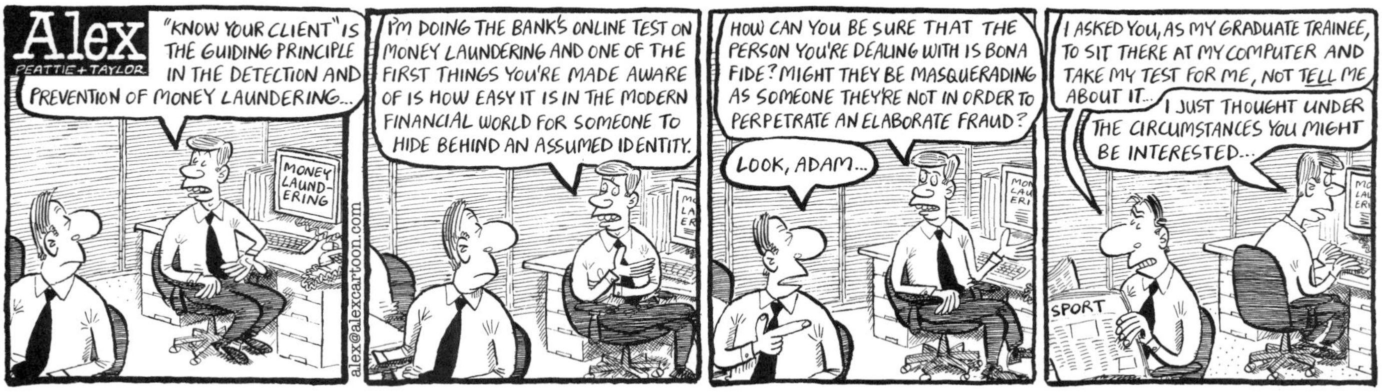
Alex
PEATTIE + TAYLOR
"KNOW YOUR CLIENT" IS THE GUIDING PRINCIPLE IN THE DETECTION AND PREVENTION OF MONEY LAUNDERING...
MONEY LAUNDERING
I'M DOING THE BANK'S ONLINE TEST ON MONEY LAUNDERING AND ONE OF THE FIRST THINGS YOU'RE MADE AWARE OF IS HOW EASY IT IS IN THE MODERN FINANCIAL WORLD FOR SOMEONE TO HIDE BEHIND AN ASSUMED IDENTITY.
alex@alexcartoon.com
HOW CAN YOU BE SURE THAT THE PERSON YOU'RE DEALING WITH IS BONA FIDE? MIGHT THEY BE MASQUERADING AS SOMEONE THEY'RE NOT IN ORDER TO PERPETRATE AN ELABORATE FRAUD?
LOOK, ADAM...
I ASKED YOU, AS MY GRADUATE TRAINEE, TO SIT THERE AT MY COMPUTER AND TAKE MY TEST FOR ME, NOT TELL ME ABOUT IT...
I JUST THOUGHT UNDER THE CIRCUMSTANCES YOU MIGHT BE INTERESTED...
SPORT

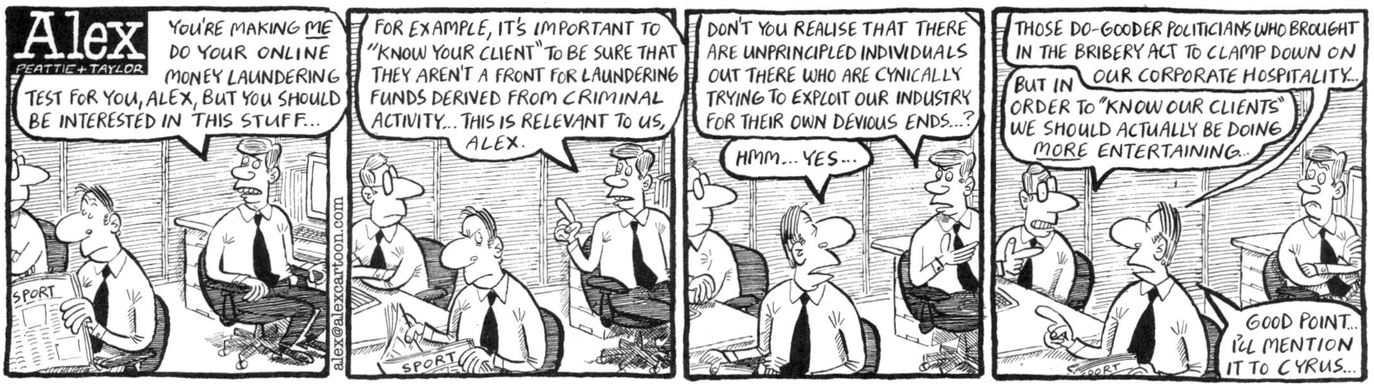
Alex
PEATTIE + TAYLOR
YOU'RE MAKING ME DO YOUR ONLINE MONEY LAUNDERING TEST FOR YOU, ALEX, BUT YOU SHOULD BE INTERESTED IN THIS STUFF...
SPORT
FOR EXAMPLE, IT'S IMPORTANT TO "KNOW YOUR CLIENT" TO BE SURE THAT THEY AREN'T A FRONT FOR LAUNDERING FUNDS DERIVED FROM CRIMINAL ACTIVITY... THIS IS RELEVANT TO US, ALEX.
alex@alexcartoon.com
SPORT
DON'T YOU REALISE THAT THERE ARE UNPRINCIPLED INDIVIDUALS OUT THERE WHO ARE CYNICALLY TRYING TO EXPLOIT OUR INDUSTRY FOR THEIR OWN DEVIOUS ENDS...?
HMM... YES...
THOSE DO-GOODER POLITICIANS WHO BROUGHT IN THE BRIBERY ACT TO CLAMP DOWN ON OUR CORPORATE HOSPITALITY...
BUT IN ORDER TO "KNOW OUR CLIENTS" WE SHOULD ACTUALLY BE DOING MORE ENTERTAINING...
GOOD POINT... I'LL MENTION IT TO CYRUS...

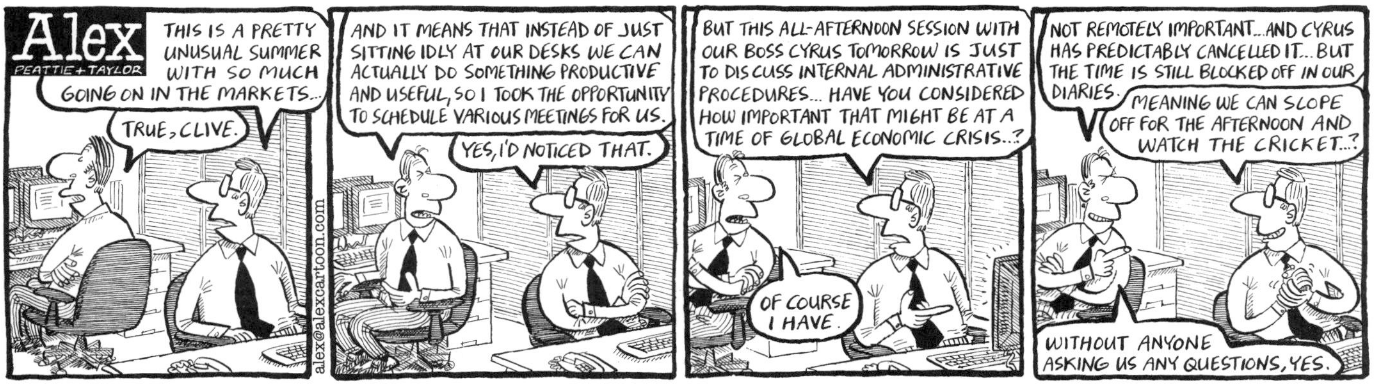
Alex
PEATTIE + TAYLOR
THIS IS A PRETTY UNUSUAL SUMMER WITH SO MUCH GOING ON IN THE MARKETS...
TRUE, CLIVE.
AND IT MEANS THAT INSTEAD OF JUST SITTING IDLY AT OUR DESKS WE CAN ACTUALLY DO SOMETHING PRODUCTIVE AND USEFUL, SO I TOOK THE OPPORTUNITY TO SCHEDULE VARIOUS MEETINGS FOR US.
YES, I'D NOTICED THAT.
alex@alexcartoon.com
BUT THIS ALL-AFTERNOON SESSION WITH OUR BOSS CYRUS TOMORROW IS JUST TO DISCUSS INTERNAL ADMINISTRATIVE PROCEDURES... HAVE YOU CONSIDERED HOW IMPORTANT THAT MIGHT BE AT A TIME OF GLOBAL ECONOMIC CRISIS...?
OF COURSE I HAVE.
NOT REMOTELY IMPORTANT... AND CYRUS HAS PREDICTABLY CANCELLED IT... BUT THE TIME IS STILL BLOCKED OFF IN OUR DIARIES.
MEANING WE CAN SLOPE OFF FOR THE AFTERNOON AND WATCH THE CRICKET...?
WITHOUT ANYONE ASKING US ANY QUESTIONS, YES.

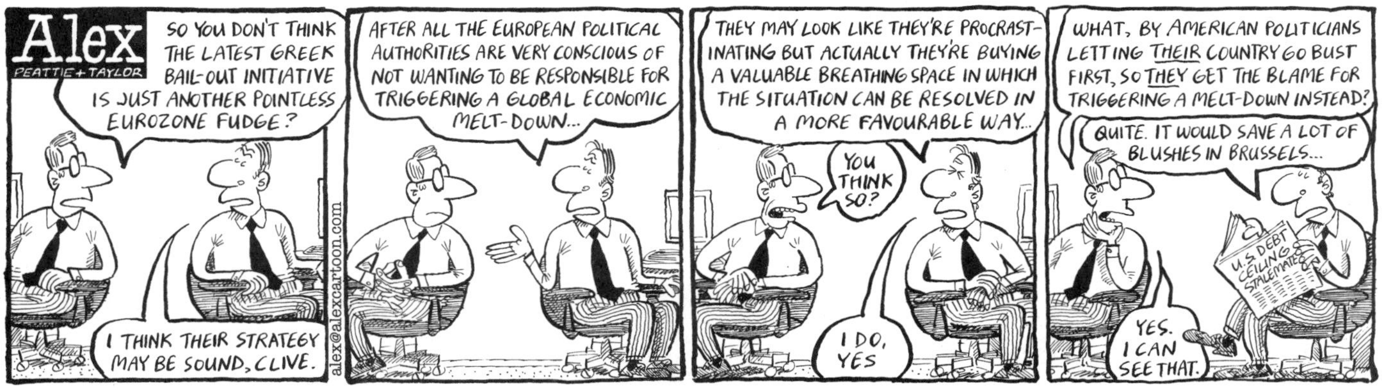
Alex
PEATTIE + TAYLOR
SO YOU DON'T THINK THE LATEST GREEK BAIL-OUT INITIATIVE IS JUST ANOTHER POINTLESS EUROZONE FUDGE?
I THINK THEIR STRATEGY MAY BE SOUND, CLIVE.
AFTER ALL THE EUROPEAN POLITICAL AUTHORITIES ARE VERY CONSCIOUS OF NOT WANTING TO BE RESPONSIBLE FOR TRIGGERING A GLOBAL ECONOMIC MELT-DOWN...
alex@alexcartoon.com
THEY MAY LOOK LIKE THEY'RE PROCRASTINATING BUT ACTUALLY THEY'RE BUYING A VALUABLE BREATHING SPACE IN WHICH THE SITUATION CAN BE RESOLVED IN A MORE FAVOURABLE WAY...
YOU THINK SO?
I DO, YES
WHAT, BY AMERICAN POLITICIANS LETTING THEIR COUNTRY GO BUST FIRST, SO THEY GET THE BLAME FOR TRIGGERING A MELT-DOWN INSTEAD?
QUITE. IT WOULD SAVE A LOT OF BLUSHES IN BRUSSELS...
U.S. DEBT CEILING STALEMATE
YES. I CAN SEE THAT.

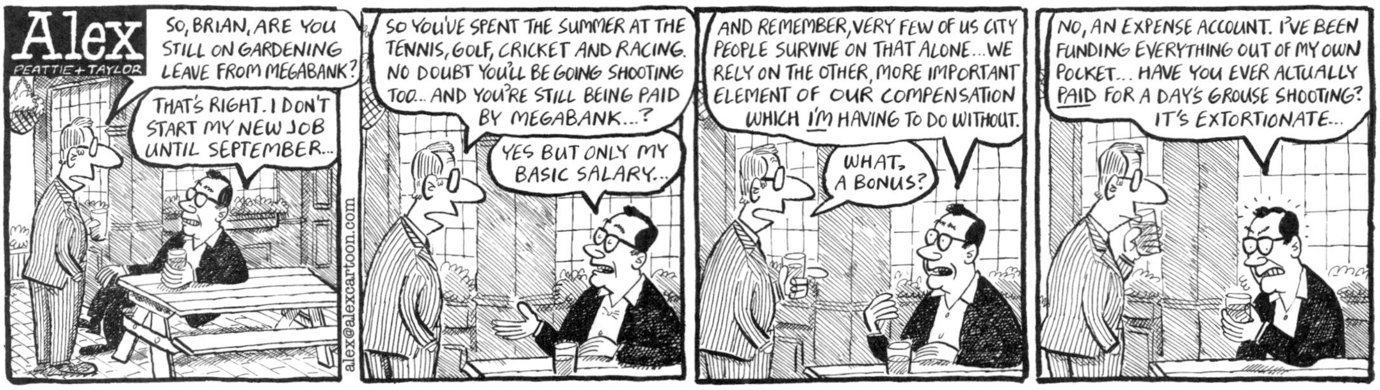
Alex
PEATTIE + TAYLOR
SO, BRIAN, ARE YOU STILL ON GARDENING LEAVE FROM MEGABANK?
THAT'S RIGHT. I DON'T START MY NEW JOB UNTIL SEPTEMBER...
alex@alexcartoon.com
SO YOU'VE SPENT THE SUMMER AT THE TENNIS, GOLF, CRICKET AND RACING. NO DOUBT YOU'LL BE GOING SHOOTING TOO... AND YOU'RE STILL BEING PAID BY MEGABANK...?
YES BUT ONLY MY BASIC SALARY...
AND REMEMBER, VERY FEW OF US CITY PEOPLE SURVIVE ON THAT ALONE... WE RELY ON THE OTHER, MORE IMPORTANT ELEMENT OF OUR COMPENSATION WHICH I'M HAVING TO DO WITHOUT.
WHAT, A BONUS?
NO, AN EXPENSE ACCOUNT. I'VE BEEN FUNDING EVERYTHING OUT OF MY OWN POCKET... HAVE YOU EVER ACTUALLY PAID FOR A DAY'S GROUSE SHOOTING? IT'S EXTORTIONATE...

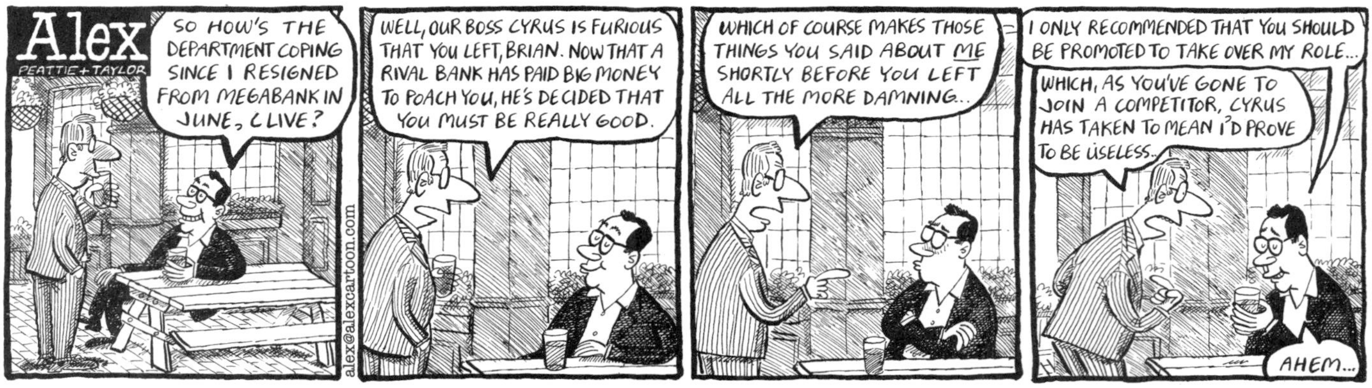
Alex
PEATTIE + TAYLOR
SO HOW'S THE DEPARTMENT COPING SINCE I RESIGNED FROM MEGABANK IN JUNE, CLIVE?
alex@alexcartoon.com
WELL, OUR BOSS CYRUS IS FURIOUS THAT YOU LEFT, BRIAN. NOW THAT A RIVAL BANK HAS PAID BIG MONEY TO POACH YOU, HE'S DECIDED THAT YOU MUST BE REALLY GOOD.
WHICH OF COURSE MAKES THOSE THINGS YOU SAID ABOUT ME SHORTLY BEFORE YOU LEFT ALL THE MORE DAMNING...
I ONLY RECOMMENDED THAT YOU SHOULD BE PROMOTED TO TAKE OVER MY ROLE...
WHICH, AS YOU'VE GONE TO JOIN A COMPETITOR, CYRUS HAS TAKEN TO MEAN I'D PROVE TO BE USELESS...
AHEM...

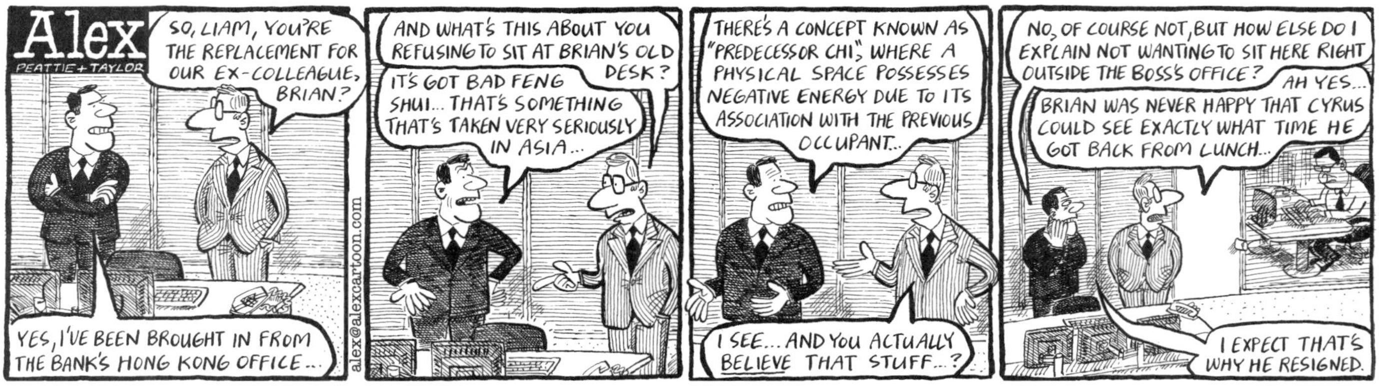
Alex
PEATTIE + TAYLOR
SO, LIAM, YOU'RE THE REPLACEMENT FOR OUR EX-COLLEAGUE, BRIAN?
YES, I'VE BEEN BROUGHT IN FROM THE BANK'S HONG KONG OFFICE...
alex@alexcartoon.com
AND WHAT'S THIS ABOUT YOU REFUSING TO SIT AT BRIAN'S OLD DESK?
IT'S GOT BAD FENG SHUI... THAT'S SOMETHING THAT'S TAKEN VERY SERIOUSLY IN ASIA...
THERE'S A CONCEPT KNOWN AS "PREDECESSOR CHI", WHERE A PHYSICAL SPACE POSSESSES NEGATIVE ENERGY DUE TO ITS ASSOCIATION WITH THE PREVIOUS OCCUPANT...
I SEE... AND YOU ACTUALLY BELIEVE THAT STUFF...?
NO, OF COURSE NOT, BUT HOW ELSE DO I EXPLAIN NOT WANTING TO SIT HERE RIGHT OUTSIDE THE BOSS'S OFFICE?
AH YES...
BRIAN WAS NEVER HAPPY THAT CYRUS COULD SEE EXACTLY WHAT TIME HE GOT BACK FROM LUNCH...
I EXPECT THAT'S WHY HE RESIGNED.

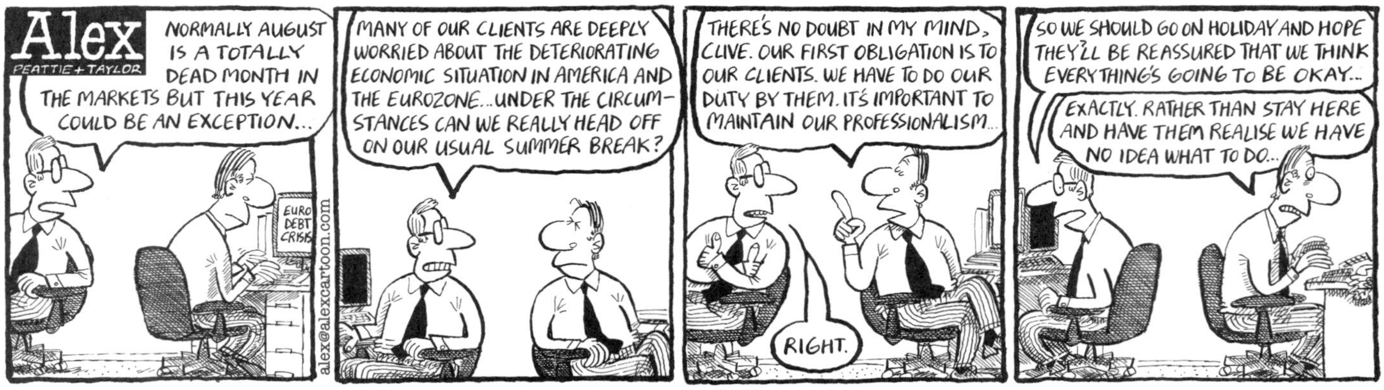
Alex
PEATTIE + TAYLOR
NORMALLY AUGUST IS A TOTALLY DEAD MONTH IN THE MARKETS BUT THIS YEAR COULD BE AN EXCEPTION...
EURO DEBT CRISIS
alex@alexcartoon.com
MANY OF OUR CLIENTS ARE DEEPLY WORRIED ABOUT THE DETERIORATING ECONOMIC SITUATION IN AMERICA AND THE EUROZONE... UNDER THE CIRCUMSTANCES CAN WE REALLY HEAD OFF ON OUR USUAL SUMMER BREAK?
THERE'S NO DOUBT IN MY MIND, CLIVE. OUR FIRST OBLIGATION IS TO OUR CLIENTS. WE HAVE TO DO OUR DUTY BY THEM. IT'S IMPORTANT TO MAINTAIN OUR PROFESSIONALISM...
RIGHT.
SO WE SHOULD GO ON HOLIDAY AND HOPE THEY'LL BE REASSURED THAT WE THINK EVERYTHING'S GOING TO BE OKAY...
EXACTLY. RATHER THAN STAY HERE AND HAVE THEM REALISE WE HAVE NO IDEA WHAT TO DO...

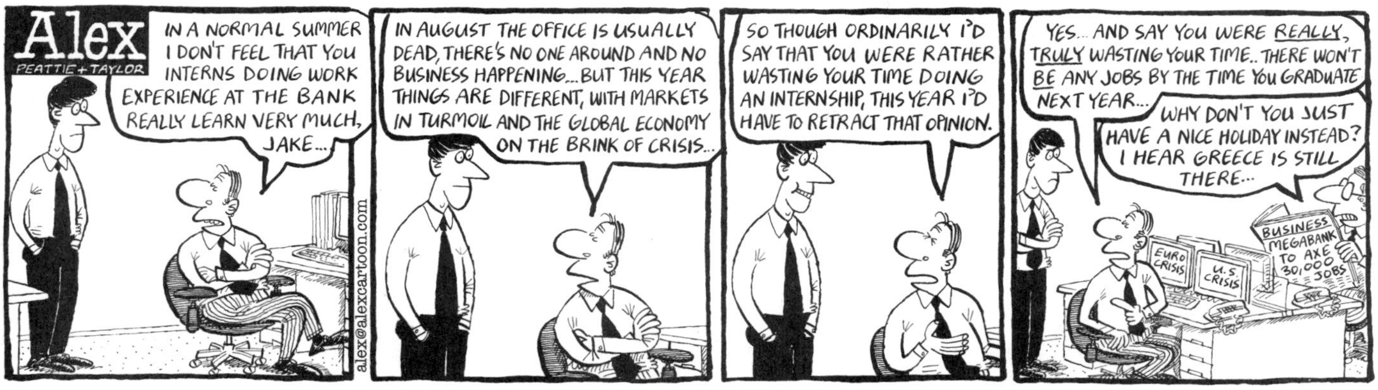
Alex
PEATTIE+TAYLOR
IN A NORMAL SUMMER I DON'T FEEL THAT YOU INTERNS DOING WORK EXPERIENCE AT THE BANK REALLY LEARN VERY MUCH, JAKE...
alex@alexcartoon.com
IN AUGUST THE OFFICE IS USUALLY DEAD, THERE'S NO ONE AROUND AND NO BUSINESS HAPPENING... BUT THIS YEAR THINGS ARE DIFFERENT, WITH MARKETS IN TURMOIL AND THE GLOBAL ECONOMY ON THE BRINK OF CRISIS...
SO THOUGH ORDINARILY I'D SAY THAT YOU WERE RATHER WASTING YOUR TIME DOING AN INTERNSHIP, THIS YEAR I'D HAVE TO RETRACT THAT OPINION.
YES... AND SAY YOU WERE REALLY, TRULY WASTING YOUR TIME.. THERE WON'T BE ANY JOBS BY THE TIME YOU GRADUATE NEXT YEAR...
WHY DON'T YOU JUST HAVE A NICE HOLIDAY INSTEAD? I HEAR GREECE IS STILL THERE...
EURO CRISIS
U.S. CRISIS
BUSINESS
MEGABANK TO AXE 30,000 JOBS

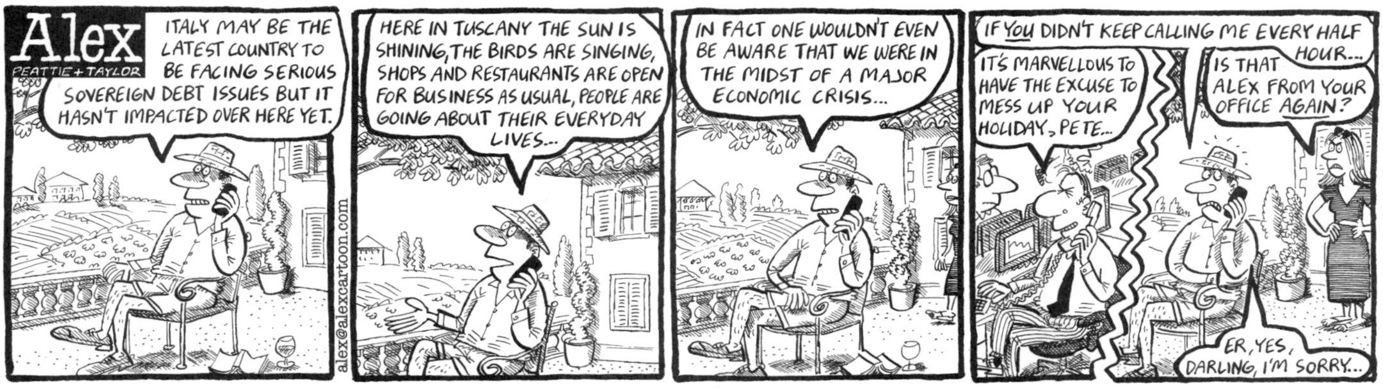
Alex
PEATTIE+TAYLOR
ITALY MAY BE THE LATEST COUNTRY TO BE FACING SERIOUS SOVEREIGN DEBT ISSUES BUT IT HASN'T IMPACTED OVER HERE YET.
alex@alexcartoon.com
HERE IN TUSCANY THE SUN IS SHINING, THE BIRDS ARE SINGING, SHOPS AND RESTAURANTS ARE OPEN FOR BUSINESS AS USUAL, PEOPLE ARE GOING ABOUT THEIR EVERYDAY LIVES...
IN FACT ONE WOULDN'T EVEN BE AWARE THAT WE WERE IN THE MIDST OF A MAJOR ECONOMIC CRISIS...
IF YOU DIDN'T KEEP CALLING ME EVERY HALF HOUR...
IT'S MARVELLOUS TO HAVE THE EXCUSE TO MESS UP YOUR HOLIDAY, PETE...
IS THAT ALEX FROM YOUR OFFICE AGAIN?
ER, YES, DARLING, I'M SORRY...

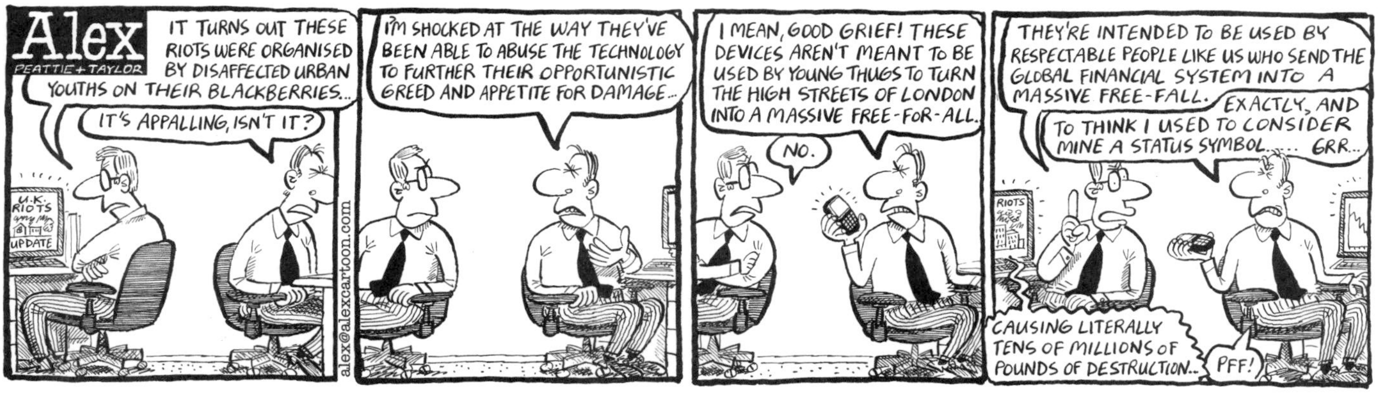
Alex
PEATTIE+TAYLOR
IT TURNS OUT THESE RIOTS WERE ORGANISED BY DISAFFECTED URBAN YOUTHS ON THEIR BLACKBERRIES...
IT'S APPALLING, ISN'T IT?
U.K. RIOTS UPDATE
alex@alexcartoon.com
I'M SHOCKED AT THE WAY THEY'VE BEEN ABLE TO ABUSE THE TECHNOLOGY TO FURTHER THEIR OPPORTUNISTIC GREED AND APPETITE FOR DAMAGE...
I MEAN, GOOD GRIEF! THESE DEVICES AREN'T MEANT TO BE USED BY YOUNG THUGS TO TURN THE HIGH STREETS OF LONDON INTO A MASSIVE FREE-FOR-ALL.
NO.
THEY'RE INTENDED TO BE USED BY RESPECTABLE PEOPLE LIKE US WHO SEND THE GLOBAL FINANCIAL SYSTEM INTO A MASSIVE FREE-FALL.
EXACTLY, AND TO THINK I USED TO CONSIDER MINE A STATUS SYMBOL..... GRR...
RIOTS
CAUSING LITERALLY TENS OF MILLIONS OF POUNDS OF DESTRUCTION..
PFF!

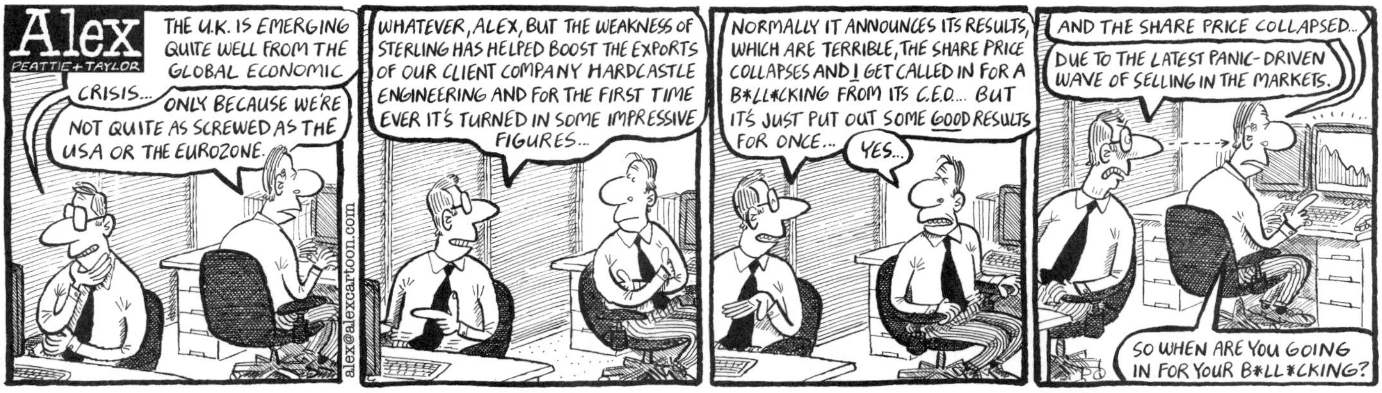
Alex
PEATTIE+TAYLOR
THE U.K. IS EMERGING QUITE WELL FROM THE GLOBAL ECONOMIC CRISIS...
ONLY BECAUSE WE'RE NOT QUITE AS SCREWED AS THE USA OR THE EUROZONE.
alex@alexcartoon.com
WHATEVER, ALEX, BUT THE WEAKNESS OF STERLING HAS HELPED BOOST THE EXPORTS OF OUR CLIENT COMPANY HARDCASTLE ENGINEERING AND FOR THE FIRST TIME EVER IT'S TURNED IN SOME IMPRESSIVE FIGURES...
NORMALLY IT ANNOUNCES ITS RESULTS, WHICH ARE TERRIBLE, THE SHARE PRICE COLLAPSES AND I GET CALLED IN FOR A B*LL*CKING FROM ITS C.E.O.... BUT IT'S JUST PUT OUT SOME GOOD RESULTS FOR ONCE...
YES...
AND THE SHARE PRICE COLLAPSED...
DUE TO THE LATEST PANIC-DRIVEN WAVE OF SELLING IN THE MARKETS.
SO WHEN ARE YOU GOING IN FOR YOUR B*LL*CKING?

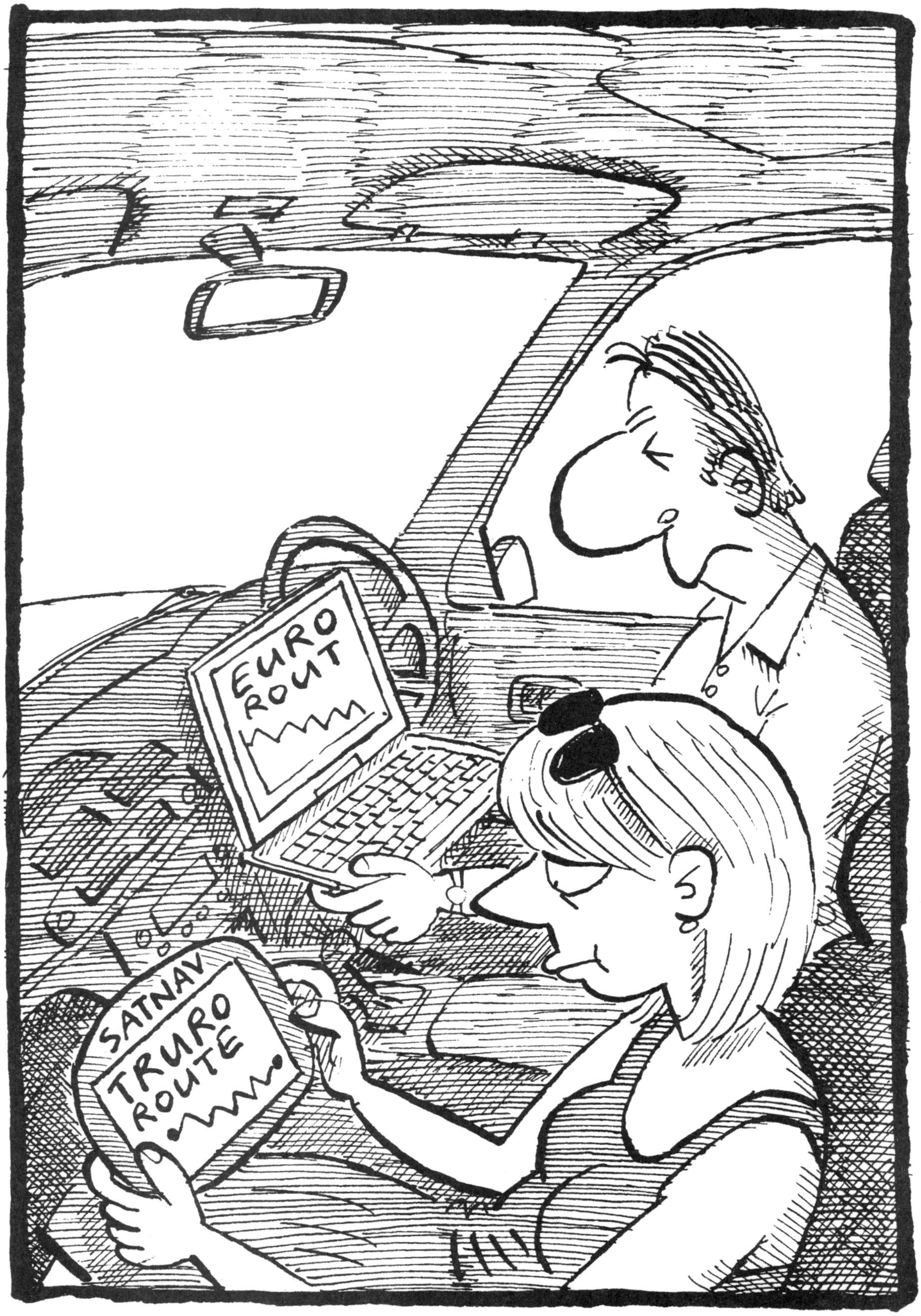
EURO
ROUT
SATNAV
TRURO
ROUTE

ALEX WENT ON HOLIDAY TO CORNWALL...

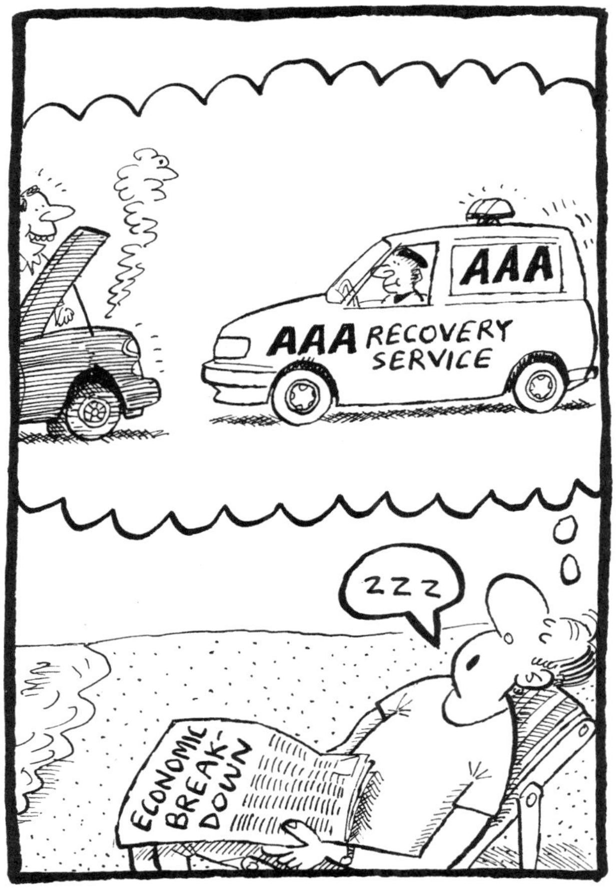
AAA
AAA RECOVERY SERVICE
ZZZ
ECONOMIC BREAK-DOWN

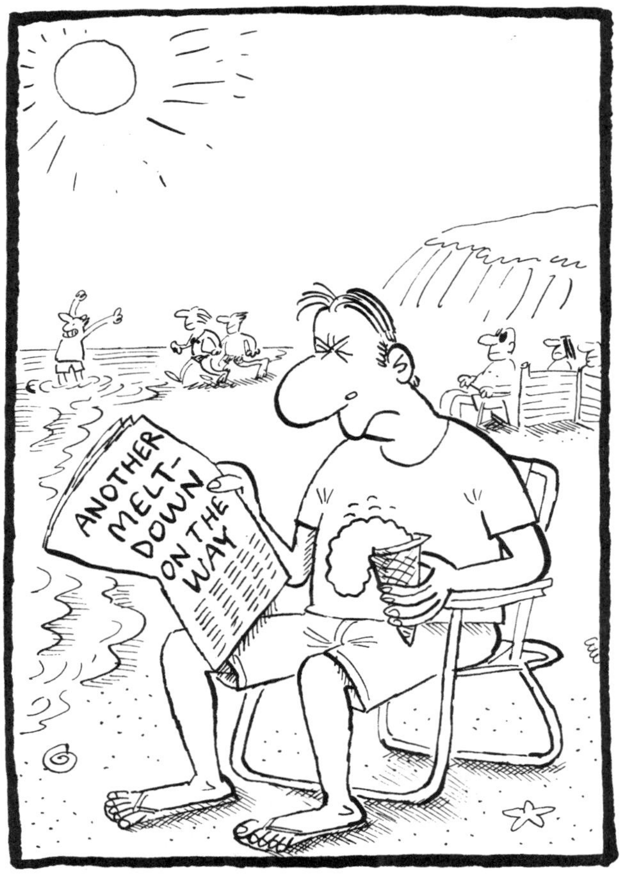
ANOTHER MELT-DOWN ON THE WAY

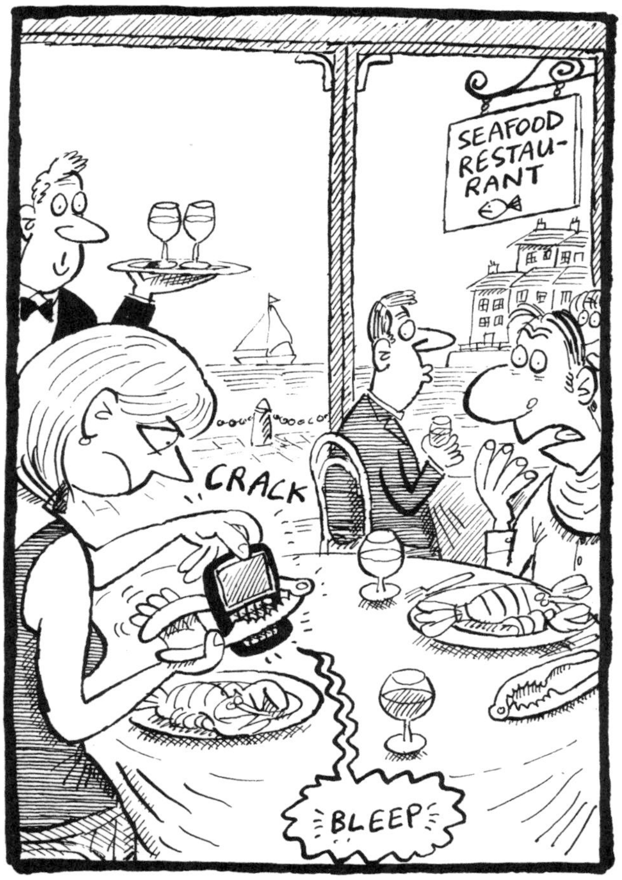
SEAFOOD RESTAU-RANT
CRACK
BLEEP

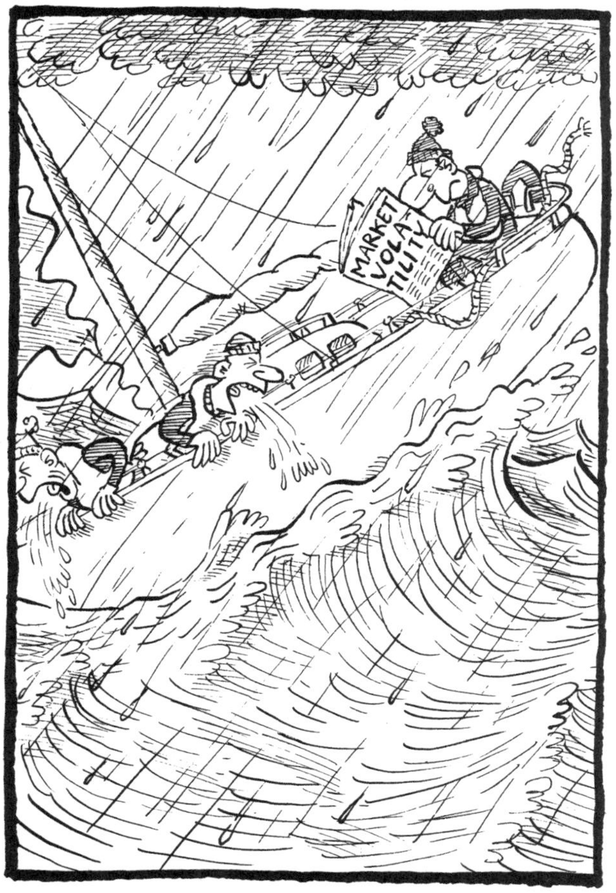
MARKET VOLA-TILITY

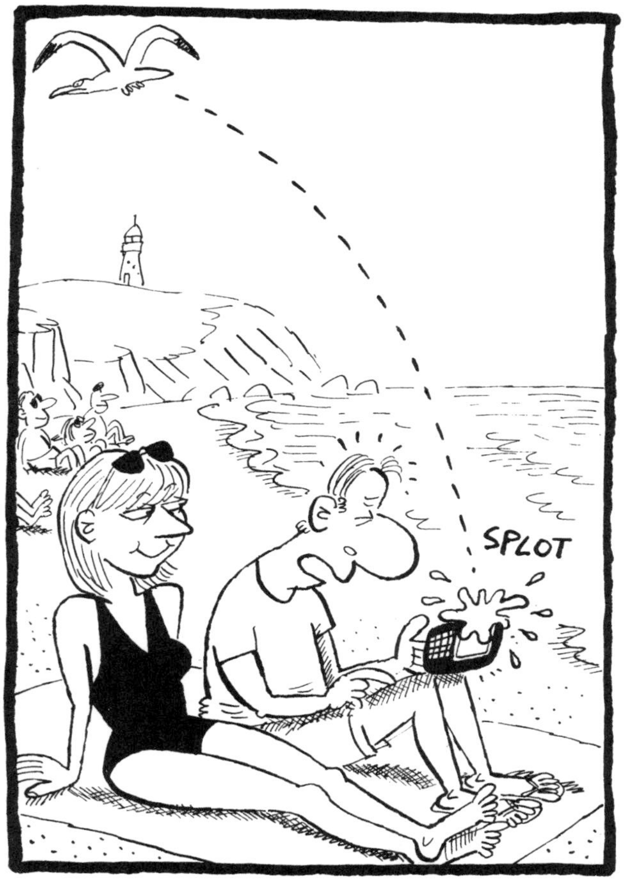
SPLOT

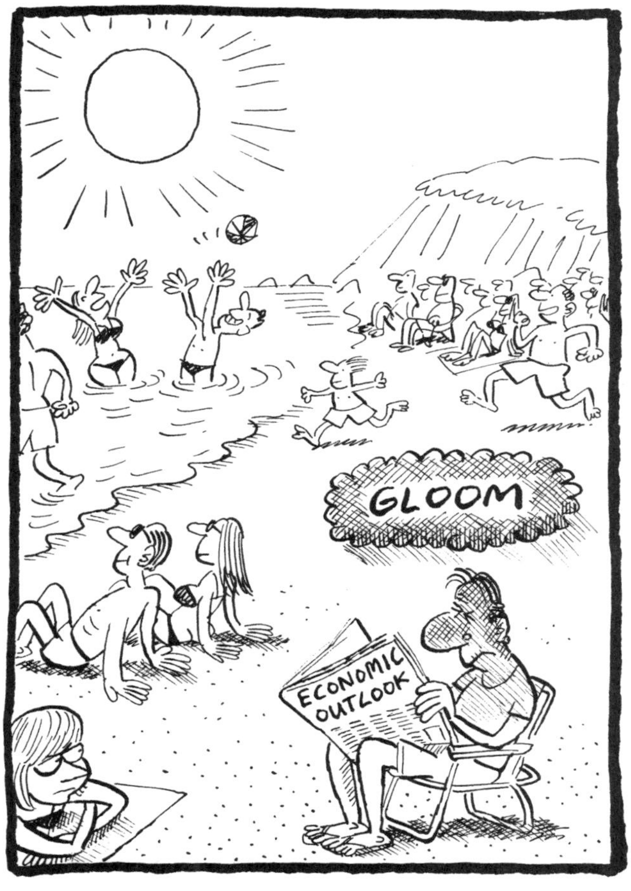
GLOOM
ECONOMIC OUTLOOK

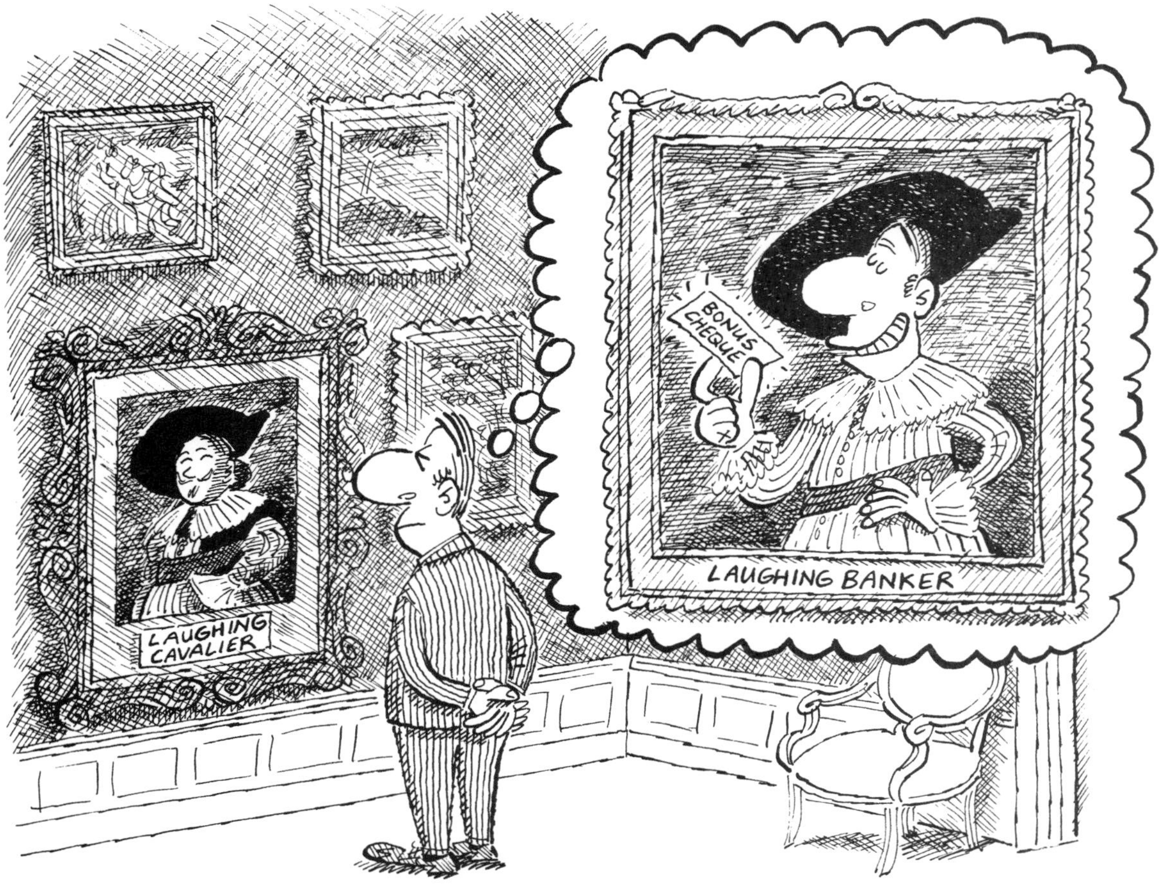
LAUGHING CAVALIER
BONUS CHEQUE
LAUGHING BANKER

Also available from Masterley Publishing

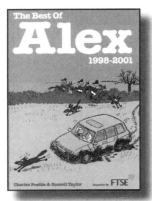

The Best Of
Alex
1998-2001
FTSE

The Best of Alex 1998 - 2001
Boom to bust via the dotcom bubble.

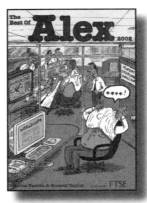

The Best Of
Alex
2002
FTSE

The Best of Alex 2002
Scandals rock the corporate world.

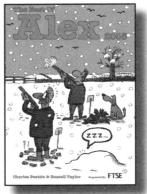

The Best Of
Alex
2003
ZZZ...
FTSE

The Best of Alex 2003
Alex gets made redundant.

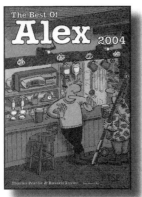

The Best Of
Alex
2004

The Best of Alex 2004
And gets his job back.

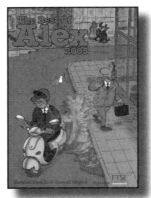

The Best Of
Alex
2005

The Best of Alex 2005
Alex has problems with the French.

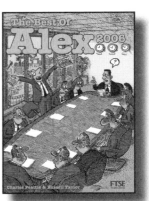

The Best Of
Alex
2006
FTSE

The Best of Alex 2006
Alex gets a new American boss.

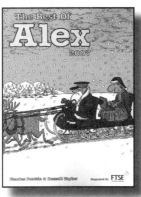

The Best Of
Alex
2007
FTSE

The Best of Alex 2007
Alex restructures Christmas.

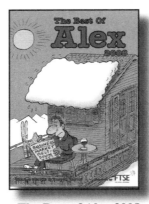

The Best Of
Alex
2008
FTSE

The Best of Alex 2008
The credit crunch bites.

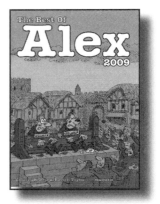

The Best Of
Alex
2009

The Best of Alex 2009
Global capitalism self-destructs.

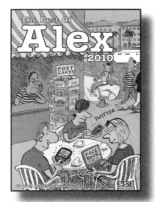

The Best Of
Alex
2010

The Best of Alex 2010
But somehow lurches on.

Celeb
The Original Gary Bloke From
PRIVATE EYE

Celeb
Wrinkly rockstar Gary Bloke.

All books cost £9.99 plus p+p.
Cartoon originals and prints are also for sale.
They measure 4 x 14 inches and are signed by the creators.

For further details on prices:
Tel: 020 8374 1225
Email: alex@alexcartoon.com
Web: www.alexcartoon.com

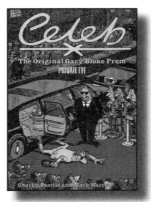